Written with Lead

William Weir

WRITTEN
WITH
LEAD

Legendary American
Gunfights and Gunfighters

Archon Books 1992

First published 1992 as an Archon Book, an imprint of The Shoe String
Press, Inc., Hamden, Connecticut 06514

The paper used in this publication meets the minimum requirements
of American National Standard for Information Sciences—Permanence of
Paper for Printed Library Materials, ANSI Z39.48–1984 ∞

Library of Congress Cataloging-in-Publication Data

Weir, William, 1928–
Written with lead : legendary American gunfights
and gunfighters / by William Weir.
p.   cm.
Includes bibliographical references and index.
Summary: Examines eighteen episodes in American history
involving firearms, heroes, and the popular portrayal
and mythic nature of guns and gunfighters.
1. United States—History.   2. Violence—United States.
3. Firearms—Social aspects—United States.
[1. United States—History.   2.Firearms.]
I. Title
E179.W43   1992   973—dc20   91-46338
ISBN 0-208-02319-4

Contents

Foreword
American Myths

Mention "myth," and the average person thinks of stories, usually bloody ones, involving Mycenaean Greeks or ancient Teutons. Every culture has its myths, though, including our own. Ours are kept alive not by wandering bards and court poets, but by script writers and novelists. With the modern academic veneration of epics like the *Iliad*, the *Odyssey* and even *Beowulf*, we tend to forget that these tales were the ancient equivalent of prime time television. Mythology is always popular culture—the culture of the people. Myths reflect the life of the people who own them. Because myths are rooted so deeply in a people's collective outlook on life, they are told again and again.

One historian reports that the St. Valentine's Day Massacre has been recreated on the screen no less than five times. The gunfight at the O.K. Corral has been filmed at least twice as many times. The life and death of Billy the Kid has inspired more than 40 films, plus television productions, novels, ballads and even a ballet.

At first glance, George Armstrong Custer and Achilles seem to have little in common. Custer, riding over the prairies with a revolver and a carbine, doesn't look like Achilles, clanking around the walls of Troy with a shield and a spear. But both are warriors. Both are brave (although Custer, lacking an impervious hide and a maternal connection to Olympus, would seem to be braver). And both are impatient with details and with any authority but their own. Both, too, are filled with overweening pride, although Achilles, unlike Custer, finally conquers his when he appears before Priam. In the end, though, both he and Custer receive the reward every good myth provides for those afflicted with *hubris*.

The same themes occur in myth after myth. "Pride goeth before the fall," says the Bible, and the result of *hubris* may be a well-aimed arrow outside bronze age Troy or a well-aimed bullet in the wilderness of 18th century New York. The traditional tragic hero doesn't have to be a great king with a paranoid personality. He can also be a great republican statesman with a paranoid personality. Or two great, paranoid statesmen, like Alexander Hamilton and Aaron Burr. Legends about small bands of heroes are not limited to spearmen like the Spartans at Thermopylae. They're also told about riflemen like the Texans at the Alamo.

The basic stories are the same; only the details differ. Roland relied on his sword; Harry Tracy on his carbine. Odysseus took his revenge with a bow; Hymie Weiss with a tommy gun.

The prominence of guns in our myths is very American. Shootouts are a world-wide phenomenon these days, but only in the Western Hemisphere do they figure so prominently in myth. This country was founded by a violent revolution. While revolution is a common means of national birth in the Americas, That is definitely not so in Europe or Asia. There's been plenty of violence in those places, but it hasn't been used to create nations. India, for example, existed long before the British Raj. And the violence that accompanied the British departure was aimed at other Indians. Even in Africa, revolutionary movements that defeated the colonial powers were seldom great wars, like the American Revolution. For the most part, the colonialists in Africa simply decided that colonies weren't worth the trouble to keep. Our country's violent beginnings, plus centuries of warfare against the continent's original inhabitants—conducted by ordinary citizens as well as official armed forces—may be responsible for the smell of gunpowder that permeates our mythology.

There are other theories. Oscar Wilde said, "Americans are great hero worshipers, and they take all their heroes from the criminal classes." Actually, we choose our heroes from all classes—criminals, like Jesse James, and honest burghers like the Minnesotans who destroyed the James gang; enthusiastic career soldiers, like Custer, and reluctant amateur soldiers like Alvin York; straight cops like Pat Garrett of Lincoln County, New Mexico, and bent cops like Wyatt Earp of Tombstone, Arizona.

Most of these diverse heroes have one quality in common: they are anti-establishment. That's another distinctively American trait. Both before and after the American Revolution, the United States was settled by Europeans who were fleeing the establishments in their old countries. This, and our revolutionary origins, makes United States culture markedly different from that of our northern neighbor, Canada. English-speaking Canada was founded by people fleeing revolutionary America. The typical Canadian hero is an anonymous Mountie, rather than a colorful outlaw. Our anti-establishment bias may be the reason that, although the overwhelming majority of shootings occur in war, so few American myths have a military origin. When they are connected with war, there is usually another factor. None of the Americans at the Alamo, for example, was a professional soldier. General Custer was a professional soldier, but he was many more things, besides, and he lived on the periphery of the military establishment.

There are two exceptions to the rule that most military actions don't make myths: the Battle of New Orleans and the Civil War.

New Orleans became legendary partly because—except for some Indian massacres—it was the most lopsided victory ever won by U.S. troops. A more important reason is that much of Andrew Jackson's army was composed of rifle-armed frontiersmen—anti-establishment forces by definition—and he received considerable help from a pirate, Jean Lafitte. Then there is the oddity that although the battle was fought after the signing of the peace treaty, it turned what was at best a tie into an American victory. The war was supposedly fought over the impressment of American seamen, a matter not even mentioned in the peace treaty. After New Orleans, though, impressment never happened again.

The Civil War was the greatest turning point in American history: the only event more important was the Revolution itself. It spawned enough myths and legends to fill at least another volume—far too many to fit here. In this book we look at the Civil War as an environmental change, like the push westward and the Great Depression. Many of the stories here, like those of Jesse James, Billy the Kid, the O.K. Corral fight, the Little Bighorn battle and the Hatfield-McCoy feud have their roots in the Civil War. Others, like the Burr-Hamilton duel and the Alamo fight, point up some of the attitudes that led to the war.

The flavor of most American myths, though, is anti-establishment, individualistic and violent, with most of the violence being performed with guns. The result of all these factors is a mythology that, like the ancient myths, follows certain universal themes, but also has features that are distinctively American. That's so, of course, because all our myths are products of the great American common myth, or common heritage—the foundation, settlement and development of the United States of America from a handful of struggling colonies on the eastern seaboard of a vast, mostly empty continent to a world superpower. All phases of this development—the Revolution and its repercussions, fights with the Indians, settlement of the frontier by the most turbulent elements of society, disruption of traditional lifestyles by industrialization, the growth of central government—have produced conflicts. And the conflicts have produced myths based on shared values. By studying them, we can get new insights into ourselves as a people.

Take the highly publicized United States homicide rate. The rate of individual murders in this country is higher than in Europe, Canada, Australia, New Zealand and Japan. But not for more than a thousand years has any European country or Japan experienced anything like our three hundred years of Indian wars. The short-lived Maori fighting in New Zealand is by no means in the same class; the settlement of Australia was accompanied by many murders of the aborigines, but no fighting to speak of. Even in Canada, settlement of the west was accomplished with little fighting. In none of the countries against which our murder rate is compared has the majority ever enslaved another race. Nor have any of those countries experienced the waves of immigration the United States has, and none has had anything comparable to the California gold rush (not even the Canadian Klondike gold rush) or the Wyoming-Montana cattle boom.

It's not hard to find countries that have had similar experiences. They begin on the south bank of the Rio Grande and continue to Tierra del Fuego. The U.S. homicide rate compares to the Latin American the way a .22 rifle compares to a 16-inch naval gun. No city in the United States compares with Medellín, Colombia, where the population of one million produces 5,000 murders a year. Nor is any U.S. city in the same league as Rio de Janeiro, where free-lance death squads will kill anybody for anyone who can pay their very reasonable prices.

There is murder in Europe, of course, but they usually give it another name—"war" or "purge"—and it's approved by the powers that be. As this is being written, a war is going on in Northern Ireland between groups of people who have no observable differences except religion. Another is being fought in what once was Yugoslavia by people whose only obvious differences are religion and the alphabets they use to write the same language. Not long ago, there was a short but bloody civil war in Romania.

This is not something new. In the twentieth century alone—*leaving out the two world wars*—there were two wars among all the Balkan states, plus wars between Greece and Turkey, Poland and Russia, and Russia and Finland (twice). There was an unsuccessful war for independence in Hungary, and a successful war for independence in Ireland, followed by a civil war in the newly-independent state. The Irish war for independence came two years after Britain crushed a revolt in Dublin. There were two civil wars in Russia (not including the 1991 coup and counter coup), one in Hungary, one in Spain and another in Greece. In addition, there was something like civil war in both Germany and Austria. This, of course, is not counting the wars Britain, France, Germany, Italy and Russia and Spain fought in Africa and Asia. In no other continent, not even Asia, has there been any comparable number of wars.

Then there were purges. Genghis Khan, the Mongol conqueror, at one time held the murder record for having caused 20,000,000 deaths in his lifetime. Josef Stalin beat that record in a few years during his purges of kulaks, dissidents and otherwise inconvenient people. Other notable purges have been Adolf Hitler's purge of the Jews, the Turks' purge of the Armenians, and the many Russian pogroms against Jews.

In Europe, whose area is roughly equal to that of the United States, violence tends to be collective; in the United States, individual. That's pretty much the way other activities are conducted in the two areas. Latin America and most of Asia have both kinds. One exception is Japan, where suicide seems to be a substitute for homicide until war provides the opportunity for large scale atrocities. Africa, in the relatively short history of most of its independent states, seems to be following the European model.

In short, our homicide rate is a national tragedy, but when all things are considered, it is hardly the international disgrace we've been told it is. When it comes to killing people, we have a lot of competition. And, fortunately, we're lagging behind most of the competitors.

This is not meant to imply that Americans are better than other people—just that we're different. And knowing our mythology helps understand why we are different.

According to the dictionary, "myth" is "a traditional story of ostensibly historical events that serves to unfold part of the world view of a people." There's another definition: "an ill-founded belief held uncritically by an interested group." We'll look at myths in that sense, too, in stories that concern people as diverse as Alexander Hamilton and Wyatt Earp and organizations as different as the FBI and the Mafia.

Like many of the ancient myths, ours are based on real events, though often distorted in the retelling. There can be tremendous distortion in a millennium or two of retelling—so much that it's impossible now to determine what *really* happened during the Trojan War. Fortunately, that hasn't happened with our modern myths. We can still see the facts and how those facts fit the universal themes of all myths. The incidents described here are all old enough to have been recounted many times, in many ways, but they are too recent for the facts to be hidden.

THE

AGE

OF

REVOLUTION

One

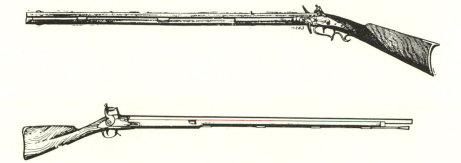

One Scalp and Three Shots Change the World

October 7, 1777, Bemis Heights, New York

"It will be like a regatta on the Thames," the general had told his friends. The general, John Burgoyne, known to his friends as "Handsome Jack" and to his soldiers as "Gentleman Johnny," was nothing if not confident. He had good reasons. He had been a member of Parliament for 15 years, was a successful playwright and a lieutenant general. Popular in high society, he was also adored by his troops for having abolished such traditional punish-

Top: Rare double barreled "Kentucky" rifle of the type used by Tim Murphy at Saratoga. In spite of the name, this type of weapon was usually made in Pennsylvania. Below: Regulation British "Brown Bess" musket—sturdy, quick to load and, compared to the rifle, wildly inaccurate.

ments as flogging. And now, in the wilderness of the New World, the 53-year-old general was about perform his crowning achievement—ending the rebellion in America.

His "regatta," using an inland navy built on Lake Champlain, took Burgoyne all the way to Ticonderoga, reputedly the strongest fortress in North America. The navy had been built last year when the rebel chief, Benedict Arnold, used a smaller fleet to stop a British drive down the Champlain-Hudson valley. The larger British fleet destroyed Arnold's, but it was then too late to continue the march.

Burgoyne had improved on the 1776 plan. Now, he would be met on the Hudson by the British army in New York City under General Sir William Howe. Another British force under Lieutenant Colonel Barry St. Leger was marching down the Mohawk River to meet them both in Albany. Burgoyne had explained to the ministers in London that his plan would isolate New England, the cradle of revolution, and crush the rebellion.

Ticonderoga proved to be no problem. Temporary Brigadier General Simon Fraser, an officer Burgoyne had personally selected, led the advance guard around the fortress and discovered that a mountain overlooking Ticonderoga was unoccupied. Burgoyne put his artillery on the mountain, and the rebels fled. Now he was moving across country, from Lake Champlain to the Hudson. The rebels had felled trees across the road. That was tiresome, but the army was still advancing. The rebels could do little to stop it.

Arnold, a brilliant, prickly former pharmacist who loved only four things—himself, fighting, gold and glory, in that order—was no longer the top rebel commander. He had been replaced by a cautious, unimaginative provincial magnate named Philip Schuyler.

In the American northern headquarters, Major General Philip Schuyler knew that Burgoyne's army outnumbered his more than two to one. Burgoyne had 7,500 men, 42 cannons and a baggage train with hundreds of carts. His personal wardrobe alone filled 32 carts. Brigadier General Arnold had bought some time for the Americans in 1776, but Schuyler hadn't been able to increase his force.

To the south, General George Washington was watching Howe closely and afraid to detach any troops from his already-outnumbered army. Schuyler attempted to raise troops locally without much success. He was a descendant of Hudson Valley patroons, an aristocrat to his fingertips, immensely wealthy, haughty and arrogant. He was not popular with the few small farmers in northern New York. The democratic New Englanders, reflexively anti-aristocrat, cordially detested him.

Further, while a good administrator, Schuyler was a slow-moving general. About all he did to oppose Burgoyne's advance was order any farmers in the way to burn their crops and evacuate their farms, taking their animals with them. Most of the farms were east of the Hudson in the modern state of Vermont. Significantly, Schuyler left his own vast landholdings in New York untouched. Burgoyne was later to stay in Schuyler's manor house and resupply his army from Schuyler's stores.

Burgoyne's advance, while slow, seemed as inexorable as a glacier's. Not all Americans despaired as Burgoyne's British and German regulars, supported by Tories and Indians, slogged through the forest. Some were delighted. Especially delighted was a pretty, 23-year-old woman named Jane "Jenny" McCrea. Her fiance, David Jones, was a Tory lieutenant in the British vanguard.

When he took Ticonderoga, Burgoyne issued a bombastic proclamation calling on all loyalists to rise and threatening to loose his Indians on rebel sympathizers. These recalcitrants would suffer "devastation, famine and every concomitant horror that a reluctant but indispensable prosecution of military duty must occasion." To be fair, Burgoyne saw the Indians only as a threat to the rebels. He forbade them to take scalps and said he would pay only for live captives. The real reason for the Indians was to act as scouts. Unencumbered by heavy equipment or the need to march in ranks, they could move swiftly through the forest and locate the enemy.

As Burgoyne was dispatching his Indians, young Jenny McCrea decided she couldn't wait for her David to come and rescue her from the despicable Whigs. She left home and moved in with an elderly relative named Mrs. McNeill who lived north of Albany on the edge of the forest. Her cabin was isolated, but it would be safe. Mrs. McNeill was a first cousin of General Simon Fraser, David's commanding general and Burgoyne's most trusted subordinate.

On July 27, two days before Burgoyne's army reached the river, Jenny McCrea met the first members of the British force. Two Indians broke into the McNeill cabin, grabbed both women, stripped them and hustled them into the woods. The Indians intended to collect the bounty for live captives.

Hours later, a badly shaken Mrs. McNeill reached her cousin, General

Fraser. She told him what happened to their young relative, Jane McCrea. On the way, the Indians had quarreled about who would get the bounty for the young woman, apparently believing there would be a larger reward for a beautiful girl than for an old woman. One of the Indians, known to the whites as Wyandot Panther, lost the argument. He threw a childish tantrum, shot the girl and scalped her. All that was left of Lieutenant Jones' eager fiance was a bloody scalp.

Burgoyne was outraged. He ordered the Indians to be hanged for murder. Then St. Luc de la Corne, the French-Indian leader of Burgoyne's scouts, appeared. He said if the general hanged the murderers, he would take all the Indians and leave Burgoyne without native scouts.

Gentleman Johnny was as handsome, brave and witty as he appears in Bernard Shaw's *The Devil's Disciple*. But he had feet of clay. After St. Luc de la Corne's threat, he figuratively took off his boots and showed them to the world. He pardoned the Indians. The army was disgusted, but the rebels, when they learned what happened, spread the word far and wide. Burgoyne had given his enemies the propaganda break of a century.

Indian atrocities—and atrocities against the Indians—were nothing new in the colonies. But this time, the Indians had been employed by the civilized, humane Gentleman Johnny Burgoyne, a man as well known in the colonies as he was in England. And the victim was not merely innocent, she was an ardent Tory. The message was clear: the British cared nothing about whether colonist were Tories or Whigs; they were waging barbaric warfare on all Americans.

Burgoyne thought he needed the Indians for his next venture, collecting loyalists and supplies east of the Hudson. He organized an expedition under one of his German officers, Lieutenant Colonel Friedrich Baum. Baum would take 300 Tories, Canadians and Indians, 150 British light infantry under Captain Simon Fraser (another of General Simon Fraser's cousins), 100 German *jägers* (riflemen) and grenadiers, 170 dismounted German dragoons—heavy cavalry equipped with long broadswords as well as muskets and bayonets, thick boots and leather breeches—two artillery pieces and a band. All of the officers took batmen. In all, there were about 800 men.

This array was to march secretly through the jungle-thick woods and swamps of western Vermont and contact local Tories. Baum spoke no English, but he had Philip Skene, a local Tory who had assured Burgoyne that the country was full of Tories, along as a political advisor.

The rebel forces, of course, were able to track Baum's movements precisely.

"We shall win, or Molly Stark will be a widow tonight," John Stark said as he swung into the saddle to lead his 1,500 New Hampshire militiamen. With the odds he had, if he didn't win, she should have been a widow.

Seth Warner joined Stark near Bennington, dashing ahead of his 500 Green Mountain Boys, the army of the independent republic of Vermont. While Warner and Stark planned their battle, another 500 militiamen, this group from Massachusetts, joined them. The Jane McCrea story was beginning to get a reaction. In a country where every free male over 15 owned a musket or a rifle, that was serious.

Baum took up a position behind the Woloomsac River and spread his forces thinly over a long front. He kept the Indians, under St. Luc de la Corne, in reserve on a plateau behind the main line.

Stark and Warner hit both of Baum's flanks then made a frontal attack with their main body. The British line collapsed everywhere. St. Luc de la Corne and his Indians disappeared at the first shots. Baum and his dragoons tried to make a stand on a hilltop. An American shot blew up the German's ammunition cart. Baum ordered his dragoons to hack their way out with broadswords, but a minute later, he was killed. What was left of his force surrendered.

The Green Mountain Boys arrived at the end of the battle, but there was more to come. A new force of Germans, 700 men and two cannons under Lieutenant Colonel Heinrich Breymann, was approaching. The Germans were incredibly brave and unbelievably stupid. They marched in line through the forest, stumbling around trees and dressing their lines every few steps. When they had a straight line, they'd load and fire a volley. The militia dodged from tree to tree as they fired. Breymann tried to withdraw. The retreat threatened to turn into a rout. He ordered his drummers to beat a slow roll, the international code for "I request a truce." To the New England rustics, the drum roll was so much noise. The retreat became a rout.

While this debacle was going on in the east, a new disaster for Burgoyne was shaping up in the west. St. Leger had entered the Mohawk Valley expecting to find a Tory stronghold. There was a reason.

Many years before, an Irish-born fur trader, William Johnson, had been inducted into the formidable Mohawk Nation and had risen in it to become a chief. He had been married to the daughters of two Mohawk chiefs and had led Iroquois warriors in battle after battle in the French and Indian War. He became Sir William and Royal Superintendent of Indian Affairs.

Johnson built up an enormous fur trading empire. He brought over another Irishman, John Butler, to help manage it and imported dozens of

Irish and Scots tenants and retainers. From his castle, Johnson Hall (now Johnstown, New York), Sir William wielded almost medieval control over the small farmers along the Mohawk River. Johnson died in 1774. It wasn't apparent immediately, but his empire died with him.

In 1776, Brigadier General Nicholas Herkimer led a force of militiamen to Johnson Hall, drove off its Mohawk and Scots Highlander garrison and captured Sir John Johnson, Sir William's son. Johnson was paroled on the condition that he would not fight against the patriots. He promptly broke parole, took his nephew, Colonel Guy Johnson, and a number of his tenants and fled to Montreal. There he organized a Tory regiment, the Royal Greens. John Butler and his son, Walter (the jury foreman in Stephen Vincent Benet's *The Devil and Daniel Webster*), followed suit and created Butler's Tory Rangers.

St. Leger's force included elements of both the Royal Greens and the Tory Rangers. He was joined by 1,000 Mohawks under their English-educated chief, Joseph Brant, Sir William Johnson's brother-in-law. But he found few local Tories. Butler's and Johnson's troops were not popular. The Mohawks were loathed and feared. When they heard the Indians were coming, the local men ran to join Herkimer's militia army.

St. Leger found his way to Albany blocked by rebels who had reconstructed and garrisoned old Ft. Stanwix. He besieged the fort, but Herkimer led his newly-enlisted militiamen up to relieve the siege. Guy Johnson, commanding the Tories and Mohawks, laid an ambush near Oriskany and sprang it as the militia neared the fort. The militia fought back fiercely. Herkimer was wounded, but he sat on the ground puffing his pipe and directing his men. Rain and darkness put a temporary end to the fighting. When the sun came up, the Tories and Indians had fled back to their lines around the fort. The militia, however, were too cut up to continue on. They retreated, and Herkimer died a few days later.

But a second relief column was on the way, this one led by Benedict Arnold. The saturnine Connecticut general had few men—Schuyler had none to spare—but he had an idea. He found a half-wit named Hon Yost Schuyler (no relation to the general) in jail as a Tory sympathizer. The Indians regarded the mentally retarded as innocents incapable of telling lies. Arnold told Hon Yost he could be free if he would go to Ft. Stanwix and tell the besiegers that the famous General Arnold was coming with an overwhelming force of rebels. Hon Yost did as he was told, and the Mohawks decamped. St. Leger and his Tories marched back to Canada. Burgoyne would never meet them in Albany.

He wouldn't meet Howe, either. Lord George Germain, secretary of state for colonies, had approved Burgoyne's plan for ending the war. But he had also approved Howe's plan for ending the war. Howe's plan called for capturing the rebel capital, Philadelphia. Howe sailed to Philadelphia, leaving a small force under General Sir Henry Clinton. Clinton eventually marched a little way up the Hudson. Then he stopped. There would be no linkup in Albany with any other British forces.

The rebels, though, were gaining strength daily. The unpopular Schuyler had been removed. Arnold was his logical successor, but Arnold was a New Englander, and New England already had its quota of major generals, Congress decided. The command went to Horatio Gates, a retired English officer who was popular with the New Englanders. Reports of the Jane McCrea murder had been circulating through the colonies for some time, and volunteers from New England and elsewhere swelled the ranks of the Continental army. As soon as he took command, Gates exploited the situation by sending an indignant letter about the murder to Burgoyne. That gave Jane McCrea's story more publicity and brought in even more volunteers. Soon Gates had one and a half times as many men as Burgoyne, and his force was still growing.

Burgoyne's was shrinking. Desertion became a problem in the British camp. Gentleman Johnny finally reinstated flogging, prescribing 1,000 lashes for deserters who were captured.

George Washington sensed that something important was about to happen in the north. He sent Daniel Morgan and 1,000 riflemen to aid Gates.

Morgan's Riflemen and their commander were legends in their own time. Morgan had been a wagoner in the French and Indian War. He'd had a dispute with a British officer, who struck him with the flat of his sword. Morgan, a tall, muscular man, laid the officer out with one punch. The officer had Morgan flogged. From that day on, the only thing Morgan wanted to do with the British was kill them. That was unfortunate for the British, because they recognized him as one of the most talented commanders on the American side.

Morgan's Riflemen were the elite of frontier Indian fighters. They and other frontier riflemen in the Revolution were among the first of a unique American type that would persist for the next hundred years. Called pioneers, long hunters or mountain men, they were the first representatives of European civilization in thousands of miles of total wilderness. Over that century, their lifestyle and even their clothing would change very little. Morgan's Riflemen wore hunting shirts instead of uniforms, and each carried a long, custom-made rifled flintlock of uniquely American pattern. The rifle was quite different from the musket, every householder's weapon in the settled part of the colonies. The musket had advantages: it was faster to load—important in regular military tactics—it could take a bayonet, and it could fire shot as well as single balls. That made it the choice of townsmen, who had more use for a shotgun than a big game rifle and who had to have a military weapon for militia musters.

The musket's one disadvantage was its inaccuracy. The musket could, if the marksman was in luck, hit some part of a target the size of a man at 80 yards. The rifle could hit a six-inch, or smaller, circle at 200 yards. If your life depended on hitting an elusive deer or an advancing Indian, the rifle was a most necessary piece of equipment. Rifles quickly became popular with frontiersmen.

The original American rifles had been copies of weapons brought over by German and Swiss immigrants to Pennsylvania. Because lead was scarce on the frontier, gunsmiths learned to reduce the bore from a .60 or .70 inch diameter to .40 or .50. To get the most from the equally scarce powder, they lengthened the barrel to get complete combustion. The long barrel also meant a longer sight radius, which made aiming more accurate. The marksmanship the frontiersmen demonstrated with these pieces amazed American townsmen and foreign soldiers. Even the German *jägers* were impressed.

Among these ace marksmen, one of the stars was a frontiersman named Tim Murphy. Murphy loved shooting more than anything else, and all his wealth was tied up in his rifle. It was a double-barrel, over-and-under gun, with a flash pan and frizzen on each barrel. After firing the top barrel, Murphy would pull a catch and rotate the bottom barrel to the top position, lining it up with the cock that held the flint.

Although Gates now outnumbered Burgoyne, he decided on a defensive battle and entrenched a plateau called Bemis Heights. He was afraid his raw recruits wouldn't be able to cope with Burgoyne's Indians (most of whom had already deserted).

To the outgunned Burgoyne, an offensive fight was just fine. Gentleman Johnny never refused a challenge; no one had ever seen him shrink from risking everything on one throw of the dice. To lead the attack, he chose Simon Fraser, whose cousin Jane had been murdered by the Indians. If Fraser had any personal misgivings about the campaign, he didn't let them show. Personal disaster was no stranger to that Scottish aristocrat. In 1745, he had commanded a regiment in the army of Bonny Prince Charlie. His father, chief of the Fraser Clan and Lord of Lovat, had been beheaded. Young Simon had been pardoned, however, when he volunteered to raise a regiment to fight in America. That was more than a generation ago, and Fraser's permanent rank was still only colonel. He had lost his title, been disinherited and now his cousin had been murdered. He had received little from the crown but his life. If it was his fate to fight for the Hanoverians, though, he would fight as well as he could.

Fraser, reinforced with what was left of the German *jägers* and grenadiers—2,000 men in all—swept wide around Gates' left flank to take a hill overlooking the American entrenchments. Burgoyne himself, leading 1,100 of the British infantry, would strike at the center of the fortifications. Major General Baron Adolph von Riedesel, commander of Burgoyne's Brunswick contingent, would take his Germans, with the rest of the British infantry, around Gates' right and cut his communications.

Gates wanted to stay in his trenches. Arnold raged at him to attack the enemy columns as they were on the move. At last Gates gave him permission to send Morgan's men out to protect the left flank. Morgan made first contact with the Canadians and Indians who formed Fraser's right flank and drove them back. Filled with a premature feeling of victory, Morgan and his men chased them wildly through the woods. In a clearing, they ran right into Fraser's light infantry. That was a different matter. The bayonet-armed light infantry scattered the bayonetless riflemen back into the forest. Morgan gobbled frantically on the turkey call he used instead of bugle to rally his men. Arnold brought up the Continental regiments of Colonels Joseph Cilley and Alexander Scammell to stop Fraser. After heavy hand-to-hand fighting these troops, too, were were driven back.

Burgoyne ordered a general advance. Arnold noticed a gap open between Fraser's corps and the British center. He threw Brigadier General Enoch Poor's brigade into it. The battle swayed back and forth. The fire of Morgan's sharpshooters wiped out gun crews and drove British infantry out of the clearings. Time after time, Burgoyne himself rallied his troops and led bayonet charges to retake his guns from the Continental infantry. Arnold's entire division was now engaged, but it was facing two-thirds of Burgoyne's entire army. Arnold rode back to headquarters and demanded reinforcements. Gates reluctantly sent up one brigade, Brigadier General Ebenezer Learned's, but he ordered Arnold not to go back to the front.

Riedesel, hearing firing, marched to the sound of the guns. His troops hit Arnold's unsuspecting division on its right flank while the commander was confined to headquarters. Dusk was falling, and the Americans left the field to the British.

It was a Pyrrhic victory. The British lost 600 killed wounded or captured. One brigade, 350 strong at the start of the battle, had only 60 men and
five officers. The Americans lost 65 killed, 218 wounded and 33 missing.
Gates' army was still increasing, while desertions from Burgoyne's were also
increasing. Burgoyne fortified his position. Most of his line was protected by
a deep ravine, with a secondary trench system in front of it. On the western
end of the ravine, his right, he built a horseshoe-shaped redoubt. On the left
of his line, near the river, he built another system of redoubts for his camp.
He waited for an attack that never came. Gates stayed in his own fortified
positions and continued to accept volunteers.

By October 7, Gates had 11,000 men; Burgoyne, about 5,000. Gentleman Johnny, the gambler, prepared one last stroke.

Once again, Simon Fraser, commanding Burgoyne's right, led the ac-
tion. He flanked the American left, behind a light screen of Indians and
Canadian militia. Morgan urged an immediate attack with a strong force
against Fraser. Gates consented to send only two brigades, Morgan's to hit
Fraser's right, and Poor's to attack his left. Poor, his brigade swollen to 800
men, let the British light infantry fire one volley, then charged with bayonets.
The British, outnumbered four to one, fell back toward the western redoubt.
Morgan had farther to go, but his riflemen and light infantry soon had
Fraser's right wing in retreat. Gates decided to add Learned's brigade to the
fight. That brigade moved hesitantly against Riedesel's experienced Germans
until a little man on a bay horse appeared. Arnold, after a knock-down-drag-
out fight with Gates, had been relieved of his command and confined to his
tent. Unable to contain himself, he broke arrest and rode to the nearest
fighting. Three times he charged the Brunswickers, and the Germans withdrew toward the British western redoubt.

Fraser rallied his own brigade, the 24th Foot, and tried to turn the tide.
The British began to regain lost ground.

Morgan called Tim Murphy, his best available marksman. He pointed to
Fraser, riding from point to point on a big gray horse.

"Kill that officer," he said.

Murphy rested his rifle barrel over a log, took aim and fired. The bullet
passed through the mane of Fraser's horse. The sniper rotated his rifle barrels
and fired again. A bullet chipped a piece off Fraser's saddle. Aides rushed to
the general and begged him to make himself less conspicuous. Fraser told
them generals were supposed to make themselves conspicuous. Murphy
reloaded his rifle—only the top barrel this time. He didn't have time to load
two barrels: his target might move away any second. He fired. Simon Fraser
slumped in his saddle and fell off the horse. It was the mystical third shot, but

all sources agree that Murphy fired three times. The aides picked the dying Fraser up and dashed toward the redoubt. When the British troops saw the general leaving the field, they swarmed after him, leaving all of their other wounded on the ground.

Gates' other troops spontaneously left their own earthworks and moved toward the British. Benedict Arnold led them on a charge right into the enemy's western redoubt. A wounded German soldier fired at Arnold and struck him in the thigh. Arnold fell off his horse but stopped his men from killing the German.

"Don't hurt him," he said. "He's a fine fellow. He only did his duty."

Burgoyne's troops streamed back the the main camp. By nightfall, it was apparent that the British position had become untenable. Six days later, Burgoyne surrendered.

France had long considered aiding the Americans. Burgoyne's surrender convinced her. Spain and Holland joined France, and a colonial rebellion turned into a world war. The war would drag on for five more years, but Britain never again had a chance of recovering her colonies. One Indian atrocity and three shots fired by an obscure backwoodsman had changed the world.

There would be a United States of America.

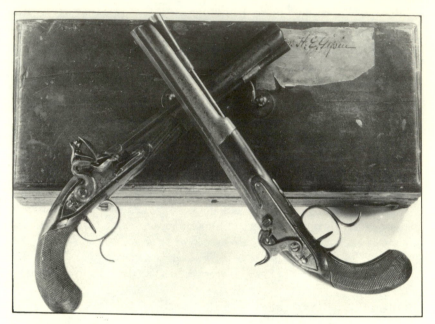

Two

Interview in Weehawken, Mystery in the West

July 11, 1804, Weehawken, New Jersey

The sun was shining brightly a little before seven a.m. Wednesday, July 11, 1804. A boat containing a rower and two gentlemen scraped onto the shore under the Hudson Palisades near Weehawken, New Jersey. The two gentlemen jumped out. One, in spite of the sun, carried a folded umbrella. The other, the one who seemed to be in charge, was a short, slim, elegantly dressed man in his late forties. He and his companion trudged to

Pistols used in the Hamilton-Burr duel. The pistol in front had been converted from flintlock to percussion so it could be used in the Civil War. The pistols have unusually sophisticated sights and are weighted to improve their balance. Pushing a trigger forward "sets" it for a light trigger pull. (Courtesy of Chase Manhattan Archives.)

the top of Weehawken Heights. A few minutes later, another boat pulled up to the river bank. Two more men in city clothes stepped out and started climbing the hill, while another stayed at the bottom of the hill with the oarsman. Again, one of the climbers carried a folded umbrella. He also had a small case. The other climber was small, elegant and exuded dignity—almost a twin of the first leader. Both parties met on the hilltop. A series of hurried conferences followed, then two shots.

General Alexander Hamilton, one-time commanding general of the army, former secretary of the treasury, one of the principal architects of the Constitution and aide to General George Washington during the Revolution, lay dying. Colonel Aaron Burr, vice president of the United States and former U.S. senator, descended the hill, his face obscured by his second's umbrella (in case of witnesses), got into his boat and was rowed across the river.

An American myth was born.

Hamilton and Burr were New York's most prominent attorneys. They were Revolutionary War heroes and uncommonly successful politicians. Their beginnings, though, could hardly have been more different.

Hamilton was born on St. Croix in the Danish Virgin Islands, the bastard son of Rachel Lavien (also spelled Levine and Lawien), the wife of a wealthy Jewish merchant, and James Hamilton, the disreputable younger son of a Scottish laird. Rachel's husband, John Michael Lavien, eventually divorced her and got a decree disinheriting Rachel's illegitimate children, Alexander and James, Jr., and forbidding her to remarry. James Hamilton abandoned Rachel, who ran a small general store. Rachel tutored Alexander and sent him to a Hebrew school in Nevis. In later life, Hamilton avoided any public reference to his illegitimacy and early education. When Rachel died in 1768, Lavien successfully laid claim to all of her property, leaving Alexander and James, Jr. without a penny.

James, the older brother, was apprenticed to a carpenter and Alexander worked as a clerk for a merchant, a family friend named Nicholas Cruger. He also wrote articles for the local newspaper. His writing attracted the attention of the Presbyterian minister for Christiansted, Hugh Knox. Knox was an American who had received religious instruction in New Jersey from the Rev. Aaron Burr, who later became president of the College of New-Jersey (now Princeton). Knox sent Alexander Hamilton to America to complete his education at King's College (now Columbia) in New York. Hamilton never returned to the West Indies. No matter how high he rose in his adopted country, though, he remained conscious that he was, as President John Adams once put it, "the bastard brat of a Scotch pedlar."

Aaron Burr, son of the minister who had instructed Knox, was also the grandson of the famous Jonathan Edwards. The Rev. Aaron Burr and his wife died of smallpox when young Aaron was two years old. Jonathan Edwards was called upon to take over the presidency of Princeton, but he died from a smallpox inoculation. His wife died shortly afterwards from dysentery. For a while, Aaron and his sister, Sally, were cared for by the Shippen family of Philadelphia—the family of Benedict Arnold's second wife, Peggy.

Later, living with his uncle, Timothy Edwards, Burr applied for admission to Princeton. He was 11 years old. The college authorities decided that was too young, but they allowed him to enter when he was 13. Once in, Burr proved to be so brilliant the administration let him skip freshman year. After more study, young Burr decided to be a lawyer. He entered America's first law school, named after his brother-in-law, Tapping Reeve, in Litchfield, Connecticut. He was, in other words, about as establishment as one got in colonial America. Burr was no more comfortable in the establishment, however, than Hamilton was out of it. Both entered the independence movement as soon as it appeared.

When war broke out, Burr joined Benedict Arnold's expedition to Quebec as a gentleman volunteer. His gallantry at Quebec earned him a commission as a major and a place on Washington's staff. He wanted action, not staff work, however, so he transferred to the field army under Major General Israel Putnam. At that time, he was 20 years old.

At the same time, Hamilton was a captain commanding a battery of artillery he had raised as a student activist. He was 19. When Howe invaded Manhattan, Hamilton, under the command of Henry Knox, Washington's chief of artillery, was preparing to make a last stand. As Hamilton was supervising the siting of his guns, a short officer in a major's uniform galloped up and offered to lead the troops to Harlem Heights by a little-known route.

Knox, who was watching Hamilton, told the major retreat now was impossible. But the major, Burr, appealed directly to the men. They cheered him and prepared to retreat. A British patrol almost stumbled on them as they were underway, but Burr and two other American horsemen drove them off. Burr's insubordination brought its reward: there was no mention of his feat in Knox's report.

During the retreat from New York, Hamilton's guns covered the rear guard. Later, Hamilton fought with conspicuous gallantry during Washington's offensive in New Jersey and was promoted to lieutenant colonel and assigned to Washington's staff. Hamilton proved to be an even better staff officer than he was a field soldier. He was a key person in the nerve center of the American Revolution.

Burr, on the other hand, was far from the nerve center and not close to action, either. Putnam had proved himself to be a man of great bravery and vast incompetence; Washington was not eager to have him involved in a major campaign. Burr finally saw some action leading a brigade, a position that called for a brigadier general, while a lieutenant colonel. Even his enemies admitted that Burr was an extremely effective brigade commander, one with loads of initiative. At one juncture, though, his initiative led him to disregard Washington's orders. He never again got a chance to command a considerable body of troops.

After the war, Hamilton was appointed a delegate to the Continental Congress from New York, having made a politically advantageous marriage during the war. He had married one of the daughters of Philip Schuyler, the aristocratic general who had failed to stop Burgoyne. Schuyler, as well as being enormously rich, was the leader of one of most politically powerful clans in the state. The handsome and charming young Hamilton had taken full advantage of his opportunities.

Burr was equally attractive to women. One of the reasons for his lack of promotions was the abundance of his amours. He, however, seemed to ignore his opportunities. He fell in love with and married, after her husband died, the homely wife of a British officer. She was 10 years older than he and had five children. Unlike Hamilton, who confessed to at least one affair after he was married and was rumored to have had many more, Burr apparently remained faithful to his Theodosia. She bore him a daughter, also named Theodosia, but died before the child reached her teens. After his wife died, Burr, an admirer of Lord Chesterfield, became notorious for his affairs.

Both Hamilton and Burr were admitted to the New York bar soon after the war. As the state had disbarred all Tory lawyers, there was plenty of work to keep both men as busy as they wanted to be. They occasionally opposed each other and occasionally worked together.

Hamilton, though, was drawn to national politics. He became one of New York's three delegates to the convention called to amend the Articles of Confederation. It was a frustrating experience. The other two delegates, Robert Yates and John Lansing, agreed with Governor George Clinton, who wanted nothing more than a loose federation of totally sovereign states. Hamilton, on the other hand, wanted a strong central government with state governors appointed by the president. The legislature appointed Yates and Lansing because of Clinton's dominance in New York politics. Hamilton's appointment was a sop to Clinton's leading opponent, Philip Schuyler.

Under this arrangement, Hamilton was able to express his ideas. But each state had only one vote and, as his two fellow delegates always voted against his ideas, his state's vote was always opposed to what he desired. Finally Yates and Lansing walked out. That was little better. Now the New York delegation had no quorum, and Hamilton couldn't vote at all.

The major architect of the draft constitution that was adopted was James Madison, although Hamilton was responsible for a number of modifications. Hamilton thought the draft provided a far weaker central government than he would have preferred, and it gave too much power to "the democracy"— the general populace. "The people," he said, "are turbulent and ever changing; they seldom judge or determine right." Nevertheless, he signed the draft, finding it far superior to the weak Articles of Confederation.

Clinton, of course, was adamantly opposed to the proposed constitution. Hamilton contacted John Jay, who, though not a delegate to the convention, shared many of his views. He proposed that they write a number of letters, to be signed "Publius," to the newspapers, explaining the constitution to the people. Jay wrote four of the first five letters; then ill health forced him to stop. To replace him, Hamilton recruited Madison. Before the state ratifying conventions were over, the letters were collected and published as *The Federalist*, one of the world's classic works of political philosophy. "Their [Hamilton and Madison's] theory," a scholar wrote in 1961, "was so comprehensive and so penetrating that it has been little modified in one hundred and seventy years."

Hamilton did more than write. He attended the New York ratification convention and led the fight for the proposed constitution. Although Clinton was president of the convention, New York ratified the constitution by a vote of 30 to 27.

When George Washington was elected first president under the new constitution, he appointed Hamilton his secretary of the treasury. For secretary of state, he chose a man who was to be Hamilton's principal ideological opponent, Thomas Jefferson. Jefferson, author of the Declaration of Independence, and America's second renaissance man (after Benjamin Franklin) was as opposed to centralized government as George Clinton. He was to found what was variously called the Republican, Democratic-Republican or Republican-Democratic party, and which is today the Democratic party. Of Jefferson's many disagreements with Hamilton, one of the strongest was over judicial review as expressed in Hamilton's seventy-eighth "Publius" letter: "The complete independence of the courts of justice is peculiarly essential in a limited Constitution. By a limited Constitution, I understand one which contains certain specified exceptions to the legislative authority; such, for instance, as it shall pass no bills of attainder, no *ex post facto* laws and the like. Limitations of this kind can be preserved in practice no other way than through the medium of courts of justice, whose duty it must be to declare all acts contrary to the manifest tenor of the Constitution void."

Hamilton and Jefferson symbolized the two extremes in American political life. There was a third force, equally strong but unorganized. People inspired by this force settled the country. The central government acquired new land, but independent individuals, each interested only in bettering himself, moved there and "won the west."

At this time, the best-known proponent of the spirit of "take care of Number One" was Aaron Burr.

Burr devoted most of his energy to living well. As one of the most expensive lawyers in New York, he earned a more than substantial income, but it was barely sufficient to support his princely lifestyle. Enormously persuasive, he could always get a loan, and he was always in debt. He occasionally supplemented his income with schemes of dubious legality, but, as he often said, "Great souls care little for small morals."

Burr wasn't unique in New York. He took a large fee from a Dutch company to lobby for favorable legislation after Hamilton's firm had broken off negotiations with the same company. Burr's lobbying technique was simple: he persuaded the legislators to see things his client's way by bribing them. But Hamilton's firm had demanded a $25,000 "loan" to Philip Schuyler's canal company. The difference was that Hamilton's firm wanted the company to bribe the lobbyist. Burr gave the bribe money to the lawmakers.

Burr showed little interest in politics until after the Constitution was adopted. About the only national issue he vehemently espoused was the abolition of slavery. Burr became a Federalist to support a friend, Judge Robert Yates, whom Hamilton, in spite of his differences with Yates at the constitutional convention, had induced to run for governor against George Clinton. Yates lost, but Clinton, seeing in Burr a potential political power, appointed him attorney general. One of Burr's jobs in office was to appoint the committee which rerouted the Boston Post Road. Some thought it was not entirely coincidental that the new route went through land Burr had recently purchased, making him a tidy profit.

Burr's style in politics was as different from Hamilton's as it was in most other things. Hamilton was an ideologue: he sincerely believed his opponents were either fools, crooks or traitors. Burr kept an eye out for personal advantage and changed party associations as easily as he changed coats.

Hamilton was a master of invective: he once wrote that Thomas Jefferson was "the atheist in religion and a fanatic in politics," a revolutionary, "a

man of profound ambition and violent passions," "the most intriguing man in the United States," an "intriguing incendiary," "the heart and soul of faction." During the French Revolution, he accused Jefferson of being a French agent. "To be the proconsul of a despotic Directory over the United States, degraded to the condition of a province, can alone be the criminal, the ignoble aim of so seditious, so prostitute a character." Those were not exceptional Hamiltonian outbursts; that was his usual way of describing rivals.

Burr seldom raised his voice and kept his language moderate. Hamilton distrusted people without land or education. Burr campaigned by shaking hands in every bar in New York. Hamilton based his campaigns on abstract ideas; Burr based his on individual self-interest. Hamilton relied on rhetoric; Burr, on organization.

While Burr was organizing a political base in New York City, Hamilton was organizing the national economy. In that first cabinet, Hamilton was one third of what was practically a triumvirate—Washington, Jefferson and Hamilton. As head of the treasury, Hamilton rescued the fledgling United States from the kind of financial instability (and the resultant political instability) that has since plagued many other new nations. His first move was to assume and reduce the national debt, foreign and domestic, including the debts owed by the states. There was a lot of opposition. Some states had already repaid most of their debts: they objected to the national government giving the non-payers a free ride. The payment of government bonds held by individuals and the redemption of Continental currency brought further opposition. Many individuals had sold their securities and currency to speculators for a few cents on the dollar. They said Hamilton was favoring those with money to speculate.

To finance debt reduction, Hamilton got Congress to impose a tax on distilled spirits. The result was the Whiskey Rebellion. While secretary of the treasury, Hamilton commanded the troops that put down the Rebellion. He also created the Coast Guard; founded a national bank, the Bank of the United States, modeled after the Bank of England; and encouraged manufacturing in the United States.

In spite of his genius as an orator, a political scientist and a financier, Hamilton always thought that his greatest strength was as a military leader. Under the second president, John Adams, he became second in command of the army after Washington. In effect, he was the commander-in-chief, the ill and aging Washington being unable to take the field. When Washington suddenly died, Hamilton became commander-in-chief in name as well as in fact.

While involved in government, Hamilton did not neglect the private sector. In the middle 1780s, he founded the Bank of New York, a "land bank," aimed at helping farmers. A little later Hamilton and Burr joined in agitating for a privately-owned water company in New York. Burr formed such a company and got the state legislature to give it the right to form other businesses. He then used most of the water company's capital to found (without the investors' knowledge) the Bank of Manhattan. Burr's bank soon overshadowed Hamilton's Bank of New York. It's still in business. Today, it's called the Chase Manhattan Bank.

In New York, though not yet in the nation, Hamilton and Burr were often linked in the public eye either as collaborators or opponents. In spite of their differences, the two rising lawyers were so similar in age, charm, appearance and intelligence that they became in the minds of their partisans good and evil twins. Which was the good twin and which the evil depended on your politics.

Burr and Hamilton had more in common than charm, looks and intelligence. Both were inveterate schemers. Most of Burr's schemes aimed at letting him continue living like royalty. Most of Hamilton's were for what he conceived to be the good of the country. Hamilton's schemes, though, were potentially far more destructive.

During the Adams administration, Hamilton, as acting commander of the army, ardently favored a war with France. He had two reasons: (1) He saw the French Revolution as the incarnation of all the evils of "democracy." (2) He expected France to force Spain to transfer Louisiana back, giving him a chance to lead an invasion force into the territory and annex it to the United States. He did not intend to stop at Louisiana. As he said in 1799, "If we are to engage in war, our game will be to attack where we can. France is not to be considered as separated from her ally [Spain]. Tempting objects will be within our grasp." Those "tempting objects" included not only Louisiana but East and West Florida, Mexico and all of South America. As commander of the U.S. Army, Alexander Hamilton could be the conqueror of a new western empire for the United States. It was not a wild idea. Mexico seethed with sedition and from 1800 on was to be torn by attempted revolutions. Spain was no longer a great power. Without the French to back her, she was hardly a power at all. A few years later, Hamilton's "twin," Aaron Burr, would get in serious trouble over a similar scheme.

Hamilton went so far as to open private negotiations with British officials about a joint American-British invasion of Latin America. The British plan, which Hamilton did not reject, called for an all-British fleet with some American sailors serving on British ships, taking orders from British officers—in effect, reducing the United States to colonial status. Nothing came of this plan, thanks to John Adams.

President Adams continued trying to resolve the country's differences with France by peaceful means, and he had no intention of invading Spanish territory to save it from the French. Frustrated, Hamilton urged the cabinet to seize control of the government while Adams was in Massachusetts. Fortunately for the development of democracy, nothing came of this idea, either.

Although both were Federalists, Adams and Hamilton could hardly have been less friendly. The feud may have begun in Adams' first campaign. Hamilton, the Federalists' political strategist, knew that Adams was not likely to take direction from "that creole." Hamilton preferred the more malleable Thomas Pinckney of South Carolina, a man whose credentials didn't approach those of the flinty Bostonian. He worked behind the scenes with Federalist leaders so that Pinckney, running for vice president, would get more electoral votes than Adams, running for president. At that time, the candidate with the most electoral votes became president, and the candidate in second place became vice president. Hamilton suggested to South Carolina Federalist leaders that they simply throw out all votes that were not for their native son, Pinckney. To others, he suggested that they vote for Pinckney and for some harmless candidate, like Aaron Burr, rather than Adams. Hamilton's scheme backfired. His machinations split the Federalists. Pinckney not only didn't get as many votes as Adams; he didn't get as many as Thomas Jefferson, the Republican candidate. Jefferson, the leader of the evil "Jacobins," as Hamilton called the Republicans, became vice president.

Meanwhile, as attorney general in a Republican state administration, Burr had decided he was really more of a Republican than a Federalist. Burr, the born aristocrat, felt that he had more in common with ordinary people than with those Hamilton, the low-born alien, referred to as "the good, the wise and the rich."

In New York's first election for the U.S. Senate, the Federalists chose Philip Schuyler and Rufus King. Hamilton's clique had picked King, a move that enraged the Livingstons, New York's second great political clan. If the Schuylers had one of their own, the Livingstons said, there should have been a Livingston senator.

Because senate terms were to be staggered, one of the seats was for a short term. That was Schuyler's seat. In the next election, the Livingstons joined the Clinton faction and elected Aaron Burr.

Although Burr knew how to win votes, he didn't know how to placate political leaders. Upon election to the Senate, he did not immediately resign his attorney general position, although that job had been promised to a Livingston stalwart. He didn't consult the Clinton machine on his votes, either.

In a very short time, Burr had alienated Hamilton and the Schuylers, the Clintons and the Livingstons. On the national scene, his lack of party discipline and his obvious ambition aroused the distrust of Thomas Jefferson. Jefferson came to see the New Yorker as a threat to his own presidential ambitions and, after he had achieved the presidency, to the chances of the Jefferson's Virginia friends, Madison and Monroe. In Hamilton's eyes, Burr began to replace Jefferson as the Prince of Darkness.

Hamilton said, "Burr will certainly attempt to reform the government a la Buonaparte. He is as unprincipled and as dangerous a man as any country can boast—as true a Cataline as ever met in midnight conclave."

Hamilton did his best to keep the Cataline from office. In spite of Republican clamoring, Washington, who relied on Hamilton, refused to appoint Burr ambassador to France. When war with France seemed likely, during the Adams administration, Burr offered his services. Adams recommended to Washington that he be appointed a brigadier general. Washington, who had selected Hamilton as his second in command, said that Burr, although "a brave and able officer" had "equal talents at intrigue."

Concerning this decision, Adams said of Washington, "He has compelled me to promote, over the heads of Lincoln, Gates, Clinton, Knox and others, and even over Pinckney, one of his own triumvirate [Washington's three major generals], the most restless, impatient, artful, indefatigable and unprincipled intriguer in the United States, if not the world, [Hamilton] to be second in command under himself, and now dreaded an intriguer in a poor brigadier [Burr]."

In the presidential election of 1796, Hamilton's politicking, by splitting the Federalists, came close to inadvertently getting Burr a national office. Jefferson, the Republican candidate for president, got only three votes less than Adams, the Federalist candidate. Burr was 38 votes behind Jefferson— mostly because Jefferson, who had almost absolute control of Virginia, prevented his running mate from getting more than one vote from his fiefdom.

Burr could still get votes in New York. He was elected to the state assembly and proceeded to confound both Republicans and Federalists. He proposed a freer bankruptcy law, and criticized the Alien and Sedition Acts, both good Republican positions. He demanded the abolition of slavery in New York, which was a good New York Republican position, but hardly one the national party espoused. He worked for stronger fortifications in New York Harbor, a position agreeable to Federalists, but not Republicans.

In 1800, Burr again ran for vice president. Hamilton again tried to keep Adams from the presidency. Instead of Thomas Pinckney as his candidate, this time he had Charles Cotesworth Pinckney, a new vice presidential candidate. In closed-door sessions, Hamilton tried to get the electors to vote for Pinckney and throw away their presidential votes on favorite sons, thus keeping Adams' vote below Pinckney's. The Republicans asked their electors to vote for both Jefferson and Burr, expecting that Jefferson's greater fame would give him the greater number of votes.

In a pamphlet intended for Federalist leaders, Hamilton attacked Adams as a man unfit for the office. Burr managed to get a copy of the pamphlet before it was distributed and sent it to the newspapers.

Its publication effectively destroyed Hamilton's political career.

Enraged, Hamilton shifted his fire from Jefferson to Burr. He wrote to friends that Burr was "bankrupt beyond redemption, except by the plunder of his country . . . If he can, he will certainly disturb our institutions, to secure himself permanent power, and with it wealth."

Hamilton, though, had lost most of his influence with the Federalists. And the Federalists had lost most of their influence with the voters. Jefferson and Burr tied in electoral votes, because some Federalists thought the one-time Federalist from New York might not be as bad as Jefferson. The election went to the House of Representatives. Hamilton took up his pen again, but it was Burr, not Hamilton, who decided the election.

Under the procedures in force at that time, in the event of an electoral vote tie, the House would vote for one or the other of the two candidates, with each state casting one vote. The Federalists were the majority party, but they controlled only eight of the 16 states. A candidate had to have nine states to be elected.

Burr had earlier written to his friend, Samuel Smith of Maryland—an even closer friend of Jefferson: "It is highly improbable that I shall have an equal number of votes with Mr. Jefferson; but if such should be the result, every man who knows me ought to know that I should utterly disclaim all competition . . . and I now constitute you as my proxy to declare these sentiments if the occasion shall require."

When it became known that there would be a tie when the votes were officially counted, Smith and others close to Jefferson tried to get Burr to say he would resign if elected president. That, however, was further than Burr would go.

Albert Gallatin, another friend of both Burr and Jefferson, was minority leader in the House. As leader of the Republican representatives, Jefferson counted on him to see to it that he and Burr were elected to the offices for which the party had nominated them. Gallatin, though, had an even greater concern. If the House became hopelessly deadlocked, the representatives could elect a president of their own chosing. As the majority was Federalist, the new president would undoubtedly be a Federalist. The Republicans, who had a majority of the voters, saw that possibility as a usurpation. Many vowed to fight. The governor of Pennsylvania promised to call up his state's militia and march on Washington in the event of a "usurpation." More than a choice of Republican candidates was at stake. There was a strong possibility of civil war.

Gallatin could see that there was some sentiment for Burr among the Federalists, but none for Jefferson. He sent a letter to Burr which was delivered February 12, 1801, after the House had begun voting and a deadlock was confirmed. For a century and a half historians have debated what Gallatin wrote. Burr destroyed the letter and never disclosed its contents. In the 1960s, the journal of a contemporary, Benjamin Betterton Howell, came to light and ended the debate. According to Howell, Burr sent for two of his supporters, Peter Townsend and John Swartwout and "laid before them a letter from *Albert Gallatin* informing Burr what was going on—telling him that the election was in the hands of Genl Smith of Maryland—Lynn [Linn] of N Jersey & Edward Livingston of NY—who held the balance of those three states, that they were friendly to Burr—*but to secure them he must be on the spot himself*, and urging him by all means to hasten to Washington without an instant's delay." Townsend told Howell that he and Swartwout urged Burr to leave immediately. Burr packed his bags, but he never left for the capital. Why, no one knows. At the last minute, he may have decided it would be ungentlemanly to renege on his pledge to abstain from competition.

The Federalists caucused on February 16. Burr had offered no specific concessions to his former party. Would Jefferson? Representative James Bayard of Delaware asked Representative John Nicholas of Virginia if Jefferson would preserve the Hamiltonian financial system, if he would keep the navy and if he would retain low-level government employees. Nicholas said he would and claimed to know Jefferson's mind, but he refused to ask the candidate directly. Bayard next asked Samuel Smith the same questions. The next day, Bayard reported to his colleagues, Smith said he had talked with Jefferson and the Republican leader answered each question affirmatively.

On the next vote, Bayard and all members of the South Carolina delegation cast blank ballots rather than vote for Jefferson, but the tie was broken and Jefferson elected.

In spite of what has been taught to generations of school children, Hamilton's opposition to Burr simply wasn't an important factor in the election of 1800. It's unlikely, therefore, that it had anything to do with what happened in Weehawken.

Burr's even-handedness as presiding officer of the Senate angered Republican leaders. Under the Constitution, the vice president has little to do. Jefferson gave Burr no more to do than the Constitution demanded. He totally ignored Burr, his vice president, in matters of patronage, deferring instead to Governor Clinton. Burr decided to run against Clinton for governor of New York.

In his home state, Burr was faced by a combination of the Clintons and Livingstons, aided and abetted by Thomas Jefferson, on the Republican side. And those Republicans were allied with Alexander Hamilton and what remained of the Federalists. Burr offered his leadership, as an independent, to all men of good will, both Republican and Federalist.

What followed for the next two years was the most scurrilous war of words yet seen in New York politics. In the end, Burr lost by 30,829 to 22,130. He seemed to take defeat philosophically. But his career and Hamilton's were continuing to run on parallel tracks. Now both were washed-up politicians.

At this juncture, Burr learned of a letter sent by Dr. Charles Cooper to Philip Schuyler, Hamilton's father-in-law. Somehow, the letter got published in the *Albany Register*. The letter referred to a Federalist campaign strategy meeting. It said in part:

"I beg leave to remark, sir, that the anxiety you discovered when his Honor the Chancellor [Robert Livingston] was about to be nominated, induced me to believe that you entertained a bad opinion of Mr. Burr, especially when taken in connection with General Hamilton's harangue at the city tavern . . . . I could detail to you a still more despicable opinion which General Hamilton has expressed of Mr. Burr."

Burr asked a long-time follower, William P. Van Ness, to take a letter to Hamilton asking him to affirm or deny whether he had offered any opinions about him that could characterized as Cooper had. Hamilton sent back a rambling reply quibbling about what could be "more despicable" than "despicable." He ended the letter with, "I trust, on more reflection, you will see the matter in the same light with me. If not, I can only regret the circumstance, and must abide the consequence." The last phrase was the traditional invitation to a challenge.

Just what the "still more despicable opinion" was has intrigued historians ever since. Burr probably heard it second-hand, and he wanted a confirmation or denial from Hamilton. Burr apparently had shrugged off such political insults as being "a Cataline" and a potential dictator and thief. The insult must have been extremely personal.

Burr tried again, but got another evasive letter. Correspondence continued, carried by Van Ness and Nathaniel Pendleton, a lawyer friend of Hamilton. Finally, Burr challenged Hamilton to a duel.

It was illegal to issue or receive a challenge, and a duelist who killed his opponent could be charged with murder. Nevertheless, dueling was common among those who considered themselves gentlemen. Hamilton had been a second in one duel and was almost a principal in two others. In one of these disputes, with James Monroe, Burr, as Monroe's second, had been able to talk the disputants out of the use of lethal weapons. Hamilton's son Philip had recently been killed in a duel with a Republican politician who challenged him after the young man finished heckling his speech. Five years before, Burr had challenged and fought Hamilton's brother-in-law, John B. Church, following a deliberate insult by Church. In spite of legend, Burr was neither an experienced duelist nor a dead shot. That was his only duel up to this time, and his performance was not impressive. He completely missed Church, and the latter knocked a button off Burr's coat without otherwise harming him.

Bloodless duels were not at all uncommon at this time. Although principals were well advised to make out their wills and otherwise settle their affairs, as both Hamilton and Burr did, the shooters frequently missed. If both principals missed, they could elect to have another go at each other, but few were so bloodthirsty: they had proved their courage and satisfied their honor and were content to have coffee together. It was considered bad form to use rifled pistols in the British Isles and America: they made killing too easy.

Duels were the last vestige of the medieval custom of trial by combat, when it was believed God would not allow an innocent person to lose. By the seventeenth century, some swordsmen, like the real Cyrano de Bergerac, had developed such skill that little was left to chance or the Almighty. Gradually, pistols became the weapon of choice. Smoothbore pistols were inherently inaccurate, and the sights on the typical dueling pistol were rudimentary— seldom even including a rear sight. A proper duelist didn't use sights anyway.

He pointed ("presented") his pistol and fired as soon as the signal was given. Gunsmiths put great effort into building dueling pistols that pointed in line with the arm to eliminate the need for aiming.

The .54 caliber, 16-inch-long flintlock pistols Burr and Hamilton used were a bit different from normal dueling pistols. For one thing, they had adjustable target sights. For another, they had what was called at that time concealed hair triggers—the same as the single set triggers used today in the "free pistol" event in international target shooting. The normal trigger on the weapons used in the Burr-Hamilton duel took a pull of around 10 pounds to fire the pistol. If the trigger were "set" by pushing it forward, the trigger pull was reduced to a half-pound. A 10-pound single-action trigger pull today is considered heavy in a pistol. A half-pound pull, unless the trigger had been deliberately set just before firing, is considered too dangerous to use. The mechanical details of these pistols, which belonged to Hamilton's brother-in-law, John Church, are important. They may be responsible for what happened at the duel. Hamilton owned a fine pair of correct English dueling pistols, but he borrowed Church's for the duel with Burr.

At least 10 days before the duel, Hamilton told his second, Nathaniel Pendleton, according to a statement Pendleton issued *a week after the duel*, he had decided "not to fire at Col. Burr the first time, but to receive his fire and fire into the air."

In a paper he wrote that was sealed and not to be opened unless he died, Hamilton said, "I have resolved, if our interview [the code word for duel to avoid later prosecution] is conducted in the usual manner, and it pleases God to give me the opportunity, to throw away my first fire, and I have thoughts even of reserving my second fire—and thus giving a double opportunity to Col. Burr to pause and to reflect."

This resolution to withhold his first and perhaps even his second chance to fire, could indicate a number of things. One of them is that Hamilton may not have thought much of Burr's marksmanship. One reason could have been Burr's performance in the duel with Church. And the way things turned out, there could have been another reason.

Certainly, Hamilton didn't seem to worry about the duel. The week before it was to take place, both he and Burr attended a Fourth of July dinner held by the Society of Cincinnati, a veterans organization both men belonged to. Burr was his usual reserved self, but Hamilton appeared extraordinarily gay. At one point, he hopped up on a table and sang a Revolutionary War song.

On Weehawken Heights, Burr and Van Ness arrived first, as had been arranged. After the Hamilton party arrived, Pendleton and Van Ness measured the ten paces that were to separate the principals. They cast lots to see who would have the choice of position and who would give the command "Present!" Pendleton won both times. As Pendleton handed Hamilton his pistol, he asked if he wanted the trigger set.

"Not this time," Hamilton said, perhaps indicating that he intended to fire for effect in the next round.

There is no evidence that Burr even knew his pistol had a set trigger.

Hamilton sighted his pistol several times, then put on his glasses, sighted it again and said he was ready. Those are not the actions of a man who plans to fire into the air.

"Present!" Pendleton yelled.

Both pistols came down and went off almost simultaneously. Van Ness later testified that Hamilton fired first; Pendleton said it was Burr. What is certain is that Hamilton did not fire into the air. His bullet hit a tree branch about seven feet above and four feet wide of Burr's head. That was pretty poor marksmanship if he were aiming at Burr, but, considering the inaccuracy of a smoothbore pistol, exceedingly dangerous if he were not. Burr's marksmanship, on the other hand, could hardly have been better. The ball hit Hamilton in the right side, the side turned toward Burr, and lodged in his spine.

In 1976, an authority on antique pistols, Merrill Lindsay, examined the pistols—now owned, ironically, by the Chase Manhattan Bank. He discovered the secret set trigger, which could be set by the pistolman without his second's knowledge. He believes Hamilton set the trigger to give himself an advantage over Burr.

"With his pistol, hair trigger set," Lindsay wrote in the *Smithsonian*, "Hamilton, I maintain, booby-trapped himself that morning of July 11 in Weehawken. Tensely, the two men faced each other. As Hamilton lowered the gun on its target, he was holding a little too tightly and accidentally fired before he had Burr in his sights. Burr squeezed hard and slow, and put an aimed shot into Hamilton."

It may have been that, once again, Hamilton was too tricky for his own good. If so, this time, the mistake was fatal.

Hamilton fell, and Burr rushed forward. Van Ness, though, jumped in front of him and pushed the diminutive Burr back.

"Col. Burr then advanced toward Genl H-----n," the seconds wrote in a joint statement issued immediately after the duel, "with a manner and gesture that appeared to Genl Hamilton's friend to be expressive of regret, but without Speaking turned about and withdrew—Being urged from the field by his friend, as has been subsequently stated, with a view to prevent his being recognized by the Surgeon and Bargemen, who were then approaching."

As soon as he reached the city, Burr asked the surgeon, Hamilton's friend, Dr. David Hosack, to let him know Hamilton's condition. Burr had seen many dead men in the Revolution; some of them, perhaps, he had killed. They were all strangers, though—not men he had worked with, quarreled with and partied with for almost three decades. He was shocked.

So were the state and the country when Hamilton died, about 31 hours after the duel. People remembered that Hamilton had done as much as any man living to give the new republic a sound foundation. Forgotten was the Hamilton who had cried, "The 'people?' Your 'people,' sir, is a great beast." Generally unknown, of course, was the Hamilton who had unofficially plotted foreign policy with foreign powers and the Hamilton who had tried to incite a coup d'etat.

Only one thing mattered. The father of the Constitution had been killed by a New York ward heeler. Now nobody had any doubt about which twin was the evil one. We all like our heroes to be pure and our villains to be purely evil. Who cares today whether Cain was a good father or whether Esau was a gourmet cook? The Clinton faction took advantage of this heaven-sent opportunity to fan popular indignation against Burr.

Crowds paraded in front of Burr's house chanting:

> Oh Burr, Oh Burr, what hast thou done,
> Thou hast shooted dead great Hamilton!
> You hid behind a bunch of thistle,
> And shooted him dead with a great hoss pistol!

New York indicted Burr for issuing a challenge; New Jersey, for murder. Burr traveled south, explored Florida, still Spanish territory a year after the Louisiana Purchase, then returned to Washington to preside over the Senate.

The most important matter to come before the Senate was the impeachment trial of Samuel Chase, an associate justice of the Supreme Court. The trial was a key event in Jefferson's struggle with John Marshall, chief justice of the United States. Marshall had been inaugurated the same day Jefferson became president and Burr vice president. (It must have been an interesting Inauguration Day: all three top officials despised each other.) From the day he took office, Marshall had been developing Hamilton's doctrine of the independence of the courts and the need for judicial review of legislation. Jefferson maintained that the president, having been elected by the whole country, should be the arbiter of what was constitutional.

For a while, Burr suddenly found himself wooed by Jefferson and his followers. The president found a way to express his favor. The year before, May 2, 1803, he had purchased Louisiana from Napoleon. (Jefferson had had to choose between an ideal—weak central government—and a good deal—a million square miles for four cents an acre. Fortunately for all of us, he took the pragmatic approach.) The French had, as Hamilton expected, forced the Spanish to give it back to France, which then sold it. Now Louisiana needed officials to govern it. Jefferson appointed J. B. Prevost, Burr's stepson, judge of the superior court of New Orleans, James Brown, his brother-in-law, secretary of the Louisiana Territory (the northern portion of the Louisiana Purchase, with its capital in St. Louis), and James Wilkinson, Burr's closest friend, governor of the Louisiana Territory. Wilkinson was also commander in chief of the army.

Burr's dignity and fairness as presiding officer at the trial were admitted by all. He favored neither side, and Chase was acquitted.

On the opening day of the Senate, Senator William Plumer of New Hampshire had written in his diary: "This is, I believe, the first time that ever a Vice President appeared in the Senate the first day of a session. It certainly is the first time, & God grant it may be the last, that ever a man, so justly charged with such an infamous crime [the murder of Hamilton], presided in the American Senate." At the conclusion of the trial, Plumer wrote: "Mr. Burr has certainly, on the whole, done himself, the Senate & the nation honor by the dignified manner in which he has presided over this high & numerous Court."

It was a performance Jefferson never forgot.

Three days after the trial, Burr's term as vice president expired. There is no transcript of his last speech to the Senate, but it left hardened politicians sobbing like children.

Burr knew he no longer had a political future in his home state. He conferred with General Wilkinson, whom he had known since the Quebec expedition, and went west. What Wilkinson and Burr plotted is still the subject of argument. It's certain that Burr had revived Hamilton's old dream of an invasion of Spain's ramshackle empire. There were also rumors that he planned to separate the western states and the Louisiana Purchase from the United States

Secession conspiracies were nothing new in the infant United States. Shortly before the duel, Federalists in New England hatched a plot to secede from the rest of the country. They approached, without success, first Hamilton, then Burr, to lead the proposed confederation. Separatist movements in the West appeared, too. Spain had defied the Treaty of Paris that ended the Revolution by claiming the northern boundary of West Florida (the Gulf coast west of the peninsula) to be 100 miles north of the treaty boundary and by refusing free passage down the Mississippi. John Jay negotiated a trade treaty with Spain that recognized Spanish control of the Mississippi's mouth, but it was not ratified.

In 1786, though, most westerners had not heard that the "stab-in-the-back treaty" had not been ratified. A movement, called the Spanish Conspiracy began, aimed at getting the western states to secede from the union and deal with Spain themselves.

Burr's friend, General Wilkinson, was a leader of the conspiracy.

It's become impossible to pinpoint the details of Burr's scheme, because Burr and his agents told so many people so many conflicting stories.

In the course of his diplomatic career, Henry Adams uncovered secret letters from Anthony Merry, the British ambassador to the United States, to his government. Merry was violently anti-American, and Burr apparently told him what he wanted to hear. One dispatch from Merry said:

> Mr. Burr . . . has mentioned to me that the inhabitants of Louisiana seem determined to render themselves independent of the United States, and that the execution of their design is only delayed by the difficulty of obtaining previously an assurance of protection and assistance from some foreign Power, and of concerting and connecting their independence with that of the inhabitants of the Western parts of the United States, who must always have a command over them by the rivers which communicate with the Mississippi. It is clear to me that Mr. Burr (although he has not yet confided to me the exact nature and extent of his plan) means to endeavor to be the instrument of effecting such a connection. He has told me that the inhabitants of Louisiana, notwithstanding that they are almost all of French or Spanish origin, as well as those of the Western part of the United States, would, for many obvious reasons, prefer having the protection and assistance of Great Britain to the support of France.

"Many obvious reasons" indeed! Merry, all his contemporaries agreed, was not the brightest star in the diplomatic firmament. Far different was another Englishman Burr cultivated. Colonel Charles Williamson, a British secret agent, was an intimate of men high in the British government, including Henry Dundas, Viscount Melville, Pitt's first lord of the admiralty. Williamson was recruiting American citizens for a clandestine army Britain hoped to use in the West Indies. Walter Flavius McCaleb discovered Williamson's reports to Melville and other British officials years after Adams' discovery of Merry's correspondence. Whether Williamson had the whole story is uncertain, but he was definitely a harder man to fool than Merry. According to his reports, the Burr conspiracy was aimed at invading Mexico and the Floridas with British help. Williamson also mentions, in one of his 14 letters, western separatism, but that was to be effected by another operation of which Burr was unaware.

With a small fleet in the Gulf of Mexico, Williamson told the chief of the admiralty, and an expenditure of less than 200,000 pounds, he "would expect to see 50,000 North Americans with Colonel Burr at their head far on their March to the City of Mexico."

Unfortunately for Burr, Napoleon was gathering ships for an invasion of England, and Pitt decided he couldn't afford to fish in the Caribbean.

Because he could see no help from England, Burr, with truly heroic chutzpah, turned to Spain. But the Spanish ambassador, red-headed Carlos Martínez de Yrujo, was no Merry. He had an American wife, followed American politics and kept his eyes open. Burr's agent, Jonathan Dayton, told Yrujo about Burr's meetings with Merry and offered to sell him information about the plot. Yrujo was not impressed. He already knew about the meetings and knew that Burr had designs on Spanish territory. To discredit Burr in the United States, he started a rumor—spread by Stephen Minor, a secret Spanish agent—that Burr was trying to carve off the western U.S. states and territories to create a new empire. That, of course, is what Burr led Merry to believe he was planning.

Dayton's story to Yrujo, though, was just to put the Spaniard off guard. Dayton came back and admitted that the conspirators had failed to get British support. He told a wilder story: Burr would take over the capital and kidnap the president.

That story was wild enough to intrigue Yrujo. He recommended to Madrid that his government support Burr. But the Spanish government had other information. According to its trusted "Agent 13," Burr still planned to invade Mexico. It authorized Yrujo to give Dayton $2,400, just to keep him talking.

Agent 13 was Brigadier General James Wilkinson.

Wilkinson, who has been called "America's greatest rascal, an honor to be treasured, since the competition is severe," got involved with Spain after the Spanish Conspiracy. He secretly became a Spanish citizen and a secret agent of Spain. As Agent 13, he received $2,000 a year while he was commander-in-chief of the U.S. Army. Burr never suspected.

"Burr is as far from a fool as any man I ever saw," Andrew Jackson once said, "yet he is as easily fooled as any man I ever knew."

In Jackson's fiefdom, Tennessee, Burr's proposal to go filibustering in Spanish territory made him a hero. It's possible that Jackson, an ambitious lawyer, planter, governor-elect and militia general, may also have favored western secession. The age was far more revolutionary than we usually realize. But there was, as events later proved, little popular support for secession. The Spanish conspiracy was long dead, and denser politicians than Burr would have seen that people in the western states were not longing to leave the union. There may have been such sentiment among the French and Spanish in the Orleans Territory, but they were numerically insignificant.

At the time, the United States and Spain seemed to be on the verge of war. When war came, the evidence indicates Burr planned to lead a volunteer army into Mexico. He would then make himself emperor of what had been New Spain. If the opportunity for invasion didn't come, he had other plans in the West. He had acquired title to land along the Ouachita River in Louisiana Territory. He could establish a colony there or sell the land to other speculators. While waiting to see which way the diplomatic ball would bounce, he tried to put himself in position to move.

Burr still needed money. He had been able to con some from Harmon Blennerhasset, an Irish aristocrat who had an estate in the wilderness, but that could be only pump-priming. He bought some supplies and raised a force of about 50 men and started down the river.

Just what Burr hoped to accomplish with this tiny force remains a mystery. He may have hoped to make it the nucleus of a volunteer army on the outbreak of war with Spain. He may have hoped to provoke a war by invading Mexico. Or the whole project may have been the action of an ambitious, frustrated man desperate to do something, anything, to regain the political limelight.

The "conspiracy" had been a top story in American newspapers for months, but as there was no evidence, the government could do nothing.

Then Wilkinson decided things were getting too hot and wrote to Jefferson about the "treason" being enacted on the frontier. Jefferson ordered Burr's arrest. Wilkinson instituted illegal martial law in New Orleans and tried to seize Burr. Burr gave himself up to civil authorities in Mississippi Territory. He was sure that if Wilkinson got him, he'd never get a trial. He recommended that his followers go home or settle on lands along the Ouachita River, which would be an excellent area to colonize. The Mississippi grand jury refused to indict Burr, but the judge would not release him to leave. He left anyway but was arrested near the West Florida border.

Burr was finally indicted and tried for treason in Richmond, with John Marshall presiding. George Hay, the prosecutor, was in daily contact with Jefferson, who directed the government's strategy. Earlier, Jefferson had said of Burr, "of his guilt there can be no doubt," which was certainly a prejudicial statement. There was a great deal of oratory, but Marshall ruled that the government had presented no evidence of Burr having committed a single overt act of treason. According to the Constitution, treason requires an overt act witnessed by two people. Burr was acquitted.

Burr was tried again, for the misdemeanor of organizing an expedition to invade Spanish territory. He was found not guilty again. The government kept trying. Prosecutor George Hay proposed to try Burr for treason again in other states, but Marshall ruled there was not enough evidence of overt acts in those places, either. He did allow Hay to proceed in Ohio against Burr for the misdemeanor. But Hay, now disgusted with the case and especially with Wilkinson, recommended no further prosecution. Wilkinson had given Jefferson a letter in cipher which he said had been written by Burr but almost certainly wasn't, and definitely had been doctored by Wilkinson, the falsified version of which Judge Marshall said contained no evidence of treason. Before the grand jury, Wilkinson had contradicted himself several times and barely escaped indictment. At the trial, he continually shifted ground and contradicted himself. Jefferson, though, kept this wholly unwholesome conspirator in command of the army. The War of 1812 showed that Wilkinson was even more of a disaster in wartime than he was in peacetime. He left the country and died in Mexico.

Burr, too, left the country after his legal ordeal. He traveled around Europe for four years, proposing wild schemes and having all of them rejected.

Finally, he returned to New York to practice law. His wife had died long before, his beloved grandson had died, his equally beloved daughter had been lost at sea, and he contracted a loveless marriage with a rich widow. He died September 14, 1836, the same day the widow's divorce from him was granted. Her lawyer was Alexander Hamilton, Jr.

Shortly before Burr died, American settlers in Texas revolted and gained their independence.

"There!" Burr said, "You see? I was right! I was only 30 years too soon! What was treason in me 30 years ago is patriotism now."

By that time, though, Burr, the evil twin, was too firmly planted in his countrymen's demonology—right behind his old leader, Benedict Arnold—for his reputation to ever change.

Three

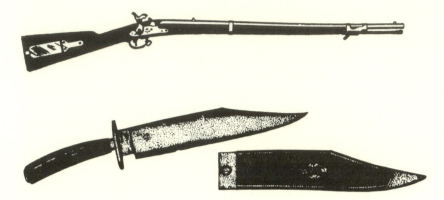

"Remember the Alamo!"

March 6, 1836, San Antonio, Texas

A flag fluttered up the staff atop the bell tower of church of San Fernando. It was not, the lookouts on the walls of the mission compound saw, the flag of the Mexican Republic. It was blood-red.

In the mission-turned fort, the co-commander, Colonel James Bowie, sent out a courier under a white flag to ask what terms the government was offering.

A Mexican staff officer gave the courier a note reading, "The Mexican Army cannot come to terms under any conditions with rebellious foreigners

Top: "Kentucky" rifle converted from flintlock to percussion operation. This specimen seems to have had the barrel shortened, too, probably to make it handier on horseback. Below: Bowie knife, patterned after Jim Bowie's. Before revolvers appeared, these were the most popular American personal defense weapons.

to whom there is no other recourse left, if they wish to save their lives, than to place themselves immediately at the disposal of the Supreme Government."

While Bowie's courier was conferring with the enemy, the other co-commander, Lieutenant Colonel William Travis, was supervising the loading of a cannon. It was the 18-pounder, largest of the twenty guns in the fort. He directed the gunners to fire at the middle of the Mexican army.

The cannon belched flame and sent a big iron cannon ball crashing into a Mexican-occupied building in San Antonio de Béjar.

"That's our answer to your 'no quarter,'" Travis said.

In the fort, called the Alamo after an army company from the Mexican town of Alamo de Parras, which had occupied it for decades, some 150 men, representing the Mexican state of Texas, were defying a federal army that eventually built up to some 5,000 men. There were not enough troops in the fort to adequately man the walls; there was not enough food for a long siege, and the command was divided between two colonels who, as their reaction to the red flag showed, did not always agree.

The results of their defiance would have astounded the wildest dreamer among them, even though the events that led to this crisis were totally unprecedented.

On October 19, 1781, Lord Cornwallis's army marched out of York-town to the tune of a popular English music hall song, "The World Turned Upside Down." Cornwallis's band leader was prophetic. The world turned and continued to turn. The world of monarchs and nobles turned upside down in France; then Napoleon made himself emperor and overturned most of the rest of Europe. In the New World, the slaves of Haiti drove out their French masters; Brazil became independent under another emperor, Dom Pedro I; and dozens of revolutionary movements sprang up in South America and Mexico.

Mexico, or New Spain, was the pride of the Spanish Empire. The Spanish focused their interest, though, on central Mexico, the land of silver mines, rich farms and a teeming population. They neglected the northern provinces and deliberately tried to empty the northeastern corner, the province called Texas. Texas was to provide a buffer zone between New Spain and the aggressive French in Louisiana. In the Spanish view, an empty expanse of dirt, grass, trees and Indians had nothing to attract an invader. Suddenly, the French were replaced by the far more aggressive Americans, a land-hungry nation of revolutionists that was growing at a frightening rate. Dirt, grass and trees, preferably without Indians, but with them if necessary, were precisely what the Americans were looking for. Problems began appearing almost immediately.

Alexander Hamilton, one of the principal leaders of the new United States of America, began calling for an invasion of the Spanish Empire even before the Americans moved into Louisiana. After the French left, Aaron Burr, the former American vice president, and General James Wilkinson began recruiting volunteers to invade Mexico as soon as war broke out between their country and Spain. At least, Burr was. What Wilkinson, a secret agent of Spain, was planning is utterly unknown.

Before long, American filibusters began appearing in Texas. These were not long-winded senators but American adventurers and soldiers of fortune—*filibusteros*, or freebooters, in Spanish. One of the first was a man named Philip Nolan, an officer who had served under Wilkinson and later unwittingly gave his name to the protagonist in Edward Everett Hale's *The Man Without a Country*.

Nolan and a small band of followers traveled the length and breadth of Texas, mapped the province, built a fort, conferred with the Comanches and gathered a herd of several hundred horses. The Spanish didn't know what Nolan was up to, so they tried to arrest him. There was a fight. Nolan was killed and his followers imprisoned.

Other Americans followed Nolan, most of them associated with one or another of the revolutionary movements that had been hatching in Mexico since 1800, when Padre Miguel Hidalgo roused his peasant parishioners in the town of Dolores.

It became obvious to Spanish colonial authorities that an empty Texas made a perfect assembly area for revolutionary armies.

The stage was set for Moses Austin, a Connecticut native who had lived in Missouri when it was Spanish territory. He boldly approached Spanish authorities in Mexico with a plan to settle colonists in Texas. His colonists would become Spanish citizens. They would farm the empty land, increase its wealth, and maintain order. No filibusters or other troublemakers would be permitted in the colony. It took Austin some time to go through channels, but finally, the military commandant of northern Mexico agreed. He gave Austin 200,000 acres anywhere in Texas he chose in return for bringing in 300 families.

Moses Austin died before he could complete his project, but his son, Stephen, took over. Austin's experiment was so successful the Spanish authorities issued more land to *empresarios* from the United States.

Meanwhile, Mexico had gained its independence in 1821 under a turn-coat royal officer, Augustín de Iturbide, who made himself emperor. Two years later, another royal officer who turned imperialist turned again, became a republican and overthrew Iturbide. His name was Antonio López de Santa

Anna. Tall, handsome and proud as Satan, Santa Anna had only one political principle.

"Were I made God," he once said, "I should wish to be something more."

In the next three decades, Santa Anna would become Mexico's chief executive seven times and be deposed seven times. His fortunes varied from prisoner to "perpetual dictator." At one point, he fled from rebel troops to the hills, only to be captured by cannibal Indians. Fortunately for Santa Anna, his enemies appeared while the cannibals were still heating up the stew pot. Santa Anna finally died in exile. During his active life, he championed everything from liberal federalism to the most extreme centralized dictatorship.

In 1824, after Santa Anna defeated the emperor, Mexico adopted a liberal constitution giving the states, including Texas, considerable autonomy. Then a man named Anastacio Bustamante seized control in Mexico City and ended all immigration from the United States. By 1828, American immigrants outnumbered native Mexicans 10 to 1 in eastern Texas. Bustamante also established military posts in Texas. One of the first was at Anahuac. A Kentucky-born mercenary, John Davis Bradburn, a colonel in the Mexican Army, came to Anahuac, abolished the settlement of Liberty, confiscated the settlers' land and jailed protesters. Settlers marched on Anahuac and drove Bradburn and his soldiers back to Mexico.

Meanwhile, Spain invaded Mexico and tried to retake it. Santa Anna, leading the Mexican army, outmaneuvered and defeated the Spanish expedition. Armed with the prestige from that battle, the "Hero of Tampico" revolted against Bustamante.

Austin and the other *empresarios* were delighted. The Texans elected a provisional council in 1832 that drew up a proposed constitution for the Mexican state of Texas. Austin took it to Mexico City, with the council's congratulations to Santa Anna on his election as president and on his winning campaigns against Bustamante.

To his astonishment, Austin was arrested as a revolutionist and imprisoned. He wrote back to his constituents, urging them to be calm. While Austin was in prison, Santa Anna finally beat Bustamante and made himself a dictator, passing decrees through a rubber-stamp congress. He marched against the liberal state governments in Zacatecas and Coahuila and ordered his brother-in-law, General Martín Perfecto de Cós, to subdue the Texans. At the same time, by pure coincidence, Stephen Austin was released under a general amnesty. He was not the same Austin who had left for Mexico City.

Santa Anna, he told the settlers, was a "base, unprincipled, bloody monster. . . . War is our only recourse. No halfway measures, but war in full."

One of Santa Anna's first moves was to reopen the military post at Anahuac. A fiery young lawyer named William Barret Travis took 25 men and a cannon to Anahuac. They fired one cannon ball, and the Mexican commander and his 44 soldiers surrendered.

The settlers heard that Cós was on his way and began to gather an army. Cós sent a detachment to the town of Gonzales to pick up a small cannon the settlers had as a defense against Indians. The settlers mounted the gun on wagon wheels and loaded it with chains and scrap iron. Over it, they hung a banner reading "COME AND TAKE IT." Cós' 100 dragoons saw 160 settlers armed with long rifles similar to those that had destroyed Pakenham's army at New Orleans, except that some of them had been modernized to use percussion caps. Percussion rifles, unlike flintlocks, were not affected by wet weather, and they always fired when the trigger was pulled. And the settlers had a cannon. They fired the cannon, and the dragoons galloped back to join Cós at San Antonio. That was October 2, 1835, the first day of the Texas Revolution. Just one week later, another group of settlers captured all the Mexican troops in the port of Goliad.

Armed settlers converged on Gonzales. More volunteers arrived from the United States. Part of one Louisiana volunteer regiment even made it to the Alamo. Of the Alamo defenders, few had been in Texas as long as six years. One celebrated defender, Davy Crockett had been in the state only six weeks when he arrived at the fort. Some volunteers came from Europe. In the roll of those who died at the Alamo, James Nowlin of Ireland is honored with James Northcross of Virginia and Andres Nava of San Antonio.

Texas had acquired, willy-nilly, an army. Three months after the fight at Gonzales, December 4, 1835, the Texas Army pushed on to San Antonio. Colonel Benjamin Miliam led 300 Texans in an assault on the town. After five days of street fighting, Cós and what was left of his 1,400-man army surrendered. The Texans allowed them to go home on condition that they never return under arms.

Most of the Texans thought the war was over. Not Sam Houston, who had just been appointed commander of the army.

Sam Houston had run away from his home in Tennessee as a boy and had been adopted by a Cherokee chief. Later, he joined the army and fought under Aaron Burr's friend, General Andrew Jackson, as a lieutenant. At that time, the War Department was in charge of Indian affairs. Because Houston spoke fluent Cherokee, and, in fact, was a member of the Cherokee Nation, he was appointed liaison to the tribe. The Cherokees told him the agents were cheating them, so he took them and their complaint directly to the Secretary of War. Lieutenant Houston appeared before starchy John C. Calhoun wearing a loin cloth and blanket and indicted the Indian agents as both an officer and a Cherokee. Calhoun didn't quite die of apoplexy, but Houston decided he was cut out more for politics than the army. With Jackson's powerful patronage, he rose in Tennessee politics and became governor when he was 30. A sudden breakdown in his marriage drove him to dispair, the bottle and the West. He eventually surfaced in Texas, where both his oratory and his military skills soon made him a leading citizen.

Houston was an early advocate of Texas independence, but Austin and other old settlers convinced him to settle for an autonomous Texas as part of Mexico. But he knew that even that would be hard to achieve. He knew Santa Anna was not going to forget about Texas: the Mexicans would be back. He urged the need to build up a regular army and prepare for war. A newly-formed Texas Legislative Council ignored him and adopted what came to be called the Matamoros Plan.

With hindsight, the Matamoros Plan, on the eve of a war for survival, seems utterly mad. In that era of conspiracies and empire-building, though, it struck many rational people as a sound idea. Under the plan, Texans would land at the Mexican port of Matamoros—300 desert miles from the North American colonies—join liberals in that city and detach all of the rich mining states of northern Mexico to make a new empire which would be the equal of either the United States or Mexico. The Legislative Council by-passed Houston and gave command of the expedition to an inexperienced officer named James Fannin.

Fannin rounded up as many troops as he could, including half of the garrison of San Antonio, and took them to Goliad, where they were to embark for Matamoros.

In Mexico, Santa Anna decided that he couldn't depend on the convicts who made up his frontier force. He began organizing a real army, one that he would lead in person.

By the end of 1835, the San Antonio garrison was starved for men and supplies. Houston knew it was madness to try to hold the Alamo, a quarter-mile of walls, with the tiny force stationed there under Colonel James Neill. He ordered Neill to blow down the walls and evacuate the fort with his guns and ammunition.

Provisional Governor Henry Smith asked William Travis, the man who had taken Anahuac, to recruit a force and take it to San Antonio. Houston wanted Travis to assist in the evacuation, but once the young firebrand arrived at the Alamo, he resolved to stay and die.

Colonel James Neill, commander at the Alamo, had to go on leave because of illness in his family and temporarily turned the command over to Travis. Many of the garrison would have preferred the famous Jim Bowie, who had led a group of volunteers to San Antonio de Béjar.

Bowie was an adventurer, duelist and knife fighter who had already become legendary in the Old Southwest. A knight in somewhat rusty armor, he had made a fortune in slave-trading as well as in lumbering and land speculation. He married a young woman named Maria Ursula de Veramendi, a member of one of the most prominent families in San Antonio de Béjar and said he planned to settle down on his plantation. But in 1833, before Bowie could fully settle down, his wife and two children died of cholera. Bowie remained an influential man in Béjar, where the family of his late wife lived.

The great knife fighter was dying of tuberculosis, however, and spent most of each day in bed. In the end, Travis and Bowie agreed to be joint commanders, but as Bowie grew weaker, so did his command function.

One living legend who didn't want to command was Davy Crockett. The former Tennessee congressman, frontier hunter and Indian fighter arrived February 8, leading a dozen riflemen he called the "Tennessee Mounted Volunteers." At 49, Crockett was one of the oldest men in the Alamo, but he said he wanted to be considered only "a high private."

Santa Anna had arrived in front of the Alamo February 23, 1836 after a winter march most of the Texans had considered impossible. There was hardly any grazing for his horses, and ferocious blizzards killed scores of troops recruited from tropical Yucatan, but the president-general crossed the desert in forced marches. He left a trail of dead animals, and not a few dead men, along the way.

For such a celebrated soldier, Santa Anna's march discipline was abominable. He plunged boldly into the desert, leaving his troops to follow as best they could. Consequently, when he reached San Antonio de Béjar, he had only about 600 fighting men and almost no artillery. The rest of the army came up in dribs and drabs. It was not until the siege was nearly over that he could surround the Alamo, and even then, his line was full of holes. The bulk of his siege artillery never got into action.

On the second day of the siege, Travis sent out a letter with a courier who was able to get through the rather porous Mexican lines.

"To the People of Texas and all Americans in the world—Fellow Citizens and Compatriots: I am besieged . . . I have sustained a continual Bombardment and cannonade for 24 hours and have not lost a man. The enemy has demanded a surrender at discretion, otherwise, the garrison are to be put to the sword if the fort is taken. I have answered the demand with a cannon shot, and our flag still waves proudly from the walls. *I shall never surrender or retreat.* Then, I call upon you in the name of Liberty, of patriotism, and everything dear to the American character, to come to our aid with all dispatch. The enemy is receiving reinforcements daily and will no doubt increase to three or four thousand in four or five days. If this call is neglected, I am determined to sustain myself as long as possible and die like a soldier who never forgets what is due his own honor and that of this country. VICTORY OR DEATH."

Travis, in the next few days sent other messages, to the *alcalde* (mayor) of Gonzales and to Fannin in Goliad asking for help. One of the messengers was a native-born Mexican, Juan Seguín, who held a commission in the Texas Army. Knowing the language and customs of the enemy, Seguín found it easy to slip through the lines.

In Goliad, Fannin still hadn't shipped out to Matamoros. When he heard the Mexicans were in San Antonio, he started for the Alamo, but a wagon broke down, then Fannin changed his mind and went back to Goliad. In Gonzales, a company of volunteers did march to the Alamo and pass through Santa Anna's lines March 1. Three days later, Travis told the garrison that if anyone wished to avoid death in the Alamo, he could leave now. Only one person, a soldier of fortune named Louis Rose, went over the wall. He, too, passed through the Mexican lines.

Although Santa Anna had a reputation among Mexican civilians and foreign soldiers of being something close to a military genius, his leadership had serious flaws. Mexican soldiers knew it. Details like perimeter security were beneath Santa Anna. He had an overwhelming force: who cared if a few rebels escaped from the doomed fort? More serious was his impatience when it took too long to properly prepare an attack.

Santa Anna, in spite of having ordered "no quarter" apparently expected a quick surrender. But the siege dragged on. Mexican sappers dug trenches ever closer to the walls, and infantry on both sides exchanged shots. In these exchanges, the Texans, with their long rifles, had a clear edge. One man firing from the walls attracted the attention of Captain Rafael Soldana of the Mexican Army.

He was "a tall man with flowing hair." He wore "a buckskin suit with a cap all of a pattern entirely different from those worn by his comrades. This man would rest his long gun and fire, and we all learned to keep a good distance when he was seen to make ready to shoot. He rarely missed his mark, and when he fired, he always rose to his feet and calmly reloaded his gun, seemingly indifferent to the shots fired at him by our men. He had a strong, resonant voice and often railed at us. This man I later learned was known as 'Kwockey' [Crockett]."

Lieutenant Colonel Juan Enrique de la Peña of the Mexican force recorded Santa Anna's irritation at the length of the siege. "Our commander became more furious when he saw that the enemy resisted the idea of surrender. He believed as others did that the fame and honor of the army were compromised the longer the enemy lived."

Peña disagreed. "But prudent men . . . . understand that the soldier's glory is greater, the less bloody the victory and the fewer victims sacrificed." These men, he wrote, "were of the opinion that victory over a handful of men concentrated in the Alamo did not call for great sacrifice. In fact, it was necessary only to wait the artillery's arrival at Béjar for these to surrender; undoubtedly, they could not have resisted for many hours the destruction and imposing fire from twenty cannon."

By this time, the Mexican trenches were only 200 yards from the Alamo's walls. According to Peña:

> Travis' resistance was on the verge of being overcome; for several days his followers had been urging him to surrender, giving the lack of food and the scarcity of munitions as reasons, but he had quieted their restlessness with the hope of quick relief, something not difficult for them to believe, since they had seen some reinforcements arrive. Nevertheless they had pressed him so hard that on the fifth he promised them that if no help arrived on that day, they would surrender the next day or try to escape under cover of darkness; these facts were given to us by a lady from Béjar, by a Negro who was the only male who escaped, and by several women who were found inside and were rescued by Colonels Morales and Miñón.

Another of Santa Anna's flaws as a leader was his utter indifference to any life but his own. Although the Texans could not have held out much longer, and his artillery was still far away, the siege was dragging. He ordered a general assault.

Early on the morning of March 6, four columns—one led by the parole-breaker, Cós—with a total strength of about 1,100 men moved up through the trenches and charged the walls just before dawn.

Inside, Travis had been patrolling the walls all night. He had just laid down his double-barrel shotgun and stretched out when he heard cheering and a bugle call. He ran into the compound and saw the Texas gunners firing their cannons. Travis had seen to it that each rifleman on the walls had three or four loaded weapons, so the Mexican attackers were at first smothered with small arms fire as well as grape shot from the artillery.

"Our columns left along their path a wide trail of blood, of wounded, and of dead," Peña wrote. "It could be observed that a single cannon volley did away with half the company of chasseurs from Toluca . . . . The few poor ladders that we were bringing had not arrived because their bearers had either perished or had escaped. Only one [ladder] was seen of all those that were planned."

General Cós directed the attack at a section of 8-foot palisade covering a gap in the walls. Mexican troops crushed together at the foot of the palisade and the walls while the Texans poured a deadly fire into them. One colonel was trampled to death by his own men. Santa Anna, watching from a safe distance, ordered his reserves into the fight. In the background, the Mexican band played *El Deguello* (The Cutthroat), a traditional Spanish signal for total annihilation of the enemy.

Travis stood on the wall and fired both barrels of his 10 gauge shotgun into the milling mass, reloaded and fired again. The Mexicans hugged the foot of the wall for 15 minutes. As the human tide flowed along the bottom of the wall, it came to a timber-and-earth redoubt where the timbers had collapsed. Mexican General Juan Amador began to climb the redoubt. His men swarmed after him.

Crockett and his Tennessee volunteers were cut off, but fought furiously. Mexican Sergeant Felix Nunez remembered one of them:

He was a tall American of rather dark complexion and had on a long buckskin coat and a round cap without any bill, made out of fox skin with the long tail hanging down his back. This man apparently had a charmed life. Of the many soldiers who took deliberate aim at him and fire, not one ever hit him. On the contrary, he never missed a shot. He killed at least eight of our men, besides wounding several others. This being observed by a lieutenant who had come over the wall, he sprang at him and dealt him a deadly blow with his sword, just above the right eye, which felled him to the ground, and in an instant he was pierced by not less than 20 bayonets."

The main body of defenders, too, fought fiercely.

"Travis was seen to hesitate," Peña reported. "But not about the death he would choose. He would take a few steps and stop, turning his proud face toward us to discharge his shots. He fought like a true soldier. Finally he died, but he died after trading his life very dearly. None of his men died with greater heroism, and they all died. Travis behaved as a hero; one must do him justice, for with a handful of men without discipline, he resolved to face men used to war and much superior in numbers, without supplies, with scarce munitions, and against the will of his subordinates. He was a handsome blond, with a physique as robust as his spirit was strong."

A single bullet in the forehead dropped William B. Travis inside the compound. The Texans slowly withdrew to the stone barracks and the ruined church. The Mexicans turned their own cannons against them and blew down the doors of the barracks and fired round shot and grape into the defenders. Then the infantry burst in, firing and bayoneting. They bayoneted Bowie, still firing a pistol from his bed, and lifted him up on their bayonets "until his blood covered their clothes and dyed them red," in the horrified words of his sister-in-law, Juana Veramendi de Alsbury. The Mexicans bayoneted all the wounded and two boys, 11 and 12, who had taken refuge in the Alamo with their father, a gunner. In their blind fury, they even fired on other Mexican soldiers. With some difficulty, Mexican officers managed to save most of the women and children.

One group of men was spared, too—for a time. Peña reported:

> Some seven men had survived the general carnage, and, under the protection of General Castrillón, they were brought before Santa Anna. Among them was one of great stature, well proportioned, with regular features, in whose face there was the imprint of adversity but in whom one also noticed a degree of resignation and nobility that did him honor. He was the naturalist, David Crockett, well known in North America for his unusual adventures, who had undertaken to explore the country and who, finding himself in Béjar at the very moment of surprise, had taken refuge in the Alamo, fearing that his status as a foreigner might not be respected. Santa Anna answered Castrillón's intervention in Crockett's behalf with a gesture of indignation and addressing himself to the sappers, the troops closest to him, ordered his execution. The commanders and officers were outraged at this action and did not support the order, hoping that once the fury of the moment had blown over, these men would be spared; but several other officers who were around the president and who, perhaps, had not been present at the moment of danger, became noteworthy by an infamous deed, surpassing the soldiers in cruelty. They thrust themselves forward, in order to flatter their commander, and with swords in hand fell upon these unfortunate, defenseless men just as a tiger leaps upon its prey. Though tortured before they were killed, these unfortunates died without complaining and without humiliating themselves before their torturers.

Santa Anna had all the bodies of the Americans burned, and all the Mexican dead were buried in a mass grave. His losses have been estimated at

600 dead—a high price for a fort held by 182. But the full price would be much, much higher.

Santa Anna sent for one of the women, Susanna Dickerson, and sent her east with an escort to tell the settlers what happened. The same thing would happen, he said, if he encountered any more resistance.

The Texans, though, had already made their decision. On February 29, just six days after Santa Anna hoisted his "no quarter" flag, 59 delegates arrived at the village of Washington-on-the-Brazos to write a new constitution for an independent Republic of Texas. The only question now was how to prosecute the war.

The Matamoros Plan had come to an ignominious end. The Mexicans had attacked Goliad, and the vacillating Fannin decided to retreat. When he was six miles from Goliad, 1,400 Mexicans surrounded his 400 men. After two days of fighting, the Texans surrendered to General Jose Urrea on the conditions that they would be treated with honor and paroled to the United States. They were held for eight days, then orders came from Santa Anna to kill them all. Only a handful managed to escape.

Its attempt at grand strategy having failed, the Texas government turned to Sam Houston. Houston would have agreed with a later American military leader, George S. Patton, who said, "Fixed fortifications are a monument to the stupidity of man." There would be no more Alamos. Houston planned to use his new country's greatest resource—empty space. The last time Santa Anna confronted empty space, his army had straggled out into a weeks-long column.

Houston and his tiny army retreated before Santa Anna for six weeks, picking up strength steadily. The Mexican supply lines stretched farther and farther, and Santa Anna had to peel off detachments to take other objectives. The Mexican president, burning towns along the way, saw no problems, however. The Texas rebels were being routed.

On April 20, he believed he had Houston and his army bottled up in a maze of bayous along the San Jacinto River. Houston had 800 men and two six-pounder cannons, "the Twin Sisters." Santa Anna had only about 750 of his 5,000-man army, but around 9 a.m., General Cós arrived with 500 more. Supremely confident, Santa Anna and his whole army took a siesta.

The Mexican army was all asleep, its muskets stacked, when Houston ordered the attack at 3:30 p.m. The Texans moved silently through the woods and across the open field in front of Santa Anna's army. Suddenly three fifes and a drum broke into "Come to My Bower," a slightly bawdy popular song, and the Twin Sisters belched double loads of grape shot. The Texans, screaming "Remember the Alamo!" dashed into the Mexican camp and cut down Santa Anna's troops with musket, rifle, bayonet and sword. Only a few groggy Mexicans were able to put up any resistance. Santa Anna fled in his carpet slippers and hid in the woods.

It took an hour and a half to conquer the Alamo. It took only 18 minutes to destroy Santa Anna's army. The killing took longer, though. The panic-stricken Mexicans had nowhere to flee. They were were trapped by rivers and bayous. Just before the battle, Erastus "Deaf" Smith, Houston's chief scout, had destroyed the only bridge out. The Mexicans fled into the water, and the Texans lined up and shot them down like ducks in a shooting gallery.

Colonel John Wharton tried to stop the massacre at one bayou. A soldier told him, "Colonel Wharton, if Jesus Christ were to come down from heaven and tell me to stop killing Santanistas, I wouldn't do it, sir." Wharton put his hand on his sword, but the soldier stepped back and cocked his rifle. Wharton went elsewhere.

In the end, the Texans killed 600 and captured 650. They lost two dead and 23 wounded. Houston sent out patrols to find Santa Anna before he could rally the rest of his troops.

Two days later, the Texas general was sleeping when he felt someone grasp his hand and shake it. He looked up and saw Santa Anna. One of his patrols had found the president-general wearing a blue work suit. They didn't know who he was, but when they saw his fine linen shirt and jewel studs, they knew they had an officer. When they brought him back with the other prisoners, one of them shouted, "El presidente!"

As Houston looked up, Santa Anna said, "That man may consider himself born to no common destiny who has conquered the Napoleon of the West." Then the author of two major massacres added, "And now it remains for him to be generous to the vanquished."

"You should have remembered that at the Alamo," Houston said.

Many of the Texans wanted to put Santa Anna before a firing squad, but Houston had another idea. He had Santa Anna order all his troops back to Mexico. The dictator then had to sign a treaty recognizing the independence of Texas.

When he got home, His Most High Excellency, the President-General, Napoleon of the West and Hero of Tampico was lucky to be allowed to live as plain Señor Santa Anna in his villa near Santa Cruz. But it's hard to keep a bad man down. In a few years, Santa Anna was back on top and leading his people into a new war. That war, caused by the U.S. annexation of Texas, resulted in an even greater territorial loss to Mexico.

Because of what happened at a ruined mission church in one of the most remote cities in North America, the United States gained Texas, Oklahoma, New Mexico, Arizona, California, Nevada, Utah and half of Colorado. That's pretty important. The big reason we remember the Alamo, though, is because a comparative handful of people looked at an overwhelmingly large enemy army, flying a "no quarter" flag and decided freedom is worth dying for.

EXPANSION

AND

GROWING

PAINS—

THE INDIANS

Four

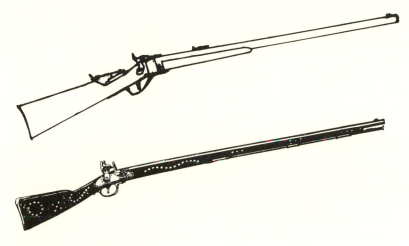

Long Shot

June 29, 1874, Adobe Walls, Texas

People in town could see their dust before the half-dozen riders appeared on the horizon. The six traveled steadily, neither slowly nor fast. Five wore army uniforms, and the sixth wore a buckskin shirt and a feather in his hat. When they rode up to the town corral, one of the buffalo hunters present asked them what they wanted.

"Looking for stolen horses," said the civilian, a half-Cheyenne army scout named Amos Chapman. "The boys still are," he said, nodding toward the soldiers, "but I'm going to have a drink and meet them later." Chapman dismounted and waddled over to the sod-sided saloon with the gait of a man

Top: Sharps "Big Fifty," the most powerful and accurate rifle of its day, standard equipment for buffalo hunters. Below: Indian trade gun decorated with brass tacks. Indians liked short guns for use on horseback and often preferred flintlocks, as percussion caps could be hard to obtain.

who spent most of his waking hours on a horse. The soldiers rode off across the endless grassy plain.

Behind Chapman there was murmuring. Indians weren't popular at Adobe Walls. Neither were soldiers. Especially unpopular were people looking for stolen horses. Someone suggested that Chapman might be a spy. Maybe for the soldiers, maybe for the Indians. Either way, it might be a good idea to hang him.

That was a strange idea, but Adobe Walls in June of 1874 was a very strange place.

The whole town consisted of a corral, a saloon, two stores and a blacksmith shop. A restaurant was going to be built, but there were no houses. The town existed to serve nomadic buffalo hunters—themselves, very strange people. Buffalo hunters worked at a profession unlike any other in the world, one that had just come into existence and would disappear within a decade. Fugitives from the law (including horse thieves) mixed with adventurous youths from the East at buffalo camps. Buffalo hunter Josiah Wright Mooar hired only outlaws as skinners. They didn't complain about their wages, and they weren't likely to run away. Buffalo hunters and their skinners were the product of a couple of technological developments: leather workers had discovered a cheap way to tan bison hides and gun makers had devised powerful, long-range rifles that made it easy to kill the great beasts. These developments made it possible to earn a great deal of money shooting buffalo.

The hunters were the product of something else, too, although none of them recognized it. They were in the first wave of an unprecedented movement—the settlement of the Great Plains of North America.

The early nineteenth century had been an age of revolution and enormous changes of national boundaries in both Europe and the Americas. Just past mid-century, the revolutionary age had come to a crashing climax and ended where it began, in the Western Hemisphere. In North America, the gory American Civil War put a permanent end to the continual secession conspiracies. In Latin America, Paraguayan dictator Francisco Solano López's attempt to dominate southern South America resulted in the War of the Triple Alliance, proportionately one of the bloodiest wars in all history. The Triple Alliance—Argentina, Brazil and Uruguay—virtually annihilated Paraguay.

The western world's age of revolution had been succeeded by an age of expansion. National boundaries had become fairly stable, although there were still changes of government in Europe and Latin America, particularly the latter: no Latin Hamilton had appeared to give the new nations a blueprint for financial and political stability. Mexican indebtedness led to Napoleon III's attempt to establish Maximilian of Austria as emperor of Mexico during the American Civil War. After the French were driven out, European expansion was limited to Africa and Asia. But that expansion was the business of an elite, primarily the military. Ordinary citizens who wanted to go elsewhere came to the United States.

Under pressure of this immigration and a high birth rate, the U.S. population pressed ever westward. The movement stopped temporarily when it reached the end of the timber—a line extending roughly from central Texas to western Minnesota. The settlers were stymied by the Plains Indians, as the Spanish and Mexicans had been before them. The pioneers' principal weapon, the muzzle-loading long rifle, was developed during a century of fighting the forest Indians, who traveled on foot and by canoe. It was less efficient fighting the horse archers of the plains. The long rifle was clumsy on a horse and could not be easily reloaded. The pioneer's secondary weapons, the long knife and the tomahawk, were almost useless: the Plains Indian usually avoided close combat with an armed enemy.

The revolver, introduced in Texas during combat with the Comanches, gave the white man an edge in mounted combat. The rifle developed rapidly. The flintlock became extinct: the percussion lock, using a separate primer cap loaded with fulminate of mercury, was far more reliable. Powder and lead were no longer in such short supply, so gunmakers made larger caliber weapons, which had the power necessary to kill such animals as bison and grizzly bears. Because they might have to be used on horseback, the new "plains rifles" had shorter barrels.

The next step was a giant one. Breech-loading became general. With a muzzle-loader, a shooter had to stand up to load a rifle. With a breech-loader, he could remain under cover, not exposing himself any more than when he was firing. Reloading was faster, too. A number of breech-loading systems were tried in the early nineteenth century, but most of them leaked gas at the breech. In 1848, Christian Sharps invented one of the most successful. It featured a sharp-edged breech block that sheared the end off the usual paper cartridge when it closed, exposing the powder to the flash from the priming cap. When metallic cartridges were invented, dozens of breech-loading systems appeared, and the Sharps was adapted to the new ammunition. For decades, the Sharps was still the favorite of target shooters and buffalo hunters—people who wanted the utmost accuracy. The buffalo hunters' favorite Sharps was chambered for the .50-110 cartridge—a brass cartridge case containing a .50 lead bullet and 110 grains of black powder. Some of these Sharps "big 50" rifles weighed 15 to 20 pounds to dampen the recoil. Many had telescopic sights.

The Indians adopted guns whenever they could get them. Their favorite piece was the Winchester carbine, a repeater that took heavy pistol cartridges like the .44-40 and the .38-40. It and the revolver, another Indian favorite, could be used easily on horseback. The white man had more guns, of course, but the Indian's horsemanship, his stealth and, especially, the mobility of his villages kept the odds even.

What tipped the scales was the demand for buffalo hides in the East and in Europe.

About 1870, there was an unbelievable number of bison on the plains. General Philip Sheridan estimated it at about 100 million—more than twice the human population of the whole country. And Sheridan would be happy to see the bison all dead. The entire Plains Indian economy depended on the buffalo. If there were no bison, the Indians would have to choose between starvation and the reservation.

A buffalo hunter got from a dollar to $4 a hide, but an efficient hunter could make as much as $100 a day. Buffalo hunting was a business based on mass killing. Each hunter had a wagon, several horses and from three to 20 skinners. He would pick a good spot some distance from a herd so the noise of his rifle wouldn't disturb the animals. Then he'd set up a pair of crossed sticks as a rifle rest and shoot one bison after another, some as much as a half-mile from where he was firing. The skinners went to work when the first buffalo fell, using horses to pull off the hide. Some hunters used two rifles, so one could cool off while the other was being fired. Others used water to cool the gun barrel. One hunter, Tom Nixon, killed 140 buffaloes without moving from his stand. Between September 15 and October 20, 1875, Nixon killed 2,173 buffalo. Another hunter, Orlando "Brick" Bond, killed 300 in one day. Wright Mooar killed 20,000 buffalo in his life, and Doc Carver, a Nebraska dentist, killed 30,000.

These days, when we read about the slaughter of the bison, we feel revulsion at the waste and destruction of the environment. In the 1870s, though, elimination of the bison was national policy. It was the only way, national leaders believed, to settle the Plains. Or at least, the only way short of killing all the Plains Indians. Army officers often gave hunters free ammunition.

By 1874, the buffalo had been nearly exterminated in western Kansas. Hunters who had been based in Dodge City moved south into the Texas Panhandle, an area that was still Indian country—an Indian hunting ground guaranteed by treaty. The Texas Panhandle is nothing like the Texas of Stephen Austin and Sam Houston. Geographically, it's more like Kansas— flat, but high above sea level, semi-arid, scorchingly hot in summer, sub-arctic in winter, with a short autumn and a shorter spring, and a wind that howls across thousands of miles of level space all year long.

In March 1874, Charlie Myers, a Dodge City merchant and former buffalo hunter, decided to move his business to be near the hunters. He hired a 23-year-old freighter and ex-hunter called Dirty Face Jones. Jones hired more wagons and recruited hunters to guard the caravan before they got to the hunting grounds. Among them were a 20-year-old hunter called Bat Masterson, Billy Dixon, a buffalo hunting veteran of 23, and Jim Hanrahan, who took a stock of liquor along with his hunting outfit and planned to start a saloon. Tom O'Keefe packed his anvil and blacksmith tools. Altogether, there were 30 wagons and 50 men in the caravan. Soon after it left, Charles Rath, another former hunter and Dodge City merchant, loaded up a wagon with $20,000 worth of merchandise to compete with Myers. He brought along a Swedish-born carpenter, Andy Johnson, to make windows and doors.

On the Canadian River, the hunters and merchants encountered the ruins of an old fur-trading fort called Adobe Walls. It had been built by William Bent in 1843 but later abandoned because of attacks by the Kiowas and the Comanches. In 1864, Colonel Kit Carson defended the roofless walls against an Indian attack. When the hunters arrived, the walls were only four or five feet high.

They built a new camp about a mile away, but kept the name Adobe Walls, even though it had no adobe walls. The corral was a palisade. Myers' store, built against the side of the corral, had palisade walls and a sod roof. O'Keefe's blacksmith shop was built the same way, while Hanrahan's saloon and Rath's store had thick sod sides and sod roofs. Sod, rather than adobe, was the normal construction material on the grassy High Plains. Dirty Face Jones had to haul the logs for the corral and the palisade-sided buildings from some distance down the Canadian.

Soon Adobe Walls was sending wagon-loads of hides to Dodge City for shipment back east. The wagons going back brought guns, powder, cartridges, lead and all the necessities of life on the plains. One wagon in June brought a young couple, William and Nancy Olds, who planned to start a restaurant.

It was a growing and thriving community that Amos Chapman visited June 18. When he met Jim Hanrahan, the scout disclosed that he really wasn't looking for stolen horses. He was bearing a message from the post traders at Camp Supply. They wanted their fellow traders at Adobe Walls to know that a large band of Indians was planning to attack the town June 27. The permanent residents of Adobe Walls agreed to share the secret with the Mooar brothers, Wright and John, who were leaving the next day. If they told all the buffalo hunters, though, the hunters would all clear out and leave the stores at the mercy of the Indians.

Hanrahan had heard the mutterings about hanging Chapman. He told the scout, and Chapman agreed to hide in the Mooars' wagon until the brothers left for Dodge.

Life at Adobe Walls continued as usual until the night of June 26. Buffalo hunters came and went. Hanrahan found that he was too busy running the saloon to hunt. He asked Billy Dixon, who had only three skinners, if he'd like to become his partner. Dixon agreed.

In the meantime, out on the plains, life was anything but pleasant. The buffalo hunters and the railroad builders had driven a wedge through the swarm of buffaloes. Now the buffaloes were said to be in either in the "northern herd" or the "southern herd." And the Indians were disappearing with the buffaloes from Kansas and Colorado. The Cheyennes split into northern and southern branches, and the army patrolled the central area to keep them out. In the Panhandle, the southern Cheyennes and the Comanches were short on food. The Indian agents delivered only half the food promised, and the buffalo hunters had now moved into this hunting ground. The buffalo provided the Plains Indian with food, clothing and shelter. Now, the Comanches saw, these wasters from unknown lands to the east had come to the southern High Plains to destroy the source of life here.

The Comanches scheduled a sun dance, a ceremony common to all Plains Indians. Before the dance, Comanche couriers carried the peace pipe to the Kiowas and the Cheyennes, inviting them to the feast and a council.

Quanah Parker, son of a Comanche chief and a captive white woman, presided at the council. Stone Calf led the Cheyennes, and Lone Wolf the Kiowas.

Stone Calf recounted the many crimes committed by the whites against the Indians, including the Sand Creek Massacre in 1864 and the Washita Massacre perpetrated by George Armstrong Custer in 1868.

Lone Wolf added more broken promises by the whites, and said he would not, as the whites wanted, settle down and till the soil.

"I am a warrior," he said. "I am not going to sit down and do women's work to get food. I want to drive the white man from our hunting grounds. I want to go on a war trail this summer and kill so many that they will go away."

Quanah Parker told the other chiefs about a new shaman who had arisen among the Comanches. His name was Ishatai, which has been variously translated as Little Wolf, Wolf's Hindquarters and Coyote Droppings. Ishatai said he had communed with the Great Spirit and learned to make magic which would stop the white man's bullets.

Ishatai, of course, was only the latest of a long line of Indian prophets going back to Tecumseh's brother, Tenskwatawa. Magic to undo western technology has been a dream of all tribal societies. The last reported magical bullet-proofing took place in what is now Zaire in 1964-5.

Parker told the chiefs the Comanches had picked a perfect target to hit first—a white settlement near the old Adobe Walls fort. It was not only a white settlement, it was a settlement of the whites who were the greatest threats to their way of life—the buffalo hunters.

When the time for the threatened Indian attack drew near, Hanrahan grew nervous. The Indians usually attacked just before dawn. How could the merchants be sure the hunters would be awake? He and Dixon conferred and hit on a scheme.

Sometime after midnight, when all the hunters had stopped drinking and were asleep, Dixon went out behind the saloon and sawed a piece of timber to an exact length. Then he drew his revolver and fired one shot into the air.

"The ridgepole!" Hanrahan yelled. "Clear out! The ridgepole is breaking!"

The hunters, most of them sleeping outside the saloon, threw off their blankets and rushed to the distraught Hanrahan, standing outside the sod building.

"I heard it crack. It sounded just like a pistol shot," Hanrahan said. If the ridgepole broke, everyone knew, the heavy sod roof would smash every bottle and keg in the saloon—a disaster of the first magnitude. Nobody could see the crack in the 2½ foot diameter log that held up the roof, but they didn't have time to look closely. Billy Dixon pushed his way into the saloon dragging an eight-inch diameter log.

"Let's see if we can brace it with this," he said. Miraculously, the log was just the right length. The hunters wedged it under the ridgepole and everyone relaxed. After the excitement, most of them felt they should have a drink before going back to sleep.

As a result, few of them were sound asleep when the sky turned gray just before dawn. They heard the "Charge" call on a bugle and the war whoops of hundreds of Indians, as the Comanches, Cheyennes and Kiowas charged Adobe Walls.

The hunters scrambled into the thick-walled buildings and barred the heavy doors. Only two didn't wake up. The Shadler brothers, Ike and Shorty, were asleep in their wagon when the Indians reached them. The Indians shot them and scalped them before they woke up.

Billy Dixon thought that the Indians would, as usual try to run off the horses. He started for the corral, but saw that the attackers were heading for the buildings. They were after blood, not horses. He ducked into the saloon just ahead of another hunter, Billy Ogg, who had sprinted a quarter of a mile to get to the building. Andy Johnson and Tom O'Keefe took shelter in Rath's store along with hunters and Rath's employees. Some of the men were still in their underwear, but each had at least one buffalo rifle and a bandolier of cartridges. Altogether, there were 28 men and one woman, Nancy Olds, forted up in Adobe Walls.

On the first charge, some of the Indians rode right up to the buildings and struck the doors with the butts of their lances. This earned them much honor among their peers, but did nothing toward taking the settlement. More effective, at least potentially, was Quanah Parker.

"I got up to the houses with another Comanche," the chief said later. "We poked holes in the roof and shot in."

Parker and his companion didn't hit anyone, but two Indians were killed, one the son of Stone Calf. A Comanche went down in front of Rath's store. Parker dashed over and, demonstrating incredible strength, leaned over while still in the saddle, picked the man up and carried him away.

The bugle sounded again and the hunters noticed the bugler, a black man who was probably a former soldier. The Indians pulled back. The Indians were using the bugler to signal their forces. Many of the hunters had served time in the army, though. They knew from the calls what the Indians would do next. They heard the charge call again. By now, the sun was up and the hunters and merchants could see their enemy. Billy Dixon later reported:

> There never was a more splendidly barbaric sight. . . . Hundreds of warriors, the flower of the fighting men of the southwestern Plains tribes, mounted on their finest horses, armed with guns and lances, and carrying heavy shields of thick buffalo hide, were coming like the wind. Over all was splashed the rich colors of red, vermilion and ochre, on the bodies of the men, on the bodies of the running

horses. Scalps dangled from bridles, gorgeous war bonnets fluttered their plumes, bright feathers dangled from the tails and manes of the horses, and the bronzed, half-naked bodies of the riders glittered with ornaments of silver and brass.

The hunters fired their rifles, most of them .50 caliber Sharps, through the windows. Others dug loopholes through the sod. Warriors and horses began to drop. This time, the Indians did head for the corral. Billy Tyler, a hunter, ran out of Myers' store to the stockade, but the Indians inside the corral fired at him through the fence. He was hit and fell in front of the doorway. The people in the store pulled him in, but Tyler was dying.

As the fighting continued, Tyler began to call for water, but there was no water. Finally, a cook called Old Man Keeler said, "Give me a bucket."

Keeler went through a window, followed by his dog. The Indian fire from the corral, 60 yards from the pump, was so heavy one of the hunters said it looked as if the palisade was on fire. Keeler held the bucket and worked the rusty pump handle as bullets landed all around him. Then he ran back to the store. His dog was hit 20 times, but the old man handed the bucket through the window and climbed in himself. Still untouched, he glanced through the window and said, "I'd like to get the devilish Indians who shot my dog."

Bat Masterson gave Tyler a drink and wiped cool water on his face. Then Tyler died.

The Indians gave up trying to get in by 10 o'clock. They pulled back and began circling the settlement so the hunters would exhaust their ammunition. Ishatai told the warriors that after leaving the camp, someone had killed a skunk, thus destroying the power of his medicine. Nobody believed him. From that day until the end of his long life, Ishatai was a man in disgrace.

The Indians tried sneak attacks. Billy Dixon saw a feather-bedecked horse wandering near the buildings. He shot the horse, and an Indian, hiding behind the animal, started to run. Dixon shot the Indian, too.

Next, the Indians appeared at long range and fired volleys at the buildings. Dixon and Hanrahan decided to run from the saloon to Rath's store, where there was more ammunition. They ran through a couple of volleys to reach the store. The men in the store wanted Dixon, a famous marksman, to stay with them, so Hanrahan took a sack of cartridges back alone.

Firing got less frequent as the day went on, but Indian casualties were mounting. Hunters killed Quanah Parker's horse and Lone Wolf's horse. Quanah Parker himself was shot; the black bugler was killed.

Firing stopped completely at night. The next day, the Indians stayed mostly out of range. One group moved up cautiously. In the exchange of fire, the hunters shot the horse from under Ishatai, the disgraced medicine man.

Henry Lease, one of the hunters in Myers store, volunteered to ride to Dodge for help. He took two revolvers and a Sharps "big 50," but nobody expected to ever see him alive again. They were wrong, but they wouldn't know it for several days.

On the third day, 15 Indians appeared on a ridge line. One of them made "a contemptuous gesture" toward the settlement. Billy Dixon adjusted the telescope sight on his big Sharps rifle and fired. There was a long pause, then the Indian who made the gesture toppled off his horse and lay still. The other Indians galloped away.

That seemingly impossible shot—the range was later found to be 1,538 yards—ended the siege of Adobe Walls. It was obvious that the white men had medicine Ishatai had never thought of. The besiegers gathered in tribal groups and began to move away. It was many days, though, before the besieged knew that they were out of danger.

By that time, the Comanches, Cheyennes and Kiowas were attacking easier targets than Adobe Walls. Before they were finished, they would kill 190 whites in Texas, New Mexico, Colorado and Kansas.

At the settlement, of course, no one knew the Indians were leaving. They might, however, have suspected that the siege was lifted, because that afternoon, more buffalo hunters arrived at Adobe Walls and helped fortify the town. The next day, a sentinel on the roof of Myers' store saw Indians, but they were riding away. Nevertheless, everyone moved inside. William Olds, the would-be restaurateur, started down the ladder from the roof of Rath's store. His rifle went off accidentally, and he fell dead at his wife's feet.

A little more than a week after the first charge by Quanah Parker and his allies, a relief column from Dodge City, summoned by Henry Lease, arrived at Adobe Walls.

The settlement was not destined for a long life. The buffalo soon got scarce even in the Panhandle. Fewer and fewer hunters worked that territory. Billy Dixon and Bat Masterson became army scouts. Dixon later won the Medal of Honor after he and three soldiers drove off a large band of Indians. A year after the Adobe Walls fight, Dixon made another spectacular shot, killing an Indian a full mile away while helping defend a town in Kansas. Masterson became a lawman and wrote a chapter of his own into the folklore of the West. By summer's end, Adobe Walls was abandoned, and the Indians still around burned the buildings and the corral. The Indians didn't stay long to gloat: they couldn't exist without the buffalo. In the place of the big shaggy bison came the longhorn steer. Dodge City, the buffalo hunters' metropolis, became a cow town.

Adobe Walls was abandoned, but not forgotten. As long as there were buffalo hunters, and long after there were none, men would talk about the fight against Quanah Parker and how Billy Dixon hit an Indian nine-tenths of a mile away. The young buffalo hunter took his place in the folklore of the West, along with Paul Bunyon and Mike Fink. Much later, Wright Mooar told of Dixon's even more significant shot—the one that induced the sleeping hunters to help Jim Hanrahan fix his ridgepole. By then, the story brought a laugh even from those who had been fooled.

To the Indians, though, the Adobe Walls fight was not something to chuckle about around campfires.

While the fighting at Adobe Walls was going on, other buffalo hunters continued to wipe out the great Panhandle herds. A month or two after the fight, most of the Comanches, Kiowas and Cheyennes who still lived on the bison had retreated to Palo Duro Canyon, a valley invisible from the flat surface of the Plains. There the buffaloes survived, and the Indians who depended on them.

One day short of three months after the attack on Adobe Walls, soldiers raided the Palo Duro. Quanah Parker, Lone Wolf and a handful of their followers escaped. On February 25, 1875, though, Lone Wolf and his starving band surrendered. Three months later, so did Quanah Parker.

The Indian attempt to drive away the buffalo hunters had been seriously beaten by the white man's technology. But there would be another time.

Some of the relatives of the Cheyennes at Adobe Walls helped bring it about, just two years later.

Five

Last Stand

June 25, 1876, Little Bighorn River, Montana

Lieutenant Colonel George Armstrong Custer watched the whole Seventh Cavalry pass before him in a column of fours, Indian scouts in the lead, pack mules in the rear. Custer, "Armstrong" to his friends, "Autie" to his family and "General" (a courtesy title based on his Civil War rank of major general) to everyone else, shook the hands of the officers seeing him off. Then he wheeled his horse around to overtake the column and march at its head.

Colonel John Gibbon, commanding another of the columns which were to converge on the Sioux camp, called after him, "Now Custer, don't be greedy. Wait for us."

Gatling gun on wheeled mount. This model has a one-inch bore and was designed to outrange rifles. The weapon was fired by turning the crank on the right rear of the gun. A gun like this could fire at the rate of 600 shots a minute. A lighter gun could fire as fast as 1,000 shots a minute.

"N-No. I won't," Custer stammered back—an ambiguous reply if there ever was one.

The current plan of the expedition's commander, Brigadier General Alfred Terry, called for Custer to march up the Rosebud River, cross the lodgepole trail discovered by the Seventh's Major Marcus Reno and verify that the Indians were on or marching down the Little Bighorn River. At the same time, the main force under Gibbon and Terry would march up the Little Bighorn. The Sioux would be caught between the two columns.

Because Custer was an experienced Indian fighter, Terry allowed him considerable discretion on the march. But he was to take five days on his march to give Gibbon's infantry and artillery time to get in place. Under no circumstances was he to take on the Sioux alone. The government did not have 1,250 men under Terry and Gibbon marching through he Yellowstone River country to count the buffaloes.

Custer had other ideas. In the years since the Civil War ended, he had been carefully cultivating business leaders, politicians and the general public. The national Democratic convention was about to begin. The public was getting disgusted with the corruption of the Grant administration. If he could win a major victory—not participate in, but win—at this time, Custer believed, he might well end up president.

That did not seem a wild idea to a man who, two years after finishing at the bottom of his class at West Point, became a general at the age of 23.

In the army, they called it "Custer's luck." Luck had arranged for the young officer to be noticed by a succession of generals—George McClellan, Alfred Pleasanton and Philip Sheridan. It was hard not to notice Custer. He wore a blue sailor shirt with a red cravat and kept his blond hair long. At the end of the war, during the great review held in Washington, Custer in all his finery broke ranks and galloped past the parading soldiers and the reviewing stand, garnering greater applause than any of the units in the parade. He later said that a little girl had thrown a bouquet at him, startling his horse. Those acquainted with Custer's horsemanship took that explanation with a grain of salt.

The generals were less impressed by Custer's appearance than by his performance, however. As a lieutenant on McClellan's staff, Custer would ride to where the fighting was thickest and report what he saw accurately and concisely. The general didn't have many officers cool enough to do that. That kind of performance impressed Pleasanton so much he had Custer promoted first to captain, then to brigadier general in the Volunteers. The Volunteer Army was a wartime force existing side-by-side with the Regular Army. All Regular Army officers held ranks in the Volunteer Army, usually considerably higher than their permanent ranks. As a brigadier general, Custer commanded a brigade in Pleasanton's cavalry. A week after his promotion, he was commanding the Michigan cavalry brigade at Gettysburg. The charge of his brigade drove Lieutenant General J. E. B. Stuart's supposedly invincible Confederate cavalry from the field, where it was positioned to support Pickett's charge.

The next year, General U. S. Grant reorganized the Army of the Potomac. He created a single cavalry corps, like Stuart's, and gave the command to Major General Philip H. Sheridan. "Little Phil" Sheridan, 33, later called "Bear" by the Indians because of his stubby legs, long powerful arms and thick neck, saw much of himself in the tall, athletic Custer. He saw the same love of combat and ability to inspire troops. It may not have occurred to him that Custer's exploits were based on pure fearlessness—a trait some later said indicated only that Custer didn't have the sense to know when he was in danger. He didn't see the pettiness, cruelty and self-absorbtion that Custer was to display in peacetime. By then, the two cavalry leaders had become lifelong friends, and for Sheridan, personal loyalty was almost a religion.

When Sheridan got an independent command in the Shenandoah Valley, Custer went with him. After the Union victory at Winchester, Custer got command of a division. When he cut off Lee at Appomattox, Custer was promoted to major general. As a popular hero, he was outranked only by U. S. Grant, William T. Sherman and Sheridan.

At the end of the war, Sheridan was sent to Texas with an army of occupation, and Custer commanded one division of 4,000 men. The ostensible reason for the troops was to provide garrisons in Texas during the reconstruction. Texas is big, but it didn't take a force the size of Sheridan's army to maintain order. The real reason was to provide moral support for Benito Juárez, the legitimate president of Mexico, who was fighting Napoleon III's puppet emperor, Maximilian. At that moment, the U.S. military machine was larger than that of France, Prussia or any other European power. It was so powerful that warhawks in the United States urged President Andrew Johnson to use it to take over Canada. Johnson had seen all the war he wanted to, however. Nevertheless, he did not like European powers thinking they could seize American countries for non-payment of debt. He sent Sheridan to Texas to drop a gentle hint. "Napoleon the Little" took the hint. The French troops went back home, and a few months later, Maximilian went before a firing squad.

The Texas army may have been good foreign policy, but the troops didn't appreciate it, as Custer soon learned. His new command was completely different from the enthusiastic warriors who had followed him in

Virginia. The Civil War was over; the Union had been preserved, and the volunteers didn't see why they should be marching around Texas instead of going home. There were desertions, abuse of civilians and all kinds of problems. Custer responded with Draconian discipline. And the troops responded with mutiny.

In 1866, the volunteer army was disbanded, and Major General Custer became Captain Custer. At Sheridan's urging, he was made a brevet major general. That was an honorary title, but it allowed him to be addressed as "general," carried certain perquisites and gave him preferment when openings for higher ranks appeared. Sheridan also lobbied to have his protege made a colonel in the regular army, but all he could get for Custer was lieutenant colonel.

The Mexican government offered Custer a commission as adjutant general of Juárez's army at twice his major general's pay. Custer jumped at this chance to get back into a real war. He asked for a year's leave of absence from the army. General Grant and Secretary of War Stanton endorsed the application. President Johnson, though, was not happy about the prospect of United States officers becoming part-time filibusters, so Custer missed the chance to be a Mexican hero.

As a lieutenant colonel in the peacetime army, Custer became second in command of a new regiment, the Seventh Cavalry. In 1867, the commander, Colonel Andrew Jackson Smith, became commander of the Military Department of the Upper Arkansas, and Custer became, in practice if not name, commander of the Seventh Cavalry.

His first year of command was frustrating to Custer. He set out in pursuit of hostile Indians, but the Indians didn't stay and fight. They just packed their tipis and moved to parts unknown. Custer did earn an Indian nickname—"Hard Ass"—because he could stay in the saddle so long during his pursuits. In camp, Custer surrounded himself with a clique of officers, one of them, his brother Tom. With his wife, Custer's clique was known to the rest of the regiment as "the royal family."

One of the officers not in the royal family was Captain Frederick Benteen. Benteen had been breveted a colonel for gallantry on the western frontier and was considered a competent officer. He had, however, a personality quirk that led him to hate almost everybody. He especially hated the flamboyant Custer. To him, Custer was an eastern soldier who, knowing nothing of the nuances of Indian fighting, was incompetent to command a unit on the frontier.

Custer did have trouble understanding the Indians. Sherman complained that he was too trusting of chiefs like Pawnee Killer, a Sioux, who professed to be for peace while his band was burning white settlements. During a second parley with Pawnee Killer, some Sioux led one of Custer's companies into an ambush and were saved only by the quick thinking of Captain Louis Hamilton, a grandson of Alexander Hamilton.

"Hard Ass's" endurance might have excited the admiration of the Indians, but it drew none from his men.

In 1868, Custer, isolated in a frontier fort, decided he wanted to see his wife, Libbie. He took four officers and 72 men with him on a forced 150-mile march—55 hours of almost unbroken travel. Horses and men broke down. At one point, Custer noticed that his spare mare was misssing. He sent a sergeant and six men back for it. Indians shot two of the troopers. Custer refused to take time to look for them. Near Fort Hays, 20 of the men deserted. Custer pushed on. He joined Libbie at Fort Riley and prepared to escort her personally back to his command. But the next day he was arrested.

He was court-martialed for being AWOL from his command, overworking horses, using government property for private business, failing to look for the two men shot by the Indians, ordering deserters to be shot without trial and refusing medical attention to wounded deserters. The court found him guilty on all counts. He was suspended from rank and command and forfeited all pay and allowances for one year. General Grant approved the findings of the court, but remarked on its extreme leniency considering the charges. Custer's luck was still working.

His luck struck again. Ten months after the sentence, Sheridan called him back to active duty. "Little Phil" wanted his old comrade back for a winter campaign against the Sioux and the Cheyenne on the Washita (Burr's Ouachita).

Custer followed a trail made after a recent raid and came to the village of Black Kettle, a Cheyenne chief ardently dedicated to peace. He didn't check to see if the trail went beyond Black Kettle's village. Only hours after Black Kettle had told other chiefs at a council that they had to make peace, the Seventh Cavalry rode into his village from four directions, slaughtering sleeping men, women and children. Mostly women and children. Black Kettle and his wife were among the first killed. Custer's men burned the lodges and killed all the Indians' horses. It wasn't a complete massacre, like the Chivington raid of 1864. (Also against Black Kettle's band.) When most of the shooting was over, Custer did tell his men not to kill a group of women found on the edge of the village.

In the attack, Major Joel Elliott charged right through the village and found himself surrounded by Cheyenne and Arapaho warriors from villages downstream. Custer feinted at attacking the villages downstream, then pulled out under cover of night without making a serious effort to find Elliott, who by this time was dead with all of his men.

Today, pro-Custer historians refer to this affair as their hero's "victory on the Washita."

Custer followed another trail a few months later with half of his regiment. Riding ahead of the troops, he and his adjutant, Lieutenant William Cooke, encountered a group of warriors. The officers made signs indicating that they had come in peace, and the warriors escorted them into one of two nearby villages. In the village, they met Medicine Arrows, one of the most powerful of the Cheyenne chiefs, and a shaman named Little Robe. The four shared a peace pipe, the colonel not quite understanding what was happening. The shaman spilled some ashes on Custer's boot and told him, in Cheyenne, that if he broke the peace he had sworn to, he and all his men would be killed. Then the rest of the cavalry came up, and Custer led them away.

During the Washita campaign, Custer apparently learned to bear his separation from Libbie. He found a new companion, a 17-year-old Cheyenne girl named Monahsetah who had been captured on the Washita. According to Indian tradition, she bore his baby late in 1869.

There are indications that Libbie, too, found agreeable male companionship during Autie's absence. The object of her affection was an officer of the regiment, Lieutenant Thomas Weir, a witty, intellectual alcoholic.

Interestingly, Custer's letters to his wife frequently praised Monahsetah, and hers to him spoke well of Weir. Custer wasn't entirely pleased with that.

"The more I see of him [Weir] Little one," he wrote, "the more I am surprised that a woman of your perceptive faculties and moral training could have entertained the opinion of him you have."

Neither affair seriously impeded the marriage of Armstrong and Elizabeth Custer. It didn't even impair Custer's relations with Weir, who, while never a member of "the royal family," had stood with Custer at the 1865 mutiny of the Third Michigan Cavalry and at his recent court-martial. He remained a Custer loyalist to his death.

When the war on the plains died down, Libbie Custer joined the colonel at his frontier posts, frequently entertaining women friends from her home town, Monroe, Michigan. Custer did a fair amount of entertaining, too. Publicity about his "victory" over Black Kettle made him a celebrity in the East, and important men were always arranging to go hunting with him. Armstrong was an avid hunter: wherever he went—even to battle—he brought along a pack of hunting dogs. Before long, he had taken a specimen of about every type of game found on the Plains.

When he heard the Seventh was to take on garrison duty in the former Confederate states, Custer took a leave and went to New York and Washington looking into alternative careers. He didn't find anything that looked interesting, but he did make a lot of contacts with financiers and railroad moguls.

The leave stretched into seven months, but Custer finally returned to active duty with two companies of the Seventh stationed near Louisville, Kentucky. While his men were chasing moonshiners, the general wrote magazine articles about his experiences and began a book, *My Life on the Plains*. The writings spread his fame as a soldier and frontiersman and gave him a new celebrity: he was now a respected author. He still entertained famous men, such as the Russian Grand Duke Alexis, who went buffalo hunting with Custer and Buffalo Bill Cody. But Custer was getting bored.

Sheridan again came to the rescue. The Northern Pacific railroad wanted to cross the Sioux hunting grounds in Montana and needed military protection. Sheridan sent the Seventh Cavalry.

The Seventh had a new nominal commander, Colonel Samuel D. Sturgis, but Custer again was the field commander. In 1873, Custer led 10 companies of the Seventh into the Yellowstone River country. The other two companies, under Major Marcus Reno, were guarding the railroad crews. With Custer's troops were 19 infantry companies and two Rodman guns under Colonel David Stanley, who commanded the whole column. Stanley was a quiet man who had little to say on the infrequent occasions he was sober. General Terry, who commanded the military department, predicted the march to show the flag would be a "big picnic."

And so it was. Custer hunted daily. His band provided entertainment every night. There were a couple of fights.

In the first, the Sioux employed their ancient stratagem and drew Custer and some of his troops into an ambush. The Indians were not, however, prepared for the rapid fire of the breech-loading Springfield carbines the troops carried. Custer and his detail held them off until the rest of his cavalry arrived and chased the Indians away.

The second fight involved some 500 warriors who attacked Custer and 450 troopers. The numerical odds were almost even, and the Indians had to attack across a river. Attacking that way, civilized troops would be most unlikely to succeed. It wasn't surprising, then, that Custer drove the Indians off. What was surprising was that the Indians attacked at all. In the past, whenever Indians attacked, they had overwhelming numerical odds. The Sioux, it seemed, had lost the Indians' traditional fear of soldiers. This was a radical change in plains warfare, but it was completely overlooked by the military authorities. And all that American newspaper readers learned was that Custer had racked up two more glorious victories. Custer's friends with the Northern Pacific Railroad were ecstatic.

The big news, though, was that the Sioux had changed. In 1866, a Texas cattleman named Nelson Story drove a herd of longhorns to Montana. At Fort Leavenworth, Kansas, Story and his 30 cowboys heard that the whole Sioux nation, led by Red Cloud, had taken the war path. Story bought a brand-new type of rifle, the Remington rolling block, for each of his men. The Remington was a breech-loader, simpler and stronger than even the Sharps, and fast to reload.

As happened eight years later at Adobe Walls, the Indians were victims of a technological gap. A young war chief named Crazy Horse attacked the cowboys, who drew their wagons into a circle. Crazy Horse's men circled Story's outfit, trying to draw its fire so they could charge after the first volley. But the first volley never ceased. And the rifles' power was so great that when they had ridden out of the cowboys' range, the Indians had also ridden out of their sight. Story brought his cattle to what is now Bozeman, Montana, and established the cattle industry in the North. The bison, and the Indians who depended on them, were pushed out of another corner of the Plains.

Ten years after his encounter with the cowboys, Crazy Horse was still a war chief. But he was a smarter war chief: he had changed the centuries-old tactics of the Plains Indians. The results were obvious—except to the soldiers. Crazy Horse had led the Sioux in both of their encounters with Custer during the Yellowstone expedition.

Most of the Oglala Sioux stayed on the reservation except during the summer hunts in their Montana hunting ground. Crazy Horse and his immediate followers, though, refused to recognize the treaty. They stayed in Montana with Sitting Bull, the great Hunkpapa Sioux chief who refused to have anything to do with the *Wasichu* (white men). Before long, most of the young Sioux on the reservation, along with warriors of the northern Chey-enne, would join Crazy Horse and Sitting Bull. The reason: Custer's next expedition.

In 1874, Custer led an expedition into the Black Hills, reserved for the Sioux by treaty. Its stated purpose was to find locations for a couple of forts. Its real purpose was to check out reports of gold in the Black Hills. There was gold. Custer sent back a sample of Black Hills ore with a formal report on the good news—good for gold seekers, railroads and army officers, who wanted to drive the Indians out of the hills. It wasn't good for the Indians, who called Custer's trail the Thieves' Road.

The army at first tried to block the gold hunters, then it turned a blind eye to them. A federal commission told the Sioux the United States was buying the Black Hills and they'd have to get out, treaty or no treaty.

The Black Hills alone wouldn't satisfy the government people. They wanted the Indians out of a huge area in Montana where the Sioux and Cheyenne had hunting rights under the treaty. This hunting ground was also the scene of the annual council of the Teton (western) Sioux. Indians in the hunting ground interfered with railroad operation, so the army resolved to force Sitting Bull and all his followers and allies onto a reservation.

Custer desperately wanted to lead the expedition. The operation was to be a winter campaign, a Sheridan specialty. In winter, the Indian horses were weak from lack of good grazing, making this the ideal season for attacking them. Winter in Montana, though, was even worse than winter in Kansas and the Texas Panhandle. Winter in Montana was closer to winter in Siberia. Custer's train was stuck in the snow before he could reach his post. His supplies were literally frozen in place. Nothing could happen before spring, which, in Montana, came when it was summer elsewhere. In the meantime, Custer was called to testify at the impeachment trial of Secretary of War William Belknap. President Grant saw Custer's testimony an act of disloyalty. He refused to allow Custer to return west. Sheridan, Custer's fairy godfather so often in the past, was paralyzed. Grant was an even closer friend than Custer. To the rescue came "Cump" Sherman, commander of the army, a man who always spoke his mind regardless of friendship. Grant eventually relented. Custer could go to Montana. The field operations, though, would be commanded by Terry. And, Sherman added, Custer would not be allowed to take any newspaper correspondents along. Custer ignored that provision and invited Mark Kellogg, a young law student acting as a correspondent for the Bismarck *Tribune* and the New York *Herald*. By the time Custer was back in the field, the expedition had been delayed half a year.

The plan Terry put in operation called for three converging columns. One, under Terry's direct command, numbered 1,000 men, including 750 from the Seventh Cavalry. That would travel up the Yellowstone River, meet a steam boat carrying supplies, and move west. Another 1,000 men under Colonel John Gibbon would march east through Montana. Brigadier General George Crook would lead a third column north from Wyoming. Somewhere in the wilderness, Sheridan expected these troops to find the Sitting Bull bands.

Gibbon moved first. His scouts located a large Indian village, but it moved before he could do anything about it. He didn't notify anybody about his find. Gibbon didn't want to advertise that he had let Indians escape. The chief fear of the army hierarchy at this time was that the Indians would get away.

The Indians weren't trying to get away. Incensed over the loss of the Black Hills, reservation Indians were riding into Montana in unprecedented numbers. The lure was not only hunting: they knew that the white soldiers were going to attack Sitting Bull's people, and they wanted to fight. One tipoff to white intentions came in March, when Joseph Reynolds, one of Crook's colonels, attacked a Sioux village near the Powder River. Reynolds drove the Indians off and burned their village. Then the Indians counterattacked. Reynolds withdrew. He was later court-martialed for cowardice. These Indians were not going to run at the sight of a blue uniform, but that fact didn't register with the army brass.

When Terry reached his jumping-off place, he changed his plan and sent for Gibbon. Gibbon's troops were to join Terry's—minus the Seventh Cavalry—and march down the Yellowstone to the Bighorn River. Custer, with the Seventh, would go south along the Rosebud, then turn back to the Little Bighorn, a tributary of the Bighorn. If all went according to plan, Crook's column should meet Custer's on the Rosebud unless somebody found the Indians first. In that case, all columns would converge on the enemy.

Before Custer left, Terry offered him three Gatling guns. Custer declined. The Gatling guns, he said, would slow his march. Actually, the Gatlings were a model designed to be broken down and carried on pack saddles. Evan Connell, in *Son of the Morning Star*, says "They frequently malfunctioned, and the bullets they sprayed from six or ten barrels—depending on the model—would have been effective only against a mass attack, such as might be expected in Europe. British redcoats might march into the fire of Gatlings with heads up and arms swinging, but American Indians were less disciplined."

The Gatling, mounted on a light artillery carriage, was certainly a clumsier weapon than a modern machinegun. The firing mechanism was operated by a man who turned a crank. As the circle of barrels turned, a cartridge dropped from a gravity-powered magazine, was loaded, fired and the empty shell ejected. But a light Gatling with a strong gunner could fire at a rate of 1,000 rounds a minute, a high rate even for a modern automatic machinegun. Connell's objection is specious: three years after Custer left the three Gatlings behind, the British took two Gatlings to Zululand. The Zulus were perhaps the most militarily sophisticated of all "uncivilized" peoples. They had already wiped out a British army many times the size of Custer's force. Although the Zulus were masters of taking cover and although the Gatlings jammed several times, they mowed the Zulu warriors down in clumps and ended the Zulu War. Against a mass attack—the kind Custer eventually faced on the Little Bighorn—machine guns were even more horrendous. A few years after the Zulu War, the British took a new type of machinegun, the Maxim, to the Sudan. The Maxim was the first automatic gun—it dispensed with the crank—but its effect on the enemy was the same as the Gatling's. A witness at the Battle of Omdurman who saw machine guns used on the Sudanese Dervishes called the action "Not a battle but an execution. . . . the bodies were spread evenly over acres and acres."

Another weapon the cavalry left behind was the saber. On Terry's orders, all sabers stayed at the supply base. Sabers were awkward in the boondocks, and, the general said, Plains Indians did not fight hand-to-hand. That meant that, unlike the infantry, which kept its bayonets, the cavalry would be unarmed if it ran out of ammunition.

Custer had, for the first time on a campaign, all the companies of his regiment. He had his "royal family," including his brother, Tom, his brother-in-law "Jimmi" Calhoun and a third brother, Boston, who joined the group as a "guide." The general's 18-year-old nephew, "Autie" Reed, had joined him as a "herder." Even Libbie's friend, Tom Weir, now a captain, was with him as a company commander.

Neither Custer nor Terry knew it, but Crook had already found some of the Indians. He met them on the Rosebud, south of where Custer was marching. Crazy Horse commanded the Indians. When Crook's cavalry charged them, they faded away in front and attacked the soldiers on their flanks. The warriors mauled Crook's column severely. Crook retreated to Wyoming without notifying Terry. Also while Custer marched, the reservation Indians began to reach Sitting Bull's camp, drifting there in small groups. On June 24, Custer's scouts found the trail formed by dragging tipi poles. Custer now knew where the Indians were. He didn't plan to wait for Terry and Gibbon. He wanted news of the victory to reach the Democratic convention before it nominated a candidate for president. The troops and their horses got little rest the night of the 24th. They were back on the trail soon after midnight.

That morning, Custer's Crow scouts climbed a hill known as The Crow's Nest. One of them pointed to the village. The officer in charge of the scouts, Lieutenant Charles Varnum, pulled out a spyglass, looked and said, "I don't see a thing."

"Look for nest of worms," said Mitch Bouyer, the French-Sioux scout. "Big pony herd far off look like tangles of fish worms."

Charley Reynolds, another guide, looked through the glass and said, "That's the biggest pony herd any man ever saw together."

Custer came up and looked. He couldn't see the village, either, but he took the word of his scouts.

Then some other scouts told him they had seen Sioux or Cheyenne warriors, and the hostile Indians had found some rations that fell off a pack horse. Custer was afraid they had been discovered. If he didn't move fast, the Indians would flee.

Actually, the Indians who found the rations were traveling toward the village, but hadn't reached it. The village at this point stretched four or five miles along the Little Bighorn and included between 3,000 and 5,000 warriors—the largest concentration of Indian fighting men ever seen north of the Rio Grande—and thousands more women and children.

Custer ordered his troops to get ready to move. He was elated. Others were not. The Arikara scouts said *"Otoe Sioux!* (too many Sioux!)" and began to sing their death songs. Mitch Bouyer told Custer, "If we go down into that valley, neither of us will come out alive."

Custer's only concern was that the Indians might escape. He ordered Benteen to take three companies and search the waterless badlands to the south. They could round up any Indians still hidden and block any others from escaping. Why Custer, outnumbered at least five to one, would detach a quarter of his force on what could reasonably be expected to be a wild goose chase, he never explained.

When he got close to the village, Custer sent his adjutant, Lieutenant Cooke, to tell Reno, leading three companies, to advance toward the tipis directly across the river "and charge afterward, and you will be supported by the whole outfit." He sent another courier to Benteen, telling him to bring up his troops. By that time, Benteen, seeing nothing but barren hills and knowing that he was marching away from any possible action, had turned around. A third courier went to Captain Thomas McDougall, who had one company guarding the pack train, telling him to bring his troops and the pack train forward. Custer didn't wait for any reinforcements. He sent one more courier, his trumpeter, John Martin, to Benteen and started north with five companies, about 300 men. With no communications but mounted couriers, Custer had in effect abandoned seven of his 12 companies and was advancing on the largest Indian army in history. There could be no explanation but an irrational belief in his own invulnerablity.

The Indians had expected an attack from the south, so their strongest group, Sitting Bull's Hunkpapa Sioux, were there. Most of the Hunkpapas had rifles, many of them repeaters. At the north end of the camp, were the weakest group, the Cheyennes, who were generally armed with bows and arrows.

Reno and his three companies were charging right at the Hunkpapas. As Reno neared the village, there were shots. He halted his men, had them dismount and form a skirmish line. An Indian woman in the camp thought the commander of the soldiers "must be crazy. We were all surprised. He could have ridden in and killed everyone."

The surprise didn't last long. Gall, Sitting Bull's adopted brother and chief lieutenant, rallied his warriors and sent the women and children to the rear. The Hunkpapas were soon pouring a devastating fire on Reno's troops. Reno's force fell back across the river. The Indians shot Reno's horse handlers, crossed the river on his flank and ran off many of the horses. Reno ordered a retreat to a line of cottonwoods. The Indians kept pressing, and the retreat became a rout to the bluffs overlooking the river. Reno saw no sign of "the whole outfit" Custer had promised would support him.

On the way to the north flank of the village, Custer split his command. One three-company battalion, under Captain Myles Keogh, he posted dismounted on a ridge. He sent a two-company battalion, under Captain George Yates, galloping toward the Little Bighorn and the Cheyenne camp. Where Custer went is unknown. He was probably with Yates. One theory is that Custer was posting his two battalions to support a charge by Benteen. He had not, however, sent any additional messages to Benteen.

Benteen was far away. He had headed back toward the main force, but it would be a while before he got there.

Before he did, the Sioux and Cheyenne Nations fell on Custer. About 30 Cheyenne warriors held the ford of the Little Bighorn as the troops approached, but they were quickly reinforced. The Sioux had seen Custer's northward march along the ridgeline. They crossed the river behind him and worked their way up the ravines. Custer and Yates, about to be surrounded, retreated to the bluffs. Keogh, still lightly engaged, saw that they were in trouble and moved his battalion to link up with them.

Upstream, Crazy Horse, the Oglala Sioux war chief, got Gall and many of his warriors to join him in the attack on Custer's force, which he saw as the main enemy.

Hunkpapa and other Sioux riflemen opened up on the troopers, forcing them to keep their heads down. Some of the soldiers killed their horses and used them for breastworks. Crazy Horse led a wide sweep which completely surrounded Custer's troops.

Below the brow of the bluffs, where the soldiers couldn't see them, Sioux and Cheyenne bowmen loosed their arrows high into the air, so they fell on the troops from above. In 1066, Duke William of Normandy used the same tactics to weaken the Saxons. After 810 years, the technique still worked. When the Indians thought the soldiers had been sufficiently softened, they sent in their suicide squads—young men sworn to die fighting the white men. The suicide squads had lances, hatchets and war clubs. Most of the soldiers had only empty guns. None, of course, had sabers.

The departure of Gall had eased the pressure on Reno, but his battalion was still in trouble. When Benteen's troops appeared from the south, the first soldiers they saw were Reno's. They joined Reno's men, and the Indians faded away to fight Custer's men.

Tom Weir waited for Major Reno to give the word to link up with Custer. The order never came. Finally, Weir left his foxhole without permission, got on his horse and began riding toward the sound of the guns. His orderly followed him. His executive officer, Lieutenant Winfield Scott Edgerly, thought the captain had Reno's permission, so he ordered the rest of the company to mount and follow Weir. Major Reno's mind seemed paralyzed, so Captain Benteen, the second ranking officer, took over command and led the troops after Weir.

"We saw a good many Indians riding up and down and firing at objects on the ground," Edgerly said later. The "objects on the ground" were the dead bodies of Custer and his command. There was nothing to do but go back to their entrenchments.

The Indian warriors were joined by old men and women in stripping and mutilating the bodies of the slain. The Sioux couldn't find Custer. Although the Cheyennes knew him as Hard Ass and his Crow Scouts called him Son of the Morning Star (because of his fondness for pre-dawn attacks), the Sioux called him Long Hair. And Custer, following orders from Washington, had had a haircut not long before the battle.

Two Cheyenne women recognized his body. When some Sioux warriors came to scalp and mutilate the corpse, the women asked them to leave it alone, because it was the body of a relative—the husband of Monahsetah and the father of her second child. The Sioux settled for a token mutilation, cutting off one finger joint. The women then pierced Custer's eardrums with sewing awls. That was to improve his hearing in the next life, they said. In this life, he had not heard Little Robe's warning after he smoked a peace pipe with Medicine Arrows.

In the Sioux camp, there was disagreement over whether they should risk more lives attacking Reno and Benteen or wait for thirst to take care of the soldiers. The next day, Sioux scouts informed the camp that many more soldiers—Terry's column—were approaching. The Indians broke camp and faded into the hills.

Terry found survivors of Reno's and Benteen's troops awaiting another attack. They buried the dead and returned to civilization.

Weir's failure to save Custer—something he could never have done— seemed to affect his mind. On the way back, he shunned all human company and began acting very oddly. He was immediately ordered to New York for recruiting duty. In St. Louis, he wrote to Libbie Custer, "You know I can't tell you now but will someday tell it to you. . . . I have so much to tell you that I will tell you nothing now." In New York, he wrote to her, "I know if we were all of us alone in the parlor, at night, the curtains all down and everybody else asleep, one or the other of you [Libbie or Autie?] would make me tell you everything I know."

He never told, whatever it was. Six months after the battle, Thomas Weir, depressed and so nervous he couldn't swallow, died. One acquaintance said it was pneumonia. Another, that it was "melancholia and congestion of the brain."

Reno was given command of a tiny outpost of Fort Lincoln. He became scandalously involved with a married woman, got into a fist fight in the officers club and challenged another officer to a duel. A court-martial sentenced him to dismissal, but President Rutherford B. Hayes commuted the sentence to two years suspension. Back on active duty he got into another fight. While he was awaiting trial, he was caught peering into the bedroom of the regimental commander's daughter. He was dishonorably discharged.

Benteen took to drinking. Drinking was hardly uncommon in the frontier army, but Benteen's got so bad he was court-martialed in 1887 and sentenced to dismissal from the service. President Grover Cleveland commuted the sentence to a year's suspension, but three days after Benteen came back on duty, he applied for and received a medical discharge.

Custer's career did not end like those of Weir, Reno and Benteen. It might have, had he lost and survived. If he'd won, he probably wouldn't have become a presidential candidate. If he had run for president, it's even less likely that he would have been elected. He would probably become, like George Crook or Nelson Miles, a fairly successful Indian fighter forgotten by all but professional historians.

As it turned out, Custer is remembered by everyone. He is a modern Achilles, the golden-haired buckskin cavalier, incomparably audacious, incredibly brave, who died fighting against impossible odds. It takes little reflection to decide which role Autie would have preferred.

The Custer luck was alive to the end.

The Indians, as usual, were out of luck.

Custer's "Last Stand" was the heaviest defeat the U.S. Army ever suffered at the hands of the Indians. That, though, says more about the Indians' lack of success than it does about the magnitude of Custer's defeat. A single cavalry regiment had been defeated—because of the gross incompetence of its commander—with a loss of less than 300 men.

The American public, however, became hysterical. The defeat was called a "massacre." The nation's *beau sabreur*, the famous frontiersman, the celebrity general, had been killed. Cries went up from all parts of the country to avenge Custer. Buffalo Bill, as an army scout, killed an Indian in an obscure skirmish and announced that he had taken "the first scalp for Custer." Within a few months, the army launched a massive offensive. Troops converged on the Yellowstone country and the Black Hills.

Sitting Bull's enormous concentration of Sioux and Cheyenne would have had to break up even if soldiers had not appeared. The Montana prairie couldn't support that many people in one place. That winter the army attacked the scattered villages one by one and drove Indian families out onto the freezing plains. The year after the battle on the Little Bighorn, Crazy Horse surrendered. When he saw that the soldiers were going to put him in a cell, he tried to escape and was killed.

Sitting Bull and his band fled to Canada, but the Canadians, saying they weren't "British Indians," refused to give them a reservation where they could support themselves. The Northern Cheyenne were sent to the Indian Territory (modern Oklahoma). There, unused to the climate and the miserable food they received from the Indian Agency, many sickened and died. A few struck out north for their old home, but most were killed by soldiers and civilian frontiersmen on the way.

The army promised Sitting Bull a pardon if he returned. In 1881, he and 186 followers did come back. Instead of a pardon, though, the old chief and shaman got jail. Eventually released on a reservation, Sitting Bull, alone of all the Sioux chiefs, refused to sign a new treaty. A newspaperman asked him how the Indians felt about giving up their land.

"Indians?" Sitting Bull exploded. "There are no Indians left now but me!"

The only white man Sitting Bull ever liked was Buffalo Bill. Somehow, Cody got the chief to agree to appear in his wild west show. As far as Sitting

Bull was concerned, Buffalo Bill Cody, the man who took "the first scalp for Custer," was the only white man who ever kept his word. When the chief left the show, Cody gave him one of his prized show horses.

Off in the wilds of Nevada, a Paiute named Wovoka, announced that he was Jesus Christ, returned to earth a second time as an Indian. He had come to teach all Indians a new dance. In the spring, when the new grass was high, he said, a tidal wave of earth would sweep over the world and bury all the white men and their works. But those who did this dance, the Dance of the Ghosts, would be carried up into the air and, when the wave had passed, be set down with the ghosts of their ancestors in a land where there would always be plenty of buffalo. The Ghost Shirts the dancers wore, Wovoka said, would make all the white man's bullets miss them.

The Ghost Dance religion spread like a prairie fire through all of the Indians of the West. Sitting Bull was not a believer, but he had no objection to his people dancing. Somehow, the whites got the notion that he was behind the Ghost Dancing, which they took to be dangerous agitation. They asked Buffalo Bill to talk him into coming to Chicago for a conference. Then someone became afraid that Cody would learn they meant not to talk with Sitting Bull, but to arrest him. The showman's mission was cancelled, and the authorities sent a company of Indian police to arrest the chief. As Lieutenant Bull Head tried to arrest Sitting Bull, one of the chief's followers produced a rifle and shot the officer. Bull Head and a Sergeant Red Tomahawk fired at Sitting Bull, killing him.

Sitting Bull's horse, trained to perform at the crack of a gun, sat down, extended one hoof, stood up and did what the onlookers took to be an equine version of the Ghost Dance.

The death of Sitting Bull spread alarm through all the Sioux Ghost Dancers. Big Foot, a Minneconjou Sioux chief, and his people set out for the village of Red Cloud, the last important Sioux chief, hoping that Red Cloud could protect them. En route, they met a battalion of the Seventh Cavalry. Its commander, Major Samuel Whitside, said he had orders to take them to the cavalry camp at Wounded Knee. The soldiers herded the 120 men and 230 women and children into the fort grounds and started to disarm them.

One Indian held out. He said he had paid a lot for his rifle and wanted compensation. A soldier tried to take it away from him. There was a shot. The soldiers raised their carbines and fired wildly into the mostly unarmed Indians. Two Hotchiss cannons joined in the slaughter. Among the soldiers were Lieutenants Varnum and Edgerly, who had been at the Little Bighorn. When the troops stopped shooting, 300 of the 350 Indians were dead.

That was December 28, 1890. Three centuries of Indian wars were over. Actually, except for the fighting retreat of Chief Joseph and his Nez Perce, the last real combat took place fourteen and a half years previously, on the Little Bighorn River—the last stand, not just of Custer, but of all the Indian peoples.

EXPANSION

AND

GROWING

PAINS—

THE GUNFIGHTERS

"Get Your Guns, Boys"

September 7, 1876, Northfield, Minnesota

There were eight of them, well-dressed, superbly mounted men. Each had a carbine hanging from his saddle and a pair of revolvers beneath his long linen duster. Sometimes they traveled together; sometimes they split into two or three parties. Usually, Charlie Pitts rode with Bill Chadwell. Clell Miller stuck with the three brothers, Cole, Bob and Jim Younger. Frequently conferring together were the other two brothers, Frank and Jesse James.

The James gang was exploring new territory. Chadwell, a native of Minnesota, had convinced Missourian Jesse James that banks would be easy plucking in the north. The gang's usual haunts, the Missouri-Kansas border

Top: Smith and Wesson Schofield revolver, caliber .45, Jesse James's favorite sidearm. When opened, the Schofield ejected all cartridge cases automatically, making reloading quicker. Below: Frank James preferred the grip and balance of Remington's "Frontier" revolver, caliber .44-40.

country, had been racked by more than two decades of guerrilla warfare, regular warfare and rampant outlawry. People there were suspicious and often armed.

The Jameses were veterans of that two decades of violence. In their teens they had followed Confederate guerrilla leaders William Clark Quantrill and "Bloody Bill" Anderson. When the Civil War ended, Jesse and Frank refused to give up violence. They continued it for their own benefit rather than for a cause. Some Confederate sympathizers saw them as resistance fighters, rather than crooks—especially because their victims were banks and railroads, those shock troops of the new financial/industrial world that was pressing in on the agricultural Midwest. Those sympathizers, though, were merely cheerleaders. They wouldn't turn in the Jameses, but they wouldn't help them. Meanwhile, the banks and railroads were getting more wary and better armed. They were adapting to the culture of violence.

While men from Minnesota, as from everywhere else, had participated in the Civil War, the war itself had stayed far from the state's borders. The people were peaceful farmers, many of them recent immigrants from Scandinavia.

The gang rode at a leisurely pace, stopping at small towns and looking over the banks. Jesse decided that the bank in Mankato would be their first job in Minnesota. Four gang members went shopping in the town to plot escape routes, and Jesse changed a five dollar bill in the bank itself while he looked over the setup. At noon the next day, the bandits approached the bank, but they saw a large crowd of citizens standing on the sidewalk. One of them suddenly pointed to Jesse James and said something to the others. The whole James gang put spurs to their horses and galloped out of town. Jesse James never learned that the man pointing to him was merely admiring his horse.

The gang moved on to Northfield, where the bank was part of a block of buildings on Bridge Square. The square and Division Street, which the bank faced, was Northfield's business district.

Shortly after 2 p.m., Charlie Pitts, Bob Younger and Jesse James rode across the wooden bridge that gave Bridge Square its name. They hitched their horses in front of the bank, sauntered up to the corner and stood in front of a general store. Five minutes later, Cole Younger and Clell Miller came ambling down the street on their horses. Miller tied his horse next to the other three while Younger stopped in the middle of the street and pretended to tighten his saddle girth. Jesse James, Bob Younger and Charlie Pitts entered the bank.

Present in the bank were Joseph Heywood, the acting cashier, F. J.

Wilcox, an assistant bookkeeper, and A. E. Bunker, a teller. Heywood stood up to greet the visitors. The visitors pulled revolvers and told him to open the vault.

"There's a time lock on it," Heywood said. "I can't open it."

Pitts struck him across the face with his revolver and knocked him down. He drew a bowie knife and shouted, "Let's cut his damned throat." Bob Younger grabbed Heywood and dragged him over to the the vault door. Younger and Pitts both threatened to shoot the cashier, but he refused to try to open the door. (It later turned out that the door was unlocked. Someone had forgotten to spin the combination dial after closing it.) As a final measure of intimidation, Pitts fired at Heywood, grazing his face. The slug put a hole in the vault door.

Meanwhile, a vacationing college student, Henry Wheeler, whose father owned a drug store across the street, had noticed the elaborately casual strangers hanging around the bank. So did J.A. Allen, who owned a nearby hardware store. Allen started to enter the bank, but Miller grabbed him, stuck a revolver in his stomach and said, "Keep your goddam mouth shut." Allen tore loose and ran down the street yelling, "Get your guns, boys. They're robbing the bank." Miller and Cole Younger vaulted into their saddles and dashed after the merchant. Allen ducked into his hardware store before they could reach him.

When Miller grabbed Allen, Wheeler ran into the square, shouting "Robbery! Robbery! They're at the bank!" Miller fired at him and missed. Wheeler dashed into the drug store.

Suddenly, Frank James, Bill Chadwell and Jim Younger appeared. They galloped down the street screeching rebel yells and firing their revolvers. "Get in! Get in, all of you!" Frank James shouted.

Inside the bank, Bob Younger joined Jesse James in trying to intimidate the other two bank employees. Pitts noticed Bunker, the teller, inching toward a drawer. He jumped up, pulled out the drawer and took out a derringer.

The three outlaws temporarily gave up trying to find someone to open the vault, and started looking for the cashier's till. Bunker took advantage of their distraction and sprinted for the rear door. A fusilade of missed shots followed him. Pitts ran after him and took careful aim when Bunker reached the alley. The bullet tore through the teller's shoulder but didn't stop him.

Pitts ran back inside and screamed, "The game's up. Pull out or they'll be killing our men."

Pitts' warning was a little late.

As soon as he reached his father's drug store, Wheeler went looking for his gun. Then he remembered he had taken it home. Knowing that there was an old army carbine and some cartridges in the baggage room of a hotel a few doors away, he ran there, seized the carbine and carried it to an upstairs room.

While Wheeler was finding a gun, Allen was standing in his hardware store, loading guns and passing them out to passers-by. In his excitement, he loaded the first shotgun with light bird shot. He passed it and some bird shot cartridges to Elias Stacy, who promptly blasted Clell Miller off his horse. The light shot didn't penetrate deeply enough to cause a serious wound, but it covered Miller's face with blood and blinded him.

With the bandits galloping through Division Street and the square, yelling and firing at anybody on the street, Northfield had become a war zone. And into the war zone walked Nicholas Gustavson, a Swedish immigrant.

"Get back!" a citizen yelled at him. But Gustavson, unable to understand English, smiled, waved and plodded on. Seconds later, he was riddled with bullets.

Pitts' warning, followed by the sounds of battle, convinced Jesse James that it was time to leave. The gang dashed out of the bank, and Jesse, the last to leave, turned and coolly shot Heywood in the head.

A. E. Manning, who owned another hardware store, joined the battle as the three robbers were leaving the bank. He saw Jesse James and Bob Younger crouching behind their still-tied horses. Manning shot the nearest horse in the head. He tried to eject the shell and reload, but the rifle wouldn't eject. Manning ducked back into his store, ejected the shell with a ramrod and returned to the street. Cole Younger saw him, fired and missed. Manning fired back and wounded the outlaw in the shoulder. Seventy-five yards down the street, Bill Chadwell, the Minnesota outlaw, turned his horse around and charged toward the hardware merchant. Manning shot him dead. An autopsy later showed he had hit Chadwell in the heart.

As Chadwell fell, young Henry Wheeler poked his old carbine through a second-floor window and fired as Cole Younger raced by. The shot took off the bandit's hat, but missed him. Wheeler reloaded and saw Clell Miller, back in the saddle again, but still blinded, firing his revolver. Wheeler fired, and Miller slid off his horse with blood gushing from his mouth. In a few seconds, he was dead.

Bob Younger, the man whose horse Manning had shot, was crouching behind a hitching post. He pegged a shot at Manning, but missed. Manning jumped behind the corner of a building and maneuvered to get a better shot at Younger. Younger, in turn, began stalking the merchant. Younger moved into Wheeler's field of view, and the boy fired his carbine. The big bullet shattered Younger's elbow. Younger shifted the gun to his left hand and fired again at Manning and again missed.

Manning dashed across the street to get a better shot at Bob Younger. Wheeler reloaded his carbine. The Missourians were still galloping around the square, but they were not intimidating the citizens. More and more Northfield men appeared with guns. Jim Younger was hit in the face; Frank James, in the leg. Unarmed men joined the battle. One of them yelled, "Stone 'em! Let's stone 'em." Rocks began to fly from all the side streets.

"We're beat! Let's go!" an outlaw shouted.

Bob Younger lurched into the street, waving his good arm. "Hold on. Don't leave me. I'm shot," he shouted. Big Cole Younger, also wounded, turned back for his brother. As he reached him, a charge of buckshot gave Bob a second wound in his right arm.

The James gang charged across the bridge and out of town, firing their revolvers, trailing blood and leaving two of their number dead on the street.

They were out of Northfield, but by no means out of trouble. Word of the raid was telegraphed to all the nearby towns. By a stroke of Jamesian luck, the telegrapher at Dundas, three miles south of Northfield, was having lunch while his sounder clicked out the alarm. The bandits passed through Dundas before anyone knew about the attempted robbery. Posses quickly organized in other towns. There were a few clashes with isolated possemen—Jesse James took a bullet through the thigh in one—but the robbers always managed to elude the law in Minnesota's dense woods.

For four days, the outlaws were able to dodge the posses. But in the course of the pursuit, they had lost their horses. And they were only 15 miles from Northfield. Finally, Jesse and Frank James said that the wounded Bob Younger was slowing them down, making it impossible for them to escape. Cole and Jim Younger refused to abandon their brother, and Charlie Pitts sided with them. The James boys took their share of the loot and set out alone, stealing a horse from a farm on the way. Somehow, they managed to get back to Missouri.

The Youngers and Pitts weren't so lucky. They wandered through the woods for more than a week, but finally they were spotted. A posse, led by Sheriff James Glispin and Capt. W. W. Murphy, a Civil War veteran, closed in on them. The four outlaws, hiding in a thicket of willows, wild plums and grapevines, were hemmed in by a steep bluff and a river. Murphy assumed command of the posse and asked for six volunteers to go in after the bandits.

The assault party included Murphy, Glispin, Col. Thomas Vought, another Civil War officer, B. M. Rice, G. A. Bradford, C. A. Pomeroy and S. J. Severson.

A bullet came out of the thicket, smashed Murphy's pipe and lodged in his pistol belt. He ordered an advance. The posse began firing and moved into the jungle, where four desperate men waited. Bradford and Severson were slightly injured, but the outlaws' fire seemed to slacken.

"Do you men surrender?" Sheriff Glispin called. There was a short period of silence, then a voice said, "I surrender." Bob Younger rose from the underbrush, his left hand held high. He reached down and threw his revolver in front of him. "They're all down except me," he said.

When the posse reached the scene of the Youngers' last stand, they found Charlie Pitts dead, the bank's derringer still in his pocket. Cole Younger was riddled with eleven bullet holes. Jim Younger had five wounds. Bob Younger, the only one able to stand, had two wounds, but they had been festering since the attempted bank robbery, two weeks before.

Somehow, all three of the Youngers lived to receive long prison sentences, but Bob never got out. He died of tuberculosis in 1889.

Jesse and Frank got back to Clay County, Missouri, but promptly lit out for other parts of the country. The brothers, with Jesse's wife, went to Kentucky, then to Tennessee. Jesse took his family to California, but both brothers eventually returned to Clay County. They recruited a new gang and robbed a stage coach, a bank and two more trains, but the stickups were bungled affairs, and the James brothers spent most of their time in hiding. On April 3, 1882, Bob Ford, a member of the new gang, killed Jesse James for the reward. A few months later, Frank gave himself up and was tried. He was acquitted, largely because of post-war politics in Missouri, but the James gang was history.

Actually it had been history for six years—ever since a handful of ordinary citizens outshot the famous outlaws on the streets of Northfield, Minnesota.

Each of the many screen reenactments of the Northfield shootout has been a bonanza for stunt men. Bodies pitch from roofs, bodies fall out of windows and bodies roll down staircases as the outlaws blast away. Actually, the ferocious James gang killed only a stunned and unarmed cashier propped up against a vault door and a Swedish immigrant who must have thought the yelling and shooting were part of some strange American celebration. They wounded an unarmed teller who went on to help alarm the town. By contrast, the amateurs—a student and some shopkeepers—had killed two armed and mounted bandits and wounded four others.

The bank in Northfield was far from the first Jesse James and his gang tried to hold up. Their robbery techniques were well tried and, until this time, successful. The touble in Northfield was that the citizens would not be intimidated. It may have been that Jesse James' reputation carried less weight in Minnesota than in Missouri. It may have been that the gang was just unlucky in meeting people like J.A. Allen and A. E. Bunker, who demonstrated to others that the famous bandits could be defied. Whatever the reason, from that point, everything went downhill for the James gang.

Jesse James, unwounded in the stick-up, was later hit as he fled back to Missouri. Charlie Pitts, who also escaped unscathed, was killed a few days later. That was when a sheriff and six more ordinary citizens walked into a thicket hiding four armed desperados and brought them all in.

Because he had been a Confederate guerrilla and because he robbed banks and railroads, Jesse James, although a cold-blooded murderer, became a kind of folk hero.

Nevertheless, it has been universally acknowledged that the real heroes in his career were the ordinary Minnesotans who destroyed the James gang.

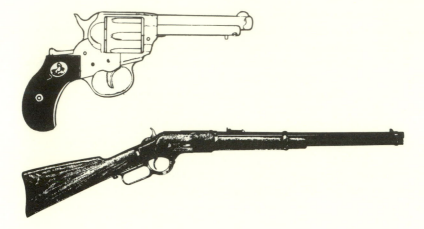

Seven

A Shot in the Dark

July 14, 1881, Ft. Sumner, New Mexico

The figure was silhouetted in the doorway for an instant. The sheriff, crouching beside his host's bed, noted that the newcomer made no sound as he walked. He had no hat, and he was carrying a large knife in one hand and a revolver in the other. The sheriff watched him glide over to the bed and speak to the man in it.

"*Pedro, quién son ellos hombres fuero de su casa?*" he asked. Then he looked directly at the sheriff, hidden in the shadows. He seemed to start.

"*Quién es? Quién es?*" he shouted. The pistol came up.

The sheriff jerked his .45 Colt single action from his holster at fired at the

Top: Colt .41 caliber "Thunderer", the double-action revolver Billy the Kid was holding when he died. The weapon was faster than a single-action, and fit small hands. Below: Winchester Model 73, caliber .44-40, the rifle Billy is holding in the only known photograph of him.

dim shape of the newcomer. Blinded by the flash of his own gun, he fired again and felt something strike the headboard of the bed beside him. He dashed for the doorway, almost colliding with the host.

"Don't shoot!" the host yelled as the two men outside drew their revolvers.

"It was him. I recognized his voice. I think I got him," the sheriff said. He ducked out of the doorway and hid behind the thick adobe wall.

The host went to a neighboring dwelling and returned with a lighted candle. He cautiously put the candle on an outside window sill. The sheriff peeked through the door. Flat on its back, the sheriff saw, was the lifeless body of Henry McCarty, alias Henry Antrim, alias William Antrim, alias Billy Bonney, alias Billy the Kid.

For Sheriff Pat Garrett, it was a moment of mixed emotions. He had killed the most dangerous and elusive criminal in New Mexico Territory, if not the nation. But he knew that he had done it only through the purest luck. Moreover, Billy was a happy-go-lucky kid of 21, always ready to help a friend and able to find a laugh in the grimmest circumstances. Garrett knew, too, that here in old Fort Sumner, now a town on Pete Maxwell's ranch, Billy had many friends, and they might be seeking revenge.

Garrett conferred with his host, Pete Maxwell, who agreed to let the sheriff and his deputies stay at his house for the night. The crowd gathering outside looked hostile.

The sheriff examined the body and the room. Billy had been hit once, just above the heart. He must have died almost instantly. The sheriff's second shot ricocheted off the wall and hit the headboard of Maxwell's bed. The outlaw's double action Colt Thunderer had not been fired. Billy had apparently taken off his boots before he came to Maxwell's house. That was why he made no noise. He must have been staying nearby.

In spite of what everyone had always told him, Billy the Kid had not died with his boots on. It was a strange end to a strange career—as strange as it was short.

Billy the Kid was born Henry McCarty in New York September 17, 1859. Both his parents were immigrants from Ireland. His father, Michael McCarty, died while Henry was a small child. His mother, Catherine, moved to Indianapolis with Henry and his older brother, Joseph, by 1868. There Catherine met William Henry Harrison Antrim, a Civil War veteran and a teamster. In 1870, Bill Antrim and the McCartys moved to Wichita, Kansas, where Catherine ran a successful laundry business. Catherine, with Bill's help, homesteaded a quarter-section of land outside Wichita, but because she had tuberculosis, she abruptly sold the land and moved to the supposedly more salubrious climate of New Mexico. She and Bill Antrim were married in Santa Fe March 1, 1873. They settled down in Silver City, a mining camp.

Nineteen months after her marriage, Catherine McCarty Antrim died. "Uncle Bill" Antrim spent most of his time in the hills looking for silver. He arranged for Henry and Joe, who had both taken his last name, to stay with friends.

Henry, short and skinny for his age, was a good student, but, said a friend, "he got in the wrong company." "The wrong company" was an older youth called "Sombrero Jack" Schaffer, who liked to get drunk and steal things. Henry never liked liquor, but he went along with the stealing. Once the sheriff caught him with a load of stolen laundry. To give him a good scare, the sheriff locked Henry in a cell for the night. The sheriff left the jail for an hour, and when he returned, Henry was gone. The boy had climbed up inside a chimney and taken off for Arizona. He was 15.

For the next two years, Henry Antrim worked as a cowboy and a cook in Arizona. As before, he gravitated toward the "wrong company" and branched out into horse-stealing and petty theft. He also learned to play monte very well and was able to make money gambling. On November 17, 1876, he was arrested for stealing a cavalryman's horse. He tried to run, but was shackled and locked in the guardhouse. The next day, the justice of the peace who arrested him found Antrim gone "shackles and all." Henry had thick wrists but small hands. He apparently had slipped one hand out of his handcuffs and used that freedom to liberate himself completely.

According to tradition, he crossed into Mexico and teamed up with a Mexican rustler named Segura. What happened there is strictly apocryphal, but Henry Antrim returned to the United States speaking Spanish as if it were his native tongue.

The laughing, joking "Kid Antrim" was generally popular with the people of Fort Grant, Arizona. The one exception was "Windy" Cahill, a huge, muscular blowhard of a blacksmith. Cahill delighted in taunting the slender Kid and pushing him around. One night in a Fort Grant saloon, he knocked Antrim down. The Kid produced a revolver and fired. Cahill died the next day, and the Kid disappeared.

Antrim surfaced in New Mexico as a member of the Jesse Evans outlaw gang. How the 17-year-old Kid happened to meet Evans, southern New Mexico's leading bandit, is not known. Men on the run tend to frequent the same places. They may have met in the United States or in Mexico, and the Kid, still an adolescent seeking a purpose for his life, attached himself to the slightly older Evans. The Kid had learned quite a bit about theft on his own. Now he was taking a post-graduate course.

In October 1877, the Evans gang stopped at some ranches near Seven Rivers in the lower Pecos valley. Jesse Evans, Frank Baker, Tom Hill and George Davis stayed at the Hugh Beckwith ranch. Billy Antrim (he had begun using his stepfather's first name now) stayed at the neighboring Heiskell Jones ranch. The Evans gang's primary business was rustling, and many of the small ranchers were their business associates.

Billy's choice of a stopping place proved fortunate. On October 17, Sheriff William Brady of Lincoln County and a posse surrounded the Beckwith ranch and arrested the four gang members for stealing horses and mules from Richard Brewer and John Tunstall, two Lincoln County ranchers.

The remaining members of the Evans gang, including Billy, made plans to break their comrades out of jail. While they were working out details, Billy began to get acquainted with the small ranchers in the area. He learned that this part of New Mexico was a different world from any he had known before.

Unlike Arizona, central and eastern New Mexico was no howling wilderness before Americans began to settle there in the late nineteenth century. White men had settled in the territory before the Pilgrims came to Massachusetts. And the natives they found were not just the nomadic Navajos and Apaches. Pueblo Indians had been farming the river valleys for centuries. The Spanish set up the same feudal society they had created in Mexico, although in the seventeenth century the Pueblos, united under Popé, chief of Tewa Pueblo, revolted and almost succeeded in driving all of the Spanish out. Santa Fe, capital of the territory, became a thriving trade center, with trading caravans from the United States making their way across the Great Plains on the old Santa Fe trail.

After the Mexican War, when New Mexico became part of the United States, American settlers began to skirt the Great Plains and trickle into New Mexico. Predominantly single men, they married into the Spanish-speaking families and operated farms and small ranches along the Pecos and Rio Grande valleys.

New Mexico was still a traditional, Hispanic land when, a few years after the Civil War, a new type of American appeared, bringing the "Gilded Age" culture of the rest of the country.

In Lincoln County, John Chisum, a Texan, drove in thousands of cattle and turned them loose on the open range. The range was owned by nobody, but Chisum acted as if it were all his. To keep the small ranchers' cattle away from his, he hired an army of cowboys whose skill with the rifle and the revolver was as important as their skill with the rope and the branding iron. To Chisum and his Texans, Hispanic New Mexicans were "natives" and "Mexicans," and not fit to be considered with "white men."

To the county seat, Lincoln, came Lawrence G. Murphy, a former army major who founded a general store. It was the only large store in hundreds of square miles. Besides selling merchandise to the ranchers, it had a contract with the army to supply cattle to the nearby Indian reservations. To sell cattle to the Indians, the primary market for beef in this corner of the country, the ranchers had to go through Murphy's store. This, of course, made Murphy an instant enemy of Chisum.

Into this growing conflict came two more players: John Tunstall and Alexander McSween. Tunstall, who had sworn a rustling complaint against Evans, was a young Englishman with polished manners, a fair amount of cash and a deep desire to become filthy rich. McSween was Tunstall's lawyer and his partner in a store he was starting in Lincoln.

The stage was set for the Lincoln County War, a very complex affair. Most versions of what happened are the simplistic, good-guys-and-bad-guys tales of Hollywood westerns.

One of the nastiest pits the evil Irishmen, Murphy and his employee, later successor, Jimmy Dolan, against idealistic Englishman, Tunstall, and the pious Scot, McSween, who are rescued by the saintly Billy. This version gives bigots a warm glow, but it ignores too many facts: Murphy had retired before the fighting started; the Kid was as Irish as either Murphy or Dolan; McSween, as his last moments demonstrate, was more psychotic than pious, and if Tunstall ever had any ideal, or even any aim in life but getting as rich as possible as quickly as possible, it was a well kept secret.

Another version has Billy the Kid leading small ranchers in the area against Dolan's store, backed by the evil Santa Fe Ring—a group of politicians led by Thomas Catron, the territorial attorney general, who were looting New Mexico as thoroughly as the contemporary Tweed Ring was looting New York. There was a Santa Fe Ring. It was evil, and it did back Dolan's store. In fact, Tom Catron held the store's mortgage. But the "small ranchers" on the Tunstall-McSween side included John Chisum, the largest and most ruthless cattle baron in New Mexico. Chisum accused all small ranchers of rustling and drove them off free land. He also retaliated against suspected rustlers by stealing their stock. Jesse Evans learned rustling as a Chisum cowboy. Plenty of small ranchers joined Dolan's forces just because Chisum had taken the other side.

The actual situation was, briefly, Tunstall decided that competing against Dolan's store was likely to be a quicker road to riches than competing against Chisum's ranch. On his part, Chisum saw "The Store" as a greater threat than Tunstall's ranch, which would have to grow a great deal to cause him serious trouble. Tunstall and Chisum made an alliance—for both, a marriage of convenience, with divorce to be expected in the near future.

Sheriff Brady had soldiered with Major Murphy, The Store's founder, and remained loyal to Murphy's protoge, Jimmy Dolan. District Attorney William Rynerson and Judge Warren Bristol were loyal to Tom Catron and the Ring. The real muscle of Dolan's side, though, was Jesse Evans, Kid Antrim's old comrade-in-arms, and his gang. Tunstall tried to buy Evans and the other gang members when they were in jail. In fact, it looks as if he had them arrested just so he could buy them. He gave them a bottle of whiskey and two new suits while they were in jail and had Brewer invite them to his ranch for breakfast when they broke jail.

He knew they'd break out, because the Kid, who was helping to plan the escape, had become a friend of Brewer. Besides, Brady wasn't anxious to keep Evans locked up. He had arrested Evans only because Tunstall and Brewer approached him with the 15-man posse they'd recruited and told him he'd better.

Under the circumstances, Evans didn't think two suits, a bottle and a breakfast were enough to purchase undying loyalty. He and his gang told Tunstall's hands they were sorry they'd stolen the boss's stock and promised not to do it again. Then they rode off.

All except the Kid.

Billy had changed his last name from Antrim to Bonney. He had a new name, and he was going to have a new life. He had been with the Evans gang long enough to see that the outlaw life promised no substantial rewards. People like Brewer, Jones and their neighbors Frank and George Coe had land, houses and families. These men, only a few years older than he, had put down roots and had opportunities to grow. To the Kid, orphaned at 14 and a fugitive at 15, that was a close approximation of heaven.

He got a job at Frank Coe's ranch. Billy looked so young Coe was dubious at first about what he could do, but he was later glad he had hired him.

"He was very handy in camp," Coe later recalled. "A good cook and good-natured and jolly."

On hunting trips, the Kid was especially welcome. He was a remarkable shot.

"He spent all his spare time cleaning his six-shooter and practicing his shooting," Coe recalled. "He could take two six-shooters, loaded and cocked, one in each hand, . . . and twirl one in one direction and the other in the other direction, at the same time. And I've seen him ride his horse on a run and kill snow birds, four out of five shots."

Will Chisum, John's nephew, remembered the Kid "always playing with his Winchester and those little .41s." The .41 Colt Thunderer, the type of revolver Billy was holding when he met Garrett for the last time, had a grip adapted to small hands. Billy's hands were unusually small, even for a boy his size. The Thunderer, moreover, was a double action gun. If its user practiced enough, he could accurately fire it much faster than the single action Colt favored by most Westerners. Its drawback was that it broke down more easily. With the care the Kid gave his weapons, that wasn't likely to happen, though.

In a frontier society, gunmanship was highly valued. "Colt's law" was proverbial. People believed, as Mao Tse-tung was to put it, "Power grows from the barrel of a gun." Billy Bonney, a master gunner, was to prove them wrong.

For the present, though, his ability with weapons, his helpfulness, his intelligence and his cheerful personality, made the Kid popular with the Pecos valley ranchers. His command of Spanish helped, too, especially with the young women, almost all of whom were Hispanic. Coe couldn't pay him much, but Dick Brewer signed Bonney on to the Tunstall ranch. The Kid now had a good job at steady pay, and he seems to have considered Tunstall a father substitute. He didn't plan to spend his life working for wages, though. Billy began thinking of starting his own ranch with another Tunstall hand, Fred Waite, a Chickasaw from the Indian Territory.

Then the war began. Dolan claimed Tunstall's partner, McSween, had cheated his mentor, Major Murphy. He charged McSween with embezzlement, got criminal warrant and a court order to attach the lawyer's property. Sheriff Brady sought to attach Tunstall's property, too, assuming that McSween was also partner in the ranch. He sent a posse, led by Deputy Sheriff Billy Matthews and including Jesse Evans and several of his gang members, to seize Tunstall's livestock.

Tunstall left the ranch with several of his hands, including Billy Bonney, and a herd of his best horses. Posse members followed. In the pursuit, Tunstall became separated from his men. Morton, Evans and Fred Hill, a member of Evans' gang, arrested Tunstall, then shot him with his own revolver.

Bonney, the newest and youngest of Tunstall's hands, was the most enraged. He wanted to kill Morton, Evans and Hill. McSween, the lawyer, though, sent him with Fred Waite to help a constable arrest Brady for murder with a warrant issued by a friendly justice of the peace, John B. Wilson. Brady, waiting in Dolan's store with a crowd of henchmen, laughed at the warrant, ridiculed the authority of the three men trying to serve it, and kept Bonney and Waite locked up for three days.

McSween, now convinced that Brady would arrest him for embezzlement and let Jesse Evans kill him in jail, made out his will and fled from Lincoln.

Leadership of the McSween cause fell to Brewer, who organized a posse of some forty-odd men that called itself "The Regulators." The Regulators swore to enforce the warrants issued by Justice Wilson. The Regulators were mostly former Tunstall hands and small ranchers with a grudge against "The Store," plus a few gunfighters employed by John Chisum. The most formidable of all was the teenage killer everyone now called Billy the Kid. The Kid was no stranger to murder, and because of his loyalty to his boss and to his friends on the Tunstall ranch, plus his youthful desire to "belong" somewhere, he was going to learn a lot more about killing.

The Regulators' top priority was arresting Billy Morton, who led the group that killed Tunstall. They found Morton with Evans gang member Frank Baker. After a chase, the two men surrendered on condition they be brought to Lincoln alive. The posse stopped at one of Chisum's ranch houses, and Billy Bonney went fishing with Will Chisum while a worried Morton wrote a letter to a friend, stating that he expected to be murdered on the way to the county seat. One man, he said, seemed intent on killing him before they reached the jail. Evidence indicates that man was Billy the Kid. The day before, the posse had picked up William McCloskey, a Tunstall cowboy who was a friend of Morton. McCloskey told Morton and Baker that anyone who hurt them would have to do it over his dead body. That night, word came to Lincoln that McCloskey, Morton and Baker were all dead.

According to the posse, Morton had grabbed McCloskey's pistol and killed him, then he and Baker made a run for it. Because McCloskey and Morton were friends and because Morton and Baker had been mounted on slow horses, no one believed the story. Most people guessed that the possemen threatened to kill Morton and Baker, and McCloskey objected. Someone then killed McCloskey. Morton and Baker tried to run and were killed. Billy Bonney was the most vehemently in favor killing Morton and Baker and also the best shot. The only witnesses, though, were the posse members, and they stuck to their story.

Temporarily outgunned by the McSween forces, Dolan got help from the Santa Fe Ring. Governor Samuel B. Axtell declared that Justice Wilson held his position illegally, his warrants were invalid, and the only legitimate law enforcers in the county were Sheriff Brady and District Attorney Rynerson.

The Regulators lay low for three weeks. Then they met with McSween at a Chisum ranch house. What that staunch upholder of "the rule of law" told his troops is unknown but the next day, Billy the Kid, Fred Waite and four other Regulators hid behind the adobe wall of the Tunstall store corral. Brady and four deputies came walking down the street. The Regulators popped up and blew away Brady and Deputy George Hindman, walking behind him. The other two deputies ran. Billy Bonney vaulted over the wall, grabbed Brady's rifle and apparently tried to get his warrant for McSween, but another deputy shot him in the leg, and he hobbled back to shelter without rifle or warrant.

The wound didn't stop Bonney from joining the Regulators in another fight three days later. This time the target was a Dolan employee named Andrew "Buckshot" Roberts. Roberts got his nickname from a load of buckshot he carried in his shoulder that prevented him from raising a rifle high enough to sight. The posse found Roberts near an old stone mill.

Frank Coe, who knew Roberts, tried to talk him into surrendering.

"No," Roberts said. "The Kid is with you, and he will kill me on sight."

Suddenly three more Regulators appeared. Roberts raised his carbine to the hip. Regulator Charley Bowdre and Roberts fired at the same time. Bowdre's bullet went through Roberts' body. Roberts' slug hit Bowdre's pistol belt buckle, cut the belt and ricocheted into George Coe's right hand. Roberts retreated to the building, furiously pumping bullets out of his Winchester. Two more regulators were hit. The Kid counted Roberts's shots and dashed into the building after the last shot. He thrust his Winchester at Roberts and fired. At the same time, though, Roberts drove the muzzle of his empty carbine into the Kid's belly, deflecting his aim and knocking him breathless. Billy ducked out of sight. Roberts then snatched a single-shot .45-70 Springfield rifle from a wall, loaded it and laid it over a mattress.

Brewer, leader of the posse, circled the mill and shot at Roberts through a door. He missed, and Roberts returned his fire. The huge 500-grain bullet hit Brewer in the eye and blew out the back of his head. The Regulators retreated, leaving Roberts to die alone. Field leadership of the posse more or less devolved on Billy, the Regulators' top gunman.

In Lincoln, Dolan's fortunes took a turn for the worse. Despite the efforts of Judge Bristol and prosecutor Rynerson, a grand jury refused to indict McSween for embezzlement. Two of Dolan's top enforcers, Jesse Evans and Tom Hill, were out of action. They had attempted to rob a sheepherders' camp, and the sheepherders killed Hill and wounded Evans, who was then arrested. Worst of all, The Store had gone bankrupt, and Tom Catron foreclosed on his mortgage.

Then the county commissioners appointed a new sheriff to replace Brady, a man named John Copeland, who was intellectually dominated by McSween. McSween had moved back to Lincoln, and the Regulators made his house their headquarters. Now McSween, rather than Dolan, dominated the justice system, but equal justice for all was as far from Lincoln County as ever. And another shift was coming.

Two of Brady's deputies, George Peppin and Billy Matthews, claimed to be legitimate officers of the law and raised a new posse. For the next few months, there was a series of raids and counter-raids with long-range firing and few casualties.

Jimmy Dolan had not lost all his clout with the Santa Fe Ring. He wrote to Governor Axtell and had Copeland replaced as sheriff by George Peppin. The McSween people recognized Peppin no more than the Dolan people recognized Copeland. There was little color of law now in what had become a real war. The only reason for the fighting was the personal enmity of McSween and Dolan, with their followers, toward each other. Both sides built up their armies by inducing large numbers of Hispanic ranchers to get involved.

The orphaned Kid, growing up in this violent and immoral world, had become the field commander of one side. He had the boldness that let him dash into the street to get the warrant Brady was carrying but the intelligence to count Roberts' shots before exposing himself. He would soon become unquestioned leader of the McSween forces.

On July 14, the Regulators entered Lincoln. Most of Sheriff Peppin's crew were out in the country looking for them. McSween now had 60 gunmen, Anglos and Hispanics. Dolan had only a few men, most of them in the Wortley Hotel, across the street from the old Dolan store. For some reason, McSween made no move, giving Peppin a chance to come back to Lincoln with his posse.

Even so, the Regulators still outnumbered the Dolan men 60 to 40. The Regulators, though, were scattered in several places. Dolan's troops were all in the hotel and the *torreon*, a round tower built in 1862 for defense against the Indians.

Indecisive firing began after Peppin's posse came to town. As always, McSween refused to fire. He said the Bible forbad killing. It didn't stop him from hiring killers, though. Firing continued for three days until Colonel Nathan A. M. Dudley, commander of nearby Ft. Stanton, entered Lincoln with a squad of cavalry, a platoon of infantry, a howitzer and a Gatling gun. Dudley, who disliked McSween, was was blatantly violating the Posse Comitatus Act, just passed by Congress because of previous military meddling in civilian affairs. Dudley stationed the troops so that Peppin's men could fire at the Regulators without endangering the soldiers, but if the Regulators fired back, Dudley could say their were shooting at his men. Then he trained the Gatling and the cannon on Regulators in buildings outside the McSween store. The Regulators said Dudley ordered them to evacuate or he would pulverize the buildings. At his later court martial, the colonel denied he ever told the McSween forces to leave. He said aiming the guns was merely a defensive move. The Regulators, though, were hardened fighting men who would not have fled without a direct threat.

With Dudley tipping the balance for them, the Dolan men managed to get close enough to set fire to McSween's house. Billy Bonney organized the escape and plotted a route that let them leave the house without being seen. Five regulators ran out, the last being Bonney. McSween was to be next.

Suddenly, McSween yelled, "I surrender!"

Three Peppin men under Bob Beckwith went to the house to bring him in. When he saw them, McSween shouted, "I'll never surrender!" The three deputies started to shoot at McSween and the Regulators still with him. The Regulators fired back.

At about the same time, Bonney and his crew were spotted by the Dolan men. Firing became general. One of Bonney's crew was hit. McSween and two Regulators with him were killed. Bob Beckwith caught a bullet in the head and died instantly. Billy the Kid and his followers made it out of Lincoln. The Kid was now the leader of diminished army without a cause. Tunstall was dead. Brady was dead. McSween was dead. Dolan was broke and his empire bankrupt. For all intents and purposes, the Lincoln County War was over. And the *de facto* leader of the Regulators was Billy Bonney, a bright 18-year-old who had learned only: (1) how to steal, (2) how to kill, (3) that leaders of business, like Dolan—and, as he must have recognized by now—Tunstall and McSween—are hopelessly corrupt (4) almost as corrupt as leaders of government, like Brady, Dudley, Rynerson, Bristol and even Governor Axtell. The only reason for life, he concluded, is to take what you want and have fun.

The Regulators stayed together for a short time, stealing a few horses and cows while hunting down Dolan partisans. They encountered the Chisum outfit, driving their cattle north out of the war zone. For the last time, Billy the Kid resumed his on-again-off-again courtship of Sallie Chisum, old John's pretty teenage niece. The regulators started to scatter, and Billy drifted around with his new sidekick, big Tom O'Folliard, another teenager. The Kid rustled a little, gambled a lot and visited every pretty girl available.

He made old Fort Sumner his base. Pete (Pedro) Maxwell, heir to an enormous ranch, had sold the original Lucien Maxwell land grant and bought the abandoned fort and surrounding territory from the federal government. Maxwell and his family had made their homes in the houses in what had been the fort's Officers' Row. He converted the hospital, barracks and other buildings into apartments where his employees lived. Maxwell had turned the old army base into a privately-owned town, entirely Spanish-speaking.

Billy the Kid liked Hispanics. He spoke their language, admired their culture and delighted in their festivities, especially their weekly dances. He felt at home with them. Unlike most Anglos at the time, he never patronized them. The Hispanics, from the Maxwells to the poorest sheepherders, felt the same way about the Kid: he was not a foreigner; he was one of them.

Fort Sumner was remote from any sheriff's office, so it became a resort for a number of dubious people besides the Kid. Billy had no problem finding helpers for a rustling expedition. He never committed crime in Fort Sumner, however, and he was a free spender in the town. Although he didn't drink, he spent a lot of time gambling in the Sumner saloons, and became especially friendly with one of the bartenders, a long, lanky ex-buffalo hunter named Pat Garrett. His closest friendships, though, were with the young women of the area.

"Fort Sumner was a gay little place. The weekly dance was an event, and pretty girls from Santa Rosa, Puerto de Luna, Anton Chico, and from towns and ranches fifty miles away drove in to attend it. Billy the Kid cut quite a gallant figure at these affairs," said Paulita Maxwell, Pete's sister. "Billy the Kid fascinated many women. In every *placita* in the Pecos some little señorita was proud to be his querida."

One of them was Paulita Maxwell, although she always denied it. Another was Celsa Gutierrez, Pat Garrett's sister-in-law. A woman named Abrana Garcia had two daughters by him. Gossip connected him with the wife of Charley Bowdre, one of his followers, and Nasaria Yerby, the 18-year-old "housekeeper" of Tom Yerby, Bowdre's employer. Nasaria was also believed to have borne Billy's child.

One thing that tempered the Kid's fun was the knowledge that he had to keep looking over his shoulder. There was a territorial warrant for his arrest for the murder of Brady and a federal warrant for the murder of Roberts. (Roberts was thought to have been killed on federal property.) Jesse Evans and the pro-Dolan outlaws wanted their own revenge.

Billy, O'Folliard and a few of their friends rode to Lincoln and passed out the word that they'd like to smoke a peace pipe with Evans and his friends. The antagonists met, buried the hatchet and swore that none would do anything to injure the other side. Then they went to a bar to celebrate their new friendship. All except the teetotaling Billy became staggering drunk. Traveling from bar to bar, they met Huston Chapman, a lawyer McSween's widow had engaged to bring Colonel Dudley to justice. One of Evans' crew, a mean-tempered cowboy named Billy Campbell, thrust a revolver into Chapman's chest and demanded that he dance. The lawyer refused, and Campbell shot him dead. Another murder indictment was the last thing the Kid wanted. At the earliest opportunity, he left his new "friends" and rode back to Fort Sumner.

Billy the Kid, who had so often seen justice perverted by corrupt or incompetent leaders, was going to have a new chance to get the government off his back. A new governor had been appointed. General Lew Wallace, lawyer, philosopher, musician, sportsman and best-selling author, offered a "general pardon" to all members of the warring factions who were not already indicted.

After the murder of Chapman, Wallace came to Lincoln personally. What he learned there convinced him that Colonel Dudley had to go. He contacted some political and military associates, and the pompous colonel was no longer commander of Fort Stanton.

Soldiers and lawmen were still looking for Billy Bonney. Wallace's amnesty did not cover him. The Kid thought he saw an opportunity to get a pardon, however. Wallace was embarrassed because no witnesses would talk about the murder of Chapman. Billy the Kid wrote to the governor offering to testify in return for amnesty. He said he wanted to stop running and lead a normal life. Wallace wrote back: "I have authority to exempt you from prosecution if you will testify to what you say you know."

The governor and the outlaw met in a house in Lincoln.

"Testify before the grand jury and the trial court and convict the mur- derer of Chapman," the governor said, "and I will let you go scot-free with a pardon in your pocket for all of your own misdeeds."

Billy agreed. Wallace said he'd arrange a fake arrest and keep the Kid in protective custody until he could testify. The arrest took place as planned. The governor appeared to be somewhat surprised at the reception the notorious outlaw received in Lincoln. He wrote to Carl Schurz, secretary of the interior, "A precious specimen nick-named 'the Kid,' whom the sheriff is holding here in the Plaza, as it is called, is an object of tender regard. I heard singing and music the other night; going to the door, I found the minstrels of the village actually serenading the fellow in his prison."

Wallace did not stay in Lincoln for the opening of court. He went back to Santa Fe and his half-completed novel, *Ben-Hur*. He seemed to forget about Billy, who testified as agreed. The grand jury returned indictments against Evans, Campbell, Dolan, Peppin and even Dudley. However, Judge Warren Bristol, McSween's old enemy, released most of those indicted, and only two came to trial, where friendly prosecutors made sure they were not convicted.

Billy was to be prosecuted. Wallace left him to the tender mercies of Judge Bristol and District Attorney William Rynerson. Bristol's first move was to grant Rynerson a change of venue out of Lincoln County, where people knew the Kid. Billy took off, while Sheriff George Kimball, who knew a dirty deal when he saw one, looked the other way.

His chance to lead an honest life frustrated again, Billy the Kid stepped up his criminal activities. He might be the best gunman in the Southwest, but no power grew from the barrel of his Winchester or his Colts. He could no more change his life than a cork floating in the Pecos could change its direction. He spent a lot of time stealing cows in the Texas Panhandle, where, only five years before, Quanah Parker had attacked the buffalo hunters in Adobe Walls. Now the buffalo no longer roamed, and the Red Man had been pressed from that part of the West. Now the Panhandle was America's premier cattle country. One of the Kid's prime targets was the herd of old John Chisum. He claimed that Chisum had promised him money for fighting in the Lincoln County War but didn't pay.

His grudge didn't extend to the rest of Chisum's family. One night, he came into a Fort Sumner saloon with two of old John's brothers, Jim and Pitzer. At the bar was a loud-mouthed Texan named Joe Grant. Grant had earlier offered to bet the Kid $25 that he'd kill a man before Billy. Billy the Kid was not so far gone that he considered murder a subject for competition. Grant was drunk and had already taken another man's ivory-handled gun, replacing it with his own, because he admired it. The Kid knew Grant was going to cause trouble. He asked the Texan if he could look at his fine revolver, and took it before Grant could object.

It is dangerous to carry a Colt Single Action Army revolver with all six chambers loaded. If the hammer is down, the firing pin rests on the primer of a loaded cartridge, and a light bump could fire it. The hammer could be carried at half-cock, but it snaps easily from that position and can fire the gun. All knowledgeable gunmen carried the hammer on an empty chamber or a fired cartridge. That's the reason formal revolver competition today is based on "strings" of five—not six—shots.

As Billy examined the revolver, he turned the cylinder so that, if cocked, the hammer would fall on the fired cartridge. Then he handed it back to Grant.

When he heard the name Chisum, Grant threatened to kill the brothers. Billy told Grant the Chisums he was with were Jim and Pitzer, not John.

"That's a lie," Grant said.

Bonney turned his back on the Texan.

"Grant squared off at Billy, who when he heard the click, whirled around and 'bang, bang, bang.' Right in the chin. You could have covered them all with a half a dollar," Jim's son, Will Chisum related.

Whatever his brothers and nephew felt, John Chisum had no friendly feelings for the young rustler. He joined forces with the Panhandle stockmen's association and a secret service agent named Azariah Wild, who thought some of Billy's associates were passing counterfeit money. One of their objectives was to get a new sheriff for Lincoln County. The man they chose was Pat Garrett. With the aid of Chisum's money and political clout, they got Garrett elected.

Garrett was a friend of Billy's, but he took his new job seriously. He pushed Billy hard. Others took up the chase. A posse from White Oaks, a largely Anglo mining camp, cornered the Kid and some friends at the ranch of one of their customers. The outlaws had a hostage, a blacksmith named Jimmy Carlyle, who panicked during negotiations between the posse and the outlaws. Exactly what happened is unknown. Carlyle suddenly jumped through a window, touching off a storm of fire from both sides, as the posse thought he was a gang member trying to escape. Carlyle was riddled. Shocked by what they had done, the posse went home and the rustlers escaped.

Garrett scoured the range for the Kid and hired spies in places the Kid frequented. He sprang one ambush that killed Tom O'Folliard, but Billy the Kid escaped. Garrett trailed the Kid to a house at Stinking Springs, where he was camped with four other outlaws. Surprising the rustlers, the posse shot Charley Bowdre when he came out for water, and besieged the house. Billy the Kid had his horse inside the stone building. Ropes tied to other horses led into the building. One of the gang began pulling his horse inside. Garrett realized they were planning to mount inside and ride out. He shot the horse in front of the doorway, knowing no horse would cross the body of a dead horse. Then the old buffalo hunter cut the ropes on the other horses with his rifle's bullets. At last, tempted by the smell of cooking, Billy the Kid and his hungry followers gave up.

The federal charge against Billy, the murder of Buckshot Roberts, was dismissed. There was doubt that it had been committed on federal land, and, clearly, Billy had not shot Roberts.

The murder of Brady was another matter. The Kid would have been convicted even if Judge Warren Bristol were not on the bench. Billy was sentenced to hang May 13, 1881. Governor Wallace, his promises forgotten and letters to him from the Kid ignored, signed the death warrant.

While Garrett was out collecting taxes, he left Billy the Kid in the care of two deputies, Jim Bell and Bob Olinger. Olinger hated the Kid. He blamed him for the death of his friend, Bob Beckwith, the night McSween's house burned. On April 18, he ostentatiously loaded the brass shells of his shotgun with nine buckshot apiece, while telling Billy what such a load would do to the man who caught it. Then he took five other prisoners across the street to lunch. The Kid, in handcuffs and leg irons, asked Bell to escort him to the privy. On his return, he ran up the stairs ahead of Bell and slipped one of his tiny hands out of the cuffs—a trick he had performed before. When the deputy reached the second floor, Billy swung the handcuff like a blackjack, knocked Bell down and took his gun. Bell ran, and Billy shot him dead.

Billy the Kid scooped up Olinger's shotgun and went to a window overlooking the street. When the deputy headed back to the jail, the Kid called to him. Olinger looked up, and Billy emptied both barrels into him. He told a man on the street to toss up a pick, which he used to break the chain on his leg irons. Then he stole a horse and galloped out of town while nobody in Lincoln lifted a finger to stop him.

Garrett deputized John W. Poe, who had been hired as a detective by the Panhandle stockmen, and Thomas "Tip" McKinney. They continued searching, but the sheriff said he doubted that they would ever catch Bonney. He thought the young man had gone to Mexico.

Then Poe got a tip from a friend who had been sleeping off a drunk in a stable. As he woke, he overheard two men talking. One said that the Kid was staying in Fort Sumner. Poe told Garrett, but the sheriff seemed strangely reluctant to go to Sumner. He said he was sure Billy the Kid wouldn't return to his old base. Garrett may have been trying to rationalize his behavior. He wanted to be a conscientious and efficient sheriff, but he didn't want to send a friend to his death.

Actually, the Kid felt safe in Fort Sumner. The area was full of his friends, and he was welcome everywhere, at isolated sheepherders' camps, at ranches, at houses in the town itself. Nobody would give him away.

Finally, Garrett agreed to send Poe, unknown in Fort Sumner, to look around the town and see what he could learn. When Poe returned, he said that whenever he mentioned Billy the Kid, even in the most casual way, his respondents froze and conversation ceased.

Garrett decided that he and his two deputies should go into Fort Sumner and stake out the house of one of Billy's girlfriends. If nothing happened, they could visit Pete Maxwell, a friend of Garrett, who might be able to tell them something.

Billy was visiting a girlfriend, but not the one Garrett and his men were watching. He heard that a freshly slaughtered side of beef was hanging at Maxwell's. He felt hungry, so without bothering to put on his boots or his hat, he took a butcher knife and headed for Pete's house to get a steak.

At the same time, Garrett gave up the stakeout and went to Maxwell's house. Pete was in bed. Garrett crouched down beside him and asked if he had seen Billy the Kid.

Outside the house, Poe and McKinney saw a hatless man approach Maxwell's fence, stare at them curiously, go through the gate and enter the house. Neither had ever seen Billy the Kid before.

Before Maxwell could answer Garrett's question, the Kid entered his room.

Seconds later, Billy the Kid, cold-blooded killer or confused kid—in any case, a wasted man—was dead.

Eight

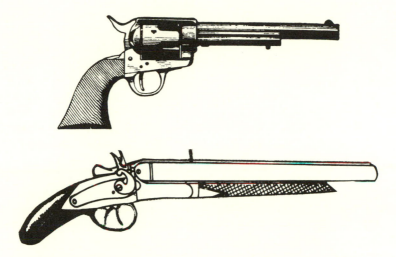

Nothing Okay at the O.K. Corral

October 26, 1881, Tombstone, Arizona

Four abreast, they strode down Tombstone's dusty Fremont Street on a cold, blustery late October day. They wore black Stetsons, white shirts with black string ties and long, black frock coats. Three were tall and broad-shouldered, the fourth, a scrawny blond man. All wore sixguns in holsters, and the skinny man carried a shotgun.

Waiting for them on the street was a group of other men, wearing

Top: Colt Single Action Army revolver, the weapon of everybody involved in the O.K. Corral fight. This weapon, in .45 Colt, .44-40 and .38-40 was the most popular revolver in the Old West. Below: Sawed-off shotgun said to have been used by Doc Holliday at the O.K. Corral.

cowboy outfits. They, too, wore revolvers, and they stood near horses with Winchester rifles in their saddle scabbards.

"Throw up your hands!" commanded the black-coated man in the middle of the line, U.S. Marshal Wyatt Earp.

Instantly, the cowboys drew their guns and began shooting. The others returned their fire, and the evil Clanton-McLaury gang, perpetrators of a reign of terror in Tombstone, was history. Wyatt Earp, his two brothers and their friend, little Doc Holliday, had cleaned up the wickedest city in Arizona.

Almost all Americans, and millions of people around the world, know this story. Wyatt Earp, frontier marshal, is to millions today the epitome of the fearless, incorruptible, straight-shooting lawmen who brought law and order to the West—from the wild and woolly cow towns of Kansas to riproaring Tombstone, Arizona. Dozens of films, a long-running television series and several biographies have spread the fame of the tall, lanky hero with the droopy mustache. The gunfight at the O.K. Corral has become as much a part of American folklore as George Washington and the cherry tree.

Unfortunately, it's not much more factual. Many of Earp's contemporaries viewed him as not as a hero but as a tough gunman who preferred to live by his wits and his gun rather than his work. He occasionally worked for the law, but he was never a city marshal, never a sheriff and never a U.S. marshal. He was, for a short time, a policeman in a couple of Kansas towns. At the time of the O.K. Corral fight, he was merely a citizen who had been temporarily deputized by his brother Virgil, the city marshal. He may have become a deputy U.S. marshal after the fight. If so, he had little time to enjoy his new position. Five months after the fight, he was on his way out of Arizona, running from a posse that wanted to arrest him for murder.

Before coming to Arizona, Earp had, besides patrolling cow towns, shot buffaloes and stolen horses for a living. His principal profession, though, was gambling. He owned the faro concession at Tombstone's Oriental Saloon, as well as a quarter of the saloon itself. He was also a silent partner in the Alhambra Saloon, where his friend Doc Holliday dealt faro. There is no record of how much—if anything—he paid for these properties. One report has it that he received the Oriental Saloon interest as a reward for protecting the Oriental from racketeering gunmen. That sounds something like the deal the Senate's Kefauver investigating committee reported in 1950 about how a Kansas City gangster became half-owner of a restaurant. "John Magniaracina acquired a 50 percent interest in the business by reason of his stature in the underworld."

How Wyatt Earp became a folk hero is a story itself.

The Wild West had been a mythic region to Americans since the days of Morgan's Riflemen. James Fenimore Cooper capitalized on his readers' fascination with the western wilderness in *The Last of the Mohicans* and the later adventures of Natty Bumppo. Thousands of copies of the (mostly fictitious) adventures of Daniel Boone and Davy Crockett were sold. When American settlement reached the Great Plains, Buffalo Bill Cody and Wild Bill Hickok replaced Boone and Crockett.

Buffalo Bill, though, was also a showman. So was Wild Bill: he appeared in Cody's show, then launched a less successful show of his own. There is no doubt that Hickok was one of the deadliest of frontier gunfighters, but the American people, then as now, took show biz with a grain of salt.

The tall, taciturn Earp was no Hickok. He was probably not as accomplished a gunman, but he was real. He was, as one historian put it, "a perfect example of the western peripheral man." Neither an out-and-out outlaw, like Jesse James, nor an honest, hard-working rancher or tradesman, like most of the settlers, he followed the turbulent outer edge of settlement from Kansas to Alaska. There were a lot of peripheral men—all of the principals in the O.K. Corral fight, for example. But Wyatt Earp's active life spanned the entire western expansion from when the Indians and the buffaloes owned the Great Plains to when the gold began to peter out in Alaska.

Born to a family that traveled to California in a covered wagon, Wyatt and his brothers later drifted east. The brothers, indoctrinated by their father that there were only two classes of people in the world, "us" and "them," were seldom separated.

In 1870, at the age of 22, Wyatt beat his half-brother, Newton, in an election for township constable of Lamar, Missouri. Wyatt's wife died less than a year later, and Wyatt left town, possibly because of troubles with his brothers-in-law. He next appears in the court records of Fort Smith, Arkansas, where he was indicted for horse theft in the Cherokee Nation. He jumped bail and reappeared in a buffalo hunters' camp near Dodge City, where he met Bat Masterson.

When cows replaced buffaloes, Wyatt Earp found his niche in the booming cow towns. He occasionally worked as a policeman, a job somewhat more dangerous than it is today, but hardly arduous, while he polished his gambling skills. A badge was useful to a gambler: he could legally carry a gun and use the power of the law to discourage sore losers.

In 1873, Ben Thompson, one of the West's most notorious killers, had a confrontation with the police in Ellsworth, Kansas. Earp later claimed that he, a simple citizen, walked up to Thompson and disarmed him, after which he was hired as city marshal. Actually, according to newspaper stories, the mayor, Jim Miller, received Thompson's guns after he made his police officers give up theirs. There is no mention of Wyatt Earp in the papers. That's because at the time of the incident, he was not within 100 miles of Ellsworth. Earp probably visited Ellsworth in 1873, but there's no record of him as a law enforcement officer there.

He was hired as a policeman in Wichita June 17, 1874, ten days before his friend Bat Masterson became embroiled in the Adobe Walls fight. Earp was one of seven cops—not counting the city marshal or his deputy marshal—in the department. When the department was cut to four cops, Earp was still there. His name appeared in the newspapers when he ran down a horse thief on foot, and he may have been the policeman who was beaten up by a vagrant he was supposed to be guarding.

According to William Smith, who was running for city marshal, the incumbent marshal, Mike Meagher, had let Earp and another policeman collect license money without turning it over to the city treasury. Smith also charged that Meagher agreed to hire Earp's brothers, Virgil, Morgan and Jim. Jim was already in Wichita, a sometime bartender whose common-law-wife was one of the town's madams. The police force, Smith said, would be turned over to the "Earp gang."

Smith had been making these charges for some time when Wyatt caught him and proceeded to beat him bloody. Meagher arrested Earp, and the town fired him. The council then voted to enforce the vagrancy law against the two Earps. Jim was out of work, and Wyatt had just been fired. Except for Jim's wife, Bessie, no Earp seemed to be making money.

From Wichita, the Earps went to Dodge City. Not because, as Wyatt claimed, the mayor telegraphed him to come and save the town, but because Dodge was the ultimate booming cow town, with gambling establishments that ran around the clock. Wyatt and Jim Earp arrived in newly incorporated Dodge City in May of 1876. Jim got a job tending bar, and Wyatt was appointed assistant marshal on the brand-new police force. The same month, Wyatt's old hunting companion, Bat Masterson, arrived and became a deputy sheriff. A little later, two more Masterson brothers and three more Earp brothers joined them.

Wyatt and Bat appear to have been better than average officers, but they still worked hard on their gambling games. Wyatt left his job several times during the winter, when the Texas cowboys were away, to go on gambling expeditions to places that still had action, such as the mining boom town, Deadwood, South Dakota.

When the big cattle herds finally by-passed Dodge, the Earps moved to Arizona. They intended to deal in mining claims. Not to dig silver ore—that was work—but to stake claims and sell or lease them to others. And, of course, to gamble with the naive citizens who had flocked to the pay dirt.

In 1879, Wyatt and Jim, with their common-law wives, Mattie and Bessie, arrived in wagons when Tombstone was only 10 months old. With them was another brother, Virgil, who had been a deputy sheriff in Prescott, Arizona, and Virgil's wife, Allie. Morgan Earp arrived a little later, and Warren Earp came after the O.K. Corral battle. Jim, a wounded Civil War vet, took part in no gun battles. When Wyatt arrived, he was 31; Jim, 38; Virgil, 36; Morgan, 28, and Warren, 19.

Virgil, a deputy U.S. marshal, got a job as a policeman; Morgan went to work for Wells Fargo; Jim became a faro dealer, and Wyatt, a stage coach guard. Wyatt, though, wanted to become sheriff when a new county was carved out around Tombstone. That job was worth $40,000 a year, a fortune in those days, because the sheriff was also the tax collector and kept 10 percent of what he collected. Wyatt became a deputy sheriff of Pima County, but resigned before the new county, Cochise, was created. He was replaced by Johnny Behan, who was also interested in the new sheriff's job.

The territorial governor, John C. Fremont, who would appoint the new sheriff, was a Republican, as was Earp. Wyatt may have believed that cutting his ties to the Democratic sheriff of Pima would enhance his chances. Behan, like the majority of Cochise County, was a Democrat. The majority of the city of Tombstone was Republican. Behan got the job, which pleased most of the county but annoyed Earp and most of Tombstone.

Another cause of friction between Wyatt and the new sheriff was Josie Marcus, a young actress who was living with Sheriff Behan. She took a shine to Wyatt Earp and was soon spending more time with him than with Johnny Behan. Mattie Blaylock, Earp's own live-in companion, was practically under house arrest. Wyatt forbade her to visit the neighbors. She stayed in her cabin and took in washing for a few pennies to live on while Wyatt was running his faro game and dealing in mineral rights. Eventually, after they all had left Arizona, Wyatt deserted Mattie and took up with Josie. Left alone, Mattie became a prostitute, then took a fatal dose of laudanum. For now though, Josie Marcus was almost as big a bone of contention between Earp and Behan as the sheriff's job.

Almost, but not quite. The Earps were learning that they had walked into a tinderbox of conflicting political, economic and historic rivalries. The Civil War ended only 15 years before. Most of the miners and townsmen were Republicans from the North. Most of the cattlemen outside of town were Democrats from the South. There was a strong criminal element in both factions.

In the town were pimps, gamblers and thieves. Among the cattlemen was a loosely organized group of rustlers who tended to follow John Ringo and Curly Bill Brocius. Most of the other cattlemen were friendly with the rustlers, and many of them bought and sold stolen cattle. A lot of Arizona cattle had been stolen from the big spreads in the Mexican state of Sonora. But a lot of Sonora cattle had also originated in Arizona.

In spite of the white-hats/black-hats treatment usually given to the Earps and their rivals, Cochise County was much like Billy the Kid's Lincoln County. Good guys were as easy to find as marsh grass in the desert.

The big difference between the Earps and Billy the Kid was that Wyatt and his brothers knew how to get what they wanted. Billy the Kid was, in a sense, a victim of circumstances. Unlike the happy-go-lucky Kid, the Earps— particularly Wyatt, a humorless conniver—created circumstances.

The Earps, not being shrinking violets, soon found themselves leaders among the Republican business people in Tombstone. (It should be noted that a large proportion of Tombstone's business consisted of saloons, gambling dens and brothels.) It pleased this faction to call itself the "Law and Order Party." The law-and-order people saw only rustlers and thieves when they looked at the cattlemen. To them, the cowboys, who had been in the area a generation before Tombstone, were the origin of all evil. There was plenty of crime—from public drunkenness to murder—in Tombstone itself, but hardly any of it was caused by the cowboys, who seldom visited Tombstone. The rustling of the cowboy faction came close to bringing about war between the United States and Mexico, but it really didn't have much impact on the citizens of Tombstone. The law-and-order people, though, found it easier to blame "them"—the cowboys—then to analyze the cause of crime in the city, which might involve some of "us."

In the beginning, the distinction between "us" and "them" wasn't as sharp as it later became. There were rumors of collusion between "the Earp gang" and the rustlers early on. On October 27, 1880, City Marshal Fred White attempted to disarm Curly Bill Brocius. As he reached for the cowboy's gun, Virgil Earp grabbed Brocius from behind. The revolver went off, wounding White fatally. White, Earp and Brocius all said the shooting was accidental, but few people at the time could understand why White, an experienced officer, reached for a cocked gun with the muzzle pointing at him. The rumor was that Brocius had performed a trick—known ever after as the "Curly Bill spin." If so, he handed the weapon to White butt first, then reversed it with a quick flip as the marshal was reaching for it and fired. The trick could be done so quickly that White, in shock from the impact of a .45 slug, could think it was an accident. But why would Virgil, who had seen the whole action, swear that it was?

It was a convenient accident for Virgil. With White dead, there would have to be an election for a new city marshal. In the meantime, the Law and Order-dominated city council appointed Virgil temporary marshal. In the special election, January, 1881, Virgil was defeated by Ben Sippy. But six months later, June 6, 1881, Sippy took an unexplained leave of absence and never returned to Tombstone. The Earp clan got the big badge it was looking for, although Wyatt still coveted the sheriff's job.

A more open connection with the cowboy faction than the possible collusion of Virgil Earp and Bill Brocius was the close friendship of Wyatt Earp's best friend, the tubercular and homicidal dentist, John H. "Doc" Holliday, with a rustler named Billy Leonard. That added still another complication to life in Tombstone after an attempted stage coach robbery on March 15, 1881.

Two men, the driver and a passenger, were killed, but the coach got away. Behan and his deputy, Billy Breckenridge, rode to the site. With him rode Marshall Williams, Wells Fargo's manager in Tombstone, and his friends, Wyatt and Morgan Earp, Doc Holliday and Bat Masterson, who happened to be visiting Tombstone. They found a trail in the snow, followed it and caught a man named Luther King, who admitted holding the robbers' horses. King identified the robbers as Billy Leonard, Holliday's friend, Harry Head and Jim Crane, all rustlers. From this point, things get complicated.

Behan and Breakenridge brought King back to Tombstone while the Earp crowd continued to look for Leonard, Head and Crane. Leaving King in the care of Undersheriff Harry Woods, Behan and Breakenridge returned to the hunt with Buckskin Frank Leslie, a bartender and onetime scout. While the posse was looking for tracks, King escaped from jail by simply walking out of an unlocked back door.

In Tombstone and Cochise County, a lot of people started saying the hunters were hunting themselves. They believed Doc Holliday was involved in the attempted stickup, and they doubted that either the sheriff's people or the Earps were really interested in finding the robbers.

Ike Clanton, a leading member of the cowboy faction, later testified:

Virgil told me to tell Bill Leonard . . . that he [had] thrown Paul [Bob Paul, the stage coach guard and candidate for sheriff of Pima County] and the posse that was after him off the track . . . and he had done all he could for them, and that he wanted him to get those other fellows—Crane and Head—out of the country, for he was afraid that one of them might get captured and get all of his friends into trouble.

Clanton, of course, had his own agenda. But a telegraph worker reported he heard shots and saw Doc Holliday racing away from the direction of the shots on a horse owned by Behan's partner in the O.K. corral ownership, John Dunbar. He added that it was "the consensus of opinion" that Holliday was not only involved but had shot the stage driver "because he knew too much."

Luther King, the horse-holder, did not name Holliday as a robber. But the hot-tempered and homicidal Holliday was part of the posse that questioned him.

Holliday's common-law wife, Big Nose Kate Elder, got drunk one night and told the sheriff that Doc had killed the driver. She later took back her statement, and the case against Holliday was dismissed for lack of evidence. Virgil's wife, Allie, reported that Big Nose Kate said Buckskin Frank Leslie had been hired by Wyatt Earp to throw the posse off the trail. To Mattie, Wyatt's wife, Kate said, "It's that sneaking con man husband of yours what's the trouble." Allie's account continues:

> Then it happened. Kate had been leanin' against the closet door, her hand on the doorknob. As she flipped around, the door flew open . . . Out of the closet came a big suitcase, spewin' out on the floor. . . . Wigs and beards made of unraveled rope and sewn on black cloth masks, some false mustaches, a church deacon's frock coat, a checkered suit like drummers wear, a little bamboo cane. Lots of things like that!

"Wyatt's disguises," Kate said. She explained that Doc had been keeping them in her house, but she demanded he move them. She told Allie that Wyatt would soon have "that stupid Virge under his thumb like Morgan!"

Both Wyatt Earp and Ike Clanton later agreed that Wyatt had approached Ike about a deal concerning the stage robbery.

Wyatt testified he had asked Clanton and Frank McLaury, a friend of the Clantons, to lure the stage robbers into the Tombstone area.

"I told them I wanted the glory of capturing Leonard, Head and Crane, and if I could do it, it would help me make the race for sheriff at the next election. I told them that if they would put me on the track of Leonard, Head and Crane, and tell me where those men were hid, I would give them all of the reward and would never let anyone know where I got the information."

On the other hand, Clanton said of Earp's proposition: "He said his business was such that he could not afford to capture them. He would have to kill them or else leave the country. He said he and his brother, Morg, had piped off to Doc Holliday and Wm. Leonard the money that was going off on the stage, and he said he could not afford to capture them . . . for they [were] stopping around the country so damned long that he was afraid that some of them would be caught and would squeal on him."

Wyatt and Morgan Earp, both with Wells Fargo connections, provided, according to Clanton, the stage robbers' intelligence.

What did Clanton say to this proposition that he betray his friends and participate in their murder?

Virgil Earp stated that Clanton came to him after talking to Wyatt and said he would set things up, as long as Wyatt got an agreement from Wells Fargo to pay a reward for the robbers either dead or alive.

Neither Clanton nor the Earps got a chance to profit from the agreement. Leonard and Head were ambushed by two ranchers who suspected them (probably with reason) of being hired assassins. The Earps spread the word that before dying, Leonard and Head confessed to the robbery and absolved Doc Holliday. Why they would have bothered to tell this to their killers, who didn't even know Holliday, nobody explained. The Earps, as we've seen, were not noted for truthfulness, and convenient dying statements were one of their specialties.

Two months later, Crane eliminated any chance that he would be captured. He, with Old Man Clanton, Ike's father, with a number of other cowboys, was killed while driving 300 head of cattle near the Arizona-Sonora border. The attackers were Mexican troops. Nobody got unduly excited, as it was assumed that the cattle had been stolen in Mexico. According to John Pleasant Gray, a rancher, Crane had been preparing to give himself up and implicate Holliday. That story, though, is about as credible as the confessions of Crane's late partners.

With the Clanton-Earp agreement now a dead letter, Virgil Earp and Johnny Behan began to complain to territorial and federal authorities about lack of cooperation from the other. After a stage was robbed September 8, 1881 near Bisbee, Deputy Sheriff Breakenridge went to the scene, accompanied by Wyatt and Morgan Earp, representing Wells Fargo. Dave Neagle, another deputy, later joined the party. So did Marshall Williams, the Wells Fargo manager (who a year later was found to have stolen thousands of dollars from his employer), and Fred Dodge, an Earp supporter who later claimed to be an undercover Wells Fargo agent. Posse members followed the robbers' trail until it was wiped out by a passing herd of cattle. The party split, with the deputies going on to Bisbee while the Wells Fargo people continued to examine the site.

In Bisbee, the deputies interviewed victims of the holdup. They learned that one robber referred to money as "sugar," an expression used habitually by Frank Stilwell, a livery stable owner and deputy sheriff. Looking around Bisbee, they found a shoemaker who had just put new heels on Frank Stilwell's boots. He even had the old heels.

In the meantime, Fred Dodge, in the Wells Fargo posse, rediscovered the trail and found a boot print. The heel of the print matched the heel Breakenridge got from the shoemaker. Both parties also learned that Stilwell had ridden with his business partner, Pete Spencer. The deputies arrested Stilwell and Spencer. This would have been a fine example of teamwork between the two factions but for one thing: each claimed to have solved the robbery alone.

Earp and the law-and-order people loudly claimed the Bisbee robbery was the latest in a string of cowboy depredations. Neither Stilwell nor Spencer was a cowboy, however. Both were businessmen, and a rancher friendly to the cowboys said that Spencer was "one of the most treacherous and low down robbers and murderers that ever was let live in any town."

Nor were the Earps in a position to talk about stage coach robbers. On September 9, 1881, the day after the Bisbee coach robbery, Virgil had seen Sherman McMasters, wanted for a stage coach robbery in February, on the streets of Tombstone and let him escape. Little more than a year later, McMasters would openly join the Earp faction and ride with Wyatt during his bloody exit from Arizona.

Nevertheless, Frank McLaury heard that the law-and-order element was organizing a vigilance committee and had appointed the Earps enforcers. He confronted Virgil.

"I understand you are raising a Vigilance Committee to hang us boys," he said.

"You boys?" asked Virgil.

"Yes, us and [the] Clantons, Hicks, Ringo, and all us cowboys."

McLaury approached Morgan, too.

"If you ever come after me, you will never take me," he said.

As tensions increased, Ike Clanton developed worries of his own. He was afraid the Earps might tell Holliday about the deal to double-cross the stage robbers. Billy Leonard had been a friend of the unpredictable little killer, and Ike Clanton was thoroughly afraid of Doc Holliday.

Ike was not reassured when Wyatt came to him with a new proposition. Since the original stage robbers were dead, this proposition was for a fake robbery. Ike and some of his friends would be the robbers, while the Earps and Holliday would be the heroic rescuers and scare off the "robbers." No one would be hurt, Wyatt said. Ike was not at all sure of that.

On October 25, Ike Clanton and 18-year-old Tom McLaury came to Tombstone in a wagon. McLaury was there to get supplies and collect a payment on cattle he had sold to Bauer's Union Market. He would be joined next morning by his brother, Frank. Ike came to drink. His brother, Billy, would meet him next morning, mostly to be sure the hung-over Ike got home safely. Ike started hitting the bars early, and by 1 a.m. he was pretty well sloshed. Feeling the need to eat, he sat in the Occidental Saloon's lunch room. Doc Holliday walked in, stopped, and stared at Clanton. He put his hand inside his coat.

"You son-of-a-bitch of a cowboy, get out your gun and get to work." Holliday said.

"I don't have a gun," Clanton replied. He had, as the law required, checked his guns.

"If you ain't heeled, go and heel yourself," Doc said.

Morgan Earp, although Virgil had appointed him a special policeman, watched the scene "with his hand in his bosom" according to Clanton. Clanton got up without touching his meal. Morgan stood up, too.

"Yes, you son of a bitch, you can have all the fight you want now," he said. Wyatt joined Morgan as they all went outside.

Outside on the sidewalk was Virgil Earp with one of his deputies, Jim Flynn. Virgil told his brothers to leave Ike alone. In Ike's version, he added "while Jim is here."

According to Wyatt, Clanton threatened Holliday and the three Earps. If he did, he must have been not only drunk but insane. Ike was no gunman, but all three Earps and Holliday were known to be both expert and ruthless.

Strangely, about half an hour later, Ike Clanton got into a poker game. The other players were Tom McLaury, Johnny Behan—and Virgil Earp. When the game broke up, Ike, unable to sleep, wandered around Tombstone. In the course of his wandering he picked up his revolver, then later, his rifle. A neighbor woman told Big Nose Kate that Ike Clanton was looking for her husband with a Colt and a Winchester.

Virgil Earp summoned Morgan to go with him to arrest and disarm the cowboy. They found Clanton staggering down Fourth Street ahead of them. They moved up behind him quietly, and Virgil bashed him on the head with the barrel of his revolver. The Earps took his guns and dragged him, bleeding from the cut on his head, to the courtroom. While they were waiting for the judge, Wyatt, Virgil and Morgan took turns taunting Ike. At one point they offered him a gun if he wanted to fight. The judge finally appeared and fined Ike $25 and court costs for carrying a weapon.

A little later, Wyatt saw young Tom McLaury walking on the street.

"Are you heeled or not?" Earp asked. McLaury said he had no weapons. Earp slapped his face with his left hand and with his right hit the unarmed boy on the head with a pistol. McLaury went down, struggled to his feet and was knocked down again with a second blow of the revolver barrel. A witness heard McLaury tell Earp "that he never had done anything against him and was a friend of his," but Earp hit him with the revolver "four or five times" and then went on. There were several witnesses to the scene, and all agreed McLaury had no weapon.

In the meantime, Billy Clanton and Frank McLaury rode into Tombstone about 2 p.m. to meet their brothers. they went to a gun shop and bought some ammunition, visited a feed store, then went through the O.K. Corral to Fremont Street, where Bauer's market was.

The threats by Holliday and the Earps, Ike's erratic behavior and threats against Holliday (and maybe the Earps) plus the Earps' pistol whipping of Ike Clanton and Tom McLaury led Tombstonians to expect trouble.

B. H. Fallehy, a Tombstone citizen, later testified, "I heard some stranger ask Ike Clanton what is the trouble; he said there would be no trouble . . . then saw the Marshal [Virgil Earp] and the Sheriff [Behan] talking; the Sheriff says, 'What's the trouble?' the Marshal says, 'Those men have been making threats; I will not arrest them but will kill them on sight.' "

Sheriff Behan found the cowboys on Fremont Street near the market and tried to take their guns. Ike Clanton and Tom McLaury said they had no guns. Behan searched them to make sure. Billy Clanton and Frank McLaury said they all were just about to leave town.

Then around the corner from Fourth Street came the three Earps and Holliday. Behan ran up to them and asked Virgil to give him time to disarm the cowboys. The "Earp Gang" said nothing as they pushed past him. Unlike the traditional picture, the three Earps were wearing mackinaws and they carried their revolvers in their hands or in coat pockets. Wyatt's coat pockets had waxed canvas linings to make it easy to draw a gun. Holliday was wearing a long gray overcoat with a nickel plated revolver in his coat pocket and a short-barrel 10 gauge shotgun in his hand under the coat.

Martha King was shopping at the butcher shop when the line of men passed its door. She saw Holliday's coat blow open, revealing his shotgun. Holliday, whom she knew, was nearest the building.

"I heard this man on [the] outside—[he] looked at Holliday and I heard him say, 'Let them have it.' And Doc Holliday said, 'All right,' " King later testified.

She tried to run to the back of the store, but got only a couple of steps before shooting broke out.

The opponents were standing close to each other. Addie Bourland, a dressmaker, standing at an upstairs window directly in front of the confrontation, saw Doc Holliday poke his Colt Single Action Army revolver right in

Frank McLaury's stomach, then he "stepped back two or three feet and the firing seemed to be general."

Other witnesses said there were two shots in quick succession, probably fired by Doc Holliday and Morgan Earp. Ike Clanton ran for dear life. Tom McLaury opened his coat to show that he had no guns, but Holliday swung up his shotgun and blasted him with a 10 gauge charge of buckshot. Morgan Earp shot Billy Clanton, and Wyatt Earp put another slug through Frank McLaury. McLaury, still standing, tried to reach the Winchester in his horse's saddle scabbard. The horse shied, so he drew his Colt single action and fired at Doc Holliday, hitting him in the hip. Morgan Earp fired again. McLaury fell with a hole just below his ear. Billy Clanton, who had yelled he didn't want to fight when the Earps and Holliday approached, was firing from the ground. He hit Morgan Earp in the shoulder and Virgil in the leg as Virgil fired at him. Morgan fell, but got off another shot. He and Virgil hit Billy Clanton. A bystander ran up to Billy, and the young man's last words were a request for more cartridges.

Wyatt Earp testified, "When I saw Billy Clanton and Frank McLowry (sic) draw their pistols, I drew my pistol. Billy Clanton leveled his pistol on me, but I did not aim at him. I knew that Frank McLowry had the reputation of being a good shot and a dangerous man and I aimed at Frank McLowry. The first two shots which were fired were fired by Billy Clanton and myself, he shooting at me and I at Frank McLowry."

Wyatt's account is impossible. In the 1930s, Ed McGivern, a trick shooter and pioneer in timing shooting stunts, proved that a person who starts to draw after his opponent has started has to be almost twice as fast as his opponent to "beat the drop." According to McGivern, "The average quick-draw performer divides his activities from start to finish into three sections or periods of time of about equal proportion. It takes him practically one-third of the time from starting impulse to get into action and get his hand on the gun, then the next third of the time is required for the necessary gripping and drawing from holster movements, and the last third of the time is used for pointing the gun at the target, and at the same time performing the finger movements necessary for firing the shot just as pointing movements are completed." To even fire at the same time as an opponent who has already started to draw, the gunman must be 50 percent faster than his opponent. To beat his shot, as Earp claims he did to that "good shot and dangerous man" Frank McLaury, he would have to be more than twice as fast. Among experienced gunmen, like all those in the O.K. Corral fight, nobody is that fast or even close to that fast.

In any unbiased court, the Earps and Holliday would have been found guilty of premeditated murder. But there was no unbiased court in Tombstone.

Justice Wells Spicer, a friend of Wyatt Earp's, held a preliminary hearing to see if the Earps and Holliday should appear before a grand jury. He permitted Wyatt Earp to read his testimony from a previously prepared paper and allowed no cross examination of the marshal's brother, although all other witnesses spoke extemporaneously and were cross examined. Morgan and Virgil, both seriously wounded, were not required to testify. Even Doc Holliday, whose wound amounted to little more than a scratch, was excused. In his decision, Spicer ignored the testimony of disinterested witnesses like Martha King and B. H. Fallehy and said Virgil was carrying out his duty as city marshal in attempting to disarm the cowboys, and his brothers and Holliday, having been deputized, were acting as they should. He made no reference to the deal between Wyatt Earp and Ike Clanton, mentioned by both Earp and Clanton in their testimony. Nor was there even a suggestion that the Earps and Holliday thought Clanton, his family and his friends knew too much.

Nevertheless, many citizens had their doubts. On October 29, 1881, three days after the fight and the day before the Spicer hearings, the Tombstone city council met to consider "grave charges" against Virgil Earp. The hearings were held behind closed doors, and at the end of them, Virgil was no longer city marshal.

In December, a grand jury was convened to hear the Earp-Holliday case despite Spicer's decision. The jury, however, was full of Earp's friends, including Marshall Williams, the crooked Well Fargo manager. The Earps and Holliday had the strong support of U.S. Marshal Crawley Dake (later removed from office for blatant corruption), and, after all, Spicer had found no reason to hold them for the grand jury. Predictably, the grand jury followed Spicer's lead. The whole situation was a brazen miscarriage of justice, but in Tombstone, the pro-Earp faction had most of the guns and all of the political power. There was no need for subtlety.

Life for the Earps did not continue as before, though. On the night of December 28, a group of gunmen hidden in the shadows opened up on Virgil Earp, leaving him with wounds that crippled him for life. The Earps began selling off their properties, and Wyatt lost his gambling concession in the Oriental Saloon. In the January 3, 1882 election, the Law and Order Party went down to defeat, and the *Tombstone Nugget* headlined the story "Exeunt Earps!"

That was a bit premature. With Virgil Earp out of action, Crawley Dake telegraphed Wyatt Earp stating he was appointing him a deputy marshal.

There is some mystery about that appointment. Almost a century later, writer James D. Horan went to the Justice Department and found that there were no records of Wyatt Earp being appointed or serving as a deputy U.S. marshal.

Whatever the records show in Washington, Wyatt Earp pinned on a badge and began gathering a posse. The posse included some rare specimens. One was Sherman McMasters, the stage coach robber. Another was Texas Jack Vermillion, who lived in a cave and had murdered a man in Flagstaff. A third was Turkey Creek Jack Johnson, a gambler who, in Deadwood, South Dakota, once invited two men to shoot it out. Turkey Creek paid a laborer to dig two graves, then went to meet his opponents. As they walked toward Turkey Creek, the two men began firing when 50 yards away. Each emptied one revolver while Johnson held his fire. When they were 30 yards away, Johnson killed one. He let the next get off three more shots, then killed him, too.

Earp took his posse out to hunt for cowboys. They didn't find any, but they thoroughly shot up the town of Charleston, containing the cowboys' favorite watering holes. On March 18, Morgan Earp was playing billiards when somebody shot him dead through the window in a door. Frank Stilwell, the stage coach robber, who was awaiting trial, was suspected.

The Earps decided to send Morgan's body by train to their parents in California. Crippled Virgil and his wife would accompany the body. Wyatt Earp and members of his posse, now including his brother Warren, escorted it as far as Tucson. Doc Holliday, Wyatt and Warren Earp and Sherman McMasters boarded the train with Winchester rifles and short, Wells Fargo-issue shotguns. When the train stopped at Tucson to let passengers eat dinner, witnesses heard seven or eight shots. Ahead of the train, they found the bullet riddled body of Stilwell, an unfired revolver still in his belt. Holliday, McMasters and the Earps had disappeared. How Stilwell happened to be at the Tucson train station is something of a mystery, too. The idea that a lone man with a revolver wanted to shoot it out with four gunfighters carrying shotguns and rifles is absurd. The best guess is that some of Earp's friends lured him there.

The sheriff of Pima County swore out a murder warrant for Wyatt Earp, Warren Earp, Doc Holliday and Sherman McMasters. He telegraphed Tombstone, but Wyatt and his posse had left.

Sheriff Behan swore in a legitimate posse, but one that also included questionable characters. John Ringo, one of the rustler leaders, was a posse member, as were most of his followers. So, too, were Ike and Phin Clanton. About the only prominent member of the cowboy faction not in the posse was Curly Bill Brocius.

The Earp posse killed a Mexican suspected, with little reason, of having helped murder Morgan. A little later, they claimed to have had a fight with nine cowboys. In this scrap, according to an account in the Earp-supporting *Tombstone Epitaph*, the Earp group drove off the cowboys and killed Curly Bill Brocius. In contrast, the *Tombstone Nugget* said there were only four cowboys and they drove off Earp's crew. The *Epitaph* ran a later account in which no cowboys were killed, but Turkey Creek Jack lost his horse.

One of the cowboys later told Breakenridge that he lined up his sights on Wyatt Earp's white shirt and fired, but Earp rode away. Earp was saved, the cowboy said, by his steel vest. According to Big Nose Kate, Wyatt Earp did have a steel vest. That she said, caused his final break-up with Doc Holliday. The dentist objected to taking risks that Wyatt avoided by wearing a bullet-proof vest.

Whether or not Curly Bill was killed became a major controversy in the Tombstone area. Earp's friends said he was, his enemies said Bill had left the state long before Earp's posse set out. It was a fact that Behan, who had recruited about every rustler in sight for his posse, did not get Curly Bill. The *Nugget* offered $1,000 to anyone who could prove Curly Bill was dead. The reward went unclaimed. The *Epitaph* offered $2,000 to Curly Bill if he would show himself. If he was alive, Curly Bill did not appear in Tombstone. Stupider men than Curly Bill Brocius would know that if he got $2,000 for proving himself alive, he wouldn't stay that way long. Not in Tombstone.

Wyatt Earp and his followers managed to stay ahead of Behan and his posse. The Earp gang finally surfaced in Trinidad, Colorado, where Bat Masterson was city marshal and a political power. In a series of adroit legal maneuvers, Masterson frustrated the efforts of Arizona to extradite the fugitives. Arizona finally gave up, and Wyatt Earp began wandering the West, gambling in about every boom town between Canada and Mexico. He tried prospecting in California and claim-jumping in Idaho. For a while, he ran a saloon in Nome, Alaska, during the gold rush there.

Eventually, Wyatt settled in California and married Josie Marcus, the actress and department store heiress he had won from Johnny Behan. He became associated with San Francisco gamblers and in 1896 was called upon to referee the fight between the middleweight champion, Bob Fitzsimmons, and a heavyweight named Tom Sharkey. At stake as a shot at the heavy-weight champion, Gentleman Jim Corbett. Although he was 35, weighed only 165 pounds and had all the finesse of a sledgehammer, Fitzsimmons was the heavy favorite because of his tremendous punching power. During seven rounds of the fight, "Ruby Bob" pounded Sharkey like a bass drum. In the eighth, he knocked "Sailor Tom" cold. Earp walked over to the unconscious Sharkey and raised his hand in victory. He said he was taking the fight from Fitzsimmons for a low blow. Earp's "smart-money" friends made a killing. But it was Fitzsimmons who got the title shot. In 1897, he beat Corbett ("the first scientific boxer") in 14 rounds and with no accusations of foul blows.

A couple of years later, Wyatt tried a little boxing himself—the informal kind—at a race track. His opponent was a man named Tom Mulqueen, a "well known horseman" according to the *Arizona Citizen*. Mulqueen had also been a professional fighter. The *Citizen* reported that Wyatt "attempted to do the horseman, but the latter knocked him glassy-eyed in the first round."

As time went on, Wyatt Earp began to attract more journalistic attention. He had lived all over and all through the mythic Wild West and was one of the few wild westerners still alive. Wherever he went, the monosyllabic Earp let reporters pry out of him the story of how he had almost single-handedly brought law and order to the West. Journalists in those days usually didn't waste time verifying facts. Wyatt's tales did not become less colorful because all his contemporaries were dead.

In the 1920s, Wyatt Earp met Stuart Lake, a freelance writer. Lake carefully listened to all Earp's lies, went to his old haunts, looked up his old acquaintances and read old newspapers. Then he wrote a story he thought would sell. *Wyatt Earp, Frontier Marshal* is the result. First, as a series in the *Saturday Evening Post*, then as a best-selling book, it founded the legend that has gone on and on. It's a fascinating book, but as historical as *The Wizard of Oz*.

All of our great epochs have had heroes. The Revolution had George Washington. The Civil War had Abraham Lincoln and Robert E. Lee. The push to the plains had Daniel Boone. The one thing the Wild West needed was an unalloyed hero to stand above the sleazy, gritty world of cowboys, miners, gamblers and gunmen. If Wyatt Earp had never existed, we'd have had to invent him.

So we did.

EXPANSION

AND

GROWING

PAINS—

LITTLE WARS

Nine

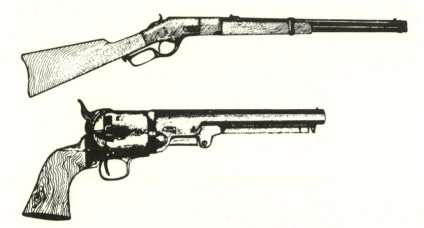

New Year's Party

January 1, 1888, Pike County, Kentucky

It was midnight when the 15 riders hitched their horses in the woods and crept silently through the snow to the dark cabin. One of them raised his Winchester and fired a shot through a window.

"That will rouse the damned sons of bitches," he said.

Inside the cabin, 24-year-old Calvin McCoy jumped from his bed and yelled, "Pa, it's the Hatfields!"

"I reckon so," said old Randolph McCoy pulling on a pair of pants un-

Top: Winchester Model 1866 in .44 rimfire, a gun popular in the Tug Valley many years after its introduction. Below: Colt Model 1851, the famous .36 caliber Navy Colt, the darling of generations of gunfighters. Its cap-and-ball amunition was cheap, and its balance was superb.

der his night shirt. Both men strapped on Colt revolvers, picked up rifles and went up to the loft, where they had cut loopholes in the thick log walls.

"Come out, Ranel," called a voice old McCoy recognized as belonging to Jim Vance, the man who led the bushwhackers who had killed his brother Harmon. Vance was the uncle of Devil Anse Hatfield, leader of the damned-Hatfields. "Come out and surrender," Vance called again.

Ranel McCoy poked his Winchester through the loophole and fired into the darkness.

"Give it to the goddam sons of bitches," Vance yelled. Fire erupted all around the house, but the .44-40 and .38-40 slugs wouldn't penetrate the heavy logs. Ranel had built his cabin to serve as a fort. On the first floor, Sally McCoy and her daughters, Alifair, Adelaide, Fannie and Josephine, stayed away from the windows.

Jim Vance could see that his raiders were making no headway. He gave an order, and Tom Mitchell ran to the woodshed and came back with a bundle of pine faggots and a stick wrapped with a kerosene-soaked rag. He placed the faggots against the house, stuck a match and lighted the torch. There was a flash and a bang from the cabin, and Mitchell stared at his hand in the torch-light. It was gushing blood from where three fingers had been. He turned and dashed for the shelter of the smokehouse while the faggots, ignited by the burning torch, began to blaze.

Inside the McCoy cabin, the defenders tried to put out the fire with the water they had brought in for the night. They ran out of water and tried milk. They still couldn't put out the fire. Alifair McCoy, 29, said she would get water from the well. Even a Hatfield wouldn't shoot a defenseless woman. She got a bucket and stepped outside.

"Stop!" said a man behind the well box. In the flickering light from the fire, Alifair recognized Cap Hatfield.

"Why, Cap," she said, "you wouldn't shoot me. I've never harmed nobody."

Cap fired. Alifair slumped to the ground and died.

Her mother, old Sally, though sick and weak, went out into the snow toward her daughter.

"Cap Hatfield—you murderer!" she screamed.

Jim Vance stepped out of the shadows.

"Get out of the way, old woman!"

"I'm a-going to Cap. He killed my girl."

Vance swung his rifle and hit Sally McCoy on the head. When she fell, he stood over her and pounded her prostrate body.

The fire continued to burn. The people in the house ran out. Calvin fell with a bullet through his heart. Ranel rounded a corner and found his way blocked by Johnson Hatfield. He fired his Colt, and Johnse spun around with a bullet in his shoulder.

Unable to find the McCoys who fled, the Hatfields burned the storehouse containing their food and rode back to West Virginia.

Back home, they reported to their clan chief, William Anderson Hatfield, known throughout the Tug Valley as Devil Anse. They had attempted to kill Old Ranel, the McCoy chief, and put an end to the feud. All they had done was kill a young man, kill a young woman and severely beat an old woman. It wasn't a very successful night. But in recent months, the Hatfields hadn't been very successful.

It wasn't always that way. In the past, Devil Anse Hatfield had always been successful.

When the Civil War broke out, Devil Anse, like Ranel McCoy and most of the men in the Tug Valley, had enlisted in the Confederate army. Devil Anse rose from private to lieutenant, but in 1863, he deserted. The war was raging right in the Tug Valley, which included parts of Logan County Virginia (later West Virginia) and Pike County Kentucky. Devil Anse, like other Tug Valley men, again including Ranel McCoy, didn't see why he should be fighting in foreign places he didn't care about when his own people needed defending.

Back in Logan County, he formed his own militia company and led it as a captain. The Yankees considered him a daring and dangerous guerrilla. His fellow guerrilla, Ranel McCoy, didn't fare so well. He was captured and sent to a Yankee prison camp. Ranel had a certain amount of luck, of course. He wasn't hanged, and the war ended before he starved to death. But Randolph McCoy, son of a dissolute father, had entered the army poor and came out poorer. He also had a personal tragedy.

His brother Harmon had fought on the other side. Few Tug Valley people had slaves, but almost all were for the Confederacy. They felt that the Confederacy, with its far weaker central government, gave them a better chance to continue the near-total autonomy they had always enjoyed. Most of the slave-holders, like Harmon, opted for the Union. Slave holders were the wealthier residents of the valley and more in contact with the outside world. They cared less about losing their slaves—few in any case—than about joining the booming economy of the northern states.

Harmon's enlistment ran out December 24, 1864. Although he had been wounded and walked with a limp, Harmon reenlisted and got a furlough. Back home, Harmon ran into Jim Vance, a member of his nephew's Logan Wildcats company.

"We hear you've enlisted to keep on fighting for Old Abe," Vance said.

"That's right. And it looks as if we're going to bring the South back into the Union in a few months, too."

"We'll have every one of Anse's Logan Wildcats over here on you, and we'll see."

McCoy hid out in a cave, but Vance and some militia members found him and killed him.

To Ranel McCoy, it wasn't right, killing a wounded soldier who was home on leave. It wasn't like killing him on a battlefield. It was war, and all that, but it convinced him that the Hatfields were no damn good.

Devil Anse couldn't care less what that old failure Ranel McCoy (12 years his senior) thought. He had been as poor as Ranel, but by borrowing on what he didn't own, suing whenever he thought he could win and financial manipulations worthy of a modern junk bond broker, Devil Anse made himself a comparatively rich and powerful man and started a massive—for the Tug Valley—timbering operation.

His aggressiveness scandalized the traditional and devout mountaineers. "You can say it is the Devil's church I belong to," he once said, referring to himself. His enemies said he was mad for money, but the Devil was more interested in something else—power. The southern Appalachians were in the midst of a crisis, and Devil Anse saw a way to take advantage of it.

The problem was land. When their grandparents came to the valley, land was plentiful and cheap. But the average family had more than 10 children (Devil Anse had 12 and Ranel had 16). It became harder and harder to acquire enough land to give each child enough to live on. Children of solid, respectable farmers had to work for wages—a less-than-respectable situation in the eyes of the independent mountaineers.

Devil Anse hired these landless sons on his timbering crews and paid them so well they were able to acquire their own land. When Anse had to sell land to repay creditors he couldn't escape, he sold it to potential followers for bargain prices. That was how people like Selkirk McCoy, related on both sides of his family to Old Ranel, became "a Hatfield." When Devil Anse had to fight for what he believed to be his rights, he was able to call up a formidable number of retainers.

Anse Hatfield's power was based on an extension of the old southern tradition that hired hands and servants were members of the family. Devil

Anse's "family" included many with no Hatfield blood, while there were many Hatfields who had nothing to do with the feud and some who actively opposed Anse.

Ranel McCoy's family, as Ranel had no economic clout, consisted only of close relatives—at the beginning of the feud, only his children.

That is not to say there was no family solidarity among the many, many McCoy cousins and the many, many Hatfield cousins. That became obvious at the "pig trial," the beginning of the feud.

Ranel McCoy lost a sow. He later saw it in the yard of Floyd Hatfield. Ranel went to the justice of the peace, Preacher Anse Hatfield, a man who, in spite of his name, was on good terms with both Hatfields and McCoys. Ranel told Preacher Anse he thought Floyd had taken his sow. He had good reasons for thinking that; in the mountains, pigs were allowed to run wild, but each had its owner's distinctive earmark. It didn't make sense to put someone else's earmark on your own pig, but the pig in Floyd's yard had Ranel's earmark. At the trial in 1878, in order to be fair, Preacher Anse selected a jury of six Hatfields and six McCoys. The jurors agreed to take a vote and render a unanimous decision to the side that got the majority. The deciding vote was cast by Selkirk McCoy. Ranel lost.

Feeling ran high on both sides, then boiled over in 1880. Squirrel Hunting Sam McCoy (so called to distinguish him from Ranel's son Sam) and Paris McCoy were hunting when they encountered Bill Staton, a Hatfield. Staton shot and wounded Paris McCoy. Squirrel Hunting Sam knocked the rifle out of Staton's hands. The two struggled hand-to-hand, then Sam McCoy managed to draw his revolver and kill Staton. As the shooting took place in West Virginia, both McCoys were tried in that state. They were acquitted on the grounds of self-defense.

In the meantime, on election day in 1880, Roseanna McCoy, Old Ranel's daughter, met Johnson Hatfield, Devil Anse's son. Devil Anse's family frequented Pike County elections, although they lived in another state. They brought along plenty of the Devil's white lightning and passed it out liberally. It was part of Devil Anse's strategy for getting friendly politicians elected on both sides of the Tug Valley.

What happened this time, though, was something neither Devil Anse nor Old Ranel ever expected. When Johnse and Roseanna met, the result was that rarest of all phenomena, love at first sight. In spite of the enmity between their families, Roseanna agreed to go home with Johnse. Anse, the sly old devil, saw an opportunity to get his back on the head of the clan that had killed his kinsman, Bill Staton. He told Johnse Roseanna could live with him, but under no circumstances could he marry her.

Johnse was a tall, handsome man with the soul of a little boy. He agreed. Roseanna wanted Johnse under any conditions, even with lack of wedlock. And the longer she stayed, the more afraid she was of what her father would do if she went home.

Eventually, Old Ranel sent Roseanna, now pregnant, a message: either she come home, or he and her brothers would go over to West Virginia and bring her back by force. Fearing that she might be the cause of killing, Roseanna went back to Kentucky after she and Johnse pledged their undying love to each other.

Back home, Roseanna's father refused to speak to her and tried not to even look at her. After several weeks, she could take it no longer and moved in with her aunt, Betty McCoy. Johnse learned where she was staying and came to visit. He still wasn't ready to disobey his father and marry her, but he said he'd return. One of Roseanna's brothers saw Johnse on one of his visits and told Ranel. The next time Johnse crossed the Tug, several of Roseanna's brothers appeared. Tolbert McCoy flashed a deputy sheriff's badge and told Johnse he was under arrest for carrying a concealed weapon. The arrest was a setup, because in those days almost every Tug Valley mountaineer in potentially dangerous territory carried a Colt six-shooter in a shoulder holster.

Roseanna was afraid her brothers would kill Johnse. As soon as they were out of sight, she got on her horse and rode to Devil Anse's house, where the Hatfields were putting up a barn, and relatives and friends from far and near were helping. Roseanna told the Hatfield leader than her brothers had Johnse. She begged him to go at once, but not to hurt her brothers.

Devil Anse and about 30 to 40 Hatfields caught up with Tolbert and the other McCoys. The old Hatfield released his son and cussed out Tolbert, but did him no harm.

Roseanna was even more estranged from her family after that. She drifted toward deep depression. Then her baby was born—a little girl Roseanna named Sally after her mother. For a few months, the young Hatfield woman seemed to perk up: she now had something to live for. Then the baby died of measles. Roseanna now devoted her life to nursing members of her family when they became ill. In good times, though, she became more and more withdrawn, and made frequent trips to the infant's grave. Once, soon after little Sally died, she was kneeling by the side of the grave and looked up to see Johnse Hatfield.

After a long embrace, he said, "Honey, I've come to marry you. We'll get married today—right now, and nobody can do anything about it."

She slowly pushed him away.

"No, Johnse," she said, "I can't marry you now. The time is past. If our baby had lived, I would have risked anything to be with you, but I can't do it now."

"Why? Don't you love me anymore?"

"Yes, Johnse, I love you. I never loved anybody but you and I never will, but you had your chance to marry me, and Anse wouldn't let you. I stayed with you anyhow, and I had our baby by myself. She died, and I went through that by myself. I went through a lot of other hurts by myself, and there's not a thing left. Not for me, anyway."

Besides, Roseanna explained, she knew that if she went to West Virginia, her father would come after her.

"I have made up my mind," she said, "to cause no more trouble. If I must suffer—and I know I will—I will suffer alone. I don't expect to be happy, for I know I never will."

Eight years later, Roseanna McCoy died. The cause, said the doctor, was that she just didn't want to live anymore.

Johnse, always a heavy drinker, went on a roaring binge after his rejection. A little later, though he never forgot Roseanna, he married her cousin, Nancy McCoy. His luck did not improve.

Before the stormy Hatfield-McCoy marriage had really begun, another election day brought another crisis. Tolbert McCoy got into a fight with Elias Hatfield, who, although a Hatfield, was not one of Devil Anse's "family." Tolbert knocked "Black Lias," also known as "Bad Lias," unconscious after a hard struggle. At that point, Ellison Hatfield, Devil Anse's brother, dealt himself in, hitting the exhausted Tolbert. According to some accounts, he got McCoy in a strangle hold; at any rate, the fight was going poorly for Tolbert. Tolbert pulled out a pocket knife and started stabbing Ellison. Bill McCoy, 16, ran to help his brother and stabbed Ellison with his own knife. Ellison pushed both brothers away and picked up a large rock. Someone in the crowd threw a revolver to Pharmer McCoy, and Pharmer shot Ellison. The big man staggered and fell to the ground.

Two constables, John and Floyd Hatfield, sons of Preacher Anse, arrested Tolbert, Pharmer and Bud McCoy, who had been mistakenly identified, instead of Bill, as the other knife wielder. Preacher Anse told them to take the brothers to the Pike County jail. They took their time—long enough for Devil Anse to round up some 30 retainers and abduct the prisoners to West Virginia.

Sally McCoy crossed the river and pleaded with Devil Anse for her sons' lives. Devil Anse said he was waiting to see if his brother would live. But, he told Sally, whether Ellison lived or died, he would return the McCoy boys alive to Kentucky. Sally could do nothing more. She went home to wait.

Ellison died. Devil Anse and a couple dozen followers took the McCoy brothers alive, over to Kentucky. Then, having fulfilled his promise to Sally McCoy, he had his followers tie them to three pawpaw bushes and shoot them dead.

A coroner's jury found that the boys met their death at the hands of persons unknown. Ranel became livid with rage and badgered the prosecuting attorney into calling a grand jury. The grand jury in Pikeville was less impressed with Devil Anse than the Tug Valley coroner's jury. It indicted 23 Hatfields, including Devil Anse, for the murder.

The Hatfields didn't like being indicted, although West Virginia did nothing to implement the Kentucky indictments. They began raiding the McCoys in Kentucky. In one ambush, a young son of Ranel's son Larkin, was killed. With the Hatfields' numerical superiority, they could strike at will. Randolph's son, Sam, and a couple of cousins, Hense and John Scott, were ambushed just outside Ranel's house. John and Hense were wounded, but the ambushers were frightened off by another of Ranel's sons, Calvin, who rushed at them firing a revolver in each hand.

Another raid on Ranel's house ended even more ignominiously. Fifteen Hatfields rode up to the cabin, but neither Ranel nor any of the other men were there. There was only old Sally and two of her daughters. The young women ran up to the loft to count the Hatfields, but one of them tripped over some loose logs in the loft. The falling timber made such a racket the Hatfields thought the whole McCoy clan was in the loft and getting ready to open fire. They all jumped on their horses and rode away.

Over in West Virginia, Tom Wallace, Cap Hatfield's hired man, said he thought so many raids had been foiled because someone was giving the McCoys information. That someone, he believed, was Mary Daniels, Nancy McCoy Hatfield's sister. Mary lived in West Virginia, but she had frequent contact with her relatives. Wallace didn't mention the fact that he had been living with Mary Daniels' daughter, but the girl had left him. He blamed her mother.

One night when Bill Daniels was away, 12 masked men burst into the cabin containing Mary Daniels and her mother-in-law. They wore masks, but one was identifiable. There was a white streak right in the middle of his dark brown hair. Tom Wallace was the only man with a scalp like that. They pulled old Mrs. Daniels out of bed, knocked down young Mrs. Daniels, and beat both women with the cow's tail, leaving both unconscious. Old Mrs. Daniels was crippled for life.

Ranel's son Jeff killed a man in a fight entirely unrelated to the feud. Fearing arrest, he went to West Virginia and looked up Nancy McCoy

Hatfield, Johnse's wife. Nancy told him what had happened to Mary Daniels and how Tom Wallace had been identified. Jeff went up to Cap Hatfield's cabin, saw Tom Wallace working in the yard and shot at him. Wallace ran into the cabin, and McCoy, after some fruitless shooting, left to wait for a better opportunity. It never came. A few days later, Cap Hatfield and Tom Wallace got the drop on him near the Tug river. Jeff McCoy jumped into the Tug and swam for Kentucky, but as soon as he reached the western bank, a Hatfield bullet cut him down.

After Jeff's funeral, his brother, Lark McCoy, went Wallace hunting in West Virginia. It wasn't too hard. Nobody except Devil Anse's personal "family" had any sympathy for Wallace. It wasn't long before Lark came back to Kentucky with Tom Wallace in tow. He put Wallace in the Pikeville jail, but someone apparently paid off the jailer. Wallace escaped and, believing even West Virginia was too hot for him, lit out for Virginia, due south of Pike and Logan counties. Lark McCoy put out the word that he'd pay a reward for Tom Wallace dead or alive.

Several weeks later, two men plodded up the muddy road leading from Virginia. They reached Lark McCoy's cabin, and one of them halloed for him. Lark came out.

"Are you Larkin McCoy?" one of the men asked.

"I'm Lark McCoy. Who are you?"

"We've got something for you," the stranger said. "This." He reached into his saddle bag, took out a package and handed it to Lark.

McCoy unwrapped the package. It was a scalp—dark brown with a white streak through it.

None of the feudists knew it, but at this time, outside forces were about to dramatically change the course of the private war between the Hatfields and McCoys. Millionaires in New York, Philadelphia, Boston and Pittsburgh were casting avaricious eyes toward the Tug Valley. The valley, and similar valleys in southern Appalachia, were treasure troves of coal and timber—treasures that were largely ignored by a handful of subsistence farmers who valued nothing but independence. Devil Anse had, to be sure, begun large scale timbering, but Devil Anse was only a big fish in a very small pond. The sharks and barracudas were moving in.

Operators like Devil Anse could never really exploit the valley's resources because there was no decent transportation. When the Hatfields cut a quantity of timber, they made a raft and tried to float it down the narrow, rocky Tug and into the Ohio. The outside exploiters were not thinking of rafts. They were thinking of railroads. Railroad and mining interests began negotiating with the state governments. In at least one instance, the state and a railroad agreed on a price per acre for all the land the road wanted. Anyone along the proposed right-of- way had to sell for that price. There were no negotiations.

One embarrassment for Governor Simon Bolivar Buckner of Kentucky was that the feud had given his state the reputation of being a dangerous place. That reputation made it hard to attract capital. Buckner, then, was unusually attentive when his old friend and campaign contributor, Perry Cline, came to visit. Perry Cline was Randolph McCoy's lawyer, and Ranel had been after him to do something about putting teeth into the indictments. Cline was also a bitter enemy of Devil Anse Hatfield, who years before, had sued the lawyer and won 5,000 acres of timberland from him. Cline got Buckner to reactivate the indictments, now five years old. Buckner also told Cline he could organize a posse and go after the Hatfields in their own home territory. That might put an end to the feud. At the very least, it would shift the fighting to West Virginia and help restore Kentucky's reputation.

To head the posse, Cline found a young man named Frank Phillips. "Bad Frank," as everyone called him, was the sort of person who drifted west to places like Tombstone and Deadwood at this time. Ranel's family joined Phillips' posses enthusiastically, but so did citizens of Pikeville who seldom even visited the Tug Valley. Pikeville was strongly Unionist, and the descendants of Union Civil War veterans were anxious to get a crack at Devil Anse Hatfield, the most unreconstructed rebel in the hills. In 1870, testifying for a West Virginian who had killed a black man, Devil Anse explained that the killer had been ordered to shoot the man by "Colonel H. M. Bentley, then commanding officer in this section of the state in the Confederate States army." The fact that the murder had occurred five years after the end of the Civil War didn't bother Anse. It didn't bother the court, either. It acquitted Anse's friend.

The feud no longer consisted of sporadic raids, and the Hatfields no longer had the initiative. Jim and Calvin McCoy captured Tom Chambers and put him in the Pikeville jail. Bad Frank, Jim McCoy and a crowd of Kentucky possemen swept through West Virginia and captured Selkirk McCoy. He, too, was securely jailed. There would be no more Tom Wallace escapades.

Devil Anse bided his time and planned. On New Year's Eve, 1887, he sent his forces out to get Ranel McCoy, the author of his family's troubles.

When his "New Year's party" failed, Anse knew he couldn't win. But he kept trying.

Nancy McCoy Hatfield stopped trying. Her relationship with Johnse had gone from bad to worse—six years of quarreling with him over his drinking, his womanizing, his subservience to his father and the fighting with her relatives. Johnse was frequently away days at a time. One night when Nancy was sleeping alone, Johnse sneaked into the house and pointed a shotgun at her. Fortunately, he was dead drunk. Nancy took the gun away from him and put him to bed. She believed Johnse's malevolent brother Cap had talked him into trying to kill her. A few days later, Johnse asked her to go for a walk with him. Nancy walked a short distance, then noticed Cap Hatfield hiding behind a rock. She went back to the cabin. The next time Johnse went away, Nancy took her two children and returned to Kentucky. A few weeks later, she moved in with Bad Frank Phillips.

Devil Anse had no time to meddle in his son's domestic affairs. He had his hands full trying to defend his family.

A week after the house-burning, Phillips and Jim McCoy, with 21 followers, killed old Jim Vance, whose killing of Harmon McCoy in 1865 started the first trouble between the Hatfields and McCoys.

Over the next ten days, Bad Frank and Jim McCoy led a half-dozen more raids and captured Andrew Varney, Dow McCoy, Curt McCoy, Plyant Mayhorn and Mose Christian. Devil Anse's brother, Valentine, surrendered to the McCoys voluntarily.

Devil Anse wrote to the governor, then he went to Logan County authorities and got a grand jury called. The grand jury indicted 20 McCoys for kidnapping and the murder of Jim Vance. And the sheriff deputized Devil Anse and his followers. If the McCoys could cover their depredations with a legal smokescreen, so could the Hatfields.

On January 19, Devil Anse led a posse of eight men toward Kentucky. The old clan leader had lost much of his political and economic clout to the newcomers and new ideas that were entering West Virginia as they had Kentucky. Hatfield raiding parties of from 20 to 40 men were a thing of the past.

Unknown to the posse members, between them and Kentucky, hidden in the woods bordering Grapevine Creek, were 23 McCoys led by Bad Frank Phillips and Jim McCoy. Devil Anse's luck held. Bud McCoy, impatient to get his enemies, stepped out of hiding and yelled "Surrender!" The Hatfields fired a volley and fled. The McCoys fired another volley. The net results of the so-called "Battle of the Grapevine" were two Hatfields killed and a McCoy wounded. But the Hatfields never again invaded Kentucky.

Defiant to the last, Anse sent a messenger to the McCoys. His message: "If you ever come over to this territory again, come and see me."

A week later, Frank Phillips, Jim McCoy and some 30 followers appeared outside Devil Anse's house as the Devil was preparing to eat his noonday meal. They announced their presence with a fusillade of rifle shots but for some reason neglected to surround the house. Devil Anse and the nine men with him fired back, but one by one they slipped out the back of the house and fled to the hills. Only Anse's wife, Vicey, was left to greet the McCoys.

The governor of West Virginia wrote to the governor of Kentucky, demanding the arrest of the indicted McCoys. The governor of Kentucky ignored the demand, as the governor of West Virginia had previously ignored his demand for the arrest of the indicted Hatfields. West Virginia sued Kentucky in federal court for the release of the captured Hatfields. The court ruled that it had no jurisdiction, and the U.S. Supreme Court upheld the decision.

The captured Hatfields were tried in Pike County in 1889. Perry Cline, who had tilted the balance in favor of the McCoys, defended the Hatfields. They could pay enough to make it worth his while. Valentine Hatfield, Alex Messer, Dock Mayhorn, Plyant Mayhorn, Sam Mayhorn, Andrew Varney, and Selkirk McCoy all got life imprisonment. Others got long prison sentences. One, Ellison Mounts, was hanged. Cap Hatfield had bribed Mounts with a rifle, a saddle and $500 to confess to the killing of Alifair McCoy if he were captured. Cap assured Mounts, a retarded man, that there was no risk, and if he ever did get captured, the Hatfields would tear down the jail to get him out. When he saw that the state planned to hang him and that no Hatfields were coming to break him out, Mounts told what happened and tried to change his guilty plea, but it was too late.

The feud smoldered on for a few years, but now the raiders were bounty hunters who worked both sides of the Tug. The mountaineers, suspicious by nature, had become practically paranoid as the result of the feud. The bounty hunters weren't too successful. One, Dan Cunningham, managed to capture Bud McCoy, but as he was escorting his prisoner, McCoy pulled a revolver from under his shirt and shot a hole in Cunningham's hat. The surprised bounty hunter dropped his gun and was sent on his way with a warning: if you ever come back, you'll be dead.

Johnse Hatfield was turned in to the authorities in West Virginia ten years after the trials. The Hatfields now had no clout. The West Virginia lawmen spirited Johnse into Kentucky. The court there sentenced him to life in prison. After six years, however, he saved the warden's life and was pardoned. His brother Cap, never captured, murdered two men in West Virginia, went to prison, escaped, taught himself to read, became a deputy sheriff and then a lawyer. He died as the result of old bullet wounds. Randolph McCoy died in 1914, having outlived many younger feudists. In

1911, Devil Anse underwent religious conversion, an event the minister who baptized him never tired of relating. He died in 1921.

The same year, the ferocious Matewan coal strike occurred in the West Virginia side of the Tug Valley. Private detectives paid by the mine owner tried to evict hundreds of miners. The mayor of Matewan and its chief of police declared the evictions illegal. The company detectives shot the mayor and several bystanders, but the chief of police killed seven detectives. His name was Sid Hatfield.

Sid Hatfield was not, however, descended from Devil Anse's "family." He was adopted and had been raised by one of the numerous neutral Hatfield families.

The descendants of the feudists were on the other side. Johnse Hatfield was a coal company detective. Jim McCoy was a deputy sheriff protecting mine and railroad interests. Don Chafin, the sheriff of Logan County who declared his county off limits to all union organizers, was a cousin of Vicey Hatfield, Devil Anse's wife.

The other war was over, too. In the war between the independent farmers and the big city financiers, both the Hatfields and the McCoys had lost.

Ten

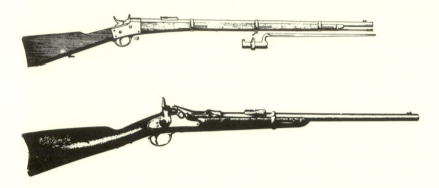

The War on Powder River

April 9, 1892, Kaycee, Wyoming

Another volley of shots ripped through the shattered window and knocked chips from the log wall on the opposite side of the cabin. Big Nate Champion finished reloading his rifle, took a pencil from his pocket and stooped down to put another entry in his pocket notebook. He scribbled right below an earlier entry that read:

> Me and Nick was getting breakfast when the attack took place. Two men was with us—Bill Jones and another man. The old man went after water and did not come back. His friend went to see what was the matter and he did not come

Top: Remington rolling block rifle. This single shot, made in a staggering variety of calibers, was sold world-wide as a military weapon and to ordinary citizens, including the defenders of Johnson County. Below: Springfield carbine, caliber .45-70, used by cavalry.

back. Nick started out and I told him to look out, that I thought there was someone at the stable and would not let them come back.

The two men—Bill Jones and the other man—were trappers who had spent the night with Champion and his partner, Nick Ray, to get out of a blizzard. Ray had just stepped through the door when a staccato blast of gunfire riddled his body. Champion ran out and dragged his partner inside as bullets splashed snow and dirt around him.

Ray and Champion were former cowboys who owned a small ranch. The cabin they were in was not theirs. It belonged to the KC Ranch (now the town of Kaycee) owned by a small rancher named Nolan. It once been a line camp for the big Frewen outfit, the Powder River Cattle Company. All cattle in Wyoming roamed the open range—land that had no private owners—and the small ranchers of northern Wyoming used each other's cabins whenever convenient.

Champion's new entry was short: "Nick is shot, but not dead yet. He is awful sick. I must go and wait on him." An hour later, he wrote: "It is now about two hours since the first shot. Nick is still alive."

Champion and Ray might have avoided trouble if they had camped anywhere but the KC Ranch. The KC had a bad reputation. At one time, it was a rendezvous spot for Kid Curry (Harvey Logan) and his Hole in the Wall Gang. Champion, considered the best shot in Johnson County, fired back at his besiegers whenever he could spot a target. That wasn't often. He wrote: "They are still shooting and are all around the house, Boys, there is bullets coming in here like hail. Them fellows is in such shape I can't get at them. They are shooting from the stable and river and back of the house."

Champion had a good idea who "them fellows" were. He had been named foreman of the independent cattlemen's roundup, run by the newly formed Northern Wyoming Farmers' and Stockgrowers' Association, which challenged the assumption of a handful of millionaires that they owned the state of Wyoming. In retaliation the Wyoming Stock Growers Association had put him on its death list.

The day wore on. Champion wrote a new entry: "Nick is dead. He died about 9 o'clock. I see a smoke down at the stable. I think they have fired it. I don't think they intend to let me get away this time."

Agents of the Stock Growers Association had tried to get Champion earlier, but he wounded two of them and the rest fled. This time, the Stock Growers had dozens of assassins, and they were persistent. Champion wrote:

Noon. There is someone at the stable yet. they are throwing a rope at the door and drawing it back. I guess it is to draw me out. I wish that duck would get out further so I could get a shot at him.

Boys, I don't know what they have done with them two fellows that staid here last night.

Boys, I feel pretty lonesome right now. I wish there was someone here with me so we could watch all sides at once. They may fool around until I get a good shot before they leave.

It's about three o'clock now. There was a man on a buckboard and one on horseback that just passed. They fired on them as they went by. I don't know whether they killed them or not. I seen lots of men come out on horses on the other side of the river and take after them."

The two men were a rancher named Jack Flagg, who was on his way to the state Democratic convention, and his 17-year-old-stepson. Flagg saw men at the KC, thought they were his constituents and rode over to greet them. They fired at him. He dashed back to the wagon, cut loose a horse, put the boy on that and both galloped to safety.

Champion continued keeping his diary:

I shot at them men in the stable just now. I don't know if I got any or not. I must go and look out again.

It doesn't look as if there is much show of my getting away. I see twelve or fifteen men. One looks like [name scratched out]. I don't know whether it is or not. I hope they did not catch them fellows who run over the bridge toward Smith's.

They are now shooting at the house. If I had a pair of glasses, I believe I could know some of those men.

They are coming out now. I've got to look out.

Well they have got through shelling the house like hail. I hear them splitting wood. I guess they are going to fire the house tonight. I think I will make a break tonight, if still alive.

The attackers took the wagon the Flaggs had left, loaded it with hay and kindling, rolled it against the cabin and set it afire. Champion wrote his last entry.

Shooting again. I think they will fire the house this time. It's not night yet. The house is now all fired. Goodbye, boys, if I never see you again.

Nathan D. Champion

Champion dashed out of the house and was cut down by four bullets. The killers found the notebook and gave it to a Chicago newspaperman they had invited to accompany them. Then the other attackers came up and fired into Champion's body. The body must have been a gory sight. The county coroner, Dr. John C. Watkins, died of a stroke when he started to examine it. He, Champion and Ray were buried the same day.

The deaths of Ray, Champion and Watkins announced the opening of the Johnson County War, sometimes called the War on Powder River, because the inhabitants referred to anything in the Powder River country as "on Powder River." The war was the fruit of a conspiracy that, in its membership, anyway, makes Aaron Burr's look like a child's daydream. Ivy-Leagued bluebloods, managing ranches for English lords and baronets, conspired with the legislature, both U.S. senators and the governor of Wyoming to defy both state and federal law and murder innocent citizens. Of course, both senators, the governor and many legislators were members of the Wyoming Stock Growers Association, as well as the Cheyenne Club and the Republican Party. There is some reason to believe that the president of the United States was a party to the conspiracy, too. He later took unusual steps to help the conspirators. And if he didn't know that something was going on in Wyoming before the war broke out, President Benjamin Harrison must have been very dull, indeed.

The object of the conspiracy was to preserve the most aristocratic society to appear in this country since the heyday of the New York patroons and the Virginia planters.

That society was the result of a boom rivaling the eighteenth century's South Sea Bubble. With the dispersal of the Indians following their last victory on the Little Bighorn, millions of acres of grazing land became available in the northern plains. A prospective rancher need pay only for housing, barns and strategically placed line camps, buy a few cows, hire a few cowboys and turn his livestock loose on the open range. Grazing was free at first; later the federal government charged a ridiculously small fee. Mother Nature would do the rest. The idea of investing in North American cattle spread across Europe like a prairie fire.

Walter, Baron von Richtofen (the Red Baron's grandfather) put it this way: "The immense profits which have been universally realized in the Western cattle business in the past, and which will be increased in the future . . . may seem incredible to many of my readers, who no doubt have considered the stories of the fortunes realized as myths. Yet it is true that many men who started only a few years ago with comparatively few cattle are now wealthy, in some cases, millionaires. . . ."

Cattle had come to the northern plains about 20 years before Baron von Richtofen published *Cattle Raising on the Plains of North America* in 1885.

But the mountain ranches in Montana that sprang from Nelson Story's cattle drive didn't have room to become big operations. When the Indians and the buffaloes were driven out of Montana and Wyoming, the big money from Europe and the East began arriving. The boom started in 1878, two years after Custer's debacle. By 1884, there were 20 huge cattle companies—half of them British—covering all of the Wyoming grazing land. Moreton and Richard Frewen, a pair of British younger sons, managed the vast Powder River Cattle Company that spread its stock all over the Powder River country. On Powder River there was also a supposed son of King Edward VII; in the Bighorn Basin was an Austrian archduke. Henry Cabot Lodge and a dozen American millionaires had interests in Wyoming ranches.

Remittance men, like the Frewens, and the Harvard-educated "young gentlemen" other companies hired to manage their ranches didn't go west to rough it. In Wyoming's capital, they established the Cheyenne Club, one of the poshest gentlemen's clubs of the Gilded Age. The Cheyenne Club was the first club in the country to have electric lights, as Cheyenne was the second city in the country to have them.

For a while, Wyoming was paradise for the young managers and for their investor bosses thousands of miles away. Summers were wet, winters were mild, and cattle multiplied on the land. Managers took to estimating the size of their herds by multiplying the number of cattle last counted by what was believed to be the rate of natural increase. They even bought and sold herds without counting them.

Then nature took a hand. The summer of 1886 was unusually dry, which meant grass was sparse, which left the cattle weak as winter approached. The winter of 1886-7 was horrendous, even by Wyoming standards. Huge quantities of snow fell, making it difficult for cattle to move, let alone dig for grass. Then a south wind melted the top layer of snow, and a north wind froze it solid. Cattle could no more get through that ice than they could have gotten through armor plate.

By spring, some herds—those moved up from the south—had decreased by 90 percent. Most ranchers lost more than half of their stock. And because ranch owners had been figuring the size of their herds by "natural increase" rather than counting them, their losses seemed even higher.

The cattle bubble had burst. Many of the European nobles and American millionaires sold out at huge losses. Many did not, though. They sent outraged telegrams to their managers demanding explanations.

The managers didn't want to say that they had miscalculated the effects of winter. Ever since the Sioux campaigns, even Europeans were aware of the kind of weather you could expect on the northwestern plains. Still less did the managers want to admit that their glowing reports of stock increase were based not on nose counts but on hasty calculations based on theoretical "natural increase." So they all sent back the same answer:

Thieves.

It was not a totally unsubstantiated answer. There were thieves—lots of them. Many small ranches got their start because of their owners' skill with a running iron -- a straight iron used to change cattle brands.

On the Great Plains, cattle brands, like the Kentucky mountaineers' earmarks, were the only way to tell one owner's livestock from another's. Once a year, the owners held a "roundup" to group cattle by brands. Unbranded calves followed their mothers and were given the appropriate brand at the roundup. One problem was the few mavericks—calves that had lost their mothers. Owners of adjoining herds were usually able to negotiate which mavericks belonged to which. Often, though, a crooked cowboy might get to the maverick first and give it his own brand.

The absentee owners, knowing little or nothing about either cattle or the country, accepted the explanation, although there was just no way thieves could have accounted for any but a tiny fraction of their losses—not even if all the growth of small ranches came from rustling rather than the vaunted "natural increase" that did so much for the big ranches.

The owners accepted the explanation, but they demanded action to thwart the thieves.

The gentlemen cattlemen in the Cheyenne Club took steps. First, they blackballed any cowboy who had a head of his own stock. In an area where 99 percent of all jobs concerned cattle, a blackballed cowboy could starve. The law forced otherwise honest men to steal enough cattle to give them at least a meagre income. Next, the WSGA got the state legislature to pass a "maverick law," making every unbranded stray calf the property of the Wyoming Stock Growers Association. After roundups, supervised exclusively by the WSGA, the Association would sell mavericks to the highest bidder. This froze out the small ranchers two ways: (1) the WSGA would not allow them to join, and (2) they couldn't afford to bid on the mavericks. As, presumably, at least some of the mavericks came from the small herds, the WSGA was depriving the little ranchers of their property without due process of law.

But the big ranches had a problem that even the maverick law couldn't help. The Homestead Act of 1861 gave every citizen the right to stake out a claim to 160 acres of federal land. If the homesteader lived on the land for seven years, it was his. The Indians were gone, and the railroads had been built. Barbed wire fences began appearing on the prairie, especially on land with stream banks and on land surrounding springs and ponds.

Ranch managers encouraged their cowboys to cut fences. But farmers who found their crops destroyed by cattle did not turn the other cheek. The homesteaders were not the meek-and-mild peasants of Hollywood westerns. Anybody who could scratch a living from the lonely Wyoming prairie was a tough cookie, one prepared for all kinds of trouble. Cattle began dying of a new cause—rifle bullets. Some cowboys, too, found themselves staring at the wrong end of a gun.

To the ranchers, people who killed cattle were the same as rustlers, and rustlers must be brought to justice. Even those who didn't kill cattle were "land rustlers," some cattlemen said. It made no difference to them that the "nesters" had legal title to the the land they used, and the cattlemen did not.

Bringing rustlers to justice was easier said than done. Rustling was hard to prove, and as the Wyoming Stock Growers Association began cracking down on small ranchers and farmers, juries were less and less inclined to convict without iron-clad evidence.

The answer was what the cattlemen called "stock detectives." The small ranchers and homesteaders called them hired murderers. The stock growers' chief detective was also the sheriff of Johnson County. His name in Wyoming was Frank Canton. In Texas, where he had once lived, it was Joe Horner. Joe Horner was an outlaw and a murderer who joined a cattle drive to Nebraska to escape the law. He became a lawman in the north and killed a number of outlaws. Reading about his career, it's difficult to escape the conclusion that Canton liked to kill people and acquired a badge so he could do it legally.

Frank Canton didn't keep his Johnson County badge long. The big ranchers on Powder River considered him "the country's leading peace officer," but during Canton's term, the big ranchers and their minions ceased to be a majority. When small ranchers and farmers began to be shot from ambush, the voters of Johnson County decided Canton had to go. They replaced him with W. E. "Red" Angus. In retaliation for this slight to their chief detective, the WSGA members spread the canard that Angus "rode with the rustlers."

It was difficult to defend ambushing unarmed citizens, even when the newspaper publishers were all on your side, so the lords, honorables and Ivy Leaguers at the Cheyenne Club tried another tack. They would have suspected rustlers lynched by "vigilantes," crowds of indignant citizens who could no longer put up with their depredations.

The first targets of the new tactics were Jim Averill and Ella Watson. They may have been lovers as had been alleged, but they had separate homesteads and were nextdoor neighbors only by the standards of nineteenth century Wyoming. Averill ran a general store and saloon and was a justice of the peace. He owned no cattle. He was, however, a populist who in April 1889 wrote to a newspaper attacking the WSGA for its high-handedness. Watson was a fat, 28-year-old prostitute who may have occasionally taken cattle in payment for her services. It is difficult, though, to see how she managed to combine her principal profession with ranching.

In July 1889, ten men pulled Averill and Watson out of their cabins and hanged them.

The Cheyenne Wits who planned the operation provided their victims with what the CIA would call "a legend."

According to the Cheyenne *Leader*, "Averill and the woman were fearless maverickers. The female was the equal of any man on the range. Of robust physique, she was a daredevil in the saddle, handy with a six-shooter and an adept with the lariat and branding iron. . . . Lately it has been rumored that the woman and Averill were engaged in a regular roundup of mavericks and would gather several hundred for shipment this fall."

In later stories, chubby Ella Watson would become Cattle Kate Maxwell, the rustler queen.

Killings continued. Most of the victims were innocent. Tom Waggoner, a homesteader known for his honesty, was hanged. After that, the Stock Growers appear to have had trouble organizing even an imitation lynch mob. Orley Jones, a young broncobuster was shot by a man hiding under a bridge as he was driving home on a buckboard. John Tisdale was killed from ambush as he was driving to his ranch with groceries and Christmas toys for his children. Frank Canton's horse was seen nearby. At least six persons were shot or hanged, but no one was ever tried for the murders. One of the two men Nate Champion wounded in the first attempt to kill him was briefly jailed, but he got out of jail somehow and later appeared across the state line.

The killings, most of them in Johnson County, aroused Johnson Countians against their former sheriff and his employers. To show the WSGA that they could not be terrorized, they announced that they were going to hold their own roundup, shortly before the WSGA roundup and that Nate Champion would be roundup foreman. That announcement would be Champion's death warrant.

The Cheyenne Club propagandists were already building a "legend" for Champion. He was "King of the Rustlers" and leader of all the outlaws. It was probably fortunate for Champion, although he was an accomplished gunman, that the lethal Kid Curry, the Hole in the Wall Gang's top gun, did not care what the swells in Cheyenne said and felt no temptation to play "king of the mountain" with Champion. Champion's gang was called the Red Sash Gang, according to the Cheyenne Wits: they wore red sashes to show that they were not ordinary rustlers. (Several pictures of Champion exist. In none does he wear a sash of any color.)

The "gentlemen" of the Cheyenne Club and the WSGA decided they'd have to do something drastic about Johnson County. They drew up a death list that was said to have 70 names on it. Included were Red Angus, the sheriff of Johnson County, all his deputies and the three county commissioners. Jack Flagg, the Democratic politician who narrowly avoided death at the K.C. Ranch was another. Flagg, like Averill, was a populist and a rabble-rouser.

The Cheyenne clubmen made no secret of their intentions. They did not want arrest the "rustlers;" they wanted to "exterminate" them. The two U.S. senators, Joseph M. Carey and Francis E. Warren, were in on the plot, so was Dr. Amos Barber, former lieutenant governor and now governor. Barber ordered the state adjutant general not to respond to any calls for help from local sheriffs—a clear violation of Wyoming law. None of the plotters had any worries. This was 1892 and everybody—at least everybody who counted—knew the "best people" were always right. The big ranchers were merely defending the country from anarchy.

The problem was how could they go about it.

Frank Wolcott had the answer. Major Frank Wolcott, a retired army officer who still wore his military puttees. Johnson County, he said, should be invaded as if it were enemy territory. The cattlemen would recruit an army of gunmen, give them all necessary supplies—guns, ammunition and explosives, of course, but also food, bedding and anything else necessary for an army on the move. As they marched into Johnson County, they would cut all telegraph wires leading to the outside world. Once in Buffalo, the county seat, they'd kill Angus, his deputies and the county commissioners. Then they could sweep through the leaderless county and dispose of all on the death list.

Wolcott may have had a hidden agenda. He managed the VR Ranch, owned by the Tolland Cattle Company, a Scottish corporation. Tolland's U.S. representative was a Scotsman named John Clay, who at the time was president of the WSGA. Wolcott owned Clay $80,000 which he was unable to repay. It has been suggested that his instigation of the war was done in return for forgiveness of his debt. Just before the hostilities commenced, Clay went to Scotland for a vacation.

Getting gunmen could pose a problem. Wyoming cowboys in general were not to be trusted, not even employees of the big ranches. So the Stock Growers sent Tom Smith, one of their detectives, to Texas, where he had once been a deputy U.S. marshal, to recruit gunfighters. Each man would get five dollars a day, and every time an enemy was killed, each man in the force would get $50, no matter who did the killing.

While Smith was recruiting old friends in Texas, the cattlemen bought extra horses, weapons, tents, bedding and other supplies, plus three heavy freight wagons.

The gunmen met in Denver, got in a special Pullman car provided by the railroad and started for Cheyenne. Almost at once, troubles began. The mercenaries were dressed for the climate in south Texas, which is very different from Wyoming's in early April. Dr. Charles Penrose, a blue-blooded Philadelphian who was riding with the cattlemen's army, noticed a Texan named Jim Dudley, "a big good-natured-looking party of 225 lbs. who arrived clad in nothing but a summer undershirt, trousers and shoes."

In Cheyenne, 19 of the 100 stockmen who put up money for the expedition joined the expedition. The Pullman was hooked up to a special train that included three stockcars, a baggage car, a flat car for the freight wagons and a caboose. The train was to arrive in Casper, the closest town of any size to Johnson County, early April 6.

The short run to Casper was not pleasant. The Texans, with Smith, were bunched in one end of the car, the stockmen in the other. The stockmen were ready to fight and die with the Texans, but not to associate with them. Wolcott was rearranging baggage in the baggage car when Canton walked in. The major ordered him out. Canton left in a huff and joined Smith and the Texans. Wolcott went to the stockmen and resigned his command, which was given to Canton, with Smith leading the Texans.

That seemed a minor problem when the train pulled into Casper and the gunmen started packing their horses for the 150-mile trip to Buffalo. The stockmen had checked, and the telegraph lines to the outside were down. All the supplies were in place, and there was nothing to do but ride to Buffalo and kill all the "rustlers."

The march didn't start for a while, though. Big Jim Dudley couldn't find a horse strong enough to carry him. Finally, an Englishman named W. B. Wallace traded mounts with the big Texan. When the column started moving, its wagons bogged down in the turf, muddy from melting snow. Then when they stopped for lunch, some members of the expedition tied their horses to sage brush. The horses merely walked away, taking the shallowly rooted brush with them. Then a wagon broke through a flimsy bridge. After the wagon got back on solid ground, a snow storm began. It took two days to reach the Tisdale Ranch where the cattlemen planned to spend their first night.

The next day, a man rode to the Tisdale Ranch and said a bunch of rustlers were holed up at the KC Ranch. He advised attacking them immediately. Canton objected that time was growing short, but he was outvoted. The cattlemen and their mercenaries set out at midnight, just as a blizzard started. It took them six hours to travel the 15 miles to the KC They surrounded the ranch and captured the two trappers when they came out. When Nick Ray came out, they shot him and besieged Nate Champion while he traded shots with them and wrote his journal.

After killing Champion, they started for Buffalo, but Jack Flagg and his son got there first. Red Angus hastily raised a posse and started south to meet the "invaders." Other citizens spread the word to more distant ranches.

At 2 a.m., the cattlemen's army stopped for refreshments at the ranch of an ally. Blissfully unaware of what was happening in Buffalo, they remounted—although Dudley had to try five horses before he found one that could carry him. They hadn't traveled far before their point men galloped back with word that there was a large body of armed men camped just ahead of them. The cattlemen and their hired guns stopped and milled around in confusion. Wolcott seized command again. He lined up the expedition and put them through close order drill. After a lot of of "hut, two, hee, haw," Wolcott led his army to the TA Ranch, a friendly outpost off the beaten track to Buffalo.

At the TA, Jim Dudley found a big gray horse that looked suitable. The horse didn't think Dudley was suitable. It bucked him off. His rifle struck the ground and fired. The bullet hit Dudley in the knee. He was was taken by wagon to Fort McKinney, where he died of gangrene several days later.

From the TA, Wolcott marched toward Buffalo, having outflanked the sheriff's posse. At dawn, a rider on a lathered horse—WSGA member James Craig—galloped among the "invaders" yelling, "Turn back, turn back! Everybody in town is aroused. Get to cover if you value your lives."

Wolcott ordered a retreat. Canton and Smith opposed him, saying the Texans had come too far to turn back now. Wolcott, although a pompous ass, was also a soldier. He knew that several hundred armed citizens could wipe out his 46-member expedition in minutes. The majority of the expedition agreed with him, and they all rode back to the TA. The Chicago newspaperman, Sam T. Clover, smelled serious trouble. He slipped away and rode to Fort McKinney to visit an old friend, Major Edmund G. Fechet with whom he had campaigned during the Ghost Dance War. With him went Nate Champion's journal.

The ranch house and barn were built of heavy logs and located in a highly defensible position. Wolcott had his troops build a small log fort as an outpost, dig a network of trenches connecting the buildings and raise dirt breastworks around the ranch house.

At dawn, the defenders of the TA saw the first of the "rustlers." About 50 men, led by Arapahoe Brown, an unsuccessful candidate for sheriff, had arrived during the night and dug fox holes. A little later, Red Angus brought his 40-man posse to join them. Groups of men, organized into companies of 20, arrived from Buffalo all through the day. If the invaders had fled back to Casper at the first warning, they might have had a chance. By the end of the day, there were more than 300 Johnson County men slavering for their blood.

In Buffalo, ministers called on the faithful to go out and defend their rights; a merchant offered free guns and ammunition to anyone going to fight the invaders; ladies prepared wagonloads of food for the men at the front.

Wolcott sent out a courier to telegraph Cheyenne, expecting that the lines his force had cut would now be repaired. They had been repaired, but Johnson County people cut them again. And again. And again. They didn't want any help to reach the cattlemen and their hired guns.

Finally, on the second day of the siege, two Buffalo officials did manage to get a telegram to the governor. They asked him for help against an illegal armed force that had invaded Johnson County. Barber stalled. He didn't want to send help against his friends in the WSGA. Late that night, he got Wolcott's message: the WSGA expedition was surrounded and might soon be annihilated. The governor sent a panicked telegram to his state's senators, who got President Harrison out of bed to tell him that Wyoming was in a state of "insurrection."

Wheels in Washington started turning, and on April 13, three troops of cavalry under Colonel J. J. Van Horn started out for the TA ranch. With the colonel at the head of the column were Sheriff Angus, Major Fechet and, of course, Sam T. Clover. No matter what they said about "insurrection" in Washington, Van Horn knew the score. He was going to arrest the invaders.

At the TA, the defenders had been losing hope, and friction had broken out between the cattlemen and their hirelings. At one point, Wolcott asked one of the cattlemen to choose eight gunfighters and relieve the men in the log outpost. The cattleman picked seven men. The eighth refused. Wolcott ordered him to move.

"It's too light," the Texan said. "I'd be killed."

"Which do you prefer, being killed going up the hill or being killed right here?" Wolcott asked. "You white-livered son-of-a-bitch, you will either do as ordered or I'll kill you myself."

The gunman went up the hill.

At dawn on the 13th, the defenders saw an enormous vehicle covered with heavy timbers and hay bales rolling toward them. They recognized the wheels—they had come from one of their supply wagons. Inside the ark was something else from their supply wagons—dynamite. The Texans and cattlemen fired with everything they had. They might as well have been using peashooters. The Johnson County men pushed steadily.

Just as the Johnson County citizens had reached dynamite-throwing range, attackers and defenders heard a bugle call. The ark stopped.

In no western movie did the U.S. cavalry arrive at a more opportune time.

Wolcott came out and saluted Van Horn. "I'll surrender to you," he said. He glanced disdainfully at Angus. "To this man, never."

Two of the Texans were wounded; one of them later died from his wounds. Van Horn took the rest of the expedition to Fort McKinney, where they were to be held pending trial in Johnson County for the murders of Nate Champion and Nick Ray. The invaders, however, had no reason to worry. They were, in the words of a newspaper correspondent "backed not only by the Republican machine from President Harrison on down to the state organization, but by at least twenty-five million dollars in invested capital. They have the President, the governor, the courts, their United States Senators, the state legislature and the army at their backs."

The courts gave them a change of venue, so the prisoners were whisked out of Fort McKinney and Johnson County to Fort Russell, near Cheyenne. They made part of the trip on a private Pullman stocked with champagne. At Fort Russell, the invaders were allowed to wander at will around Cheyenne. After 10 weeks, a judge ordered them confined in the state penitentiary, but, he assured the governor, they would not be forced to mingle with ordinary convicts. They were escorted to prison by an honor guard led by the state adjutant general.

Meanwhile, Johnson County authorities were trying to locate the only neutral witnesses to the murders—the two trappers. Soon after the arrest, a group of gunmen seized the trappers and hustled them to Omaha. The cattlemen's agents gave each trapper a postdated check for $2,500 and put them on a train going east. The trappers stayed hidden until the checks would become valid. When they tried cash them, it turned out that they were on a bank that never existed.

While Wolcott's army was being held, a judge ordered Johnson County to pay for their confinement—$100 a day per man. The county treasury soon went broke. The invaders were released, and there was no trial.

A newspaper editor who criticized these procedures was arrested for criminal libel and jailed for 30 days—long enough to silence his paper. Another editor, A.S. Mercer, was beaten. Mercer refused to be intimidated. He published a book, *The Banditti of the Plains, or The Cattlemen's Invasion of Wyoming. The Crowning Infamy of the Ages*. Mercer's shop was burned down, and a judge ordered all copies of the book seized and burned. A wagonload of the books escaped the bonfire, but copies on library shelves as far away as the Library of Congress were stolen and destroyed.

From the lack of punishment for the conspirators, the War on Powder River appeared to settle nothing.

Actually, it settled almost everything. In the election of 1892, Wyoming voters swept the Republican Party, the WSGA's political arm, out of power. The Northern Wyoming Farmers' and Stockgrowers' Association held its roundup as scheduled, and it continued to hold it annually, making the maverick law a dead letter. The WSGA's blackball died, too. A democratized WSGA admitted the small ranchers, and one of the defenders of Johnson County became its president. As one historian wrote, "The Johnson County cattle war marks the dividing line between the old West, under the rule of the big cattle kings, and the new West of the pioneer homesteader."

Frank Canton moved to Oklahoma, pinned on another badge and killed more people. He then moved to Alaska where he served two years as a deputy U.S. marshal. Near the end of his life, he wrote an autobiography that for sheer untruth rivals Wyatt Earp's biography. Canton, unlike Earp, never became a hero, though. It may be because he wrote the story himself, instead of letting writers pry it out of him. More probably, too many people knew of his activities in Wyoming. Snipers who kill unarmed people from ambush don't make good hero material.

Frank Wolcott, the dauntless enemy of rustlers, made his last appearance in official records when he was arrested for cattle rustling.

TIME

WARP

Eleven

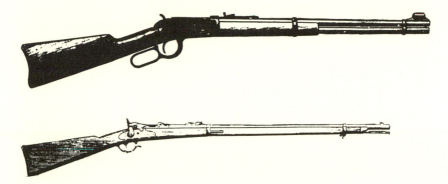

"The Most Remarkable Man-Hunt"

August 5, 1902, Davenport, Washington

A sullen column of stripe-suited convicts shuffled out of the chapel and lined up in the courtyard of the Oregon State Penitentiary near Salem. It was June 9, 1902, 16 months after a pair of outlaws called Butch Cassidy and the Sundance Kid took a boat for Argentina, 18 months before a pair of mechanics named Orville and Wilbur Wright staged the world's first manned airplane flight.

Top: Winchester Model 1894 .30-30 carbine, the gun Harry Tracy used to shoot his way across the Northwest. Below: Springfield .45-70 rifle, the weapon of the National Guardsmen who chased Tracy, as well as of the regular U.S. Army. Some militia units used it until after World War I.

After headcount, Guard Frank Girard took charge of the foundry detail and marched the convicts to their work location. There, Girard turned the detail over to guard Frank B. Ferrell while two convicts, a fair man of medium build and a saturnine man, lean to the point of emaciation, moved toward a work bench covered with newspapers.

"Ready, Dave?" the fair man whispered. The dark man nodded almost imperceptibly.

Both reached under the newspapers and came up with .30-30 Winchester carbines that had been smuggled in.

"Oh my God!" Ferrell yelled. An instant later, the fair convict fired, and Ferrell fell with a bullet through his heart. Girard dashed out of the foundry. Dave, the dark convict, fired but missed.

While the other prisoners scurried away from the shooting, the two armed convicts walked over to a 12-foot ladder. A lifer named Frank Ingram tried to get out of the way, but nervous, he stumbled into Dave. The gunman fired, and Ingram fell writhing to the floor while blood poured from his right leg.

The gunmen carried the ladder out into the courtyard, and Dave suddenly pointed to the wall.

"Harry—up there on the wall!" he yelled.

The convict called Harry dropped his end of the ladder and raised his carbine. The "clunk" of the falling ladder was drowned out by Harry's shot. One hundred fifty yards away, Guard S. R. T. Jones fell off the wall. He was dead before he hit the ground.

Harry and Dave put the ladder against the wall and calmly climbed up, while bullets from the guards' rifles knocked chips off the wall. The convicts leaped from the wall, began running and disappeared around a corner. Two guards, B. F. Tiffany and Duncan Ross, jumped off the wall and ran after them. As they rounded the corner, they almost stumbled on the crouched convicts who poked their .30-30s into the guards' bellies. Both guards dropped their own rifles. The convicts marched the two guards ahead of them while the other guards on the wall held their fire.

Then one of the guards fired a shot. Harry immediately shot Tiffany dead. Ross thought fast and threw himself flat as Dave fired. The two convicts, thinking him dead, dashed for the woods.

Harry 'Tracy, 27, and Dave Merrill, 28, were loose, and western Oregon went into an uproar. Merrill, a Washington man who had been sticking up stores and bars in Portland, was known as a bad actor. But his partner, Harry Tracy, was absolute poison.

First arrested for stealing a keg of nails in Montana, the teenage Tracy fled to Salt Lake City and became a burglar. Arrested and sent to a road gang,

Tracy escaped by braining a guard with his shovel. He made his way to the Hole in the Wall in Wyoming and joined Butch Cassidy's Wild Bunch.

Tracy became friendly with a couple of robbers named Swede Johnson and Dave Lant. One day Johnson had the bad judgment to kill a resident of the Hole in the Wall. The small ranchers in the Hole didn't mind sheltering outlaws as long as they committed their crimes elsewhere. Johnson had to leave in a hurry. Tracy and Lant went with him. Trapped barefoot in a freezing mountain pass with his two companions, Tracy killed a posseman named Valentine Hoy. The posse retreated and waited for the cold to do its work. Johnson and Lant wanted to surrender. Tracy said he'd shoot them if they tried to.

When the sun went down, and the temperature dropped far below zero, Tracy relented and allowed the other two to give up. Not until the moon was high, however, did Tracy, now almost dead, stagger out of the pass and into captivity.

As he was recovering, Tracy took up whittling. Anticipating John Dillinger, he carved a wooden gun and covered it with tinfoil, then used it to break out of jail. Recaptured, he resorted to cruder methods. As the sheriff was serving him breakfast, Tracy knocked the officer out and locked him in his own cell. Then he set out for the Northwest, where he met a small-time thug named Dave Merrill. A little later, he married Merrill's sister.

It took train robber Tracy a while to get accustomed to life in a big city. The first job he and Merrill pulled in Portland was to hold up the Second Street trolley car and take the watches and wallets of all the passengers. His brother-in-law convinced him it was more profitable to rob stationary targets, though, and Tracy and Merrill became a two-man crime wave in Portland, Seattle and Tacoma. Then Dave Merrill's brother, Ben, who had occasionally helped the pair, confessed and implicated the other two early in 1899. Portland detectives captured Merrill, but Tracy ran for it. Pursued by police, he ran to the railroad and jumped aboard a passing train, held a gun to the engineer's head and told him to make his iron horse gallop. But a conductor pulled the brake cord and Tracy got 20 years in the penitentiary.

Now Tracy was free again. This time, he was in his natural environment—the wilderness, not the confining streets of a city. And he had a rifle, not the pistol he was forced to make do with in Portland. Pistols were often handy, but outside of town they were mostly backup weapons. What Tracy didn't realize was that the wilderness had changed in the five years since he had ridden with Butch Cassidy. Cassidy knew it: that's why he left the country while Tracy was in prison.

As soon as word of the escape reached Salem, the local sheriff summoned every man who owned a gun (virtually every voter in the county) to join the posse. He didn't get that many possemen, of course, but he got at least 200, plus a company of national guardsmen. It looked as if the convicts' taste of freedom would be a short one. Certainly, no one expected that this escape would launch the wildest manhunt in the history of the now-disappearing Wild West.

The next day, the sheriff learned that Tracy and Merrill had slipped through his lines, entered Salem and robbed two posse members of their clothes, guns and buggy, then drove through the streets of Gervais, 15 miles away, waving their hats and yelling to passers-by. Shots were later exchanged, but the convicts disappeared.

One ally of the fugitives was geography. At that time, except for a couple cities of 100,000—Portland and Seattle—and the somewhat smaller Tacoma, the whole area west of the Cascades was covered by the earth's only temperate rain forest, towering trees growing out of a rank mass of four-foot ferns that limited visibility to a few feet. The second night after their escape, Tracy and Merrill were able to bed down in the timber less than 100 yards from where the posse was milling around outside Gervais. Scattered through this jungle were small towns, some no more than crossroads settlements, and tiny farms and stump-ranches. There was plenty of room to hide.

There were also plenty of people to hide from. Whenever Tracy appeared, telephone calls alerted all the authorities where he had been and where he seemed to be heading. Lawmen and militia rushed to meet him over a thickening network of railroads.

By June 11, there were three National Guard companies and hundreds of deputies surrounding the area where the outlaws were last seen. There were also bloodhounds, some imported from Washington.

"A spokesmen for the manhunters predicted that Tracy is so hemmed in he will be caught in a few hours," the June 12 issue of the *New York World* reported.

While the paper was being hawked on the sidewalks of New York, Tracy tapped on the door of a farm house near Monitor, Ore., about 40 miles from Salem and close to Portland. When Henry Aker opened the door, the convict greeted him with the words that would chill citizens the length and breadth of the Northwest for the next two months.

"I'm Tracy," he said. He added, "My friend and I would like to have breakfast with you." Tracy and Merrill entered guns first and kept the Aker family covered as they ate. A nearby mill whistle startled the fugitives before they finished their ham and eggs. They jumped up and dashed out of the cabin.

Hysteria had begun to grip the region. Portland set up special arsenals for the police. A Portland cop shot a man he described as "a desperate-looking character" but who was neither Tracy nor Merrill and who had committed no crime. Two surveyors were shot by nervous possemen. Several hunters and tramps were lucky enough to run into posse members who arrested, instead of shooting, them.

The fugitives, meanwhile, slipped through the lines again, stole a team and drove right through Portland. At the Columbia, they forced three fishermen to row them across into Washington. Before they left, they promised each man $50 for his help.

The authorities in Washington fared no better than those in Oregon. Posse members and fugitives again swapped shots near Vancouver, Washington, but the only casualty was a deputy sheriff shot by another deputy. Although they had bloodhounds, some brought in from Idaho, Indian trackers and most of the Washington National Guard, the posses chased shadows and rumors all over western Washington. When they found a place the convicts had actually been, they were always too late.

On June 30, a haggard, red-eyed man walked into an oyster camp on Puget Sound run by Horatio Alling.

"I'm Tracy," he told Alling. "I'm hungry. Fix me some breakfast." Alling noticed that Tracy was alone, but he was too frightened to ask about Merrill. He just told the cook to hop to it.

While Tracy was covering Alling, the cook and a third man in the camp, two more oystermen entered. Tracy asked if they had a boat. They said they did, and the captain was getting ready to shove off.

"Bring him here." Tracy ordered.

The fishermen returned with Captain A. J. Clark and his son.

"Pleased to meet you, Captain," Tracy said. "How far can that boat of yours travel?"

"This is one of the latest type gasoline launches. It can travel 1,000 miles without refueling."

"That's good, because you're going to take me to Seattle."

The captain said it took four men to handle the boat. Tracy chose him, his son and the two men who had recently arrived, Frank Scott and John Munro. He tied up the others and left.

Once off shore, Tracy seemed to relax. Somebody asked him about Merrill.

"That two-faced rat! I saw a newspaper story at one of the farms we stayed at that said Merrill had tipped off the cops when we were in Portland. [The paper's information was garbled, it was Ben Merrill, Dave's brother, who had informed on him.] He denied it, and we agreed to fight a duel. We started back-to-back, and we were going to take ten paces, turn and fire. I knew he was going to turn around at the ninth step, so at the eighth, I put the rifle over my shoulder and fired. That didn't do the trick, so I gave him two more shots."

Tracy seemed to be in a good mood, he told jokes and entertained the oystermen with tales of his experiences. Once, as they passed the federal prison on McNeill's Island, Tracy asked Clark to pull in close to the island.

"For God's sake, why?" the captain asked.

"I want to knock a few of those damned guards off the wall."

"Harry, if you do that, they'll fire back. We've done everything you've asked. Don't make us endanger ourselves."

Tracy reluctantly agreed to give up his guard-shooting project.

When the boat landed a little north of Seattle, Tracy shook hands with all the oystermen and promised to send them money as soon as he had a stake. He then tied them up and took one of the crew, Frank Scott, with him to make sure nobody gave the alarm for a while.

As they walked down the railroad line towards Seattle, Scott said, "Look Harry, I'm a poor fellow working for wages, and the wages at these damned oyster fisheries aren't high. If you tell me where you left Merrill, I could find his body and claim the reward."

"They'll only beat you out of it, Frank, but I'll tell you anyway. You can find the body under a couple of big logs near the Northern Pacific line north of Chehallis."

When he got back to the oyster camp, Scott quit to look for Merrill's body. Finding even a full-size body in the rain forest wasn't easy, though. Weeks went by before a woman picking blackberries found the decomposed remains of Dave Merrill.

Word that Tracy was in the Seattle area quickly reached Sheriff Edward Cudihee of King County, who deputized everyone he could find and scattered small parties of possemen all through the woods north of Seattle. One such group near Bothell saw a suspicious-looking cabin. The posse included two newspaper reporters, Karl Anderson and Louis B. Sefrit of Seattle, as well as Deputy Sheriffs John Williams, L. J. Nelson and Charles Raymond.

"This is our place," Raymond said when he saw the cabin. The posse members crept into the woods. Raymond touched Sefrit on the arm and pointed to an enormous stump they could just make out through the pouring rain.

"That's exactly where I believe he is," the deputy whispered. "Let's . . ."

He never finished.

Tracy, rifle at his shoulder, bobbed up behind the stump and fired. Anderson dropped as a bullet grazed his skull, but the cold puddle he fell into revived him. Raymond took two bullets through the chest. Tracy fired at a movement in the brush, and Williams lurched into the clearing, his shirt dripping blood. He fell next to the dead Raymond, seriously, but not fatally wounded. Tracy dashed into the woods and made what the *Portland Oregonian* called "a tremendous leap down a declivity."

Out on the road, Tracy hailed a passing buggy and told the driver, Louis Johnson, that he was a posseman going into town. When they passed a big house in the Seattle suburb of Fremont, Tracy had Johnson stop the buggy and come to the door with him.

When Mrs. R. H. Van Horn answered the door, the outlaw told her and the astonished Johnson, "I'm Tracy."

With the muzzle of his carbine, he directed both Johnson and Mrs. Van Horn into the house.

"I'd like some food," he told the woman. "Be quiet, and no harm will come to you."

A roomer named Butterfield came downstairs, and Tracy took his dry clothes.

"I haven't enjoyed a meal so much in three years," Tracy said when he'd finished dinner. "I don't want to tie you up," he told the hostess. "Will you promise you won't say anything about me being here?"

"I will for tonight. But not for tomorrow morning."

There was a knock on the door. Mrs. Van Horn got up while Tracy covered Johnson and Butterfield.

"Not a word," he cautioned.

It was the butcher's delivery boy. Mrs. Van Horn mouthed the word "Tracy" as she took her delivery. The boy understood. He whipped his team into town to spread the alarm.

Sheriff Cudihee grabbed Portland policeman E. E. Breece, Deputy Game Warden Neil Rawley and posseman J. L. Knight and dashed for Fremont.

Cudihee took up a position where he could cover the buggy; the other three formed a semi-circle across the street.

As Tracy passed him, Breece jumped out and yelled, "I know you, Tracy. Drop that gun!"

Tracy whirled and fired twice, killing Breece instantly. Firing became general. Rawley fell, fatally wounded by Knight's revolver. Cudihee fired twice and missed. Tracy disappeared into the woods.

Two days later, Tracy appeared on the shores of Puget Sound and forced a Japanese fisherman to row him across. On the other side, he walked into a farm house owned by a Swedish immigrant named John Johnson.

"I'm Tracy," he announced. "Do as I say and you'll be all right. You're very lucky. At first, I planned to kill you all and stay here a couple of days, but when I saw your pretty little girl, I decided to spare you."

Mrs. Johnson set a place at the table for him.

"That's not right," Tracy said. "When I eat, I want everybody to eat, just like I was your guest."

About 8 p.m., Tracy had Mrs. Johnson prepare some food for him to eat on the road. He helped himself to Johnson's clothes. Then he made the Johnsons' hired man, John Anderson, row him back across the sound.

Word of Tracy's excursion across Puget Sound got back to Seattle. Cudihee chartered an electric launch and a sea-going tug to carry his posse. The sheriffs of Jefferson and Clackamas counties chartered two more tugs. Two Coast Guard cutters joined the search, as well as hundreds of volunteer riflemen in privately-owned boats. This small navy sailed up and down Puget Sound and never saw two men in a small white skiff.

Tracy kept Anderson to carry his supplies. The two men hid in a ravine all day after landing on the eastern shore of the sound. Then they started walking east along the railroad tracks.

While they were resting in some bushes, they heard voices. Tracy investigated and saw two young women, a little girl and a teenage boy picking salmon berries. He stepped out in front of the boy.

"Hey, wait a minute, my boy," he said. "I guess you've heard of me."

"Why certainly, you're Tracy," 26-year-old Ada McKinney said with a laugh.

"No, I don't know who you are," 18-year-old May Baker said with a chill in her voice.

"Well, I am Tracy," the outlaw said and made a small motion with his carbine.

Both women gasped. After a short silence, Mrs. McKinney said, "Well, Mr. Tracy, I'm glad to meet you." But she stepped in front of her six-year-old daughter, also named Ada.

"I never would have known you. You're much better looking than your picture," Miss Baker said.

"Ah, now you're jollying me. But don't be afraid. I've never harmed a woman in my life." The murderer smiled and doffed his hat.

The women told him they were visiting their aunt, Mrs. Charles Gerrells, who lived a short distance down the tracks. He told 13-year-old Charlie Gerrells to run ahead and tell his mother she had a couple of guests for dinner.

"Tell her I bring no harm to her or hers," he said dramatically.

When they got to the house, little Ada began to cry. "Now, now, little girl, don't be afraid," Tracy said. "Nobody will hurt you. I won't let them." He gave Charlie Gerrells two watches to pawn and asked him to buy two revolvers and a box of cartridges.

When he got to Renton, the nearest town, Charlie Gerrells told everyone he met that Tracy was at his house. The local sheriff sent four deputies to get the train he had arranged to have ready to take deputies anywhere they were needed. The train was full of passengers, however, and the conductor wouldn't let the lawmen have it. After arguing half an hour, they got an engine and a caboose. Then the sheriff, who had also telephoned Sheriff Cudihee in Seattle, was late. The four deputies took the caboose themselves and positioned themselves north and south of the house. An hour and a quarter later, their boss arrived with a posse. Still later, Cudihee appeared with another posse.

Tracy was getting water in the back yard when Cudihee's train went by. He knew the law had arrived. Completely unflustered, he went back in the house, put a record on the phonograph and asked May Baker to dance.

"I wish I were home," Miss Baker said.

"I'd be happy to walk you home."

She didn't get a chance to answer, because somebody knocked on the door. Tracy grabbed his carbine, and Mrs. Gerrells answered the door. It was two idlers from Renton who thought it would be quite a joke to go the the house and ask for Tracy. Mrs. Gerrells told them the outlaw certainly wasn't in her house, and the two men left, blissfully unaware of how close they had come to death.

The arrival of the two men showed Tracy that the lawmen had not completely surrounded the house. If they had, the two wiseacres would never have reached the front door. He saw more posse members creeping through the underbrush. Little Ada McKinney saw them, too, and began to cry. She ran to Tracy.

"Now, now, little girl. I wouldn't let anyone harm an innocent little thing like you," the killer said. He turned to Mrs. McKinney and Miss Baker. "I hate to have ladies see me in these unpressed pants," he said, "I'm going to get a new pair from a deputy." He stepped out of the back door and waved goodbye.

As Tracy was leaving by the back door, Cudihee, in front, gave his posse orders to advance. The other posse wanted to get into the act, so they moved up, too. Tracy, hidden in dense brush, saw a gap in their line and went through it it.

Cudihee put bloodhounds on the trail. They hit a dead end at a river, picked it up on the other side and lost it again. The dogs recrossed the river. Possemen could tell from their baying that the quarry was near. Suddenly, the baying changed to howls of pain. They had hit the red pepper Tracy put on his tracks. By the time the hounds were able to smell again, Tracy was long gone.

Gone, but not forgotten. The *Portland Oregonian* reported, "The Tracy whom May Baker, an 18-year-old girl of Seattle, will always remember is a gallant, tender-hearted man with a prodigious love of little children, a conversationalist of brillancy, a merry-hearted josher, a man with a decided respect for womanhood, but above all, a man with an iron nerve."

Tracy doubled and redoubled on his trail, robbed farmers and ranchers. Pursuers were everywhere. There was no way to ditch them. But no one could pin him down. Cudihee, still on the trail, though often far out of his jurisdiction, surrounded a couple of suspected hiding places, but found nobody. At one town, Tracy called the sheriff on the telephone.

"Hello, Sheriff, I just wanted to cheer you up. Even if you haven't caught Tracy, you've come closer to him than the others. You're the only one who's talked to him."

Tracy engaged in two more shootouts, leaving several wounded deputies. In the last fight, he was hit in the hip with a double 0 (.34 caliber) buckshot, but limped on. As pursuit intensified, another Tracy began to emerge—one quite different from the merry outlaw.

Tracy stopped at an isolated cabin owned by a couple named Johnson, which seems to have been the most common name in Washington. Tracy sent E. M. Johnson to Tacoma to borrow money and buy a couple of revolvers. But he didn't kid around. When deputies found them, both Johnson and his wife, who stayed with Tracy as a hostage, were suffering from what the newspapers called "nervous prostration."

Tracy worked his way east over the almost unexplored Cascades. He came down to the dry, sunny plains of eastern Washington. It was country— unlike the spooky rain forest and the desolate mountains—to cheer the heart of the former Wyoming long rider.

On July 31, he stopped at the ranch of W. A. Sanders and S. J. McEldowney near Wenatchee, six miles from the Columbia River. He helped himself to a couple of horses and told McEldowney to go with him to the ferry. Mrs. McEldowney began to cry.

"Damn it, man, your wife will cry all night, won't she?" Tracy asked. "You stay here. I'll go alone."

Three days later, Tracy showed up at the Eddy ranch, near Davenport, a semi-arid area about 70 miles from Idaho.

"I'm Tracy," he told Louis Eddy. "I don't want to hurt you or rob you. I just want to swap horses."

After looking at the Eddy horses, the outlaw said he'd stay at the ranch for a while until his own horses got some rest. On the way to the ranch, he had met a youth named George Goldfinch and taken him along to point out the way to the ranch. The next night, he let Goldfinch go, but told him he'd kill the Eddy brothers if he told anyone that Tracy was there.

It took Goldfinch a day to make up his mind. Then, on August 5, he sent a wire to Sheriff Gardiner of Lincoln County. A railroad man named Joe Morrison overheard Goldfinch dictating his message. Morrison got four friends, Deputy Sheriff C. A. Straub, Dr. E. C. Lanter, Maurice Smith and Frank Hillengren. They rode out to the Eddy place and spoke to Lou Eddy. He told them Tracy was there, but "he'd kill me and my brother if he knew I told you. He looks unarmed, but he has a revolver hidden under his shirt."

The vigilantes saw Tracy helping Eddy's brother fix a barn door. Smith and Lanter headed for the barn; the other three moved to block a possible retreat.

Tracy spotted them and dashed into the barn. He came out with his hat and rifle. He sprinted for a wheat field and ran about 600 yards while the vigilantes churned off shot after shot. Tracy fired back, but the sun was in his face, and he didn't hit anyone. He ducked behind a rock outcropping at the edge of a wheat field and fired again. The vigilantes took cover.

After a few minutes, the manhunters noticed a small dust cloud moving through the wheat and up a hill. They started firing at the dust. The cloud reached the top of the hill and stopped. There was one shot from behind the crest of the hill. The vigilantes surrounded the field and waited.

After several hours of waiting, Sheriff Gardiner arrived with a posse. A little later, dogged Ed Cudihee arrived with his posse. It wasn't until the next day any of the posse members dared to enter the wheat field.

By then, Tracy had been dead 12 hours.

When Tracy had reached the rock outcropping, a bullet hit him in the thigh. He'd rammed a handkerchief into the wound and started crawling. A second bullet had cut an artery and broken a bone in his lower leg. With blood spurting from the wound, the outlaw had crawled another 75 yards.

He'd realized he was losing consciousness rapidly. If he passed out, they might take him back to prison. Too weak to raise his arms, he'd taken his revolver in his left hand, rolled to his left side and blown his brains out.

The *Portland Oregonian* called his death "intensely tragic." The *New York Times* summary of his career approached the fulsome:

"The death of Harry Tracy by his own hand ends perhaps the most remarkable man-hunt in the annals of crime. Since June 9 last, Tracy, hunted by Indian trackers, bloodhounds, hundreds of officers of the law, the state troops of Washington, and unnumbered volunteer bands of vigilantes, with a price on his head that amounted to a fortune, traveled over 1500 miles of wild country and defied capture to the last.. . . . he killed six officers of the law, slew his fellow fugitive, David Merrill, in a duel fought while men and hounds were on his heels, wounded nearly a dozen other officers of pursuing parties, and terrorized the people of two states.. . . The criminal exploits of Frank and Jesse James, the Youngers, Murel and all the desperate outlaws of the West, pale beside the determined and daring courage of the Oregon convict."

Souvenir hunters stripped Tracy's body. A dozen women claimed to be his wife. A reasonably good five-cent cigar and a cocktail were named after him. At least three stock companies put on plays based on his life.

Tracy was, of course, a spectacular outlaw. In two months he had killed more men in gunfights than Billy the Kid had killed in the entire Lincoln County War. His devil-may-care attitude and sense of humor were never seen in Jesse James or his surly Missouri bank-robbers. And no Western character ever surpassed him for sheer toughness.

But both Billy the Kid and Jesse James had died two decades before Tracy. The new century brought more than the airplane. There was a network of interurban railroads, and telephones were widely available. In the relatively densely populated Pacific Coast of Oregon and Washington, these posed problems Billy the Kid or even Butch Cassidy never had to cope with. Lawmen could outrun any horseman by train, and they could convey instant, detailed information to other lawmen. Anywhere Tracy went, he found a posse waiting.

Tracy, like the Indian tribes a generation before, was technologically outclassed. Traveling on foot or on horseback, he couldn't get away from lawmen who had access to trains and rapid communications. He was an anachronism. But he was also a generation too early. People who remembered accounts of the great manhunt for Tracy would later read similarly breathless stories of hunts for other desperate characters who, driving the fastest automobiles available, were often able to outrun the law or evade roadblocks because there were too many roads to block.

So numerous were those chases in the 1930s that most people forgot for a time the man who had chilled the northwest with his simple introduction:

"I'm Tracy."

Twelve

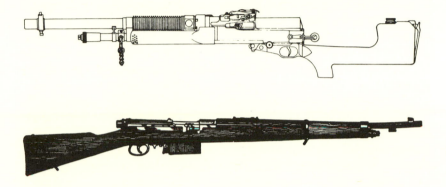

Viva Villa!

March 9, 1916, Columbus, New Mexico

"I was awakened about 4 a.m. by the sound of shots," recalled Buck Chadborn, a rancher, cattle inspector and deputy sheriff in Columbus, New Mexico. "Jack Thomas, another deputy sheriff, was working for me on my ranch and staying at the house. We both jumped up, grabbing our clothes and our guns. At first we thought the commotion was just some cowboys celebrating."

First Lieutenant John B. Lucas had returned from Fort Bliss, outside El Paso, where he had been playing polo with other cavalry officers. He had just

Top: Benét-Mercié machine rifle, caliber .30-06, used against Villa's raiders at Columbus, New Mexico. Below: Mondragón semi-automatic rifle, caliber 7 mm., used to assassinate Villa at Parral, Chihuahua, Mexico. The Mondragón was the first semi-auto rifle used in war.

made sure his .45 was loaded and had taken off his boots when he heard firing.

Colonel Herbert J. Slocum, commander of Camp Furlong, slept soundly. Two days before, he had heard two Mexican cowboys, Juan Favela and Antonio Muñoz, tell how a large band of armed men had captured an American cowboy they were working with and had chased them over the border. To Slocum, this was just one more story about the whereabouts of Pancho Villa, a bandit-turned-revolutionary who inspired more newspaper stories than all the other leaders in Mexico's six-year-old civil war. Villa, after all, was Mexico's problem. And if he crossed the border, Villa would have problems of his own. Most of the regular U.S. Army was strung out along the Mexican border because of occasional raids by guerrillas of one faction or another.

While Slocum slept, shadowy figures in big sombreros approached the wire fence along the border as soon as the moon was down. They cut the wire and walked silently, the vanguard dismounted, up a drainage ditch leading to town. About a mile from Columbus, the 500 Mexicans divided into two columns, one aimed at Camp Furlong and the other at Columbus, a tiny garrison town housing about 300 civilians. There was no electricity in Columbus, and no street lights of any kind. All of the kerosene lamps in the houses had been blown out hours before. The Mexicans didn't hesitate. They seemed to know exactly where they were going.

Private Fred Griffin of K Troop, 13th Cavalry, who was on guard duty, heard footsteps in the darkness. He faced the noise, and brought his Springfield to port arms.

"Halt! Who's there?" he challenged.

The answer was a rifle shot that hit him in the stomach.

Griffin leveled his rifle and fired, again and again, operating his bolt action weapon with a speed born of long training. Then he sank to the ground and died. When the sun came up later in the day, three dead Mexicans were found near Griffin's body.

Lieutenant James P. Castleman, the officer of the day, dashed out of the guard shack when he heard the shots. He ran right into one of the Mexican raiders but shot him down with his .45 automatic. He kept going and met some men from F Troop, out of uniform, but carrying rifles and ammunition. Castleman guessed that the raiders would head for the bank. He led his men toward the center of town. They were fired on by, and drove off, Mexican troops five times in 500 yards. One man, Private Thomas Butler, was hit four times, but kept up with his comrades until he received a fifth wound, a mortal one.

Castleman's troops got to the bank before the raiders. They took up prone positions and fired down Main Street at the flashes of the Mexicans' guns.

Meanwhile, Lucas had grabbed his pistol and dashed barefoot toward his command, Machine-Gun Troop. The machineguns were locked in the guard shack, so Lucas led the troop there. The lieutenant and two men set up one of the machineguns and aimed at a group of Mexicans. The gun jammed. Lucas ran back to the guard shack and got another gun. Lucas loaded the gun, and Corporal Michael Barmazel fired. Barmazel aimed low and sprayed bullets toward the flashes of Mexican rifles. As fast as Barmazel emptied one clip, Lucas slipped in another. The rest of Machine-Gun Troop joined them with the two remaining guns.

The machinegun of the 13th Cavalry was called the Benét-Mercié Machine Rifle in the U.S. Army. (The British called the same weapon the Hotchkiss Light Machinegun Mark I, and the French called it the Model 1908.) It was designed by an American, Laurence Benét and a Frenchman, Henri Mercié, at the French Hotchkiss plant, which had been founded by another American, Benjamin Hotchkiss. It weighed only 27 pounds, making it the one of the earliest light machineguns. Instead of a belt, its cartridges were held on a steel strip, or clip, containing 9, 14 or 30 rounds. Like many early designs, the Ben-A, as the soldiers called it, was a bit tricky, especially if you had to clear a jam at night.

After the fight, there were reports that the machineguns were useless because they had jammed. Actually, Lucas' troopers got three of their four guns firing immediately and cleared the jam in the fourth within minutes. All through the attack, there were at least two guns in action all the time, each churning out bullets at the rate of about 10 a second. Altogether, the machineguns fired 20,000 rounds. To Lucas, it seemed that he and his handful of gunners were holding off thousands of Mexicans.

The raiders reached the town's only hotel. One guest, Walton Walker, was pulled away from his wife and shot on the stairs. The Villistas took took two other men, Dr. H. M. Hart and Charles Miller, into the street, robbed them and killed them. Steven Burchfield, hearing the commotion, opened his door and told the raiders in fluent Spanish he would give them all the money he had. He pulled bills and coins from his pockets and threw them into the hall. While the invaders were scrambling for the loot, Burchfield ran into his room and went down the fire escape.

Outside, the Mexicans roamed the streets, firing at any window that showed a light.

The Villista column that attacked Camp Furlong had tough going from the start. Their primary target was the stables, but the cavalrymen were awake and armed when they got there. These regulars were not like Custer's, unfamiliar with their weapons because the government didn't "waste" money on practice ammunition. They were products of intensive training with the relatively new Springfield Model 1903, caliber .30-06. Not only that, they were the army's elite. In the recent fighting in the Philippines, cavalrymen, though they seldom fought mounted and traveled almost as much in boats as on horseback, were the equivalent of World War II's paratroopers—highly mobile shock troops. The raiders scared some horses, but they never reached the stables.

The Villistas tried to hide from the troopers' fire behind the thick-walled adobe cook shacks. The cooks and KPs, though, had been up and working before the Mexicans crossed the border. In each cook shack were Winchester Model 97 12 gauge pump shotguns. The cooks used them to supplement army rations with wild game. Now they used them on the Villistas. At the range they were used—a few feet—their birdshot loads were as deadly as buckshot. A group of raiders broke down the door of one cook shack, but the first cook threw a pot of scalding coffee in their faces, and a KP killed the blinded men with a wood-chopping hatchet.

Lucas noticed the action around the cook shacks and turned one of his guns on them. The shacks were bullet-proof, but the Ben-A mowed down the Mexicans outside.

Buck Chadborn and Jack Taylor had hidden their wives and children in a cyclone cellar and ridden into town.

"By the time we got into town, there were several buildings burning," Chadborn recalled. "In the light from the fire, we could see a milling mob of Mexicans wearing the big sombreros and crossed gun belts of Pancho Villa's followers. There were bands of them, shooting and yelling 'Viva Villa!' and 'Viva Mexico!' The Commercial Hotel was blazing. I remember a couple of Customs men, Jolly Garner, the nephew of John Nance Garner, and Ben Aguirre, saving a woman from the second floor of the hotel. They got her out and down to the ground by lowering her with sheets tied together. The hotel burned clear to the ground.

"The raiders were plundering and looting the burning stores of every-thing they could carry out. Many of them were just kids. I remember one dead boy about fourteen holding a pair of women's black patent slippers. Another dead boy had his hands full of candy."

Chadborn, Taylor and another friend of Chadborn's, Dick Rodriguez, began organizing citizens to fight the raiders.

The Mexicans were suffering heavy casualties, particularly from the machinegun fire. Machine-Gun Troop, though, was also taking casualties. Corporal Barmazel was hit in the jaw and splashed blood all over his gun, but he bound up the wound with a handkerchief and went on firing. Sergeant Mark Dobbs was hit in the liver early in the action but continued to fire. He was still firing when he died.

As dawn broke, Chadborn said, it suddenly became quiet. The Mexicans began pulling out. He, Taylor, Rodriguez and a few other civilians followed them, firing as they went.

Major Frank Tomkins ran to Colonel Slocum and asked permission to pursue the retreating raiders.

"Mount up a troop and take the offensive," Slocum said. Tomkins mounted H Troop.

On the way, Tomkins noticed a movement in the brush and went over to investigate. It was a woman, Mrs. J. J. Moore, who had been shot in the leg. She said the Villistas broke into her house during their retreat, killed her husband, ripped a ring from her finger and shot her.

Lieutenant Castleman, the OD, arrived with F Troop and joined Tomkins in the chase. The Mexicans crossed the border and posted a rear guard on a ridge. Tomkins ordered a mounted pistol charge, and the Villistas jumped on their horses and fled. The American troopers dismounted and opened fire with Springfields, killing 32 Villistas.

The troops and armed civilians continued the chase at least 15 miles into Mexico. Along the way, they passed bodies, dead and wounded horses and equipment—including two machineguns—left behind by the Villistas. After they turned back, the troopers counted nearly 100 Villista bodies on the way to town. Altogether, almost 200 of the 500 raiders had been killed. In Columbus, 17 Americans, including nine civilians, had been killed.

Tactically, Villa's raid had been a fiasco for the famous guerrilla leader. But that's how things had been going for him lately.

He could always remind himself that things had once been much, much worse.

General Villa had been born plain Doroteo Arango to peons on a large ranch in Durango, the state just south of the border state of Chihuahua. He was born under the *Porfiriato*, the reign of Porfirio Díaz, who ruled Mexico for three decades as if it were his personal property.

Benito Juárez, who defeated Maximilian, had died early in his fourth term. He was succeeded by the chief justice, Sebastián Lerdo de Tejada, who scheduled a new election. Lerdo was a candidate; so was Díaz, who had distinguished himself fighting the French. Lerdo won the election, but made enemies during his term. When he announced that he would run for reelection, Díaz revolted, overthrew him and took his place. Díaz, who through the Juárez and Lerdo administrations denounced reelection of presidents and governors as undemocratic, refused to run for another term. His successor, Manuel Gonzales, served one term that convinced Díaz that the country needed him. He ran for president and won. After that, he not only changed his views on reelection, he arranged things so that he and the governors he favored never had to worry about losing a bid for reelection.

Under Díaz, Mexico turned into a modern state. Crumbling and abandoned mines were made productive again. Agriculture was mechanized. Harbors were dredged, and railroads criss-crossed the country. For the first time that anyone could remember, Mexico's treasury had a surplus and the country exported more than it imported. Capital from the United States and Europe poured into Mexico. Theodore Roosevelt called Porfirio Díaz "the greatest statesman now living." Count Leo Tolstoy called him "a prodigy of nature." Andrew Carnegie said Díaz "should be held up to the hero worship of mankind."

But while Mexico became richer, most of her people became poorer. They went from primitive conditions to abject misery. It was not that Don Porfirio neglected them. He aided and abetted the process. Díaz and his advisers saw that Mexico needed capital. To get it, he extended special favors to foreign investors and rich Mexicans.

Anita Brenner, an American who lived in Mexico during the Porfiriato, said, "Justice was carried out according to an unwritten, unbreakable law which required that a case be settled in rigid observance of who the attorney was, who the client. Cases involving a foreigner against a Mexican were decided according to the principle that the foreigner must be right, unless word came from Don Porfirio, exceptionally, to discover otherwise. In the remotest places judges understood the fine points of these usages, and could interpret skillfully the precept taught by the U.S. State Department that Americans were guests and must be spared the judicial annoyances unavoidable to Mexicans; that every American working and living in Mexico, from plant manager to gang foreman and oil driller, and every company that had American money in it—even if it were only one red cent, said the Embassy— had the same kind of extraterritorial immunity."

In 1883, Díaz enacted a law to encourage foreign colonization of rural Mexico. It authorized land companies to survey public lands. For this service, they would receive one third of the lands surveyed and would be allowed to purchase the rest at cut-rate prices. The law defined public land as any land to which no one had a legal title. Most of the land in Mexico was occupied by people whose ancestors had been farming it centuries before Cortés arrived.

Hardly any of the owners could produce a document proving the land was theirs. Every Indian village had an *ejido*, a tract of land held in common by the villagers. No documents covered ejidos, either.

By the beginning of the twentieth century, 134 million acres of the best land in Mexico had passed to a few hundred fabulously rich landowners, both foreign and Mexican. More than half of all rural Mexicans were peons on the *haciendas* of those landowners. In Chihuahua, bordering Texas, the extended Terrazas-Creel family owned almost the entire state. Not only land, but mines, factories, granaries, railroads, telephone companies, sugar mills and meat packing plants. Don Luis Terrazas owned eight times as much land as the King Ranch. His son-in-law, Don Enrique Creel, served several terms as Chihuahua's governor and was Mexico's secretary of foreign relations.

On the estates owned by the Terrazas-Creel family and the families of the other hacendados were literally millions of peons, like the parents of the boy who became Pancho Villa. A peon was not like an American tenant farmer. He was more like a medieval serf, except that a serf had some rights. A peon was bound to the land, like a serf, but, unlike the serf, he could be evicted at the pleasure of the landlord. He worked all day, sometimes seven days a week, on the landlord's crops. Sometimes he couldn't tend his own until the sun set. He had to buy all necessities at the hacienda store at inflated prices, then was taxed for the privilege of trading at the store. He went deeper and deeper into debt, of course, and had to pay that debt through free labor for the hacendado. A peon who tried to leave the hacienda was considered a thief, someone who tried to steal from the landlord, and could be arrested and punished by the law as well as the landlord. The hacendados had almost as much control over their peons as U.S. planters once had over their slaves. And that control led to the same sorts of abuses.

Young Doroteo Arango, born into his father's debt, was a peon and a *vaquero*, or cowboy. One time, Doroteo left the hacienda and was punished with a flogging that left scars on his back for the rest of his life. He learned to ride a horse and to shoot. In the wilds of Durango, with jaguars, cougars, wolves and coyotes threatening the cattle, a rifle was a necessity of life. Even peons had them. One day, the son of the hacendado raped Doroteo's sister, and the boy found a new kind of target for his rifle.

They had flogged him for leaving the ranch; 16-year-old Doroteo couldn't even imagine what they might do to him for killing the crown prince. He fled to the mountains and made his way to Chihuahua, living on wild game as he traveled. Across the state line, he managed to get a few odd jobs, using a new name, Francisco Villa—the name of a bandit locally famous in Durango.

In southern Chihuahua, the new Francisco Villa fell in with some modern bandits, the gang of Ignacio Parra. The attraction was mutual. Villa learned that the bandits were people like himself, poor *mestizos* (of mixed Indian and white ancestry) who had been oppressed by the hacendados. Moreover, he learned that they were doing what he always yearned to do: they were paying back the rich by stealing their cattle and their money. On their part, Parra and his men saw a tough teenager, already a killer and a fugitive, who hated the rich and who would make a great bandit.

He proved to be even better than expected. Young Francisco, now universally called Pancho (Frank), was the first man into every dangerous situation. Among people who adore macho, he was the most macho in the gang. So when Parra was killed in a stage hold-up, Villa took over leadership of the band.

Don Pancho became the kind of bandit who inspires ballad singers. He may have been the greatest cattle rustler in history. He certainly gave more free meat to to the peons than any man in history. He hated hacendados and priests, whom he considered hypocrites and con men, and any native of Spain. He considered Spaniards representatives of a nation of thieves and thought they wanted to put Mexico back into a colonial yoke. His one political ideal at this time was the formation of national butcher shops, which would sell meat to the starving peasants at nominal prices.

He actually put this idea into practice. He became a butcher in Chihuahua City and sold his meat at prices determined by the customer's ability to pay. No matter how little he charged. he made a profit: the meat came from cattle stolen from the big haciendas. The advantage to Villa was that the butcher shop gave him a respectable front, let him live in town and gave him access to community leaders.

One of these leaders, Abrán González, told Villa about a hacendado who had turned against his own kind. He had risen against the almighty Don Porfirio, who had slaughtered strikers, peons and protesters without number in the last few years. This hacendado, Francisco Madero, was trying to raise an army to drive Porfirio Díaz out of power.

Villa volunteered to help Madero. He joined the revolutionary army as a captain; two years later, he was a colonel—of cavalry, of course. Villa, with his keg-like body, short legs and long arms, looked like that other great horse soldier, Phil Sheridan. Like Sheridan, he appeared awkward on his feet but turned into a centaur on a horse.

With several revolutionary armies closing in on him, Díaz embarked for Europe and Madero became president. Still in the army, Villa and a general named Victoriano Huerta had a dispute over a horse. Huerta condemned

Villa to death. He was standing in front of a firing squad, looking at an open grave, when Francisco Madero's brother, Raúl, rushed up with a reprieve from the president. Villa was sent to prison, but he escaped six months later after having learned to read and write. He fled to the United States and lived for a while in El Paso.

Meanwhile, there was another revolt. Huerta arrested both Madero brothers and had them tortured and murdered. Then he made himself president. Huerta has been called a reactionary, but he actually did more to help the people than Madero, who fought for political, rather than economic, reform. Huerta's good intentions, though, were far outweighed by his methods. He based his rule on firing squads, assassination and torture.

Villa was outraged at the murder of the men who had saved his life. He got together eight friends, bought some guns and ammunition and rode across the border early in 1913. They rode through the first town they came to shouting "Viva Villa!" and about every man with a horse and rifle flocked around the legendary bandit chief. The famous brigand, a symbol of the old Mexico, had become to the people in villages the harbinger of Mexico's democratic future.

Villa sent men all through Chihuahua recruiting. Through villages, farms and ranches Villistas rode, chanting a song translated as:

> Compañeros of the plow,
> Starving, tired and dirty,
> There's but one road to follow now,
> So grab your thirty-thirty!

And they did. The Winchester Model 1894 carbine (Harry Tracy's favorite rifle) in .30-30 caliber was practically Everyman's weapon in the western United States and northern Mexico. If they didn't have .30-30s, the men of Chihuahua took whatever they could find that would shoot. Within 30 days, Villa had 3,000 cavalrymen with rifles, revolvers and machetes that they used in place of sabers.

Villa seemed to be everywhere in Chihuahua state. Moving behind a far-flung screen of cavalry, his columns marched north, south, east and west singing the plaintive *Adelita* or the sardonic *La Cucuracha*. Finally, only three Chihuahuan cities remained under Huerta's control—Torreón, the city of Chihuahua and Juárez. On October 1, 1913, Villa's cavalry charged the federal lines outside Torreón and burst into the city. On November 3, they appeared outside Chihuahua City, 300 miles north. Once again, Don Pancho launched his patented wild cavalry charge, but this time the Huertistas were prepared. They repulsed the Villistas with a storm of rifle and machinegun fire.

Villa realized that charging machineguns might be *macho*, but it wasn't war. He called off the attack. He then captured a troop train en route to Chihuahua from Juárez and put the captured federal forces under guard. Forging the train commander's name, he sent a telegram to the commander in Juárez, a General Castro, saying that his engine had broken down and he needed a new engine and five additional box cars. When the additional rolling stock arrived, Villa sent another telegram: "Large forces of rebels approaching from south. Wires cut between here and Chihuahua. What shall I do?"

Castro wired back: "Return at once."

Villa loaded his own troops on the box cars and ordered the train back to Juárez. At midnight, November 15, the train got to the border city, the major overland port of entry between Mexico and the United States. Immediately the box car doors slammed open, the Villistas swarmed out and took the city before most of the garrison was awake. Eight days after the capture of Juárez, the federals counterattacked and were severely mauled. On December 8, Chihuahua City surrendered, and Villa proclaimed himself the governor of the state of Chihuahua. One of his first official acts was to give anyone who asked for it a tract of 75 acres, non-transferable for 10 years.

Technically, Villa's forces were supporting Venustiano Carranza, the governor of neighboring Coahuila. Actually, Villa and Carranza despised each other. To Carranza, Villa was just a bandit, cruel, ignorant and opportunistic. To Villa, Carranza was a former Díaz senator, an hacendado who cared only for personal power. Carranza had no military ability. He relied on Álvaro Obregón, a farmer from Sonora who never let machismo interfere with intelligence. The fourth great revolutionary figure came not from the north, but from Morelos, a state a little south of Mexico City. Morelos was sugar country, not cattle country, a land of Indian villages that Díaz had given to the hacendados. The Morelos leader was Emiliano Zapata, a short, slight Náhuatl Indian with piercing eyes and a single war aim—land reform.

Villa and Zapata were natural allies. Villa, the mestizo who considered himself an Indian, and Zapata, who was pure Indian, believed they were the only real representatives of Mexico's masses. Carranza was a rich white hacendado. Obregón wasn't rich, but he was white and, although born poor, he had worked his way into Mexico's tiny middle class.

Of the four, Villa was by far the star of the revolution as far as the American public was concerned. American mercenaries enlisted in his army, dozens of U.S. correspondents rode with his men. All newspaper readers knew of his bravery, his impetuousness, his generosity and his concern for the peons. Less well known was his darker side. He financed his war effort with wholesale robbery, and any priests or Spanish nationals he came across were lucky to escape with their lives.

In the United States, Villa paid cash for thousands of Winchester carbines and millions of rounds of ammunition. He could buy as much as he wanted: his credit was good. U.S. President Woodrow Wilson had lifted his country's arms embargo on the Mexican revolutionists, although he continued it on the Huerta government. Faced with Mexico's confusing array of leaders, Wilson seemed to favor Villa. His secretary of state, William Jennings Bryan, called Villa a "Sir Galahad" in spite of years of robbery and murder because he, like Bryan, was a teetotaler.

Meanwhile, in Mexico City, Huerta decided to follow Don Porfirio's example. He went to Veracruz and took a ship for Europe. Obregón, leading the Carrancista forces, was the first rebel into the city. Villa was approaching with his 40,000 cavalry, called the *Dorados* (the golden ones). Villa was in a foul mood: Carranza had cut off his coal supplies so he couldn't take his army south by train. Obregón went north to appease him.

When Obregón arrived, Villa announced that he would be shot at once. Smoothly, Obregón pointed out that such an action would dishonor the name and reputation of the "Centaur of the North." Villa listened, and dismissed his firing squad. Over dinner, Villa burst into tears and told Obregón, "Pancho Villa does not kill defenseless men, and least of all thee, little comrade, who art my guest."

Villa was later to bitterly regret changing his mind.

Villa, Zapata, Obregón and Carranza met at Xochimilco on the outskirts of Mexico City. They agreed on Eulalio Gutierrez as provisional president, mainly because he was backed by Villa, the man with the largest army. Villa himself, in a rare moment of humility, said he was not qualified to be president of the republic.

The conference settled nothing. Fighting broke out among rival factions all across the country. The soldiers in all factions added a new verse to the million or so in *La Cucuracha:*

> *Si Carranza se casa con Villa,*
> *Y Zapata con General Obregón,*
> *Si Adelita se casa conmigo,*
> *Pos se acabará la revolución.*
> (If Carranza marries Villa,
> And Zapata General Obregón,
> If Adelita marries me,
> Then the revolution will end.)

Carranza and Obregón went to Veracruz to build up their army. Veracruz had been occupied by the U.S. Navy ever since Huerta had refused to salute the U.S. flag. The navy conveniently (for the Carrancistas) pulled out. Villa and Zapata occupied Mexico City. They dawdled while they and their soldiers sampled the delights of the big city.

Obregón didn't dawdle. He and Carranza got in touch with Germany, which was anxious to keep Mexico in turmoil. Unrest in Mexico meant distraction for the United States, which was drifting closer to involvement in World War I. With new supplies and recruits, Obregón hit the other revolutionists in Puebla, just south of the capital. Zapata withdrew to the south. Next, Obregón, who had picked up a German military advisor and was a keen student of the war in Europe, turned his attention to Villa.

In April, 1915 he fortified the town of Celaya, a little northwest of Mexico City, and defied Villa to do anything about it. It was a challenge no macho man could resist. Villa sent 25,000 of his Dorado cavalry charging Obregón as they sang *La Cucuracha*. They were chopped to pieces by Obregón's quick-firing artillery, shredded by machineguns with interlocking fields of fire and hung up on the hundreds of miles of barbed wire in front of Obregón's maze of zig-zag trenches.

The Villa of 1913, inventor of the Trojan iron horse, would have stopped the slaughter and given Obregón another surprise—perhaps encirclement. The tactics Obregón used were effective on the Western Front only because the line ran from the sea to Switzerland and could not be flanked.

The Villa of 1913 was dead, though. He was buried under millions of sycophantic comments and tons of adoring newspaper stories. The Villa of 1915 knew he was invincible. He ordered another charge. And another. . . . The next day, Villa could think of nothing better than more charges, and the Dorados kept charging, regardless of loss of life. At the end of the day, when the remnants of the Dorados could barely urge their exhausted mounts forward, Obregón brought his own cavalry out from behind the barbed wire, where it had been hiding, and hit both of Villa's flanks. The Villistas were totally routed.

On June 2, Villa attacked Obregón at León, 60 miles northwest of Celaya. It was a replay of Celaya. The field was carpeted with dead Villistas and their mounts, while Obregón's losses were trifling. The Dorado cavalry had been almost annihilated.

Villa's losses convinced Wilson that the only viable leader in Mexico was Carranza, a prickly old man who was ungrateful for the help he had received and rejected Wilson's advice on how to run his country. Legal arms sales to Villa stopped.

Villa moved north to consolidate his position in his home territory. Shortly after his split with Carranza, some 1,500 men loyal to Carranza entrenched themselves in the border town of Naco, in Sonora. José Maytorena, governor of Sonora and a Villista, besieged them. Bullets from Naco, Sonora began whizzing through the streets of Naco, Arizona. U.S. General Hugh Scott mediated an agreement between the two sides that let the Villistas use Nogales, Arizona, as a port of entry and let the Carrancistas use Douglas, Arizona, opposite Agua Prieta, Sonora.

Back north, licking his wounds from Celaya and León, Villa resolved to clean out the nest of Carrancistas in Agua Prieta. That shouldn't be hard, he thought, because he controlled all lines of communications in the north. What Villa didn't know was that Woodrow Wilson let a heavily equipped Carrancista regiment enter the United States and take U.S. trains to Douglas, Arizona. From Douglas, they merely walked across the street to Agua Prieta, which they proceeded to turn into another Celaya.

After his last two defeats, Villa gave up the idea of a massive cavalry charge in broad daylight. He would attack Agua Prieta at night and surprise the Carrancistas. The Villistas deployed in pitch blackness and crept across the fields toward the Carrancista lines. Suddenly, as soon as they reached the barbed wire, rows of powerful searchlights came on, blinding the Villistas and outlining them against the night sky for Carranza's machineguns.

The searchlights were connected to power lines in Arizona.

On the heels of this defeat, Villa took his demoralized army to Hermosillo, the capital of Sonora, now occupied by Obregón's forces. Once again, faced with barbed wire and machineguns—and driven by machismo—Villa sent his reeling army against Western Front type defenses—and once again he met a bloody defeat.

Now, though, he had someone to blame for his troubles—Uncle Sam. Villa, long a friend of the United States, believed he had been betrayed. The Villistas scattered and drifted toward the border. One group fired at some U.S. soldiers in Nogales and caught a volley of well aimed Springfield bullets in return. Another fired wildly at freight yards in El Paso and killed an American trainman.

On January 10, Villista Colonel Pablo López stopped a train carrying American and Mexican mine engineers through Chihuahua. The miners worked for an American mine that had been closed during the revolution. Obregón had convinced the mine owners to reopen it and promised the protection of the government. Villa had ordered López to steal the mine's payroll.

López exceeded his orders. He stole everything, including all the property of the Mexican and American workers. Then López told the Mexican
miners, "If you want to see some fun, watch us kill these gringos." Kill them
he did, all but one American who escaped to tell the tale.

Villa must have thought killing Americans was a good idea, because he
rounded up all the followers he could find and moved on Columbus.
Whether his motive was pure revenge, or to involve the Carranza government in a war or—most likely—both, is unknown. What is known is that he
was there. Ever since 1916, people on both sides of the border have sworn
that Villa could not have been there. They are people who knew Pancho Villa
in good times and could not imagine that a man with his generosity and
sunny disposition could take out his wrath on helpless civilians.

But he did.

On March 1, 1916, Mrs. Maud Hawkes Wright was working in her
ranch house near Colonia Hernández, Chihuahua when 12 armed Mexicans
approached. She offered them the hospitality of the house, but their leader,
Colonel Nicolás Hernández told her she was a prisoner of the Division of the
North. When her husband, E. J. Wright, came home with a friend named
Hayden, they, too were made prisoners. The Wrights' infant daughter was
given to a Mexican woman and the American were put on horses and taken
away. The next day, both men were killed. Mrs. Wright went from officer to
officer asking to be reunited with her daughter. She eventually went to Villa,
who merely shrugged and told her to talk to Colonel Hernández. Hernández
refused and told Mrs. Wright she'd have to ride along with the army. They
were going to Columbus, New Mexico, he told her, to burn the town and kill
everybody in it. Mrs. Wright didn't suspect that on the eve of the attack, Villa
would set her free, saying he admired her courage. Weeks later, she was
reunited with her daughter in Colonia Hernández.

On March 7, three vaqueros saw a party of Hernandez's troops. Two of
them, Favela and Muñoz, put spurs to their horses and galloped for the
border. The third, William Corbett, knew that he had done nothing wrong,
so he held up his hands and waited for them. The Villistas took him to camp,
where he saw three other Americans, Arthur McKinney, the ranch foreman,
James O'Neil, the cook, and a black cowboy, Buck Spencer. One of the
troopers rode off and came back with Villa himself. Villa gave a command,
and his men hanged Corbett and McKinney from a tree. They spread-eagled
O'Neil on the ground, and a group of riders galloped at him to trample him
to death. O'Neil evaded them and climbed up behind one Mexican. He was
strangling the Villista when the other Villistas shot him. Spencer prayed that
his black skin would save him. It did. He was released before the attack.

Columbus, which looked like an easy target, proved to be as serious a disaster—proportionately—for Villa as Celaya. Then the American public began clamoring for revenge. The Wilson administration called up the National Guard and prepared plans for an invasion of Mexico to capture Villa. The expedition, under Brigadier General John Pershing, son-in-law of Senator Francis Warren of Wyoming (who got President Harrison to save the Johnson County invaders), was described as an effort to help the Carranza government capture the bandit Villa. Carranza had told Wilson repeatedly that he didn't want U.S. troops in Mexico, but they went anyway.

They never found Villa, although they had a few brushes with his men. Nobody would give them any information as to where Villa might be found. Pershing's expedition was a strange blend of traditional and new. The general had four airplanes, but none of them could climb high enough to clear the mountains of Chihuahua and so were useless for scouting. He had cavalry and infantry, but he also had trucks and traveled in a Dodge touring car. His personal aide, Second Lieutenant George Smith Patton, Jr., later famous as a leader of mechanized divisions, killed two Villistas with the single action cowboy-type Colt he carried in preference to the modern automatic.

Finally, Carranza's non-cooperation turned to outright hostility. Rather than engage in a side-show war in Mexico, when it looked as if the country would soon be fighting Germany, Wilson pulled the expedition back.

Villa's most serious trouble came not from Pershing or Obregón, but from a Mexican civilian. The old magic no longer worked. Few men volunteered to join Don Pancho's army. Therefore, he rounded up all the young men in one town and told them they were now his soldiers. When they saw American troops, he passed out some old rifles and a small quantity of ammunition to his new recruits and told them to defend themselves. During a counterattack, with Villa characteristically well ahead of his men, one of the recruits aimed an ancient 11 millimeter Remington rolling block at the general and fired. The bullet hit him in the leg. Villa was carried off in a wagon to parts unknown—out of action for months. When he recovered, he went back to his old trade, banditry.

Carranza finally got rid of Zapata. A Carrancista officer, Colonel Jesús Guajardo, got a message to the little Indian saying he wanted to defect. Guajardo proved his sincerity by attacking his Carrancista comrades and, after defeating them, executing his prisoners. Zapata came to an hacienda for a meeting with the officer. As he entered the courtyard, defecting troops were lined up. Guajardo raised his sword, and the troops presented arms to salute the general from Morelos. The sword flashed down; the troops leveled their rifles at Zapata and fired.

Carranza had no patent on treachery. Obregón made himself president by the simple expedient of hiring the chief of Carranza's bodyguard to kill the president, then establishing a figurehead interim president. He bought Villa off with a 25,000 acre ranch in Chihuahua. It looked as if Don Pancho would settle for the life of a country squire, while Obregón held the presidency.

Having little of it himself, Obregón feared the power of charisma. He could never, like Villa, have built eight followers into an army of 3,000 in a month. Villa's charisma had been returning. When he retired, he had built his army back up to 700 men.

On July 19, 1923, Villa came to Parral, Chihuahua, to spend the night with one of his many mistresses. The next day, eight horsemen tethered their mounts in front of a local hotel and took a room overlooking the road. Fittingly, in this mixture of the Wild West and modern times, the riders carried Mondragón semiautomatic rifles. The Mondragón, invented by General Miguel Mondragón, Díaz's rapacious chief of ordnance, was the first semiautomatic rifle ever used in combat (by German aerial observers in 1915). The Mondragón is a rare weapon today. It was never easily available to Mexican civilians.

When Villa's car appeared, the killers cut loose and hit everyone in the car. Villa and all but one of his bodyguards died. He was buried with no honors of state in a little cemetery in Parral. Three years later, his grave was opened and his body decapitated. The whereabouts of Villa's head has been a mystery ever since. One wild rumor has it that the head was taken to a Yale University secret society, Skull and Bones.

A neighbor of Villa confessed that he had led the assassination squad because of a dispute over money. He was sentenced to 20 years in prison, but Obregón saw to it that he was released in six months. Then the new president made him a colonel in the army.

In 1926, Obregón was sitting with friends in a restaurant when a young man walked up to him and put five bullets through his head. Under torture, the young man said he belonged to the Cristeros, a militant Catholic faction.

All of the revolutionary lions had been murdered. The waning years of the Mexican Revolution were dominated by Obregón's lieutenant, Plutarco Elías Calles, closer to a hyena than a lion, who became president and then controlled three succeeding presidents from behind the scenes. The fourth president, Lázaro Cárdenas, would not be controlled. He arrested and exiled Calles and put down the last armed uprising.

After a quarter of a century, the Mexican Revolution was over. Poor Mexico ("So far from God and so close to the United States," according to

Porfirio Díaz) had more than its share of martyrs, heroes, villains and hero-villains.

The only one of them that really established himself in the American imagination, though, was Pancho Villa, the man who crossed the border with eight friends to overturn the old order, who sent thousands of his followers to their death in foolish cavalry charges, who, for the first time in Mexican history, gave free food and free land to the peons, and who in a fit of fury raided Columbus, New Mexico.

Thirteen

One-Man Army

October 8, 1918, Argonne Forest, France

The mighty German Army, which had occupied France for four years, was beginning to crumble. Corporal Alvin Cullum York trudged through the misty, pre-dawn blackness with the rest of his battalion of the 82nd (All American) Division. They were planning to flank another of the temporary strong points the Germans had been setting up as they fell back from their ruptured trench line. The Yanks would cut the narrow-gauge Decauville railroad, which carried German supplies.

Along the way, York passed wounded men who had not yet been picked up. He later remembered "some of them . . . lying around moaning and

Top: German Maxim machinegun MG-08/15, portable version of the standard MG-08, caliber 8×57 mm. Guns like this almost annihilated York's battalion. Below: U.S. Rifle M-1917, caliber .30-06, the rifle used to silence the German machinegunners and capture 132 of them.

twitching. And oh my! The dead were all along the road and their mouths were open and their eyes, too."

The rangy mountaineer may have thought about how he came to be here—he, who had been a conscientious objector. War certainly was all he had expected—a dirty, bloody affair of poison gas, mangling artillery barrages and hails of bullets from hidden machineguns.

York came from the village of Pall Mall, Tennessee, a hamlet near the Cumberland Gap on the Tennessee-Kentucky border. Pall Mall was southwest of Pike County, Kentucky, about 100 miles—and 100 years—removed. The railroads and mines that had transformed Pike County never quite made it to Pall Mall. York's father had a small less-than-subsistence farm and ran a blacksmith shop. There wasn't all that much blacksmith work, and William York had plenty of time to go hunting with his son.

In the Cumberland hills, hunting was more than a sport. Without hunting, there would seldom be meat on the table. Most people didn't even have enough money for cartridges. They used loose black powder and home-cast lead balls in long percussion cap rifles like those used by their ancestors almost a century before. Rifles were passed down the family from father to son. The weapon Alvin York used had been made for his grandfather. The old rifles were accurate enough, but they had a big disadvantage. They were slow to load. If you missed your first shot at an animal, you'd have to hunt up another target. Conditions like that encouraged marksmanship.

The elder York was known as a good shot, but Alvin outclassed his father before he was well into his teens. He attended turkey and ham shoots whenever he could. The hidden-turkey shoots were especially challenging. A turkey was tied behind a log so that only its bobbing head was occasionally visible. The contestant, standing 40 yards away, tried to hit the turkey's head as soon as it appeared. To make it harder, the other contestants were allowed to try to distract the shooter. They could talk to him, move around him, even walk in front of him, ducking under the muzzle of his rifle. But nothing bothered Alvin York. His concentration on the target was total. York seldom left a shoot without a turkey.

With hunting, shooting contests and farm work, young Alvin didn't have much time for school. He attended school three weeks each summer for five years. He later calculated that he had the equivalent of a third grade education. He read his first book when he was 20—a biography of Jesse James. He acquired an old cap-and-ball revolver and practiced shooting at a tree as he galloped by on the family mule, imitating a feat attributed to James.

William York died of typhoid fever in 1911, and Alvin became the family breadwinner. He didn't win as much as he could, because he took up drinking at the illegal saloons along the Kentucky-Tennessee border.

"I was always spoiling for a fight," he recalled later. He took his revolver and a knife with him on his drinking excursions. He later allowed as how that first book he read had made "a big impression." Fortunately, he never got in serious trouble, but night after night, he would return to his waiting mother dead drunk.

Then one day, a "saddlebagger," a wandering preacher, rode into Pall Mall and began holding nightly revival meetings. There wasn't much variety in Pall Mall's nightlife, so Alvin attended one of the meetings. The preacher made a bigger impression than Jesse James. York became a regular at the meetings, and on January 1, 1915, he swore off "smoking, drinking, gambling, cussing and brawling."

A couple of years later, York got a draft notice. He wasn't happy.

"I had had fighting and quarreling myself," he said. "I found it bad. . . . I just wanted to be left alone to live in peace and love." He saw no difference between quarrels between persons and quarrels between nations. And the Bible, God's inspired word, said, "Thou shalt not kill."

He applied for conscientious objector status, but the local draft board refused on the grounds that the Church of Christ in Christian Union was not "a well recognized" sect. His appeals were rejected.

York was sent to Camp Gordon, Georgia.

"I just went to that old camp and said nothing. I did everything I was told to . . . but I was sick at heart just the same."

He was assigned to Company G of the 328th Infantry Regiment of the 82nd Division. The 82nd was called the "All American" division because the troops in it came from all parts of the country. Most of the men in York's company were city boys from the Northeast. York went into culture shock. His barracks mates were, he said, "A gang of the toughest and most hard-boiled doughboys I ever heard of. . . . They could out-swear, out-drink and out-cuss any other crowd of men I have ever knowed." But when they shot, he said, "They missed everything but the sky."

Right after he was assigned, York told his company commander, Captain E. C. B. Danforth, Jr. about his religious beliefs. Danforth told the battalion commander, Major George E. Buxton, Jr., a former newspaperman from Providence, Rhode Island.

Buxton had a long talk with York. Buxton knew his Bible as well as York. He used quotations from Luke, John, Matthew and Ezekiel to try to persuade the quiet mountaineer that "under certain conditions, a man could go to war and fight and still be a good Christian."

York asked for time to think about their discussion. He applied for a ten-day leave and went back to Pall Mall. He went into the mountains and prayed alone. He prayed all night and through part of the next day.

"And as I prayed there alone, a great peace . . . came into my soul and a great calm come over me and I received my assurance. He heard my prayer and He come to me on the mountainside. . . .

"I begun to understand that no matter what a man is forced to do, so long as he is right in his own soul, he remains a righteous man. I knowed I would go to war."

During the fighting in France, York was promoted to corporal and became a squad leader. In September, the 82nd took part in the St. Mihiel attack, the first American offensive. On September 17, the division was transferred to the Argonne Forest for an offensive that was to become the last of the war.

On October 8, 1918, Company G and the rest of the Second Battalion moved out at 6:10 a.m. without benefit of the usual artillery barrage. This was to be a surprise attack. When the early morning mists cleared, it was the doughboys who were surprised. They were in an open valley and proceeding parallel with a ridge on their left. On the ridge was a machinegun battalion of the Prussian Guards with their Maxim guns sited to enfilade the Americans.

The water-cooled Maxim, the invention of Maine native Hiram Maxim, was the first automatic—as opposed to hand-cranked—machinegun. Belt-fed and utterly reliable, the refined German version could fire 600 shots a minute for as long as its crew kept the waterjacket full and the ammunition coming—all day long, if necessary. The Maxim probably killed more human beings than any other firearm ever invented.

The German Maxim gunners opened fire, and the second battalion was almost wiped out. Everyone alive was pinned down. Captain Danforth sent three squads from the first platoon, including York's, under Sergeant Bernard Early to work around the left of the German position. They moved through the still-dense Argonne Forest and came to an open area where, besides a hut, a German major was conferring with other officers. It was the headquarters of a German machinegun regiment.

The Americans fired and charged with fixed bayonets. Most of the Germans surrendered. One fired at York, and York shot him dead. Early and his detachment were lining up the prisoners when a hail of bullets struck them. The German machinegunners on the hill had heard the shooting and turned their guns around. Early was hit six times. He called on the senior corporal to take over, but he and all his squad were dead. Only Alvin York and seven privates were still able to fight.

The seven privates were hugging the ground, hiding behind trees and still keeping the prisoners covered. Privates George Wills and Michael Saccina crawled towards groups of prisoners, keeping the prisoners between them and the machineguns. American bodies covered the area.

Alvin York was caught in the open, about 30 yards from the machineguns when the barrage began. There were between 20 and 30 machineguns.

"Thousands of bullets kicked up the dust all around us," he said. "The undergrowth was cut down . . . as though they had used a scythe."

York flopped down on the ground and aimed his rifle at the area where the guns were hidden.

"Every time one of them raised his head, I just teched him off," he said. It reminded him of a turkey shoot, "but the targets were bigger. I just couldn't miss."

York's rifle was the M-1917, not the army's beloved Springfield. The M-1917, like the Springfield, was copied from the German Mauser, but it was a British design. The Boers and their 7 millimeter Mausers had impressed the British at the turn of the century, and they decided to build a Mauser of their own, chambered for a super high velocity 7 millimeter cartridge. As tensions increased in Europe, plans to convert to a new rifle caliber were shelved. The Mauser derivative was chambered for the old .303 cartridge. All gun makers in Britain were working at full capacity to build the standard rifle, the Short Magazine Lee Enfield, so the British government let contracts for the new rifle out to American plants. When the United States entered the war, these rifles were converted to the U.S. .30-06 cartridge.

Alvin York didn't care that his rifle was classified "substitute standard." It worked just fine. German fire slackened, because the German gunners became reluctant to look over their parapets.

York stood up and assumed the "offhand" position he used at hidden-turkey shoots. He could see the heads of Germans who thought they were hidden. He resumed fire. Every now and then, a German would peg a rifle shot at him or fire an unsighted machinegun burst. York stayed as cool as he had at the contests back home, firing and reloading with five-shot clips whenever the bolt jammed back to show him the rifle was empty. He fired so fast he could feel the barrel getting hot beneath the rifle's wooden handguard.

A German lieutenant 25 yards away, distressed because nobody seemed able to hit the tall rifleman standing in the open, quietly ordered the men around him to fix bayonets and follow him. When York emptied his rifle again, the lieutenant and five enlisted men appeared out of the bushes and dashed at York.

York's right hand, reaching for a new clip on his belt, sped to the .45 automatic he, as an NCO, carried on the same belt. He drew the pistol and started firing. The German lieutenant, seeing York firing again and again, probably thought this enemy, no matter how deadly he might be with a rifle, was no better with a pistol than anyone else. Then he caught a bullet in his chest and had no more thoughts.

York later explained that he had shot at the Germans "the way we shoot wild turkeys at home. You see we don't want the ones in front to know that we're getting the back ones. ... I knowed, too, that if the front ones wavered, or if I stopped them, the rear ones would drop down and pump a volley into me." He killed all six men. Then he reloaded his rifle and shot at helmets as they appeared. By this time, he had killed 21 Germans with as many shots.

"I didn't want to kill any more than I had to," he said. "I would tech a couple of them off and holler [for them to surrender] again."

While he was firing, York sensed that somewhere behind him someone was shooting. He turned around and saw the German major holding an empty Luger.

When the major saw York turn, his face was the picture of despair. He tried out the English he had learned years before when he lived in Chicago.

"English?" he asked.

"No, not English."

"What?"

"American."

"Good lord! If you don't shoot anymore, I'll make them surrender."

The major blew a whistle, and the machinegun crews stood up and began to walk down the slope. One diehard, though, pulled the string on his "potato masher" grenade and started to throw it. An alert private in York's squad cut him down.

The fighting over, York noticed that all the buttons of his uniform jacket had been shot off and there was a hole in his helmet.

"Somehow," he said, "I knew I wouldn't be killed."

York lined up the prisoners in a column of twos. He detailed one man to help the wounded Early, who, miraculously, was able to walk with assistance. He had prisoners carry the other wounded Americans who were still alive. After placing the prisoners so they would provide cover for his men and himself back through the German lines, York asked the major the best way to reach the American forces. The major suggested a route, so York marched his column in the opposite direction. The major tried to stall. York poked him in the back with his .45.

"You should have seen the major move on down that hill whenever I pulled down on him with that old Colt. 'Goose-step it,' I think they called it. He was so little! His back was so straight! And all huffed up over the way he had to mind me."

On their way back, the Americans passed other German machinegunners. They, too, surrendered. Only one didn't. York had the major order the man to surrender twice. The machinegunner refused, so York shot him.

"I hated to do it. . . . He was probably a brave soldier boy. But I couldn't afford to take any chance, and so I had to let him have it."

As they neared the American lines, a doughboy challenged them. York moved in front of his prisoners and announced that Corporal York was bringing in some prisoners. When the column appeared, word spread through the battalion that "York is bringing in the whole damned German Army." He had 132 prisoners.

By silencing the machineguns, York enabled the division to capture the railroad and make the Germans abandon their position.

The next day, York asked Danforth to let him go back to the scene of his fight to look for wounded. The company commander let him go and take two litter bearers. There were no wounded.

"The ground in front and on both sides of where we . . . stood was all soft and torned up with bullets. The brush on either side was all torned up and there was a sort of tunnel cut in the brush behind me. Everything destroyed, torned up, killed—trees, grass, men.

"All was terribly quiet in the field. . . . Oh my, it seemed so unbelievable. I would never see them again. . . . I could only pray for their souls. And I done that. . . . I prayed for the Germans, too. They were all brother men of mine."

York was immediately promoted to sergeant. His exploit was so fantastic skeptics said it couldn't have happened the way he told it. The division commander, Major General George B. Duncan, said, after an investigation that took many months, "The more we investigated the exploit, the more remarkable it appeared." He called York "one of the bravest of men and entitled to all the honor that may be given to him."

York received the Medal of Honor, the Distinguished Service Cross, the French *Croix de Guerre* with palms, the French Legion of Honor, the Italian *Croce di Guerra* and the War Medal of Montenegro. On arriving home, he got the biggest tickertape parade in New York history up to that time, and Wall Street brokers carried him on their shoulders. In the giant, impersonal meatgrinder of the Western Front, York stood out as an individual hero.

He received all kinds of offers to write a book or make a movie, but he turned them all down. All he wanted was a ride on the New York subway, which he'd heard about and never seen, and to go back home and marry his fiance. He had no desire to cash in on having killed a lot of his fellow men.

In 1941, he was persuaded that it was his patriotic duty to allow Gary Cooper to portray his story in a movie. It won Cooper an Academy Award.

It also earned York more money than he had ever seen in his life. And that brought him more trouble than he'd had since 1918. Unfamiliar with the income tax—he seldom made enough money to have to pay it—he reported his earnings as capital gains. In 1961, the Internal Revenue Service ruled that he should have reported it as ordinary income, taxable at a higher rate. It said York, now bedridden, partially paralyzed and almost completely blind, owed the government $85,442 plus $87,155 in accumulated interest.

York, who never had any interest in high living, had already given most of the money away. He had $25 in cash, a home and farm worth $30,000, worn out farm machinery, 50 head of cattle and a four-year-old car fitted out for his wheelchair which had been donated to him by the 82nd Airborne Division. His debts amounted to $9,362. He got a veteran's pension of $135 plus $38 in Social Security and $10 as a Medal of Honor winner monthly. His annual taxable income was $4,190.97.

House Speaker Sam Rayburn launched a campaign to raise money for the old soldier. It paid off his taxes and debts and established a trust fund for him. Financier S. Hallock du Pont set up another fund that gave him $300 a month for the rest of his life.

York died September 2, 1964 at the age of 76—a reluctant hero who remained more concerned about his family and his meagre farm than any military glory.

PROHIBITION,

DEPRESSION,

AND

INTERSTATE

CRIME

Fourteen

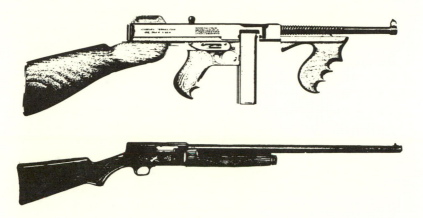

Valentine Present

February 14, 1929, Chicago, Illinois

Frank Gusenberg looked at his watch. Where could Bugs be? Bugs had called all the guys and told them a shipment of Canadian was coming in, and everybody could take his cut. Now the truck was late and so was Bugs. Everybody else was there—Frank, his brother, Pete; Adam Heyer, who owned the garage; John May, who dabbled in bootlegging when he wasn't blowing safes; Jim Clark, who preferred to rob banks with a gun; Al Weinshank, who needed the booze for his speakeasy, and Dr. Reinhardt Schwimmer, a nutty optometrist who liked to hang around gangsters.

A car pulled up. Frank Gusenberg looked through a window. It was a

Top: Thompson Submachinegun, caliber .45 ACP, the weapon used in the St. Valentine's day massacre. This is the original Model 1921/28, with an adjustable sight and two pistol grips. Below: Semiauto shotgun, a Savage here, previously the gangsters' choice (with shortened barrel).

big black Caddy, like the Chicago detectives used. Three men in police uniforms and two in business suits got out.

"Bulls!" shouted Gusenberg. Where the hell was Bugs?

Bugs Moran was outside. He was approaching the garage when the Cadillac stopped there. What a hell of a time to have a raid. He waved his two companions, Willie Marks and Ted Newbury, into a coffee shop. All ordered coffee and waited for the bulls to leave. Bugs knew he'd have to send Newbury down to precinct headquarters with bond money. The Gusenbergs always carried, so they were sure to be arrested for concealed weapons.

People living next to the garage heard what sounded like pneumatic drills. Three uniformed officers emerged from the building leading two other men. They had apparently made an arrest. A dog began to howl.

Mrs. Jeannette Landesman was disturbed by the dog's howls. She asked one of her roomers, C.L. McAllister, to go next door and see what was going on in the garage. McAllister was back two minutes later, his face white, his lips trembling.

"The p-p-place is full of d-d-dead men," he stammered.

To the newspapers, it was "the Saint Valentine's Day massacre"—seven more deaths to be added to Chicago's grim total of gang killings, a total that would reach more than 1,000 before the bootleg wars ended.

To sociologists, it was the most ignoble result so far of what reformers a few years before had hailed as "the noble experiment"—the 18th Amendment to the U.S. Constitution prohibiting the manufacture and sale of alcoholic beverages for general consumption.

To George "Bugs" Moran, it was the worst setback in a career that really began when, at 17, he quit stealing horses for ransom and teamed up with a safe-cracker named Dion "Deanie" O'Bannion. He, Deanie and a couple of Deanie's boyhood buddies, Hymie Weiss and Vinnie Drucci, formed a fairly successful burglary and safe-cracking gang. Before long, O'Bannion had money for expensive lawyers and payoffs to corrupt judges. Moran, a tall, rawboned kid with an almost ungovernable temper—he "went bugs" when he got mad, friends said—was an awkward burglar. Deanie kept him in the gang because of his loyalty and his muscle.

In 1917, Moran was arrested while burglarizing a department store. When he got out of prison in 1923, Prohibition was the law of the land, and O'Bannion had turned to bootlegging and built up a powerful mob. Deanie welcomed his old buddy back, and Bugs became one of the leaders of what the public called the North Side Mob.

Bootlegging called for a more elaborate infrastructure than burglary. A burglar can break into any place, anywhere. Bootlegging was a business that depended on steady customers. The customers had to know the bootlegger and know that they could depend on him. That tied the bootlegger to the area where his customers lived. Because there were a lot of other bootleggers, he had to defend his territory. That led to something new in American crime—the permanently employed, salaried gunman, the hoodlum.

Bank robber Alvin Karpis once explained to John Edgar Hoover, director of the FBI, what a hoodlum was. Appearing at a press conference with the recently-arrested Karpis, Hoover referred to the robber as a hoodlum. Karpis objected angrily:

"I'm no hood! I don't like to be called a hood. I'm a thief. . . . I was offered a job as a hoodlum, and I turned it down cold. A thief is anybody who gets out and works for his living, like robbing a bank, breaking into a place and stealing stuff. . . . A hoodlum is a pretty lousy sort of scum. He works for gangsters and bumps guys off after they've been put on the spot. . . . They offered me $250 a week and all the protection I needed. But I wouldn't consider it. 'I'm a thief,' I said. 'I'm no lousy hoodlum.' "

The law that led to the creation of the hoodlum was a product of two trends: (1) a growing movement to ban liquor and (2) the assumption of unheard-of powers by the federal government during World War I. "Temperance" advocates were the most intemperate fanatics of the early twentieth century—people like William Jennings Bryan, who called the bloody Pancho Villa a "Sir Galahad" because he didn't drink. They proselytized their cause vigorously. The war introduced rationing and the "spirit of sacrifice for the common good." On December 18, 1917, Congress approved the amendment and gave it to the states for ratification. The state legislatures, disproportionately dominated by rural WASPs, ratified it in about a year. The Volstead Act of 1919 banned liquor sales after January 16, 1920.

The law not only provided a new way for crooks to make a dishonest dollar, it gave crime a whole new dimension. Urban gangsterism had been a feature of American cities since before Independence. These urban gangs did not specialize, like the O'Bannion gang, in direct theft. They ran territorial rackets—gambling, smuggling, prostitution, fencing, loan-sharking, extortion and assault-for-hire—enterprises that, like bootlegging, required a stable clientele. Before prohibition, though, the gangsters had pretty much stayed in their own neighborhoods and victimized their own ethnic groups. In New York, for instance, Irish gangs dominated Hell's Kitchen; Jewish gangs, the Lower East Side; Italian gangs, Little Italy; and African-American gangs, Harlem.

To take advantage of the opportunities offered by Prohibition, the gangsters had to leave their ghettos. Among the first to move were Jewish gangsters: heavy drinking was not a cultural trait of their constituents. Actually, none of the impoverished areas that bred gangsters were the best markets for an expensive luxury product. In any city, the best markets were the big restaurants and wealthy individuals who were found downtown and in posh residential areas.

With all gangs leaving their ghettos for the bright lights and gold coasts of their cities, there were clashes. Especially since there were many more gangs than the traditional neighborhood organizations. O'Bannion, for example, had been more thief than racketeer before Prohibition. Wars alternated with peace conferences, treaties and revolts. Whenever a gang became dominant in an area, it introduced all the rackets, loan-sharking, extortion, etc., that it practiced back in its traditional neighborhood. When eventually repeal of Prohibition killed bootlegging as a way to riches, the gangs went on practicing the other rackets, but they were no longer confined to one or the other of a city's depressed areas.

As its name showed, the O'Bannion gang controlled the north side of Chicago, which included some of the wealthiest areas of the city. O'Bannion's major rival was the organization run by John Torrio and his enforcer, Alphonse Capone, which dominated the Loop and the West Side. Torrio was a New Yorker who had come to Chicago to work for his uncle, Big Jim Colosimo, who owned the city's largest string of brothels. When Prohibition became law, Johnny Torrio begged Big Jim to take advantage of the opportunities. Colosimo balked.

"We stay with the whores, Johnny," Colosimo said.

Torrio solved the problem by calling in Big Al Capone, nicknamed Scarface, a gunman he knew in New York. Capone killed Colosimo, and Torrio added speakeasy bars to his houses of ill fame.

In addition to the two big mobs, there were a number of smaller gangs that organized to take advantage of Prohibition. There were:

The South Side O'Donnells, Spike, Steve, Walter and Tommy, who turned to bootlegging and tried to move into Torrio and Capone turf. They failed. Because they made slurs against Italians, Capone respected their prejudices and sent Danny McFall and Frankie McErlane to kill them.

The West Side O'Donnells, "Klondike," Bernie and Myles, who tried to play the North Siders against Capone and got caught in the middle.

"Polack Joe" Saltis and his homicidal partner, Frankie McErlane, Capone allies who secretly plotted to eliminate Big Al while doing his killings.

And then there were the Gennas—the "Terrible Gennas," "Bloody Angelo," Pete, "Tony the Gentleman," Jim, "Mike the Devil" and Sam. They were Sicilians, born and raised in Marsala and genuine *Mafiosi*.

In spite of popular belief and romantic legend, there never was an organization called the Mafia that covered all of Sicily, and there is no evidence of anything called the Mafia in any Sicilian wars of liberation against any of the island's many invaders—Vandals, Goths, Arabs, Normans, French or Spanish. Gaetano Mosca, an Italian sociologists, says the word mafia "is not found in Italian writing before the nineteenth century." Traina's Sicilian-Italian dictionary of 1868 defines "mafia" as a neologism for bravado.

"The Mafia is not, as is generally believed, one vast society of criminals," Mosca wrote in 1902, "but is rather a sentiment akin to arrogance which imposes a special line of conduct upon persons affected by it. The mafioso considers it dishonorable to have recourse to lawful authority to redress a wrong or crime committed against him." The famous post-war Sicilian brigand, Giuliano, was a mafioso in this sense, although he operated more like Jesse James than Vito Genovese.

Perhaps the ultimate authority on the Sicilian Mafia was Cesare Mori. Mori was the head of Mussolini's largely successful drive to eliminate the Mafia in Sicily. Mori wrote:

> It has happened in certain times and in certain districts that mafiosi habitually met in groups which had all the characteristics of true association, with regular, and of course, secret, statutes, concealed badges and marks of recognition, definite hierarchies and elections of chiefs; but these were exceptional cases. . . . [The Mafia is] a system of local oligarchies, closely interwoven, but each autonomous in its own district. . . . There are no statutes. The law of *omertà* [silence] and tradition are enough. There is no election of chiefs, for the chiefs arise of their own accord and impose themselves. There are no rules of admission. When a candidate has all the necessary qualifications, he is absorbed automatically.

The Gennas brought Mafia traditions to Chicago, including the traditional Sicilian parochialism. For their mob, they recruited only Sicilians, and they strongly preferred Sicilians with roots in Marsala. They sold a rot-gut whiskey made from corn sugar and distilled in dozens of Sicilian-occupied homes.

Angelo Genna aspired to be president of the Chicago Unione Siciliana. In the United States, L'Unione Siciliana has often been confused with the Mafia, which is something like confusing the Ancient Order of Hibernians with the Westies. L'Unione was not even a single organization: it was a number of independent clubs in different cities. Big Mike Merlo's word was law among Unione members it Chicago, but it wasn't worth a hoot in New York. Wherever found, L'Unione Siciliana was a club for all Sicilians, but because of the aggressiveness of mafiosi and the submissiveness of other Sicilians, these clubs included a number of mafiosi in their leadership.

Angelo's aspirations brought him into conflict with Al Capone, who, though not Sicilian, tried to lead the Unione Siciliana through stooges. It didn't help his relations with O'Bannion, either, because Deanie was a close friend of Mike Merlo, the founder and president of Chicago's Unione. More serious was the Gennas' conflict with O'Bannion when they began selling their rot-gut in the North Side at half what Deanie charged for good whiskey. To retaliate, O'Bannion began hijacking Genna trucks. Mike Merlo had to step in to prevent a war.

O'Bannion and Torrio had agreed to a boundary line between their territories, Madison Street. Still, there was some friction, because O'Bannion continued to serve his regular customers south of the line, and Capone tried to establish whore houses in the North Side.

In modern folklore, O'Bannion is sometimes portrayed as a "good" gangster because he, unlike the Torrio-Capone combination, would not permit prostitution in his territory. He also loved flowers (his legitimate front was a flower shop), distributed food and clothing to the needy, went to church regularly and hung around with Charles MacArthur, the bard of Chicago newspapering.

It's worthwhile to remember, therefore, that Chicago Police Chief Morgan Collins said, "Dion O'Bannion is Chicago's arch criminal who has killed or seen to the killing of at least 25 men." O'Bannion carried three pistols at all times, continued to open safes in his spare time and had on his payroll many of Chicago's judges, police officials and top politicians. Once an automobile backfired, and O'Bannion, thinking it was a shot, fired at the only other man on the street, an innocent soul named Arthur Vadis, who was on his way to work. Deanie later sent a box of cigars to Vadis' hospital room.

In 1924, O'Bannion asked Torrio if he'd like to buy O'Bannion's Sieben Brewery, which made the best beer in town. The price was $500,000. O'Bannion explained that he was tired of the rackets and wanted to settle down in his flower shop. Torrio agreed and joined O'Bannion and Hymie Weiss at the brewery. Twenty minutes later, police arrived and arrested all three men. It was a first offense for O'Bannion and Weiss, which meant they would pay a fine. For Torrio, though, it was a second Prohibition offense, which meant a mandatory jail term. One of O'Bannion's paid policemen had told him about the raid in time for him to arrange the visit with Torrio.

As Deanie expected, the authorities closed the brewery down permanently. And he kept Torrio's half million.

Out on bond, Torrio made a decision: "O'Bannion's got to go!"

Almost on cue, Mike Merlo, the Sicilian peacemaker, died a natural death.

Capone got in touch with Frankie Yale, a New York gunman, then called Genna headquarters. "Bloody Angelo" sent his two top torpedoes, John Scalise and Albert Anselmi.

On November 10, 1924, Jim Genna came to O'Bannion's flower shop and ordered a $750 floral arrangement for Merlo's funeral. O'Bannion said it would be ready at noon.

A few minutes after 12, Yale, Anselmi and Scalise appeared. O'Bannion, holding a pair of shears in his left hand, held out his right in greeting.

"Hello, boys," he said. "You here for Merlo's?"

Yale grabbed the outstretched hand and pulled O'Bannion off balance while Anselmi and Scalise pumped bullets into him.

Little Hymie Weiss, multiple murderer, compulsive womanizer and the cold blooded planner of the North Side Mob, wept like a baby at the funeral. Weiss, whose real name was Earl Wajcieckowski, had known O'Bannion since both were kids in Holy Name Cathedral parochial school. Weiss vowed he'd get the killers. He had no doubt who they were and who was behind them.

On January 12, Al Capone got out of his car in front of a restaurant. A fast moving car swept down on him, and three shotgun muzzles poked through the window. Behind the guns were Hymie Weiss, Vinnie "Schemer" Drucci and Bugs Moran.

"They let [Capone's car] have everything but the kitchen sink," said a traffic copy who witnessed the incident.

Capone's chauffeur was injured, but Big Al managed to scurry into the restaurant and safety.

Johnny Torrio wasn't so lucky. Just eight days later, Weiss, Drucci, Moran and Frank Gusenberg caught the senior partner of the West Side Mob as he was coming home from a shopping tour with his wife. They blasted him with sawed-off shotguns, then Moran held his pistol to Torrio's head to give him the *coup de grace*. The hammer fell with a click; then the North Siders heard police sirens. They ran to their car and took off, leaving Torrio barely alive on the sidewalk.

When Torrio recovered, he served his term for Prohibition violation in a rural jail where, at his request, bullet-proof windows had been installed. When he got out, he turned all his rackets over to Capone and left the country. He would later return to New York as a criminal elder statesman, but he had had enough of Chicago.

Meanwhile, "Bloody Angelo" Genna did succeed in becoming president of the Unione Siciliana and defied Al Capone. Then he initiated a deal that gives new meaning to the term "fine Italian hand." He sent Scalise and Anselmi to kill Capone. They were to join Capone's gang and do away with him at their earliest convenience. Anselmi and Scalise did join Capone, but they realized he was the man with the heavy artillery, so they told him what Genna wanted them to do. Capone told them to act as if they were still secretly employed by the Gennas. Angelo Genna, he decreed, must die.

Hymie Weiss beat him to it. On May 25, 1925, Angelo Genna got into his roadster and set out to buy a house for his new bride. A big sedan, driven by Frank Gusenberg, roared up alongside him. In the car were Hymie Weiss, Bugs Moran and Schemer Drucci, O'Bannion's oldest and dearest friends, all holding shotguns. Angelo's brother, "Mike the Devil" was barely able to identify what remained of the president of the Unione Siciliana.

Bodies of minor Capone and Genna hoodlums began appearing all over Chicago. Anselmi and Scalise tried to take "Mike the Devil" for a ride, but they had trouble with the police on the way. There was shooting, and Detective William Sweeney killed Mike Genna before Capone's torpedoes got a chance to do it.

"Tony the Gentleman" knowing he was next, had gone into hiding. His top gun, Giuseppe "the Cavalier" Nerone, told him about the treachery of Anselmi and Scalise—doubly heinous because they had joined a non-Sicilian against a Sicilian. Nerone told Genna he'd round up the gang, then "Tony the Gentleman" could meet them and make plans for a comeback. Genna agreed. Nerone called Genna and said they were meeting at a grocery store. When Tony arrived, Nerone shook his hand while Scalise and Anselmi ran up behind him and shot him. Tall, rail-thin John Scalise and short, fat Albert Anselmi—the Mutt and Jeff of Chicago crime—finally hit a Genna.

It wasn't a perfect hit, though. Genna lived long enough to tell police that "the Cavalier" killed him. The cops, thinking he said Cavallaro, wasted time looking up every hood of that name. When they finally found the Cavalier, he was dead in his favorite barber chair. The North Siders had found him first. That did it for the "Terrible Gennas." The last three brothers left Chicago and never returned.

While the bodies were piling up, Al Capone had an armored car built for himself. He also sent his gunners to eliminate the North Side leadership. Twice Capone torpedoes attacked Weiss and Drucci on the street in broad daylight. Twice they missed.

Hymie Weiss decided to give Big Al a moment to remember, if he lived through it. He got a hearse and eight cars. He loaded them with gunmen, some of the hoodlums armed with a brand-new weapon that Frankie McErlane of the Saltis-McErlane group had just introduced—the Thompson submachinegun.

General John T. Thompson, late of the U.S. Army Ordnance Corps, had developed the weapon as a "trench broom." It arrived too late to play a part in World War I, so Thompson's company added some refinements and offered it for commercial sale in 1921. The military weren't interested, but a few police agencies bought the weapon. Basically, it was a small machinegun firing pistol cartridges (.45 automatic pistol) fed by a spring-driven magazine. It weighed about 10 pounds and could fire either semi-automatically or automatically.

McErlane learned of the weapon and decided it would make his favorite activity—killing people—much easier. What was good for McErlane was good for all the other mobsters. Soon the "tommy gun" began to replace the sawed-off shotgun as the tool of Chicago's top gunners. None of them, though, put it to as spectacular a use as Hymie Weiss.

Weiss's "funeral procession" headed south to the suburb of Cicero, then wound past the Hawthorne Hotel in that city—Capone's headquarters. The first car fired blanks to draw the West Siders into the street, but nobody came out. Then the Thompsons opened up. Weiss and his gunners sprayed the hotel from top to bottom. Every window was broken. The cortege stopped, and Weiss, Drucci, Moran and the Gusenberg brothers got out, each holding a submachinegun. They walked into the entrance of the hotel and sprayed the lobby. Then they calmly went back to their cars and drove off.

Al Capone, all this time, was flat on the floor of the coffee shop. He had lost no blood—indeed, no one was killed—but he had lost an immense amount of face. He called Weiss and asked for a truce. Weiss demanded, as the price of peace, Anselmi and Scalise. That was too high a price even for the cowering Capone.

Capone sent Anselmi and Scalise to Weiss, but gave them tommy guns and two backup hoodlums, Frank Nitti and Frank Diamond. They waited in a room across from Weiss's headquarters, O'Bannion's old flower shop. On October 11, 1926, Weiss, three bodyguards and his lawyer walked across the street in front of the Capone guns. Weiss, hit with ten bullets, and one of his bodyguards were killed instantly.

The next North Sider to go was Schemer Drucci. According to the official story, Drucci had been arrested was being transported downtown by the police where his lawyer was waiting with a habeas corpus writ. Drucci began bad-mouthing the cop sitting next to him, and the cop drew his gun.

The Schemer tried to take the gun from the cop and was killed. That's what the police told the press. They didn't explain why a killer like Drucci was not handcuffed, nor did they explain why the cop, Dan Healy, could think of no better way of quieting Drucci than using a gun. A few days earlier, Healy had beaten up Joe Saltis, who was also giving Capone trouble.

That left Bugs Moran top man in the North Side. Moran didn't forget Capone. On January 8, 1929, he and Joe Aiello, who had reorganized the Genna mob, killed Pasqualino Lolordo, a Capone stooge Big Al had installed as head of L'Unione Siciliana.

That was the last straw for Capone. He arranged to have Abe Bernstein, head of Detroit's Purple Gang, call Moran and tell him he could have a load of hijacked Canadian whiskey at $57 a case. Moran arranged to have it delivered to Heyer's garage, then called all his lieutenants.

Capone, meanwhile, arranged for the services of a St. Louis gunman called Killer Burke, who came to Chicago with a backup. To the out-of-state firepower, he added Mutt and Jeff, Scalise and Anselmi. To lead the expedition, he named his favorite hit man, "Machinegun Jack" McGurn. And to outfit his cast, Capone secured three police uniforms.

McGurn, born James Vincenzo De Mora (or Gebardi—accounts differ) was a former boxer whose father sold corn sugar to the Gennas for their pocket distilleries. In 1923, some competitors killed him. The competitors included some Genna gunmen, so Jack joined Capone's army, learned to use a tommy gun and had a great time mowing down Genna soldiers. While McGurn was hunting down Gennas, he heard that one of them had referred to his father as "a nickel and dimer." After he killed a victim, McGurn placed a nickel in his hand to show that he remembered. Within a month and a half, McGurn killed six of Genna's top men. Altogether, before the St. Valentine's massacre, he had personally murdered 15 men.

In between killings, McGurn, a handsome young man who resembled film star Rudolph Valentino, liked to night club. He acquired a share in a number of clubs, one of which featured a young comedian named Joe E. Lewis. Lewis quit for a better job, in spite of McGurn's warning. After a final threat on November 9, 1927, Lewis's new employer, John Fogarty, said he was going to tell Bugs Moran. He warned the comic to stay in his room and not to open his door for anyone. Lewis was sleeping in his hotel room when he heard a knock at the door. Almost by reflex, he opened the door and three hoodlums sent by McGurn entered, fractured his skull with pistol butts and cut his throat.

Lewis was found before he died and was taken to the hospital. When he regained consciousness, he couldn't use one arm and couldn't talk. He slowly regained the ability to speak with the help of Rev. J. A. Heitzer, a professor at the University of Notre Dame who met him in the hospital, and he gradually recovered the use of his limbs.

Meanwhile, Fogarty did tell Moran. The three hoodlums were found dead before Lewis got out of the hospital. Then Frank and Pete Gusenberg caught McGurn in a phone booth and sprayed him with tommy gun fire. Unfortunately for the Gusenbergs, McGurn recovered.

Frank and Pete Gusenberg didn't recognize McGurn when Capone's "cops" entered the garage. Machinegun Jack didn't come in until all seven men were lined up against the wall, including the optometrist. The North Siders weren't worried: routine searches were an annoying but harmless form of police harrassment. But this was no search. Instead, the phony cops mowed their prisoners down with tommy guns. When the police arrived, only Frank Gusenberg was alive. The cops asked who shot him. Gusenberg, with 14 bullets in him, whispered, "Nobody shot me."

The massacre almost destroyed Moran as a power in the underworld. He still had remnants of a mob, but hoods like to be on the winning side, and Moran looked like a loser.

The massacre gave Scalise and Anselmi new ideas. Their bullets had put Big Al where he was. They could put him somewhere else, too. "Bloody Angelo" had the right idea, but he had it at the wrong time. They began talking with the current head of L'Unione, a Capone stooge, and made a few discreet inquiries about what West Siders would do if something happened to Capone.

Big Al continued to heap honors on Mutt and Jeff. He invited them, with his L'Unione Siciliana puppet, to a dinner in their honor May 7, 1929. Then he informed the three that he knew of their treachery. He reached under the table, pulled out a baseball bat and bashed in each man's skull.

Capone was apparently triumphant, but he didn't feel safe. In June 1929, he attended a gangster convention in Atlantic City that included, besides all the big boys from the East, Chicago mobsters Bugs Moran and Joe Aiello. Old Johnny Torrio was the moderator. The gang lords all agreed on a truce, but Capone didn't trust them. In fact, he had information that they were going to do away with him before he got to Chicago. He apparently arranged to be arrested on a weapons charge in Philadelphia, which got him a year of safety during a rather comfortable incarceration in Pennsylvania. When he got out, he learned that a citizens' group, the Chicago Crime Commission, had labeled him "Public Enemy Number One," and federal agents were investigating him for income tax evasion. He was convicted of tax evasion in 1931 and sentenced to 11 years in prison. He was released after eight, because he was dying of syphilis.

Capone's jail sentence left McGurn with little work and less prestige. He lost his nightclubs during the Depression and he lost his mistress when his money ran out. On February 13, 1936, the eve of the seventh anniversary of the massacre, Jack McGurn was trying to forget his troubles at a bowling alley.

Three men entered the bowling alley, one of them holding a Thompson submachinegun. They riddled McGurn and left him dead on the polished wood floor. Nobody was able to identify the gunmen to the police, but it was common knowledge that the machinegunner was Bugs Moran. In McGurn's right hand, he placed a nickel; in his left, a comic valentine.

Fifteen

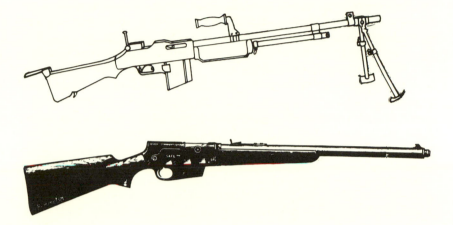

Hello, Young Lovers

May 23, 1934, Bienville Parish, Louisiana

The sidewalks were broiling in Oklahoma City that July day in 1933 when a young couple in a black Ford approached a traffic policeman.

"Watch this," the young woman in the driver's seat said to her male companion. She stopped next to the officer.

"How can I get to Sixth and Main?" she asked the cop.

As the policeman gave her directions, she slid a sawed-off shotgun, hidden by the door, into position.

Then she blew off his head.

Top: Browning Automatic Rifle, Clyde Barrow's heavy artillery. Model shown is the M-1918 A1. Barrow used the M-1918 without a bipod. Below: Remington semi-auto rifle like the .30 Remington model Frank Hamer used when he and five other officers ambushed Bonnie and Clyde.

The young woman squealed with delight. She and her giggling companion drove off.

The subject of this story is, of course, Bonnie Parker. Who but American mythology's queen of murder and rapine could do such a thing? The story has been repeated again and again, in print and in lectures, to show what ruthless, worthless, immoral creatures Bonnie Parker and Clyde Barrow were.

Nevertheless, the story smells like a catfish left too long in that Oklahoma sun. For more reasons than one:

—Clyde Barrow almost always drove when he and Bonnie Parker were together.

—By 1933, Bonnie and Clyde were so well known in the lower plains states that it would have been suicidal for them to voluntarily approach a police officer.

—Early in June 1933, when the really hot weather began, Bonnie Parker was trapped in a burning car and almost burned to death. She couldn't drive—she couldn't even walk without assistance until fall. In July 1933, when the shooting was supposed to have taken place, Bonnie Parker was totally incapacitated and frequently unconscious.·

—Finally, no traffic policeman in Oklahoma City was killed on duty by anyone in 1933.

This story, and some even more bizarre, originated in the self-serving "confession" of a bandit who traveled with Bonnie and Clyde until he decided he could make more money working by himself. W. D. Jones was by any reasonable standard a highly unreliable source, but the story gained currency because of that old standby of mystery writers and political analysts—powerful interests. Particularly one that was perhaps the most powerful in the country while he lived: J. Edgar Hoover, director of the FBI.

Hoover wanted to deglamorize crooks, especially the bank robbers who had been speeding through the back roads of the Midwest and the Middle South in the wake of the Great Depression. Torturing the truth in the interests of law and order was a Hoover technique that was later directed against the Rev. Martin Luther King, the civil rights movement and any groups the Director considered dangerous leftists.

In the case of Bonnie and Clyde, this disinformation was largely wasted effort. The couple themselves were perhaps the most ridiculous and pathetic of all legendary American criminals.

The story began in January 1930, when Bonnie, a waitress who had lost her job, decided to help a friend in West Dallas who had broken her arm. At the home of the other young woman she met a short, rabbit-face man with jug ears. She instantly fell in love.

What attracted a pretty, 19-year-old blonde who had always made excellent marks in school and was, according to her cousin, "the tenderest-hearted little thing that I ever saw" to 20-year-old Clyde Barrow has always been a mystery. Puny (5′ 6″) Clyde had had as little education as he could manage and got his kicks as a kid by breaking chickens' wings and watching them flop around. But Bonnie, a romantic by nature, had always been capable of Grand Passion. In high school, she took little interest in boys until, at 15, she noticed classmate Roy Thornton. Bonnie had his name tattooed on the inside of her thigh and married him when she was only 16. The couple moved into a house two blocks from Bonnie's mother. Bonnie was never comfortable far from her mother for very long. Roy, though, was a wanderer. He deserted Bonnie for weeks, then months, at a time. Each time he left, she went into deep depression and did not revive until he came home again. Roy's last absence, though, lasted more than a year, and when he returned in 1929, Bonnie realized she no longer loved Roy. She threw him out. Later, she learned that he had been involved in a robbery and a murder.

Not long after the split, the Dallas restaurant where Bonnie worked had to close. The Depression was beginning. About the only bright spot in her life was meeting Clyde Barrow. The feeling seemed to be mutual—or at least Clyde seemed to feel as much love for Bonnie as that self-centered psychopath ever felt for another human. After knowing Clyde a week, Bonnie took him home to meet her mother. Emma Parker spent quite a while talking to Barrow, trying to find out what sort of man her little girl was so thrilled about. Barrow could be charming when he wanted to be, and Mrs. Parker was favorably impressed. It was late when the talk ended, and she let Barrow sleep on the couch in the living room.

Early the next morning, two Dallas police officers appeared and took Bonnie's dream man away in handcuffs. Bonnie "screamed and cried, beat her hands on the walls and begged the officers not to take him," her mother recalled.

She wrote to him frequently while he waited in jail for his trial.

"I want you to be a man, honey, and not a thug. I know you are good, and I know you can make good," she wrote in a typical letter.

Clyde, though, was more interested in making an escape than in making good. He had been sentenced to two years in prison plus 12 years probation for robberies and burglaries committed around Waco with his brother Buck. While waiting to be transferred from the Waco jail to the state prison, he persuaded Bonnie to help him escape. She was to go to the house of a cellmate, find a gun he had hidden there and bring it to the jail. Bonnie found the gun, a small, flat Colt .32 automatic, and carried it in her bosom into the jail. Bonnie gave her lover the gun, then went home. While she was on her way, Clyde escaped. He was gone only a week though. He and a companion botched a burglary in Ohio and were sent back to Texas. And because of the escape, Clyde now had to serve, not two, but 14 years.

While Clyde chopped cotton at the Eastham prison farm, Bonnie continued to write letters exhorting him to "make good." The working conditions and discipline at Eastham were brutal. After almost two years of it, Clyde persuaded another convict to chop off two of his toes so he couldn't work and would have to be transferred. There was no transfer, but, unknown to Clyde, the parole board had been considering his case. About a week after his self-mutilation, Clyde was paroled.

Somehow, life was like that for Clyde.

Clyde's brother, Buck, had previously been sent to Eastham, but his departure was painless. A trusty, he simply walked away. He went to Louisiana, where he married Blanche Caldwell, a gentle country girl who persuaded him to return to Texas and give himself up. Buck came back to prison shortly before Clyde got out.

As soon as Clyde was able to walk, he left to take a construction job in Worcester, Massachusetts that his sister had arranged. He lasted two weeks. Regular work and Clyde Barrow just didn't mix.

Soon after Clyde returned, Bonnie told her mother she was taking a job as a cosmetics demonstrator in Houston. Bonnie had been gone only two days, though, when Emma Parker learned that her daughter was in jail in Kaufman, a small town near Dallas.

Instead of going to Houston, she had joined Clyde and a young thief named Ralph Fults in an attempted robbery. She had wanted an honest Clyde, but if she couldn't have that, she'd take a crooked Clyde. Unfortunately, the crooked Clyde wasn't very competent. The robbery was botched, and the three fled from the police in a stolen car. The car stuck in the mud, and the would-be robbers ran across the fields. They jumped on some mules, but the animals refused to move, so the three thieves jumped off again and ran. Bonnie lost her shoes, and Clyde had to carry her. That wasn't too hard: at 4′ 10″ and 85 pounds, Bonnie wasn't much of a load. Clyde deposited her, with Fults, in a barn and said he'd steal a car and come back.

He stole a car, but he never came back. Bonnie and Fults eventually started down the road toward Dallas, and the police picked them up. Clyde found a new partner, Ray Hamilton (who, contrary to some versions of the legend, did not know Bonnie previously) and pulled two more robberies. In the second, they got $15 in cash and about $2,500 in diamond rings, but they panicked and killed the proprietor, John Bucher.

In most versions of the legend, Bonnie is with Clyde at the murder scene. Actually, she was in a cell in the Kaufman jail, where she began writing a ballad, *The Story of Suicide Sal*. Author John Treherne said this poem "is exactly in the tradition of the contemporary ballads celebrating the criminal psychopaths who had become folk heroes of the American mid- and southwest." Noting her transformation from Clyde's would-be reformer to criminal partner, Treherne observed, "Perhaps Bonnie Parker was corrupted by cheap literature."

The grand jury that heard Bonnie's case refused to indict. She went home. Her mother tried to lay down the law. Barrow and Hamilton had just robbed two filling stations and taken their managers hostage.

"If Clyde's going to keep up the way he's been going, you're going to have to stay away from him," Emma Parker said.

Bonnie said she wouldn't see Clyde again.

Two months later, in late June 1932, her mother came home from work to find a note from Bonnie saying she had gone to Wichita Falls, a booming oil town, to work in a restaurant there. She didn't mention that Clyde and Ray Hamilton were also in Wichita Falls, planning a big robbery in Dallas. On July 31, Barrow and Hamilton took Bonnie Parker home, then stuck up the Neuhoff Packing Company and escaped over the route they had planned. They returned to Dallas, picked up Bonnie and took her to their current hideout, an abandoned farm house just outside of Grand Prairie, Texas.

Bonnie still hated to be away from her mother for long, so Barrow and Hamilton took her back to Dallas, then stole another car and left for Oklahoma. That night, they saw an outdoor country dance. Hamilton wanted to dance. Barrow pulled up near the dance, and Hamilton started to have second thoughts about the advisability of stopping. A total stranger would be noticed in a small town. Sheriff C. G. Maxwell and his undersheriff, Gene Moore, decided to investigate the out-of-state car with two strange men. They might be drinking. National Prohibition was still in effect, and Oklahoma would be a dry state for years after the 21st Amendment was ratified.

Once again, Barrow and Hamilton panicked. They shot both officers and Barrow tried to drive away. The crowd ran in all directions. The wounded sheriff propped himself up on one elbow and fired at the car. One of the dancers picked up the dead undersheriff's gun and fired into the darkness. Barrow crashed the car into a culvert and overturned it. He and

Hamilton fled on foot. A car stopped for the two men apparently stranded on the road, and the bandits took the car and its driver. Fifteen miles down the road, Clyde Barrow wrecked the new car. Leaving the hostage with his vehicle, the bandits ran to a farmhouse and stole a third car, taking the farmer's nephew hostage. They headed back toward Texas, stole a fourth car, abandoning the farmer's nephew and his vehicle. They finally abandoned the fourth car near Dallas. In their excursion, they had stolen four cars, wrecked two of them, kidnapped two men, shot two police officers and killed one of them. Their profit: zero.

A few days later, Bonnie Parker joined them at the Grand Prairie hideout. She had made her commitment. From now on, she would not merely wait for Clyde. She would go with him, wherever that might be.

Bonnie Parker was now a full-fledged member of a fraternity that was a 1930s phenomenon—the automobile bandits. The auto bandits were the spiritual heirs of the Jameses, the Youngers, the Doolins and all the other horse-mounted brotherhoods who had ravaged the Midwest in the late 19th century. Like the horsemen, the new breed were predominantly rural people who had been—if not driven, encouraged—to enter a life of crime by economic conditions. The Great Depression hit farmers particularly hard, and banks were foreclosing farms and evicting farmers at a scandalous rate. On the Great Plains, a long drought added to the farmers' and ranchers' woes. Their country became known as the Dust Bowl.

At the same time, fast, relatively reliable cars offered new criminal opportunities. And on the Plains, it was virtually impossible to block an escape route. The states were and are covered with a grid of township roads, most of them dirt, running east and west, north and south, every mile. So regular is this grid that air travelers flying low enough to see the roads can calculate their speed by counting the number of roads that cut their path in a minute.

Bonnie had chosen a life of crime, and she had chosen to spend it with the least competent of criminals. Clyde Barrow was to John Dillinger what a hardscrabble Texas tenant farm is to the King Ranch. Dillinger and his gang carefully planned bank heists, stole large amounts of money and lived comfortably between jobs. Bonnie and Clyde seldom planned anything, lived from hand to mouth by two-bit stickups, slept in the fields or in a succession of stolen cars and were on the move continuously. Occasionally, they were lucky enough to spend a couple of nights in a tourist cabin.

There may have been more behind this than Barrow's ineptness. Ralph Fults, who knew him in prison, said Clyde's whole life was changed by the experience. He developed an insane resentment of authority and a bitter hatred of all law officers. His post-prison career indicates that he had become a nihilist—a man without goals, not even the accumulation of wealth, and no interest in anything but the thrills of the moment. As for Bonnie, her only interest was Clyde Barrow.

In August 1932, Bonnie, Clyde and Ray Hamilton made one effort to hide out and let things cool down. They drove to Carlsbad, New Mexico, where Bonnie's aunt lived. On the way, though, a sheriff noticed that the license plate on their car belonged to a stolen vehicle. He stopped the bandits but found himself staring at the muzzle of Clyde's revolver. Clyde put the officer in the back seat with Hamilton, turned away from Carlsbad and took the sheriff to San Antonio, where he was released. Police blocked the road ahead of him, but Clyde, who had become an expert driver in the course of traveling hundreds of thousands of miles in stolen cars, made a U-turn and outran the police.

Two years later, on April 10, 1934, Clyde sent a letter to Henry Ford to tell him "what a dandy car you make. I have drove Fords exclusively when I could get away with one. For sustained speed and freedom from trouble the Ford has got every other car skinned . . ." A few days later, a letter to Ford signed "John Dillinger" gave a similar testimonial. Alas, this letter proved to be a forgery.

Antics like kidnapping cops and evading police traps made Bonnie and Clyde front-page news. So did their killings. A typical murder occurred October 11, 1932, when Bonnie and Clyde held up a general store in Sherman, Texas. The owner, Howard Hall, apparently resisted, and Clyde shot him dead. In the two years he was on the road, Clyde Barrow killed 12 men, a total that indicates an unusual disregard for human life.

As soon as Barrow, Parker and Hamilton got their first decent score—a $1,401 haul from the robbery of a bank at Cedar Hill, Texas, Hamilton got out. He took a train for Michigan, saying he wanted to visit his father.

Clyde wanted to be a gang leader, but now he had only Bonnie. The two bandits found two thugs who, expecting rich loot, were eager to follow the famous Clyde Barrow. The first job they pulled, robbery of a bank at Oranago, Missouri, grossed $115. That night, the two thugs slipped away. Undismayed, Clyde went after another Missouri bank while Bonnie sat outside in a car with the motor running. Clyde burst through the doors with his sawed-off, semiautomatic shotgun at hip level. An elderly man in a chair in the lobby was singularly unimpressed.

"You're a little late, young fellow," he said. "Bank's been closed for four days."

Being a bank robber in the Depression had its disadvantages.

In spite of all their traveling, Bonnie and Clyde never stayed away from Dallas long. When they were in town, they would throw a bottle containing a message into the yard of Emma Parker or Cumie Barrow, Clyde's mother. The mothers would call the rest of the families to tell them they were "cooking red beans," the code for the prodigals' return. The Barrows and Parkers would meet them at the location mentioned in the letter in the bottle.

Dallas County Sheriff "Smoot" Schmid twice tried to capture Bonnie and Clyde at these reunions, once by cutting them off with a huge earth-moving machine. Each time, Bonnie and Clyde were too alert and too fast for him. He then detailed two of his best deputies, Bob Alcorn and Ted Hinton, to track the lethal couple down wherever they were.

The knowledge that Bonnie and Clyde were in frequent touch with their families did not belong solely to the law. On December 1, 1932, a teenager named William Daniel Jones, known to everyone as "W. D." came to Emma Parker and told her he wanted to join the gang. He had known Clyde since he was a child, and his greatest ambition was to travel with the famous bandit and his girlfriend. Jones achieved his ambition when Bonnie and Clyde returned to Dallas for the Christmas holidays.

For 11 months, W. D. Jones would manipulate guns and steering wheels, participate in robberies and murders to advance his hero's interests. Then, captured in Houston, he would tell a story that nobody but police enraged by the cop-killers Barrow and Parker could be expected to believe. According to Jones, the bandits picked him up at a filling station and made him their slave. They chained him to a tree at night so he wouldn't get away. Encouraged by the apparent police acceptance of this story, Jones went on. Bonnie Parker killed a traffic cop in Oklahoma City just for fun, he said. Also, both Barrow and Parker raped him repeatedly. Barrow, according to Jones, was a homosexual and Parker a nymphomaniac. He did not try to explain the fierce attraction the pair obviously had for each other. But, then, he did not explain why he had been robbing people in Houston instead of making a bee-line to the nearest police station to seek protection. Nor did he explain why Bonnie and Clyde trusted him with machineguns or getaway cars. Or why he had proven himself worthy of their trust when he used those items.

W. D. Jones's story kept him out of the electric chair, but not out of prison. It was also marvelous raw material for the FBI's magnificent public relations machine. The only admirable thing about Bonnie and Clyde was their devotion to each other. Jones's 28-page statement provided an opportunity to taint the public perception of that relationship. The homosexual-nymphomaniac relationship—like Jones's slavery—was ridiculous, but it was repeated so often it's become a permanent part of some versions of the Bonnie and Clyde legend.

Jones got his first taste of the outlaw life on Christmas Day, 1932, when he helped Barrow and Parker steal a car in Temple, Texas. The owner objected, so Barrow and Jones shot him dead.

A few days later, police, acting on information developed investigating that murder, attempted to ambush the Barrow gang at the house of Clyde's sister in West Dallas. There was a short shoot-out, and Clyde killed Deputy Sheriff Malcolm Davis. Bonnie, driving a second car and thinking Clyde had been shot, raced away in a panic. Clyde finally caught her, and they proceeded to Missouri. Along the way, a motorcycle cop tried to stop them for speeding. They disarmed the cop, put him on the floor of the back seat under W. D.'s feet and took him for a long ride before releasing him.

In March 1933, Buck Barrow, thanks to the tears of his wife and his mother, was released from prison. He decided—over Blanche Barrow's protests—to visit Clyde and Bonnie at the apartment they had been renting in Joplin, Missouri, for the last two weeks, the longest period they had ever stayed in one place. Joplin at that time was supposed to be a safe haven for crooks if they paid the right people. Bonnie and Clyde either didn't know who to pay or didn't want to pay. At any rate, Clyde and W. D., who were out looking for a store to rob, had just come back when the police arrived at 4 p.m. April 13. Clyde killed two officers with a shotgun while W. D. and Bonnie sprayed the others with Browning automatic rifles they had stolen from a National Guard armory. A vacant police car blocked the driveway, but W. D. Jones ran out under fire and pushed it out of the way. He was wounded in the head but fought on beside Clyde Barrow. He exhibited no desire to be "saved" that day. Blanche Barrow, who had been playing solitaire when the shooting started, ran screaming from the house followed by her pet dog. The police apparently saw only a distraught female, not a gang member, and ignored her. Clyde was wounded, but got behind the wheel and roared away, with Bonnie firing a BAR out of the right front window and W. D. Jones, blood flowing from his wound, firing another BAR through the rear left window. Buck, also in the back seat, was petrified. Clyde stopped and picked up Blanche. His sister-in-law had the dog in her arms and clutched the playing cards so tightly the others had to pry her fingers open. Buck and Blanche, even if they had desired nothing more than a family reunion, were now fugitives like Bonnie and Clyde.

The Joplin police had no doubt who the killers were. Bonnie had been working on her "Suicide Sal" ballad and left an unfinished copy on a table.

The bandits also left two rolls of film, snapshots of Bonnie, Clyde and W. D. clowning around. In one, Bonnie has a cigar in her mouth, leading newspapers ever after to call her the "cigar-smoking gun moll."

The Barrow gang was now too hot to risk renting apartments or tourist cabins. They would go for weeks without seeing a bed or a shower. They washed themselves and their clothes in isolated streams, still frigid from winter. Even food was hard to get. Blanche, least known of the group, did the shopping. Clyde wore out car after car with ceaseless driving, pausing only for an occasional robbery.

Once, they kidnapped a Rushton, Louisiana, undertaker and his fiancee, dropped them off on a lonely country road and drove the undertaker's car to Minnesota. With their money running short, they stopped in Okabena, Minnesota and held up the bank. The Barrow gang's one Minnesota robbery was reminiscent of the James gang's one Minnesota robbery.

"Everybody in town seemed to know about the holdup," Clyde Barrow said later. "There was a regular reception committee waiting for us when we came out, everybody shooting left and right." The Barrows were luckier than the Jameses, though. They got $2,500 and got away unscathed.

The gang had another reunion with their families. Bonnie's mother tried to talk her into giving herself up: jail was better than the electric chair, she said.

"Clyde's name is up, Mama," Bonnie said. "He'll be killed sooner or later, because he's never going to give up. When he dies, I want to die, anyway."

Soon after they left the reunion, it looked as if Bonnie was going to die before Clyde. Surprised by a closed bridge, Clyde tried to turn around and crashed down an embankment. The car exploded and burned, with Bonnie trapped inside. Clyde tore at the car "like an insane person," Jones said later, while Bonnie begged him to shoot her. After Clyde pulled her out, he and Jones carried her to a nearby farm house. They and the farm family did their feeble best to help the woman, most of her body covered with burns.

While Clyde was kneeling by Bonnie's bedside, the bedroom door opened. Jones lost his head and fired before he could see who was coming in. He hit the farmer's daughter-in-law in the hand. The farmer managed to unobtrusively call the sheriff. The sheriff and the town marshal arrived and were captured by Clyde and W. D. The bandits put them in the car, along with the delirious Bonnie. The captive marshal, moved to pity, tried to support Bonnie to ease her pain.

At Erick, Oklahoma, Clyde tied the two officers to a tree and met Buck and Blanche, who were returning from a visit to Blanche's parents in Missouri. The reunited Barrow gang drove to Fort Smith, Arkansas, and checked into a tourist cabin. Bonnie's condition worsened steadily. Clyde left Fort Smith at noon June 19, 1933, drove to Dallas, picked up Bonnie's sister Billie and returned to Fort Smith by dawn the next day. Billie had nursing skills, and under her treatment, Bonnie began to recover. Clyde never left her bedside. Never again would he abandon Bonnie as he had the time he left her in the barn while he went to look for a car. For the first time in his life, Clyde Barrow loved another person unselfishly.

While Clyde was watching Bonnie, Buck and W. D. went out to raise money. They held up the Piggly Wiggly store in Fayetteville, Arkansas. Their descriptions and that of their car were radioed ahead, and they ran into a roadblock at Alma. W. D., driving too fast, rammed the car ahead of him and wrecked both. Town Marshal Henry Humphrey and a deputy approached. Jones and Barrow opened fire, killing the marshal and wounding the deputy. They stole the marshal's car and drove off, pursued by half the town of Alma—including two hearses filled with deputies. Jones and Barrow wrecked the police car, but they managed to hitchhike back to Fort Smith.

Clyde Barrow knew they had to move, so he ferried the gang in two trips from the tourist camp to a remote hilltop, where they camped for three nights. While they were camping, Clyde stole another car and broke into another National Guard armory to get more guns and ammunition.

Clyde especially liked the Browning Automatic Rifle, known to millions of World War II and Korean War veterans as the BAR. The version Clyde used, named by the U.S. Army the M-1918, was a 16-pound light machinegun, fed with 20 round magazines and capable of firing automatically and semiautomatically. It was longer and heavier than the Thompson favored by Al Capone and Hymie Weiss, but vastly more powerful. Instead of a pistol cartridge, it took the .30-06 rifle cartridge—the most powerful regular infantry rifle cartridge ever used in war.

Clyde took Billie back to Dallas, then the whole gang moved to a tourist cabin in Great Bend, Kansas, where Clyde continued to nurse Bonnie. By mid-July, Bonnie was usually conscious, but her legs seemed to be permanently bent, and she had to be carried.

The Barrow gang established a temporary base at Fort Dodge, Iowa, and held up three gas stations. Their funds replenished, they headed toward Kansas City. They stopped at a Platte City, Missouri, tourist camp and took two cabins with built-in garages. Instead of eating at the camp's restaurant, renowned locally for its food, Clyde sent W. D. Jones out to buy take-out sandwiches at another eatery. Somebody got suspicious and called the sheriff.

After dark, sheriff's deputies equipped with an armored car and hand-held steel shields surrounded the cabins. Suddenly one garage opened and

Clyde Barrow appeared, blasting away with a BAR. Clyde's bullets penetrated the armored car and the steel shields. The sheriff, his son and a deputy were wounded. Then Buck Barrow dashed from the other cabin, spraying the area with his BAR. He was hit and slumped backward. Clyde's car came roaring out of the garage with W. D. Jones standing on the running board and firing bursts from his BAR. Bonnie was huddled in the front passenger seat. Blanche appeared, pushed Buck into the car and climbed in herself. The deputies fired a volley as the car disappeared, cutting Blanche with flying glass.

The Barrow gang headed back to Iowa and camped in a glade known as Dexfield Park. On July 24, 1933, a posse that included Iowa National Guardsmen converged on them. Buck was shot again and mortally wounded. Blanche refused to leave him and was captured. Clyde and W. D. carried Bonnie into the woods and made their escape. Clyde was shot as they crossed a river, but he held up three men and took their car. He put Bonnie in the rear seat, then let W. D. drive as he sat in the front seat and moaned from the pain of his wound.

They stole another car and drove southwest towards Denver for three days. Then they turned an headed in another direction. Weeks later in Dallas, Bonnie couldn't remember where they went.

"We lived in little ravines, secluded woods, down side roads for days that stretched into weeks," she said. "We were all so sick that time went by without our knowing it. We lost track of the days."

There must have been a few robberies to get food, and they must have been performed by W. D., the only member of the gang fit enough to look menacing, even with a gun. Stranded near Clarkesdale, Mississippi, with a worn-out car, W. D. left to steal another one. He took a leaf from the book of his hero, Clyde Barrow. He never came back. Months later, on November 15, 1933, Dallas County deputies, acting on a tip, arrested him in Houston, and W. D. Jones sang his strange song.

Bonnie and Clyde returned to Dallas September 7. Clyde had recovered from his wound. Bonnie's condition had greatly improved, but she still couldn't walk without assistance. They didn't go far from Dallas for the next few months. During autumn, Emma Parker said, "The kids came in to see us every single night except five."

Early in November, Bonnie, Clyde and a man who was never identified held up a small refinery near Overton, Texas and stole between $2,000 and $3,000. With a little money, the couple had time to plot what they expected to be their greatest coup—breaking Ray Hamilton out of the Eastham prison farm where he was serving a 263-year term.

Clyde got a message to Hamilton telling where and when he would plant pistols in timber the convicts were clearing.

Just before the breakout date, though, Bonnie found she couldn't move without severe pain. Her mother called it rheumatism, but it was probably her still-unhealed burns acting up. It was so painful that Clyde had to drive 250 miles back to Dallas, with Bonnie screaming at every bump. Her mother and his sister rubbed her with a liniment and Bonnie said she'd be able to resume the adventure.

There was a heavy fog at the prison farm on breakout day. At the right moment, a convict named Joe Palmer dived into a bush, came up with a .45 automatic and shot two guards. Hamilton grabbed another pistol. Clyde Barrow stepped out of the mist and began firing a BAR. Next to him was James Mullen, another friend of Hamilton, armed with a pistol. Bonnie leaned on the car horn to let the escapees know where to run. Hamilton and Palmer were followed by three more convicts, Henry Methvin, Hilton Bybee and J. R. French. Mullen tried to keep all but Hamilton and Palmer out of the car, but Barrow told them all to squeeze in and headed for Houston.

Clyde dropped Bybee and French off on the way to Houston. Mullen left the party a little later. Palmer got car sick and stayed that way, while young Henry Methvin was stuck dumb at the thought of riding with the famous Bonnie and Clyde. Hamilton made up for Methvin's silence with non-stop talk. His main topic was how badly he needed female companionship and how badly he wanted to see Mary O'Dare, the wife of a former partner who was serving 50 years for armed robbery.

After stealing another car and robbing another National Guard armory for a new supply of BARs and other guns, they picked up Mary O'Dare. Barrow and Hamilton then robbed a bank outside of Dallas while Bonnie, Mary O'Dare and Joe Palmer (still sick) waited in the woods. The robbers got $2,400, $3,800, $4,128.50, $4,433, $4,800 or $6,700, depending on which account you read. Hamilton proposed that he and Barrow split the money equally, but Barrow insisted that it be evenly divided among all six. That started a quarrel between Barrow and Hamilton that never ended.

The beautiful Mary O'Dare made things worse. She was an agitator. At one point, she suggested to Bonnie that she "fix" Clyde. "Then while he's out, you take his roll and beat it." When the gang stopped in Terre Haute, Indiana, Hamilton and his girlfriend left, to the relief of the others.

Meanwhile, Lee Simmons, head of the Texas prison system, talked Frank Hamer into joining the manhunt. Hamer, a former town marshal and former captain in the Texas Rangers, was a sort of living legend. He cultivated the image of the strong, silent western lawman and had, depending on who told the story, killed between 40 and 65 alleged lawbreakers. He had undoubtedly killed a lot. Hamer possessed the invincible self-righteousness of a Reformation Calvinist. He was convinced that his opponents were always wrong, and the wrong deserved killing. Once, as a young cowboy, two village toughs made insulting remarks about him when he entered a general store. Hamer ignored them. As he came out of the store, one of the toughs advanced toward him. Hamer drew a large knife and began whittling a toothpick. Then he spat in the other's face. The other man stared at Hamer a moment, then wiped his face and walked away. Asked what he would have done if the other man had reached for him, Hamer said, "Made two pieces of him."

Clyde Barrow was less concerned about the law than about a fellow desperado. Raymond Hamilton wrote a letter to the Dallas newspapers disparaging his former partner. Barrow decided to kill Hamilton. He sent Joe Palmer to find Hamilton. Palmer left and never came back. Then Barrow saw in the newspapers that Hamilton had pulled a robbery near Dallas. He and Bonnie, with Henry Methvin, went to one of Hamilton's favorite hiding places Easter Sunday 1934.

The fact that Bonnie was willing to take part in a premeditated murder shows that while Barrow was growing more like her in his devotion to his partner, she was getting more like him. Along with her native sentimentality, there was a new callousness. Bonnie took her pet rabbit, Sonny Boy, with her. She was planning to give Sonny Boy to her mother as an Easter present later in the day.

Hamilton didn't show up as expected. Clyde and Methvin were dozing when Bonnie heard two motorcycles and gave the alarm. Two policemen were coming to investigate the parked car. Barrow, Parker and Methvin shot them down. Then Bonnie, according to a witness, walked over to the men with a shotgun. Seeing one move, she fired a blast from the shotgun into him, then laughed because his head bounced.

Other police were getting closer. The FBI was later to claim credit for putting the heat on Bonnie and Clyde, but no FBI agents ever got near them. The real heat was provided by Dallas Deputies Bob Alcorn and Ted Hinton and by Frank Hamer and Manny Gault, a Texas Highway Patrolman. Usually, Alcorn and Hinton followed Bonnie and Clyde while Hamer and Gault followed Alcorn and Hinton. They stayed on the trail through state after state, identifying camp sites by Bonnie's Camel cigarettes and Clyde's hand-rolled Bull Durhams and by the lettuce scraps Sonny Boy left.

The lawmen learned that Henry Methvin's father had a farm near Shreveport, Louisiana. Hinton and Alcorn visited the area several times early in 1934 and alerted the Bienville Parish sheriff, Henderson Jordan. At the time, though, Bonnie, Clyde and young Henry Methvin were far away. They killed a police officer and kidnapped another in Commerce, Oklahoma, and dropped their hostage off in Missouri. They were in Memphis, Tennessee, when they read in the newspaper that Raymond Hamilton and Mary O'Dare had been arrested in Louisiana. They couldn't stop moving: the pursuit was too hot.

It was tough on the pursuers, too. Ted Hinton wrote:

> We had scoured the swamps in the Louisiana back country and the smoky hills of Arkansas. We came to know each place in northeastern Oklahoma, where Bonnie had spent some time when she was growing up and where she had friends and relatives. We had met with local law enforcement people, generally no more than one or two good men in each area, and shared our experiences with them. . . . Generally, we felt that the area in which the fugitives could go without attracting attention was shrinking. We told our-selves that if their physical resources were being drained as ours were, living in our car for the most part and taking sandwiches along as we searched, then we could be reasonably sure that they would make a fatal mistake somewhere.

Hinton was right. The strain was beginning to tell on the fugitives. At the last Barrow-Parker family reunion, Bonnie gave her mother her latest ballad.

The Story of Bonnie and Clyde

You've read the story of Jesse James—
Of how he lived and died;
    If you're still in need
    Of something to read,
Here's the story of Bonnie and Clyde.
Now Bonnie and Clyde are the Barrow gang.
I'm sure you all have read
    How they rob and steal
    And those who squeal
Are usually found dying or dead.
There's lots of untruths to these write-ups;
They're not so ruthless as that;
    Their nature is raw;
    They hate all the law—
The stool pigeons, spotters and rats.
They call them cold-blooded killers;
They say they are heartless and mean;
    But I say this with pride
    That I once knew Clyde

When he was honest and upright and clean.
But the laws fooled around
Kept taking him down
And locking him up in a cell,
 Till he said to me,
 "I'll never be free,
So I'll meet a few of them in hell."
The road was so dimly lighted;
There were no highway signs to guide;
 But they made up their minds
 If all roads were blind,
They wouldn't give up till they died.
The road gets dimmer and dimmer;
Sometimes you can hardly see;
 But it's fight, man to man,
 And do all you can,
For they know they can never be free.
From heart-break some people have suffered;
From weariness some people have died;
 But take it all in all,
 Our troubles are small
Till we get like Bonnie and Clyde.
If a policeman is killed in Dallas,
And they have no clew or guide;
 If they can't find a fiend,
 They just wipe their slate clean
And hang it on Bonnie and Clyde.
There's two crimes committed in America
Not accredited to the Barrow mob;
 They had no hand
 In the kidnap demand,
Nor the Kansas City depot job.
A newsboy once said to his buddy:
"I wish old Clyde would get jumped;
 In these awful hard times
 We'd make a few dimes
If five or six cops would get bumped."
The police haven't got the report yet,
But Clyde called me up today;
 He said, "Don't start any fights—
 We aren't working nights—

We're joining the NRA."
From Irving to West Dallas viaduct
Is known as the Great Divide,
    Where women are kin,
    And the men are men,
And they won't "stool" on Bonnie and Clyde.
If they try to act like citizens
And rent them a nice little flat,
    About the third night
    They're invited to fight
By a sub-gun's rat-tat-tat.
They don't think they're too tough or desperate,
They know that the law always wins;
    They've been shot at before,
    But they do not ignore
That death is the wages of sin.
Some day they'll go down together;
And they'll bury them side by side;
    To few it'll be grief—
    To the law a relief—
But it's death for Bonnie and Clyde.

Bonnie Parker

From the family reunion in Texas, the Barrow gang went to visit Clyde's uncle, who lived near the Louisiana border. They were seen there by a suspected counterfeiter, who later tipped off the law. The police arrived two days late, though. The Barrow gang had moved to the Methvin farm.

Alcorn and Hinton, then Hamer and Gault, pulled into Shreveport May 19 for a meal and a chance to sleep in beds. The next day, they learned from the police chief that Bonnie and Clyde had been seen in a car parked by a Shreveport cafe the night before. They got away from the pursuing police car, and when the cops returned to the cafe, they learned that a young man buying sandwiches had left as soon as the bandits took off. The Texas lawmen assumed that was Henry Methvin. If so, he no doubt went to his father's farm. And Bonnie and Clyde would be back to pick him up.

On their way to see Sheriff Henderson, the Texans passed the fugitives driving the other way. The Dallas deputies recognized them; Hamer and Gault didn't. Instead of chasing Bonnie and Clyde, the lawmen set a trap.

Sheriff Jordan and a deputy, Prentis Oakley, Hinton, Alcorn, Gault and Hamer waited for two days along a stretch of road near the Methvin farm. On the third day, May 23, 1934, a Ford Model A truck chugged toward them. Jordan stepped into the road and stopped the driver, Irvin Methvin, Henry's father. He took him into the woods and handcuffed him to a tree. Hours later, just as the lawmen were beginning to think Bonnie and Clyde had left the state, the same tan Ford V-8 the fugitives were last seen driving appeared.

When Clyde saw the truck, he slowed down to investigate. The lawmen said they shouted for the bandits to surrender, then they opened fire. The waiting officers fired 167 rounds, 50 of them hitting Bonnie and Clyde. The pair were killed instantly. Bonnie still had part of a sandwich in her mouth.

Ted Hinton, looking at the mangled body of the woman he knew as a waitress in Dallas, felt no elation, but Frank Hamer made a wisecrack. "I hated to bust a cap on a woman," he said, "especially when she was sitting down."

Irvin Methvin, released from the tree, threatened to sue the officers for unlawful arrest and imprisonment. Hamer, though, told him that if he kept quiet, he'd say the Methvins betrayed Bonnie and Clyde and would use his influence to keep Henry out of the electric chair. Methvin agreed.

Henry Methvin was arrested but not prosecuted in Texas, although Oklahoma sentenced him to life for the murder of the police officer in Commerce. He was paroled in ten years. Raymond Hamilton and Joe Palmer, arrested in Missouri, got the electric chair.

The newspapers gave Frank Hamer, who made good copy, most of the credit for ending the career of Bonnie and Clyde. Henderson Jordan, who was actually in charge of the operation, got much less. Even less credit went to Bob Alcorn and Ted Hinton, the Dallas deputies who did most of the work.

The FBI, of course, also took bows. Hoover claimed L. L. Kindell, special agent in charge of the Bureau's New Orleans office "coordinated" the manhunt, but was unable to give any specifics.

Hoover had no reason to fret because of missed glory. Almost exactly two months later, on July 22, 1934, the FBI would have the major role in a more important—and much stranger—ambush.

Sixteen

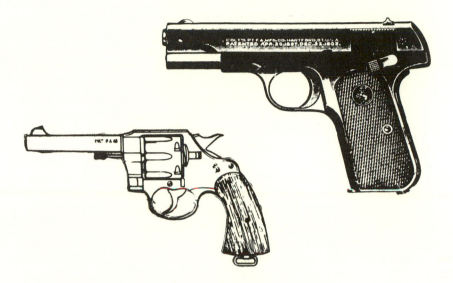

A Night at the Movies

July 22, 1934, Chicago, Illinois

Melvin Purvis chain-smoked cigarettes as he sat in the car with Special Agent Ralph Brown. "Nervous Purvis," the agents in the Chicago Federal Bureau of Investigation office called their special agent in charge. A short, skinny man who appeared to be much younger than his 30 years, Purvis didn't look like a movie G-man. He had trouble getting people to take him seriously when he joined the Bureau back in 1927, even though his father was a friend of South Carolina's powerful Senator Edward "Cotton Ed" Smith. If he was successful tonight, he'd never have that trouble again.

He was going to nail Public Enemy Number One—John Dillinger. As

Top: Colt .380 auto pistol of the type "Dillinger" was said to be carrying when shot in Chicago. Accorrding to one investigator, the gun displayed at FBI headquarters hadn't left the factory before the shooting. Below: Colt M-1917 revolver, a handgun the real Dillinger often carried.

far as he was concerned, and as far as the Director was concerned, this was the most important job he'd ever get. Dillinger was within feet of him now, inside the Biograph Theater, watching *Manhattan Melodrama*, a gangster picture starring Clark Gable. Purvis had never met Dillinger—although he'd come close to him once—but he'd know him because the famous bank robber was with someone Purvis had met, a madam named Anna Sage. When he saw Sage, Purvis would light his cigar and the agents around the theater would close in.

As the time for the picture to end approached, Purvis got out of the car, walked to the left of the entrance and, as casually as he could, selected a cigar. The doors opened and the crowd began coming out. Purvis fumbled for a match while he looked for the madam.

Then he saw her. She was wearing an orange dress that looked red in the lights of the marquee. With her was a young man and a young woman. Purvis tried to strike a light and broke the match. He struck ten matches trying to light his cigar. By the time he had the cigar going, it was all over. The young man with Anna Sage was dead. The Director would be happy.

The director of the Federal Bureau of Investigation, J. Edgar Hoover, wanted to show the country that his agents would end the crime wave that was sweeping America. Although a political conservative, Hoover saw eye-to-eye with his New Deal boss, Attorney General Homer Cummings, on this matter. Cummings espoused the whole Franklin Roosevelt philosophy that federal government must use its power to the utmost to rescue the nation from its malaise.

Part of this malaise was crime. Although, judging by local statistics (there were no national statistics until 1930), there was probably less crime in the 30s than in the 20s, the public perceived a crime wave. Newspapers were giving more space to the gang wars in New York, Chicago and other cities, and they were making celebrities out of the automobile bandits of the Midwest. Vigilante groups were formed in the Midwest. Thousands attended anti-crime rallies to protest the inaction of the Herbert Hoover administration. After the kidnapping of the son of Charles Lindbergh, currently the country's greatest hero, public outrage forced President Hoover to sign the federal kidnapping law, but he did so reluctantly. Ordinary crime—robbery, murder and kidnapping—he believed, was a matter for the states to handle.

Homer Cummings and J. Edgar Hoover took a diametrically different view of crime. They believed the interstate commerce clause in the U.S. Constitution gave the federal government the power to do far more about crime. Any crime that involved crossing state lines was a fit subject for federal action. That was the basis of the "Lindbergh law." Cummings and Hoover wanted laws that would implement that constitutional power. They also wanted laws that would strengthen the Justice Department's Bureau of Investigation. In the 20s, Bureau of Investigation agents could rarely carry guns and had to have local warrants to make arrests. Under Cummings, the agents were able to carry weapons more frequently, but the situation was far from ideal in the view of the attorney general.

On June 17, 1933, federal agents and local police officers escorted captured bank robber Frank Nash from a train at Kansas City's Union Station and prepared to put him in a car for a trip to the federal penitentiary at Leavenworth, Kansas. A group of gunmen opened fire on them as they were preparing to leave, killing Special Agent Raymond Caffrey; Otto Reed, police chief of McAlester, Oklahoma; and Kansas City, Missouri, detectives William "Red" Grooms and Frank Hermanson. Special Agents R. E. Vetterli and F. J. Lackey were wounded. Also killed was the prisoner, Frank Nash.

Whether Nash was killed by the gunmen or by Reed is still disputed, as is the identities of the gunmen. The only one positively identified was Verne Miller, a former sheriff turned hoodlum. The Bureau of Investigation claimed two more were Charles A. "Pretty Boy" Floyd and his partner, Adam "Eddie" Richetti. The evidence for this identification is shaky, to say the least, but it fit the Cummings-Hoover plan to dramatize the problem of crime. Floyd was by far the most highly publicized bank robber of the day.

Cummings announced a "war on crime" and asked for laws against interstate crime, a strengthened national police force and a high-security prison for hardened criminals. In July, 1933, the Bureau of Identification was merged with the Prohibition Bureau and the Justice Department's Division of Identification to become the Federal Bureau of Investigation, or FBI, headed by J. Edgar Hoover. Congress quickly authorized arming FBI agents and began studying how the bureau could be strengthened.

At every session of Congress, Cummings pushed for a sheaf of new anti-crime bills. To keep the "war on crime" momentum up, he and Hoover adopted a gimmick from the Chicago Crime Commission, which had labeled Al Capone Public Enemy Number One. They began proclaiming national Public Enemies Number One. The first was John Dillinger.

That was quite a distinction for a man who had been a big-time crook only 10 months and a gang leader for four months. Dillinger packed a lot into those few months, though. He robbed more banks and stole more money than Jesse James did in his 16-year career of crime. He planned carefully and conducted his robberies with a minimum of bloodshed. He himself was suspected of killing only one man—an East Chicago, Indiana, police officer named William Patrick O'Malley who had attempted to stop two unidentified robbers. Dillinger, however, always denied that he had been in East Chicago at the time. He had a flair for the dramatic—leaping over bank counters and climbing room dividers. He always seemed to be in good humor, and he cared about the comfort of hostages he took. Even before he had his own gang, the news media made Dillinger America's top criminal celebrity.

And that made him a top target in the FBI's war on crime. There were no federal laws against bank robbery at the time, though. It was not until he broke out of a jail in Indiana, stole a sheriff's car and drove it across a state line that Hoover's G-men could arrest him. Before that, though, they had been tracking him to assist local police.

Dillinger wasn't always the polished thief he later became. At 21, he was arrested after trying to rob a grocer and being chased by the intended victim. He took the advice of a prosecutor to plead guilty and throw himself on the mercy of the court. The court gave him 10 to 20 years in prison, while his companion, who pleaded not guilty, got two years.

In prison, Dillinger met more experienced criminals, including Harry Pierpont, John Hamilton, Homer Van Meter and Walter Dietrich. Dietrich tutored the others in the "Baron" Hermann Lamm method of bank robbery. Lamm, a Prussian officer, had been forced to resign his commission shortly before World War I after being caught cheating at cards. He emigrated to the United States and went into bank robbery. He depended on careful reconnaissance of the bank and its environment—escape routes, frequency of police patrols, etc. Lamm and his gang rehearsed each robbery, and the Baron timed every move. During the actual robbery, his men performed each operation on a schedule measured in seconds. Lamm's system performed perfectly until his getaway car blew a tire after one robbery and the gang stole a car that had a governor on the engine. The governor had been secretly installed by the owner's son to keep his aged father from driving faster than 35 miles an hour.

Dillinger was paroled after nine years. To get capital, he went on a robbery spree, working with as many as three gangs. In three weeks he helped stick up five banks in three states. As soon as he could, he smuggled guns into the prison so his friends could escape. Just before Pierpont and the others escaped, Dillinger was arrested for robbery and locked in the Dayton, Ohio police station. He was later transferred to the county jail at Lima. On October 12, 1933, Harry Pierpont, Charles Makley and Russell Clark broke Dillinger out of jail, killing Sheriff Don Sarber in the process.

From that point the gang, under Pierpont's leadership, but using

Lamm's method and Dillinger's flair, began making a name for itself in the Midwest.

After the escape, the gang split into two parts. Pierpont's car went on to Chicago. Unlike Bonnie and Clyde, Dillinger and Pierpont knew that crooks could hide out more safely and comfortably in a big city than in an isolated ravine. Dillinger detoured from the route to Chicago to stick up a police station at Auburn, Indiana, and steal a submachinegun, three rifles, six pistols and a thousand rounds of ammunition, plus two bulletproof vests. That wasn't enough, so after he got to Chicago, he and Pierpont went shopping again. This time, they robbed the police station in Peru, Indiana, and got another machinegun, two shotguns, several steel vests and a large quantity of pistols and ammunition. Dillinger thought that sticking up police stations was an even more direct slap at the law than looting National Guard armories like Bonnie and Clyde.

Captain Matt Leach of the Indiana State Police thought he could take advantage of the publicity the flamboyant Dillinger attracted. He told the press that the real leader of the gang was not Pierpont but Dillinger. Leach hoped to cause dissension in the gang. The plan didn't work, because Pierpont didn't care what the papers printed. But from there on, John Dillinger was America's number one bandit.

The first bank job Dillinger and the Pierpont gang pulled together was vintage. It took place the day after they robbed the Peru police station. At the Greencastle, Indiana National Bank on October 23, 1933, John Hamilton stood by the door as a lookout while Dillinger, Pierpont and Makley entered the bank and Russell Clark stayed in the car with the motor running. Pierpont and Makley held guns on the customers and staff while Dillinger jumped over the railing and ran from cage to cage stuffing money into a sack. An elderly woman walked rapidly out of the bank. Hamilton gently caught her arm.

"Better go back inside, lady," he said.

"I go to Penney's," the woman said with a foreign accent. "You go to Hell." She pulled away and walked down the street.

Makley looked at his stop watch.

"Five minutes!" he called.

Dillinger stopped filling his sack. He jumped back over the railing. He noticed a farmer standing by the counter with a small stack of bills in front of him.

"That your money or the bank's?" he asked.

"Mine."

"Keep it. We only want the bank's."

The gang members got into the car and drove off at a normal speed. They left town and drove west on township roads, avoiding a number of road blocks. When they counted the money, they had $74,782.09—far more than all the money Bonnie and Clyde had stolen in their lives.

About a month later, Leach got a tip that Dillinger would be seeing a doctor in Chicago. Leach called Lieutenant John Howe, commander of the Chicago PD's "Scotland Yard Squad." Howe invited the Hoosier to join in the capture. Capture, though, was not what Leach had in mind. He planned to have his men drive by Dillinger and blast him with shotguns as if it were a gang murder.

A fleet of squad cars came up behind Dillinger as he was driving away from the doctor's office. During a wild, 80-mile-per-hour chase through the middle of Chicago, Dillinger lost all the cars but one Indiana police car. That car pulled up near him, and a policeman began firing a shotgun.

"I think somebody's shooting at you," Dillinger's girlfriend, Billie Frechette, said as the rear window shattered.

Dillinger whipped the car around a corner at high speed, and the police car continued on. By the time the officers had turned around, Dillinger was out of sight.

"That bird sure can drive," the policeman at the wheel commented.

Before long, eight of the ten most wanted criminals on the Chicago police's list were members of "the Dillinger gang."

Dillinger, Pierpont and the others decided that Illinois and Indiana were much too warm in the winter of 1933. They went to Florida. Two days after they left, the Chicago PD's newly formed Dillinger Squad got a tip and burst into an apartment. The three men in the apartment opened fire and the police fired back with tommy guns, killing all three. The men were fugitives, all right, but they weren't associated with Dillinger and Pierpont.

After spending the holidays in Florida, the gang agreed to scatter and meet in Tucson, Arizona. They met there January 25. On January 15, the bank in East Chicago, Indiana, was robbed by two men and Patrolman O'Malley was killed. All Indiana was Dillinger-conscious, and nobody there knew he had gone to Florida. The police said one of the robbers was Dillinger. He was unhurt in the shooting, but an accomplice, at first unidentified, was hit and seriously wounded. Dillinger and members of the gang always maintained that he was in Daytona Beach at the time of the robbery. Dillinger and Billie Frechette were seen in Tucson January 18, 1934. Even if he were in East Chicago January 15, he would have had to cover some 2,000 miles in two days over 1934 roads with a 1934 car. That would be pretty fancy driving. It was important to the police, though, that Dillinger be charged with murder. How could he be the country's worst criminal if he never killed anyone?

Tucson was not a good idea. There was a fire at the hotel where two members of the gang, Charles Makley and Russell Clark, were staying. A fireman noticed them because they seemed unusually concerned about their luggage (which was full of guns). The next day he saw their pictures in *True Detective Magazine*. The firemen told the police. Makley and Clark were tracked to the meeting place, then arrested. After questioning neighbors of the house where the meeting was held, the Tucson police had enough information to round up the other gang members.

Dillinger and his friends were sent to Indiana and Ohio by the local district attorney, who ignored Arizona's extradition procedure. Dillinger would be tried for the murder of O'Malley; Pierpont, Makley and Clark, for the murder of Sheriff Sarber of Lima County.

The Tucson police asked about the rewards for the fugitives, which came to several thousand dollars. Matt Leach, sent to collect Dillinger, said he was authorized to pay only $300. Tucson detective Chet Sherman, a small young man who had posed as a messenger boy during the police assault on the meeting place, seized the six-foot Leach by the shoulders and shook him.

"You're everything Pierpont said you were," he screamed. "A dirty, double-crossing rat!"

Lodged in an "escape proof" jail in Crown Point, Indiana, Dillinger carved a wooden gun from a piece of a washboard, using a razor or razor blade, and blackened it with shoe polish. It was a convincing enough imitation for a turnkey and a deputy sheriff, who led the bandit to the jail's gun storage area, where he stole two submachineguns. He gave one to Herbert Youngblood, a black murder suspect, and locked the warden and the rest of the deputies in one of the cells. Then he stole the sheriff's car and took her mechanic and the first deputy sheriff with him and Youngblood as hostages.

The wooden gun has been a sore point with law enforcement people ever since word of it got out. James Metcalfe, who was one of the FBI agents hunting Dillinger, always maintained that it was a real gun smuggled to him by his girlfriend, Billie Frechette. John Toland, whose *The Dillinger Days*, usually follows the FBI party line, maintains that Dillinger's lawyer, Louis Piquett, bribed a crooked—but unnamed—judge to get the gun to him. He got the story from a Chicago private detective.

The Crown Point jail was guarded against assault by "Dillinger's gang" by a small army of deputies, vigilantes and National Guardsmen. Not even a judge could have passed through the cordon unnoticed, and there's no record of any judge making a visit. An extensive investigation by a grand jury blamed just about every state official but the prosecutor for various things, but found no evidence of collusion by the jail staff or any other officials. The only way Dillinger could have broken out was the way he did. He was later pictured holding the wooden gun before he sent it to his brother-in-law as a keepsake.

Out of Crown Point, Dillinger started putting together a new gang. The first man he chose was John "Red" Hamilton, who had not been picked up in the Tucson sweep. Hamilton had later been identified as Dillinger's accomplice in the East Chicago robbery, where he had supposedly been shot in the back. According to J. Edgar Hoover in *Persons in Hiding*, Hamilton had been "struck by seven bullets, ranging from the pelvic bone to his shoulder blades." If so, his recovery was complete and truly miraculous. Less than two months after the robbery, he was driving with Dillinger and a new member of the gang, a 5' 4" thug named Lester Gillis, to St. Paul and Minneapolis to meet Homer Van Meter, Dillinger's friend from prison, and two more new members, Eddie Green and Tommy Carroll, who had once been part of a gang headed by Gillis.

Little Lester Gillis wanted to be a tough guy. For some reason, he decided Lester Gillis was no name for a tough guy, so he changed it to George Nelson. "Big George," he wanted people to call him. Actually—behind his back—they called him Baby Face. His face was the only innocent thing about Baby Face Nelson. He liked to shoot people. He really didn't fit in with the Dillinger philosophy of bank robbery, but good help was hard to get on short notice.

Tommy Carroll had achieved fame in the underworld as a machinegunner. Eddie Green was known as a jug marker—one who selects and cases banks to be robbed. The one he selected was in Sioux Falls, South Dakota.

The robbery was less smooth than what Dillinger had been accustomed to, although it started with a nice touch. Red Hamilton came to town the day before and let it be known that he was a movie producer and would be shooting a movie there the next day. When the robbery began, everyone at first thought it was the movie. Things went downhill from there. Both Nelson and Van Meter proved to be excitable—Van Meter bullying a bank teller as he tried to open the vault and Nelson shooting a policeman through the bank's side window. Carroll captured two carloads of police, including the chief, without a shot. The robbers collected more than $49,000 and left at a leisurely pace with bank employees standing on the running boards. The car occasionally stopped so Dillinger could scatter roofing nails on the road to delay pursuit. Once they were reasonably clear of the law, the bandits dropped off the hostages and roared away over the township roads.

The gang's next robbery, at Mason City, Iowa, was like something scripted by Mack Sennett. Van Meter walked up to the bank president, who was facing the other way. When the president, Willis Bagley, saw Van Meter's eyes and the machinegun, he said he thought "a crazy man was on the loose." He dashed for a rear office and slammed the door on Van Meter's gun. After a brief struggle, Van Meter pulled the weapon free, but the door slammed shut. Van Meter fired through the door (slightly grazing the banker) and started rounding up hostages.

The wife of a teller called, but the switchboard operator, Margaret Johnson, said, "You can't talk to him now. The bank's being robbed."

In a steel box on the balcony, Guard Tom Walters looked through his steel vision slit. He fired a tear gas shell that hit Eddie Green squarely in the back. Then the gun jammed. He looked around for gas grenades, but there were none.

Outside, on the mezzanine, an assistant auditor found a gas grenade and tossed it down. Fumes began to fill the whole bank.

"Everybody down!" Green yelled and loosed a burst.

Margaret Johnson began crawling toward a storeroom. She reached a window and looked down on a short man wearing a cap and brown overcoat.

"Hey, you," she yelled. "Get to work and notify somebody. The bank's being robbed."

The man looked up and grinned.

"Lady, you're telling me?" asked Baby Face Nelson.

Outside, Dillinger had surrounded himself with hostages. The town police chief and a patrolman with a shotgun had spotted him, but, because of the hostages, they were afraid to fire. One who was not afraid was John C. Shipley, an elderly police judge. He pointed an equally elderly pistol through his third floor window and hit Dillinger in the shoulder. Dillinger futilely fired his machinegun at the judge and told Van Meter to go into the bank and tell everyone it was time to leave.

Inside, Hamilton had troubles of his own. He forced Assistant Cashier Harry Fisher into the vault. Fisher unlocked the barred door leading to the money vault, pushed it open and used a bag of pennies as a door stop. Hamilton grabbed the bag of pennies, thinking he had a treasure, and the door slammed shut. Fisher couldn't open it now if he wanted to. Hamilton demanded that he pass the money through the bars. Fisher did as he was told, but seemed unable to find any bills that weren't one dollar notes.

Outside, a huge crowd had collected. This time, a movie really was being shot. A free-lance photographer had been taking pictures of the Mason City business section. When he saw the crowd around the bank, he trained his camera on the action. The crowd thought the robbery was part of a feature movie and pressed forward to look at the "stars." Even when Nelson fired at a newspaper reporter and shot the secretary of the school board, the crowd was not convinced that they were looking at the real thing.

The gang forced their hostages onto the cars again, and again Judge Shipley fired from his third floor window. This time he hit Hamilton, though, like Dillinger, not seriously. (The robbers were wearing bulletproof vests.) The car rolled out of town at 15 miles an hour, burdened with hostages. An elderly hostage, Minnie Piehm, yelled, "Let me out. This is where I live!" The car stopped and Miss Piehm got off the running board as if she were on a trolley car.

The police followed the bandits. Nelson began firing a rifle. One shot hit a curious man in a car who drew too close to the strange-looking vehicle with people standing on the running boards. Nelson stopped his car and took another shot at the police car. It turned off into a driveway. Nelson got a bag of roofing nails and tried to throw them on the road. Dillinger had to point out to him that he was getting some of them under his own car.

The bandits eventually released their hostages and drove to St. Paul, where they found a friend, Pat Reilly. Reilly took Dillinger, Hamilton and Van Meter, who had also been hit, to his family doctor, the city's health officer. The doctor said the wounds weren't dangerous. Dillinger took an apartment with Billie Frechette in Minneapolis so he could rest and recuperate. The apartment manager eventually got suspicious and called the police. Minneapolis detective Henry Cummings and FBI Agent R. C. Coulter knocked on Dillinger's door. Frechette stalled them. While the lawmen were waiting, Homer Van Meter came down the stairs. Questioned, he said he was a soap salesman and offered to show them his samples in the car. When Van Meter reached his car, he opened fire. The police returned the fire. Van Meter ran and commandeered a truck. Dillinger and Frechette ran down the back stairs and out.

April 3, acting on a tip, FBI agents ambushed Eddie Green and shot him dead. They said he tried to draw a gun, but there were no weapons on the body. Two days later, Dillinger and Billie Frechette arrived in Mooresville, Indiana, for a reunion with Dillinger's father. Plenty of people in Mooresville knew the famous outlaw was in town, but nobody told the police or the FBI. A short time later, a large group of Mooresville citizens signed a petition asking Governor Paul McNutt to pardon Dillinger. After the visit, Dillinger drove to Ohio and gave money to Pierpont's family to help pay his legal expenses. He then returned to Chicago and joined Homer Van Meter in holding up the Warsaw, Indiana, police station and stealing all the department's bulletproof vests. They evaded some 5,000 Indiana lawmen and by April 17, almost the whole Dillinger gang was on its way to a northern Wisconsin hunting and fishing lodge called Little Bohemia.

The only exception was Billie Frechette. She had been picked up in Chicago by the FBI. She may have been expecting arrest. In her purse was a picture of her a few years earlier with a young man wearing a shoulder holster who looked a lot like—but was not—John Dillinger. It was odd that the pretty young Menominee Indian woman would be carrying a picture of an old flame. She was trying to get a divorce so she could marry Dillinger, and she knew that her intended was insanely jealous. He once threatened to kill her because of a mild flirtation with a one-time member of the gang.

It was the moment Melvin Purvis had been waiting for.

He got a tip that Dillinger was in Little Bohemia. He called Hoover and was told to call Hugh Clegg, special agent in charge of the Minneapolis office and place himself and his men under Clegg's command. Purvis called Clegg, but he didn't say anything about taking orders from the other man. Clegg assumed Purvis was in command. Hoover, trying to put down what later became a Purvis "cult of personality," said Clegg gave the orders, but agents who were there said Purvis ran the show.

Purvis's performance, though, was something nobody would be proud to claim.

The agents were supposed to surround the lodge. Before they could take their places, three customers came out and got into a car.

Purvis, about 100 feet away, called, "We're government agents!" in his squeaky voice. Nobody heard him in the lodge or in the car. The men in the car started the engine.

"Shoot for the tires!" Purvis said he yelled.

The agents shot at the passengers. Eugene Boiseneau, a CCC (Civilian Conservation Corps) worker, was killed. John Morris, a cook at a nearby CCC camp, and John Hoffman a gas station attendant, were wounded. While the agents and the lodge staff were looking at the victims, the gangsters in the lodge slipped out the back way and ran around the north shore of the lake behind Little Bohemia. Their wives and girlfriends hid in the cellar.

Baby Face Nelson and his wife, Helen, were not in the lodge but in one of the detached cabins. When he heard shooting, Nelson grabbed his tommy gun and went to look. He saw federal agents and fired several bursts at them before he ran around the south shore of the lake.

When Nelson started shooting, the G-men opened fire on the lodge. They later claimed that Dillinger and his men had fired on them from the second floor before leaving. It was strange, then, that all their bullets hit only the first floor. The owner of the lodge, Emil Wanatka, went to another lodge down the road. He wasn't there long before Nelson showed up. Nelson was preparing to steal another car when two FBI agents and a police officer drove up. Purvis had sent them to the lodge, Koerner's, to make a phone call. Nelson killed one FBI man and the policeman and seriously wounded the second agent. After Nelson left in the G-men's Ford, Wanatka took the dead agent's pistol and drove back to his resort. The agents and local vigilantes were still firing on the lodge.

Wanatka ran into the crowd of lawmen and shouted, "The next person who shoots a hole in my house will get hit over the head with his own gun." He dashed over to Purvis. "Your men are all dead at Koerner's," he said. Purvis merely asked him how he spelled his name. When the lawmen eventually stopped firing, the three young women accompanying the gangsters came out of the lodge.

The escape was a stinging blow for both Purvis and Hoover. The Director had already told reporters to save space for a story on Dillinger's capture.

Meanwhile, Dillinger, Hamilton and Van Meter were heading for St. Paul in a stolen car. They ran a roadblock and Deputy Sheriff Norman Dieter fired. This time, Hamilton really was hit in the back. He died a few days later.

Baby Face Nelson, who had returned to the Midwest from California, where he had been a bootlegger, headed back to the Golden State. Dillinger and Van Meter stayed in the Great Lakes region and kept low profiles while trying to get medical attention for Hamilton, then went totally underground.

On June 30, 1934, the Merchants National Bank in South Bend, Indiana was held up by four men. It was a crude and bloody affair: a police officer was killed and a citizen seriously wounded. The four were identified as John Dillinger, Pretty Boy Floyd, Baby Face Nelson and Homer Van Meter. These were also, of course, the four best-known criminals in the country. The only trouble with the identification was that Floyd was in deep cover with relatives in Ohio, and Nelson was in or en route to California. There is no reason to suppose the other identifications were more accurate. Even Melvin Purvis doubted that Dillinger was involved in the South Bend robbery.

Dillinger was spending a lot of time with his lawyer, Louis Piquett. The bandit was troubled. He didn't expect Billie Frechette to be held, but she was charged with harboring a fugitive and faced a prison sentence. He wanted to disappear. Every unsolved crime in the country was being blamed on him.

On July 20, 1934, Sergeant Martin Zarkovich and Captain Timothy O'Neill of the East Chicago, Indiana, Police Department visited Chicago Police Captain John Stege, commander of Chicago's "Dillinger Squad." They told him Dillinger was in Chicago. They could show him where the bandit was hiding—even set up an ambush for him. There was only one condition. Dillinger could not be captured. He must be killed.

Stege told the out-of-state cops he wasn't a murderer and threw them out of his office.

The East Chicago officers made another stop in the Big City. They called on Melvin Purvis. They knew Purvis still thirsted for revenge because of the little Bohemia debacle. He might not be as discriminating as Stege. They knew he was also naive. Using planted evidence supplied by the Syndicate, the heirs of Al Capone, he had recently framed a Syndicate bootlegging competitor, Roger Touhy, for a kidnapping that never happened.

Purvis snapped at the chance to get Dillinger like a hungry barracuda attacking a mackerel. He even invited Zarkovich and O'Neill to join the party.

Zarkovich explained that a certain madam named Anna Sage knew a man called Jimmy Lawrence who was really Dillinger. He was dating one of her girls, Polly Hamilton. Purvis asked to meet Anna Sage. When they met, Sage said she wasn't so much interested in a reward as in being allowed to stay in the United States. She had been convicted of running a bawdy house and the Immigration and Naturalization Service was going to deport her.

According to Purvis, he told the woman he'd see what he could do. According to Sage, he blurted out: "I'll call them off!" Given Purvis' previous impetuousness and his eagerness to get Dillinger, the second reply seems more likely.

Purvis reported the situation to Hoover. Hoover, remembering Little Bohemia, sent a thorough and deliberate special agent named Sam Cowley to head the operation. Purvis didn't object, but he didn't introduce Cowley to Sage or give him any more information than he wanted him to have. As at Little Bohemia, Purvis again took charge. When Dillinger walked into the Biograph Theater, Purvis was giving the orders and Cowley was at FBI headquarters.

Besides Purvis, the ambush party included agents Brown, McCarthy, Gillespie, Hurt, Hollis, Winstead, Lockerman, Wells, McLaughlin, Ryan, Suran, Sullivan, Glynn, Metcalfe and Campbell. Also included were East Chicago policemen Sopsic, Stretch, Conroy, O'Neill and Zarkovich. No Chicago police had been alerted to this operation in Chicago.

The FBI official story was that Purvis told Dillinger to put his hands up, and Dillinger drew a gun and started running. All the agents then shot him. Hoover wanted no individual G-man heroes. The FBI was a corporate hero, with all its agents led (from Washington) by their wise Director.

FBI folklore has it that Special Agent Charlie Winstead, standing behind Dillinger, fired three times as soon as the outlaw ducked into a crouch and began to run.

Anna Sage, christened "The Lady in Red" by the newspapers, was disappointed. The deportation order went through on schedule. The FBI gave her $5,000 and a fur coat and wished her good luck in Romania.

Homer Van Meter and Tommy Carroll were killed by police soon after the Biograph shooting. With Dillinger out of the running, Pretty Boy Floyd, who had recently surfaced, became Public Enemy Number One. On October 19, police in East Liverpool, Ohio, arrested Eddie Richetti. Richetti's partner, Pretty Boy Floyd, escaped. The Ohio cops called Melvin Purvis, who had become the country's most famous G-man. Purvis flew to Ohio and organized an FBI dragnet. Floyd appeared, tried to run and was cut down by agents' bullets. Purvis ran up to the fallen man and asked, "Are you Pretty Boy Floyd?"

"I'm Charles Arthur Floyd," he said.

Purvis said he went for an ambulance and when he returned, Floyd was dead.

Charles C. Smith, an East Liverpool police officer who was there, said Purvis asked about the Kansas City massacre.

Smith said Floyd answered: "Hell, no." adding, "I wouldn't tell you sons of bitches anything."

Then he asked Purvis, "Where's Eddie?" Purvis said Richetti was in jail.

Purvis continued asking about the massacre. Floyd raised himself on one elbow.

"I didn't do it. I wasn't in on it. Who the hell tipped you anyway?" He cursed Purvis.

Then, Smith said, Purvis turned to an FBI agent the cop called Herman Hawless [Hollis] and ordered: "Shoot him." Hollis shot Floyd twice, killing him.

With Floyd dead, Baby Face Nelson, who had recently returned to the Chicago area, achieved his dream. He became Public Enemy Number One.

On November 27, 1934, FBI agents William Ryan and Thomas McDade were en route from Chicago to Wisconsin where Nelson was reportedly seen. As they passed a car heading in the opposite direction, they thought they recognized Baby Face Nelson, his partner, John Paul Chase, and Nelson's wife, Helen. The agents made a U-turn, but so did Nelson. The FBI men checked the license plate: it was the car Nelson was reported to be driving.

McDade, driving the FBI car, saw that Nelson had made another U-turn.

"Let them come up and we can get a look at them," said Ryan, unholstering his Colt Super .38.

As the bandit car drew closer, Baby Face Nelson motioned the G-men to pull over. Chase, in the back seat, poked a Browning automatic rifle over the crouching body of Helen Nelson and fired a burst through his own windshield. Amazingly, the burst had no effect on the FBI car. Nelson and Chase had "dum-dummed" the BAR's bullets by cutting their jackets at the tip so they'd expand in flesh and make a nastier wound. They didn't understand what recent FBI tests have proved: auto safety glass causes tremendous deformation of any kind of expanding bullet. The bullets Chase had fired through his own window were too deformed to penetrate far into the FBI car.

The agents stepped on the gas.

For several minutes, the two cars engaged in a wild chase with the robbers chasing the cops. Then Nelson realized Chase wasn't hitting anything. He screeched his car around a corner and took off. Nelson left Ryan and McDade behind, but picked up a new FBI tail—Inspector Sam Cowley and Special Agent Herman Hollis. Bullets began flying again, Cowley firing a Thompson and Chase the BAR. Nelson's car sputtered. The little thief skidded into a side road and stopped. The FBI men sped past him, then stopped.

Hollis and Cowley got out, Cowley with his submachinegun, Hollis with a shotgun. Helen Gillis got out of her car and ran into a field. Nelson and Chase got into a ditch. Firing became general. For several minutes, the crooks and G-men traded shots. Then Nelson took his tommy gun and, holding it at his hip like a movie gangster, walked toward the FBI men while he swept the top of the ditch they were hiding in. The G-men fired back, but Nelson shuffled forward like a robot. One bullet hit Cowley in the head. Hollis emptied his shotgun, pulled a pistol and ran towards a telephone pole to get a better angle of fire. Nelson raised the Thompson to his shoulder and fired. Hollis fell dead.

Nelson, Chase and Helen Nelson got into the FBI car and resumed their trip.

After he'd gone a few miles, Nelson pulled over to the side of the road, stopped the car and died. He had 17 bullets in his body.

Little Lester Gillis who always wanted to be a tough guy, had died like a Public Enemy Number One. Presumably, he died happy.

It looked as if the Dillinger story would end with the burial of Baby Face Nelson. Then Jay Robert Nash, editor-in-chief of *ChicagoLand Magazine*, visited Little Bohemia in 1968. Emil Wanatka, Jr. showed him a letter he received from a man who claimed to be John Herbert Dillinger. The writing was similar to Dillinger's earlier handwriting, but not identical. But the new letter was written more than three decades later than any earlier sample of Dillinger's hand.

The letter writer referred to Anna Sage as Anna Compana—her real name was Cumpanas, but the correspondent probably wasn't an expert on Romanian spelling. He had more pertinent things to say, though.

"The man shot had black hair and brown eyes, to [sic] large for Dillinger," Wanatka's correspondent said. He also said:

"J. E. Hoover stated, 'There is every indication that the man shot is Dillinger except the proof. It's customary to send into headquarters the fingerprints of every man shot by the FBI but no fingerprints of Dillinger have come in spite of a regulation burial.'

"The fingerprints were taken of the man shot, but they did not match those of Dillinger, therefore they were not sent in, because if they were, the FBI would have to admit the wrong man was killed."

With the letter was a picture of an old man who could have been Dillinger 30 years after his supposed death.

Nash began searching out any reference to Dillinger, any Dillinger memorabilia, any persons who knew the famous bank robber. From old pictures he learned that though the man killed resembled Dillinger, he was darker and handsomer. He more closely resembled the man whose photo was found in Billie Frechette's purse. Billie Frechette, incidentally, granted Nash the only press interview in her life, because his stepfather, Jack J. Klein, had once dated her before she left the Menominee Reservation.

Nash examined "Dillinger's" glasses and gun exhibited at the FBI headquarters in Washington. The Bureau said the spectacles (all the glass of which was missing) were sun glasses. Nash learned, however, that metal rims like those of the exhibit were used only for prescription glasses in the 30s. Dillinger had perfect eyesight. The gun was even more interesting. Nash checked the serial number with Colt, the manufacturer, and learned that the weapon had not left the factory until five months after the Biograph shooting.

The official explanation of why the man killed in front of the Biograph did not look like Dillinger was that he had had plastic surgery. Nash examined the testimony of Dr. Wilhelm Loesser who was tried and convicted of performing the surgery. Loesser, a parole violator, was not even a surgeon, and his testimony about how he performed the surgery was fantasy, according to plastic surgeons Nash checked with. For instance, he spoke of using kangaroo tendons to "tighten up the cheeks." The doctors pointed out that the body would have rejected kangaroo tendons, and that there were no scars on the face of "Dillinger's" body where there would have been if Loesser had actually attempted that technique. Nor, they said, could plastic surgery have totally obliterated Dillinger's known scars.

Loesser agreed to testify only after the FBI had held him incommunicado for more than a month, the last week of it in the basement of the Bankers Building in Chicago with nothing to sleep on but the concrete floor. In return for his testimony, he received no prison time in addition to the original sentence for narcotics violation from which he had been paroled.

Other witnesses were not so lucky. James Probasco, who owned the building where the surgery was supposed to have taken place, fell 19 floors from the FBI office where he was being held. His death was listed as a suicide. According to George McKnight, an old-time Chicago reporter, the FBI in Chicago occasionally dangled suspects out of windows to persuade them to confess. Probasco had been picked up after the FBI got statements from Art O'Leary, an underworld figure associated with Dillinger's lawyer, and his cousin, Dr. Harold Cassidy. When O'Leary was released after questioning, he showed signs of cigarette burns on his face.

The FBI answered the "no fingerprints" charge by Wanatka's correspondent by showing a fingerprint card with prints, it said, that were taken from the dead man. (Obviously, many agencies had taken fingerprints of the live Dillinger.) There were some strange things about the card, though.

It was dated July 22, although Dr. Charles Parker, an assistant to the coroner's pathologist, who was with the body as soon as it went to the morgue and stayed with it until well into July 23, said nobody took fingerprints while he was on the job.

The prints were not on an FBI file card, but on a Chicago PD card, although Purvis had zealously kept the Chicago police out of the case.

Whoever filled out the card apparently didn't know the FBI's official title or the Bureau's fingerprint classification system. He also referred to the FBI agents as "government men"—an underworld term never used by the FBI in documents. It looks as if Dillinger's fingerprints were sent to FBI headquarters, but they weren't taken by FBI agents. They appear to have been taken by members of the Syndicate—a strange development, but one that fits in with a theory Nash evolved after examining more evidence.

The most damning evidence Nash obtained was a copy of the autopsy report made by Dr. J. J. Kearns. The report had been missing from the coroner's office for years. Some coroner's employees said it had never been filed. The autopsy, however, had been far from secret. A second doctor assisted Kearns and checked the results. A medical stenographer took down all Kearns' on-the-spot findings, and the doctors then checked the recorded notes. Between 20 and 30 medical students, interns and other doctors witnessed the autopsy. It was then read to members of the press and promptly disappeared.

Fortunately, Kearns kept a personal copy of the report. He gave a Xerox of it to Nash. In the report, Kearns said the body's hair was black; there was no evidence of dye. (Dillinger's hair was brown.) The body had numerous plastic surgery scars, but none fresh, as Dillinger's would have been, and none that corresponded to the operations Loesser said he had performed. The body had numerous scars, but they were all in the wrong places.

When he cut into the body, Kearns found that the man had suffered from a chronic rheumatic heart from childhood—something that would have precluded Dillinger's semi-pro baseball career, his athletic leaps during bank robberies or his enlistment in the navy.

Most important, though, Kearns said the body had brown eyes. Records from the navy and the FBI, recollections of Dillinger's friends, all say the bank robber's eyes were gray, blue or bluish gray.

When Nash looked into the shootings, he found that any nonparticipating witnesses said the man doing the shooting was a big man. Charlie Winstead, the agent generally credited with firing the fatal shot, was under 5' 8" and weighed 136 pounds. The only big men near Dillinger were the East Chicago, Indiana, cops, Martin Zarkovich and Tim O'Neill.

Two women were hit in the legs by what were said to be ricocheting bullets. According to Nash, given the angle of bullet travel shown by the autopsy and the positions of the women, the only way they could have been hit in the legs was if the man shot outside the theater were prone. That's not necessarily so. If the man killed had ducked his head was crouching when the shots were fired, the bullets could have inflicted similar wounds. They could also have hit the women in the legs, but they wouldn't be ricochets. Because of the number of lawmen behind the target, the wounds could not, of course, indicate who actually fired the shots.

After he published his book, *Dillinger—Dead or Alive?*, Nash had a phone call from an elderly woman. She said she once ran a poolroom near the theater, and when she stepped outside for some air that July 22, she saw a young man being pushed down on his face by a "large man, this fellow Zarkovich, I learned later." Then, she said "there seemed to be another man shooting at this fellow on the ground." She ducked back into the poolroom. When she came out again, she saw the young man being lifted into a police wagon. "I looked at him good. I knew this fellow. We called him Jimmy. He had been hanging around my poolroom for about three years, from about the fall of 1931. He pimped for Anna Sage."

"Jimmy Lawrence" was the alias the FBI said Dillinger had been using. There was a real Jimmy Lawrence, a small time hoodlum, living in that part of Chicago at the time.

Nash's caller said she had gone to the police, "but the Chicago cops told me—'you say something like that, lady, and you'll get a hole in your head.'" Nash asked for her name. She refused to give it. She said, "I still don't want to get a hole in my head."

Nash believes Dillinger's lawyer, Louis Piquett, who had Syndicate connections, had arranged to have Jimmy Lawrence set up as a patsy. With the phony Dillinger dead, the real one could disappear.

If the FBI found out that it had killed the wrong man, according to this theory, it would be afraid to announce it. Such an announcement would destroy the Bureau's credibility—destroy everything Hoover had been laboring to build.

Late in 1934, Melvin Purvis seemed to have dropped out of favor with the Director. Hoover assigned him to one picayune job after another. Hoover never mentioned Purvis' name after 1935. In 1935, Purvis resigned to open a detective agency, then to head Post Toasties' Junior G-Men program. Eventually he went back to practicing law in South Carolina.

It has been charged that Hoover hounded him out of the Bureau because Purvis was getting more publicity than the Director. But there may have been another reason.

History—with good reason—has not been kind to J. Edgar Hoover. Nevertheless, after the Little Bohemia fiasco, just about every other important person in the country was crying for Dillinger's blood. Homer Cummings said federal agents should "Shoot to kill—then count to ten." But Hoover ordered Cowley, "Take him alive if you can." For all his faults, J. Edgar Hoover was not a murderer.

Late in 1934, Hoover had a chance to evaluate Purvis. Purvis had helped frame an innocent man, Touhy. He had killed an innocent CCC worker, Eugene Boiseneau. He had conspired to murder John Dillinger and killed Jimmy Lawrence by mistake. He had murdered Charles "Pretty Boy" Floyd in cold blood. Hoover probably didn't know all of that, but he knew enough. The Director couldn't fire Purvis and keep the real story about what happened outside the Biograph secret. But it was utterly irresponsible to allow someone like Purvis to run around the country with a badge and a gun.

Perhaps Purvis was thinking about his accomplishments on February 29, 1960 when he selected a .45 automatic from his gun collection and blew out his brains.

Seventeen

Dutch Treat

October 23, 1935, Newark, New Jersey

O ne thing that made Dutch Schultz unusual among the gang lords of New York during the thirties was that he looked and sounded so much like a movie gangster. A muscular man with a dese-dose-and-dem accent, Schultz fancied cheap clothes and big cars. Born Arthur Flegenheimer in 1902, he had left school in the sixth grade. He later explained that he thought that was as much schooling as anybody needed. He joined a gang of blackjack-toting young thugs in his Bronx neighborhood and quickly gained a local reputation as a street fighter. His buddies nicknamed him Dutch Schultz after a legendary Bronx brawler around the turn of the century.

Top: Colt M-1911 .45 service pistol, the favorite weapon of both Dutch Schultz and his assassin, Charlie Workman. Below: Colt Detective Special, an easily concealed .38 special revolver favored by many mobsters, including Bo Weinberg, Schultz's chief leutenant and top torpedo.

He began his criminal career stealing packages from delivery trucks with a boyhood buddy, Jack Noland, the future Legs Diamond. He graduated from that to burglary, and in 1919, when he was 17, he was convicted of burglarizing a flat in the Bronx and sent to jail. He proved to be an unruly prisoner and was transferred to another, supposedly more secure jail. The additional security is questionable, because after a few months, Schultz escaped. He went back to the Bronx and was quickly recaptured. Altogether, Schultz spent 15 months behind bars, the only prison time he ever served.

Although all his life "The Dutchman" talked like a Hollywood version of an ignorant hoodlum, he was anything but dumb. What distinguished The Dutchman from hundreds of other young thieves was his business sense. By carefully choosing what to steal and by getting top dollar from the fences, Schultz raised enough money to buy into a speakeasy. He also had the acumen to remain close to Legs Diamond, an associate of Arnold (The Brain) Rothstein, the most powerful mobster in New York. Diamond organized a hijacking ring specializing in stealing contraband—liquor and stolen goods—shipped by operators too small to pay for protection. Besides Schultz, Diamond's gang included a young Italian named Salvatore Lucania, who was to become better known as Charles Luciano. Luciano and Schultz became friends and cooperated with each other in various rackets for years, not a common situation in the New York underworld of that day, where today's friend was tomorrow's enemy.

The composition of Diamond's gang is at odds with the current notion of an all-powerful Cosa Nostra controlling crime in the United States. Diamond was an Irishman. He worked for a Jew, and had a Jew (Schultz) and an Italian (Luciano) working for him.

Diamond's activities created a new gang. A lot of the small operators wanted to fight back, but they lacked the firepower. An auto mechanic who heard their gripes contacted a hoodlum he knew, and they organized a corps of crack gunmen who would escort the trucks of anyone who paid them. Their organization was known as the Bugs and Meyer Mob after the hoodlum, Benjamin (Bugsy) Siegel, and the mechanic, Meyer Lansky. Lansky was another friend of Luciano, but, as he said, business is business. The creation of the Bugs and Meyer Mob was later to have an indirect, but very serious, impact on Dutch Schultz. Siegel and Lansky had founded the modern New York underworld's first kill-for-hire organization.

Diamond's hijackings created enough turmoil in the underworld to make Rothstein withdraw his financial support and invest the money in importing foreign liquor. The Legs Diamond gang broke up. Luciano went into bootlegging for himself. He had a dispute with his old boss, Diamond. Diamond's hoods kidnapped Luciano, hung him by his hands from a tree, stabbed him with ice picks, slashed him with razors and left him there to die. He didn't die, and he earned a new name—Charley Lucky. A short time later, several members of Diamond's gang disappeared.

Schultz went into a number of enterprises. He first took over the breweries in New Jersey where "near beer," beer from which the alcohol had been removed, was brewed. His trucks got the beer before the brewers boiled off the alcohol and brought it to warehouses in New York. From there The Dutchman distributed it to restaurants and speakeasies all over Manhattan and the Bronx. These establishments were also under Schultz's "protection." He had muscled his way to a controlling position in the restaurant workers' union. Any restaurant that stepped out of line could count on a crippling strike. These endeavors were immensely profitable, but Schultz knew prohibition couldn't last. He had to branch out.

Schultz moved in on race tracks. He bought the Coney Island Race Track in Cincinnati. A key man in his organization was Otto Biederman, called Abbadabba Berman because of his mathematical wizardry. Abbadabba was a horse handicapper who also worked at the pari-mutuel tracks doing the rapid calculations needed to determine pay-offs.

Next, the Dutchman started to lean on the small numbers ("policy") racket operators in Harlem and the Bronx. He started with the biggest banker, Joe Ison. A couple of his top guns, Bo Weinberg and Abe Landau, gave Ison a ride in their car and told him the Dutchman wanted to "protect" him. There would, of course, be a small fee. Thinking of what might happen to him without Schultz's "protection," Ison readily agreed. After other bankers had come into his "combination," Schultz raised the protection premiums. Joe Ison, for instance, had to pay $1,000 a week. Within a few months, Ison went broke. He had to borrow $12,000 from Schultz to pay off his winners. Schultz gave him the money, but took two-thirds of the business and put in one of his trusted lieutenants, George Weinberg, to run it. (Weinberg's brother Abraham, known as "Bo," was the Dutchman's chief lieutenant, inter-mob diplomat and top torpedo—a kind of Machinegun Jack McGurn with brains.) Before long, Schultz controlled all the policy business in Harlem and the Bronx.

In spite of his sixth-grade education, Schultz had become an expert accountant. Still, he relied on people like George Weinberg to manage the policy business, and on Abbadabba Berman to make sure too many winning numbers did not come in. The winning number in the policy game was based on the odds on horse races as totaled by the pari-mutuel machines at Tropical Park, Florida. The first of the three winning numbers was the last digit before the decimal point of the total odds for the first three races of the day. The second digit of the winning number was the same thing for the second two races. The third and final digit of the winning number was based on the same figure for the last two races of the day. Berman kept up with the changing odds, and if it looked as if the winning number would be one that a lot of bettors had chosen, Abbadabba would call in a bet in the last seconds of betting time, thus changing the third digit of the winning number. For that, he got $10,000 a week.

There was a lot of crooked subtlety in many of the Dutchman's business practices. There was also a lot that, though crooked, was not at all subtle.

At neither the Wharton School nor the Harvard Business School will a student learn the Schultz method of beating competition. In The Dutchman's early days in the beer business, one bootlegger refused to give up his territory. Schultz and his crew beat the competitor to a bloody pulp, tied him up and bound an infected bandage over his eyes. When the competitor recovered from his wounds, he was blind. After a few instances like this, no independent operators contested Schultz's doing anything he liked.

Besides the judicious application of horrifying brutality, one of the most important skills Schultz learned was knowing who to pay off. There was no way anyone could operate a numbers empire the size of Schultz's without the authorities' knowing about it. Still less could he have sold millions of gallons of illegal beer without police interference. Schultz had a lot of important people on his payroll. The most important was the major Tammany Hall chieftain, James J. Hines. Schultz met Hines when he was taking over the policy business. According to J. Richard (Dixie) Davis, Schultz's attorney:

"The last [policy] banker to come in was a fellow named Maloney, for when he heard Schultz was forming the combination he got in touch with Jimmy Hines and got Hines' protection. . . . Schultz could not take over Maloney's bank until Hines came back from a trip to Hot Springs in the spring of 1932 and gave the okay.

"Then Schultz got Hines on his own payroll to give political protection, and that was the master stroke, for we soon found that what Hines could do was plenty. He could, and did, have cops transferred when they bothered the numbers. He had magistrates throw out good cases that honest cops had made against George Weinberg and Lulu Rosenkrantz [Schultz's bodyguard and all-around muscle]. He gave his support to a district attorney who didn't bother us much."

For his services, Hines got between $500 and $1,000 a week.

Another advantage The Dutchman had was his friendship with Charley Lucky. Legs Diamond's former employee had become one of the most powerful men in New York. The way he achieved this eminence tells volumes about what later became known (by non-Italians) as La Cosa Nostra.

The Italian segment of the underworld had been evolving from local chapters of Old World secret societies, like the Sicilian Mafia and the Neopolitan Camorra, to distinctively American groups. All of these groups identified themselves with different regions in Italy, however, and battled each other almost incessantly. The climax came with the "Castellammarese War." Giuseppe Masseria anointed himself "boss of all bosses," and not just in New York. Gaspare Milazzo, chief of the Sicilian criminal faction in Detroit, refused to recognize any boss but himself, so Masseria had him killed. Milazzo was a native of Castellammare del Golfo in Sicily. So was a New York mobster named Salvatore Maranzano. Maranzano, who spoke six languages, looked like a professor and had the instincts of a wolverine, called on all Castellamarese to avenge the murder. After a while, he didn't limit his army to Castellamarese. Luciano, a Masseria supporter, was getting static from his boss for running his own liquor importation business. Luciano called on Maranzano, then on his old friend, Meyer Lansky.

On April 15, 1931, Charley Lucky met Masseria in a restaurant and presented a plan for taking over all the rackets in New York. He excused himself to go to the bathroom. As soon as Luciano was gone, Joe Adonis, Vito Genovese and Albert Anastasia, from the Maranzano organization, and Bugsy Siegel, the muscle of the Bugs and Meyer Mob, entered. They pumped 20 bullets into "Joe the Boss."

Maranzano took Masseria's place as the preeminent crook in the Italian segment of New York's underworld. He called a meeting of other Italian-American criminal chiefs and announced a new organization. Like the current secret societies, the new group would have a formal ritual to initiate new members who had proved themselves. It would not, though, have any geographical roots in the Old Country. It would be for all Neopolitans, all Sicilians, all Italians. Members could, and should, cooperate with gangsters of other ethnic origins—even employing or being employed by them. But their first loyalty would be to the secret society, what Maranzano called "our thing," (*cosa nostra* in Italian).

Maranzano wiped out the parochialism of the old Italian gangs, a major cause of bloodletting. He wasn't against bloodletting, though. A few months after Masseria was killed, Maranzano confided to a Jewish gangster, Nig Rosen of Philadelphia, that he was going to get rid of a number of powerful Italian members of "our thing." They included Luciano; Francesco Castiglia, known as Frank Costello; Vito Genovese, and Joe Adonis. He let the contract to Vinnie Coll, an Irish gangster called "the Mad Mick" by his associates. Rosen told Costello. Costello told Luciano.

Luciano again contacted Meyer Lansky, whom he had just helped in a war with Waxey Gordon (Isadore Wexler), a West Side kingpin. He also visited Dutch Schultz, another ally. Then, as he had with Masseria, he set up a meeting with Maranzano. Instead of a restaurant, though, they would meet in Maranzano's office.

The new boss had made a rule that no guns were allowed in the office, so the police would have no excuse to make an arrest. Maranzano called Coll and told him Luciano would be in his office at 2 p.m. September 10. At 1:30 p.m. four men with IRS credentials appeared at Maranzano's office and demanded to talk to the boss. The credentials were phony. One of the "agents" was Bo Weinberg; the other three worked for one of Lansky's clients, Louis Buchalter, nicknamed "Lepke." They tried to stab Maranzano to death to avoid noise, but the old man was tougher than expected, so they ended up shooting him.

Then somebody—either Coll or the police—arrived. Weinberg later told Dixie Davis:

"I started down the stairs. I ran down three or four flights, and there was somebody coming up, so I turned around and ran back. I got in a toilet and waited a while. It seemed like hours before I got out of that joint. At last, I got in an elevator and got down to the street.

"I still had my biscuit in my pocket, because I might have to shoot my way out. I couldn't drop it and let it clatter on the sidewalk. So I wandered along and pretty soon I came into Grand Central Station.

"There's a big crowd there, all packed in, waiting for a train. I edge into that crowd and get up next to a guy who isn't looking and ease that biscuit gently into his side pocket and get away.

"I nearly die laughing when I think of when that guy put his hand in his pocket and found that gun."

The next day, all across America, old-style Italian gang lords, "Mustache Petes" in the language of Luciano's contemporaries, were killed by younger Italian mobsters, aided by other local hoods. Luciano thought big and planned accordingly.

The fruits of this second piece of treachery for Luciano was leadership, not only of the Italian underworld, but of all midtown New York gangs—on a first-among-equals basis, at least. Lucky saw that what was good for Italian mobsters was good for all mobsters. An Indian medicine man, Hiawatha, saw the same thing three centuries before when he founded the Five Nations of the Iroquois. In union, there is strength.

Luciano took what had been a working relationship of the big mobs in New York and turned it into something bigger—eventually, a nationwide syndicate. But he started with Manhattan. Costello had been working with Joe Adonis, leader of the Broadway Mob for several years. Both relied on the guns of the Bugs and Meyer Mob. Eventually, they decided it was cheaper to make Siegel and Lansky partners than to pay them by the job. Lepke (a contraction of the Yiddish Lepkele, or Louie) Buchalter, saw the need for a new gun-for-hire outfit, now that Bugs and Meyer had branched out. He took in Albert Anastasia, a bloodthirsty Brooklyn waterfront boss, and formed what the newspapers called Murder, Inc. Murder, Inc. took contracts not only from "the syndicate," but from any outsider cleared by the gang bosses.

When Luciano called for closer cooperation among the Big Town's big mobs, he had two things going for him. One was the leadership and planning he had demonstrated in the "New Sicilian Vespers" that eliminated the Mustache Petes. The other was his friendship with Lansky, the brains of the Bugs and Meyer assassination team. Knowing Dutch Schultz didn't hurt, either, but there were problems with that relationship.

One was that Dutch was an individualist who didn't want to be part of a larger whole. He was already very big and planned to get bigger. Once, commenting to an associate on the Russian revolution, Schultz said the Bolsheviks were a mob just like his mob and they had taken over a country. With the right timing, he added, his gang could take over the country.

The other problem was The Dutchman himself. In Luciano's view, he had a personality like a cheese grater, and he was scraping Lucky deeper each year. Luciano was polite, dressed conservatively and expensively, considered himself a businessman and, although he was not averse to arranging violence, he was always somewhere else when it occurred. He shunned the limelight. Lansky and Luciano were soul mates. Schultz was something else. Dutch Schultz gloried in headlines, dressed like a slob and on at least one occasion, blew out the brains of a business associate over a chance remark. At one gangster conference, he grabbed one of the prostitutes supplied by the host, took her to a bedroom and contributed to the meeting by occasionally shouting through the door.

There were other independent mobs, but they were a dying breed. As they died, Schultz grew stronger. Vinnie Coll, a former Schultz employee, declared war on Schultz when The Dutchman refused to lend him money to beat a firearms rap. Coll and his gang raided a Schultz garage and stuck up several Schultz beer trucks. There were shootings for several months. In one, Coll gunmen trying to get Joe Rao, a Schultz henchman, killed a baby by mistake. The newspapers began calling the Mad Mick "Mad Dog," and other gangsters thought Coll was giving the underworld a bad name. Coll's brother and partner, Peter, was killed by Schultz gunmen.

Coll had a strange relationship with Owney Madden, owner of the Cotton Club. Once known as Owney the Killer, Madden was a mobster of considerable prestige but declining power. Once to raise money during his war with Schultz, Coll kidnapped Madden's enforcer, Big Frenchy De Mange. But he still called the aging night club owner frequently for advice. Schultz knew about the calls and kept a man in the Cotton Club to check on calls to Madden.

"Madden was in his Harlem place, the Cotton Club, which was a hang-out for big shots," Dixie Davis recalled, "and he was called to the telephone in his little private back office."

Schultz's man followed.

"[Madden] heard Coll's voice over the wire," Davis continued, "and then he felt a nudge at his ribs. It was a shooter standing there with a gun against him.

" 'Keep talking to him,' said the shooter. 'Don't let him hang up.'

"The call was traced to a phone booth in a drugstore in 23rd Street, near London Terrace, the world's largest apartment building, where Madden lived in a penthouse. Within a few seconds, the gunmen's car was racing there from a point nearby. Bo told me it was a cop who got the call traced.

"The shooter stood there with his gun jammed into Owney Madden's ribs until the machinegun rattle came through the receiver. A gunner had calmly walked into the drugstore and riddled the phone booth while Coll was talking.

"That is the story told me by Bo Weinberg, who drove the murder car."

Waxey Gordon and Schultz coveted each other's beer empire. Shooting broke out between gang members. On April 3, 1933, less than two weeks before beer became legal, Gordon noticed a group of Schultz torpedoes entering the hotel where he was staying. He went out the window, but two of his bodyguards were killed. Ten days later, Gordon was indicted on four counts of income tax evasion. He was grateful for the safety of prison.

The federal government had begun employing income tax laws against the gang leaders. One of the first was Legs Diamond, "the outlaws' outlaw." Schultz's boyhood chum had turned against him when the Dutchman started his own mob, but he came off second best. Still, he hijacked trucks and kidnapped mobsters indiscriminately, and had been shot at so often his underworld nickname was "the clay pigeon." Legs appealed his conviction, but before the appeal could be argued in court, Bo Weinberg and a crew of Schultz gunmen killed Diamond in an Albany rooming house.

The prosecutor in both the Gordon and Diamond cases was an assistant U.S. attorney named Thomas E. Dewey. Dewey later resigned, but New York Governor Herbert Lehman, a Democrat, appointed Dewey, a Republican, special prosecutor to clean up rackets in New York. Schultz was known as a heavy contributor to the Tammany Hall machine, and the governor thought a Republican would make a more relentless prosecutor. Dewey prosecuted James J. Hines, Schultz's Tammany buddy, and got a conviction. Then he turned to Schultz.

Before he could charge Schultz, federal officers arrested The Dutchman for income tax evasion. The first trial ended in a hung jury. The next trial was moved to the upstate New York hamlet of Malone to avoid the pernicious influence of the big city. Schultz moved to Malone, mixed with local society, hired a public relations consultant and bought flowers for hospital patients. He was acquitted.

Mayor Fiorello LaGuardia announced that he was banning Schultz from New York City. The Dutchman, though, was only concerned with real dangers, not political rhetoric.

While he was out of circulation, his empire began showing signs of stress. During the summer of 1933, while he was hiding from federal agents, Schultz tried to cut the percentage of policy collectors from 30 to 25 percent. The collectors hired a hall in Harlem, held a mass meeting, and 2,000 collectors went on strike against Dutch Schultz. He agreed not to cut the percentage.

Other mob leaders began eyeing the Dutchman's enterprises.

"That loudmouth's never coming back," said Charley Lucky. He began talking with Bo Weinberg.

Then Schultz was acquitted, surprising everyone, including the judge, who dismissed the jury without thanks. He called in Bo Weinberg for an accounting of his stewardship during the trials.

"Remember that Weinberg you thought was such a nice guy?" an acquaintance asked Joe Valachi.

"Yeah, so what?" said Valachi.

"He's dead and buried. The Dutchman did it. The word is that The Dutchman found out he was playing around with the Sicilian."

Luciano, believing that Schultz was on his way out, had indeed made an arrangement with Weinberg. Schultz made other arrangements. No one ever found Bo's body.

Meanwhile, Dewey was still gathering evidence for a state case against Schultz. The gang lord decided the diminutive prosecutor was a greater threat than any of the downtown gunmen. Dewey was a problem that called for direct action. Schultz called the boys downtown and told them he had a plan to take the heat off everybody.

The plan was to kill Dewey. Every morning on the way to work, Dewey would enter a certain drug store and make his confidential phone calls in case his office phone was tapped. His two bodyguards waited outside. Dutch proposed having a man with a silenced pistol waiting in the store. When Dewey entered the phone booth, he would, like Vinnie Coll, make his last call. The assassin would then shoot the druggist and leave, walking past the bodyguards.

The downtown syndicate was appalled. Killing the special prosecutor would increase the heat on everyone a hundredfold.

"You're all chicken," The Dutchman said. "I'll do it myself."

When the syndicate learned that Schultz still had Dewey under surveillance, they decided to act quickly. They called Lepke Buchalter and offered him a contract on The Dutchman.

On October 23, 1935, two men entered the Palace Chop House in Newark, N.J. One was Charlie Workman, known as "the Bug." ("You gotta be a bug [a nut] to do what Charlie does," an acquaintance said, explaining the nickname.) The other man was probably Mendy Weiss, later executed with his boss, Lepke. The Bug wasn't happy about him. It seems Weiss' performance was not up to the Bug's standards. When the Bug started going through the pockets of his victims to check their identity, Weiss ran away, got into their car and told the wheelman, identified only as Piggy, to take off. Workman ran after him, but the car got away, leaving the Bug to walk home. When Weiss later claimed to have killed Schultz, Workman almost killed him. Only Lepke's intervention restored peace.

After his arrest, following a tip from former Murder, Inc. gunner Abe Reles, Workman said he did the job alone. Nevertheless, the bartender, Jack Freeman, Ben Bergenfeld, a waiter, and the cook, King Lou, all said they saw two men come in, do the shooting and run away.

"Lie down on the floor and stay there," Workman snapped at the bartender as the gunmen entered. Freeman dived behind the bar.

Workman and his companion walked right into the back dining room Schultz was using for an office. The Bug checked the men's room in case any

Schultz bodyguards were there. A man in an overcoat was washing his hands. He tried to close the door, but Workman kicked it open and fired one shot. He then joined his companion and shot three men sitting around a table looking at rows of figures on account books. The men behind the table tried to fire back, but the Murder, Inc. torpedoes mowed them down with 25 shots. Weiss, then the Bug, dashed out of the restaurant and disappeared.

Behind, bleeding on the floor were Bernard "Lulu" Rosenkrantz, Schultz's chauffeur and chief bodyguard, with twelve wounds; Abbadabba Berman, Schultz's mathematical genius, with wounds in the abdomen, chest and face; and Abe Landau, alias Leo Frank, a Schultz lieutenant, shot in the neck and both arms.

The man in the washroom staggered out and called an ambulance. He gave his name as Arthur Flegenheimer.

At the same time Workman and Weiss were shooting Schultz and his lieutenants, other members of Lepke's mob were fatally wounding Martin Kropier, Schultz's man in charge of operations in Manhattan, while he was sitting in a Broadway barber shop.

Dr. Earl Snavely, medical director of Newark City Hospital, said Schultz's condition was serious, but "his chances are pretty good so far."

Biederman died first. Landau, who the hospital first reported "got off lightly," died next. Rosenkrantz, who had been riddled, was the last of the three Schultz aides to die.

The Dutchman himself, mistaken for a bodyguard by Workman, lingered on. In spite of what the doctors said, he knew he was dying. He called for a Catholic priest, the Rev. Cornelius McInerney of Livingston, New Jersey, because "my wife is Catholic. I want to die a Catholic." He was baptized, made the kind of confession few priests ever hear and received the last rites of the church. A few hours later, he became delirious. A police stenographer sat by his bed and meticulously took down all his ravings.

"Max, come over here," said The Dutchman. "French Canadian bean soup. I want to pay. Let them leave me alone." Then he became unconscious and died two hours later without another word.

The syndicate chieftains divided up Schultz's rackets. For once, though, Luciano's conniving brought him no profit. With Schultz out of the way, he became the most conspicuous target for the ambitious Dewey. Charley Lucky was convicted of 91 counts of extortion and compulsory prostitution. He stayed in prison until after World War II, when his alleged services to the government in getting cooperation of the Sicilian Mafia earned him a pardon and a deportation to Italy. Joe Adonis (Giuseppe A. Doto) became the leader of the Italian "thing," but Meyer Lansky took Luciano's place as the country's biggest gangster. Bugsy Siegel, with the cooperation of Lansky and Adonis in New York and Greasy Thumb Guzik in Chicago, set up a racing wire service. Later, after a disagreement with Guzik, he closed the wire. He went west and introduced big time gambling to Las Vegas. But Siegel rejected Lansky's advice and refused to pay back $3,000,000 he had borrowed from the national syndicate. A syndicate gunman blew his brains out as he sat by a window in his mistress's home.

On Novermber 2, 1957, the top men in the Italian "thing" held a national conference in the New York hamlet of Appalachin. It was discovered by the New York State Police. A little later, a small time hood named Joe Valachi began telling Senate investigators about the Italian "thing." For years, J. Edgar Hoover, the FBI director, had been denying there was any national crime organization. It has been charged that he was unwilling to expose his agents to the bribery the mobsters had used so effectively everywhere else. Chasing the Dillingers was safer and brought better publicity. But Valachi's testimony about a secret society with tentacles everywhere could not be ignored.

Unfortunately, Valachi was in no position to take a broad view. All he saw was "cosa nostra." And a small, ethnocentric secret society was certainly easier to understand than a vast, sprawling criminal federation inhabited by every ethnic group in the United States. For Valachi, there was an excuse.

In spite of Valachi's testimony, organized crime was never really confined to one ethnic group. Luciano's ideal of cooperation has prevailed. When in 1984, Rob Marshall, the protagonist in Joe McGinniss' *Blind Faith*, decided to kill his wife, he got the word to Patsy Ragazzo, a restaurateur vaguely connected with the Thomas Lucchese crime family. Ragazzo contacted John Riccio, another New Jersey resident, who called Andrew Myers of Shreveport, Louisiana. Meyrs contacted a Shreveport crook named Ferlin L'Heureux, who gave the job to the actual killer, Ricky Dee of Shreveport. Even in the 50s, when the various families in the Italian "thing" were at the height of their power, there were, besides Lansky, prominent mobsters who would never have been able to join L'Unione Siciliana. Men like Greasy Thumb Guzik in Chicago, Mickey Cohen in Los Angeles, Snag Klein and Wolf Rimann in Kansas City were not small timers.

The FBI, however, seems to be in love with the idea of an all-powerful *cosa nostra*. For the benefit of headline writers, the Bureau gave Valachi's "thing" a name: La Cosa Nostra, literally "The Our Thing." The letters LCN, it hoped, would become as widely used as the letters FBI. Unfortunately, the FBI believed its own myth and has concentrated on criminals with Italian names.

This is almost as much of a waste as when the Bureau concentrated on the U.S. Communist Party, a third of whose members were its paid informants. Today's *"Cosa Nostra"* consists of squabbling "families" controlled by ancients who remember the good old days of Luciano (sent away at age 39) and Schultz (killed at age 34). The families seem more interested in juvenile mumbo-jumbo than in the rackets. They've been all but frozen out of the drug trade; policy rackets are rapidly slipping away from them, and unaffiliated bookies flourish in their territory. For several years, Mickey Spillane, leader of the New York Irish gang known as the Westies, used to raise money by kidnapping and holding for ransom prominent members of the five New York Italian families.

Meanwhile, Cubans, Colombians and Jamaicans are moving into organized crime in a big way, and criminals from older ethnic groups, like the Irish in New York's West Side and the WASPs in the South, continue doing what comes naturally.

Not one individual, though—certainly not the septuagenarian "dons" of the FBI's LCN—has climbed as high as the Dutchman before he planned that last, fatal step.

Eighteen

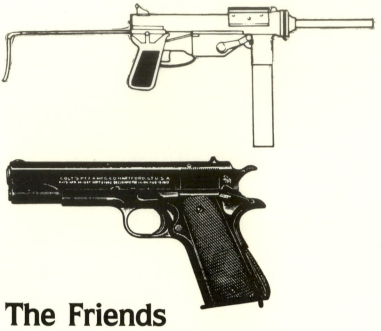

The Friends
of Specks O'Keefe

June 16, 1954, Boston, Massachusetts

It was a little before 7 p.m., January 17, 1950. Snowhill Street in Boston's North End was dark and deserted. A green Ford truck with a canvas-covered back pulled up next to the old colonial burial ground, and seven men jumped out. All seven wore identical outfits—chauffeur caps, Navy pea coats and dark pants. All but one, who had crepe-soled shoes, wore rubbers, appropriate enough on this drizzly night. In the dark, the chauffeur hats and

Top: Submachine Gun M-3, alias the grease gun, the weapon Elmer Burke used when he attacked Joe O'Keefe. It uses the same ammunition as O'Keefe's weapon, (below) the .45 auto M-1911 A1. In 1926, the government made slight changes in the grip and added A1 to the model number.

pea coats resembled the uniforms worn by the employees of Brink's, the armored car company, which had an installation nearby.

The men in the chauffeur caps strolled along the street and down some steps to a playground. They looked up at a rooftop, saw a flashlight blink on and off, then started across the playground toward Prince Street. With elaborate casualness, they sauntered along the North Terminal Garage building where the Brink's terminal was located.

The first man in the ragged line stopped at a door, put a key in the lock and opened it. The other men followed, as casually as if they were going to work.

They were, in fact, going to work. They weren't Brink's employees, though. The man with the keys was a small-time thief named Joseph James O'Keefe, 41, whose specialty until now had been holding up bookies and crap games—victims who were not likely to go to the police. He was also an accomplished burglar who had earlier opened Brink's doors without keys and removed the lock tumblers so keys could be made. Using keys to open the doors was faster than picking the locks and less likely to arouse the suspicions of onlookers. The newspapers were to call O'Keefe "Specs," a misspelling of "Specks," the boyhood nickname his freckles had earned long before he had to wear glasses. Those who knew him called him Joe.

Behind O'Keefe was Michael Vincent Geagan, 41, a longshoreman who moonlighted in crime. Originally a stickup man, he had for some time been working with a talented safecracker named Anthony Pino. Pino, who had planned this heist, was waiting outside in the truck. Geagan had a little more than average size and a lot more than average strength. He and his associates expected to do a lot of heavy lifting this night.

Geagan was followed by Henry Baker, 43, who owned a vending machine business, but was more interested stealing money directly. He had recently been released from state prison.

Thomas Francis "Sandy" Richardson, 42, followed Baker. Richardson worked with Geagan on the docks by day and drank with him and stole with him at night. He was very strong for his 145 pounds and accustomed to moving heavy loads through narrow spaces. Except for Pino's brother-in-law, Jimmy Costa, he was the master thief's closest associate.

Then came James Ignatius "Jimma" Faherty, 38. Faherty had been a steam fitter, an electrician, a clerk, a longshoreman and was currently a bartender, but, as O'Keefe later put it, "like the rest of us, he was a compulsive thief." Faherty had an estimated IQ of 160, and in prison, he was a champion debater. He was also a hopeless alcoholic.

Bringing up the rear were the youngest intruders. John Adolph "Jazz"

Maffie, 38, a Boston bookie who had been a star athlete now used his muscle to support Pino's enterprises. Stanley Albert "Gus" Gusciora, 31, was O'Keefe's regular partner in other crimes and, like O'Keefe, had no occupation but stealing.

The men made their way through the darkened building while on a rooftop opposite, 35-year-old Vincent James Costa watched anxiously through binoculars. Costa was an outside man for two reasons: (1) the rest of the gang felt he was too inept to go inside the terminal; (2) Pino wanted to keep his sister's husband out of harm's way. Costa, though, had a key job.

The gang had given up hope of opening the Brink's vault without setting off the alarm. Equally hopeless was the idea of holding up that mammoth money mover while dozens of armed employees were coming and going. Months of surveillance had established that all of the employees went home by 7 p.m. except for five men who counted money and put it in the vault. The only way to get the money in Brink's was to hold up those five after the rest of the employees had gone home, but before they closed the vault.

On his rooftop, Jimmy Costa checked to make sure the the five Brinks men were all together and the vault was open. If the men weren't together, he signaled the robbers to wait. If the vault was closed, he used his flashlight to tell them to drop the attempt. He'd already cancelled five attempts.

Down the street, in the green truck, 42-year-old Tony Pino fidgeted as he waited. Soon after he was released from prison in 1944, he had seen a swarm of Brink's trucks taking money from their downtown Boston terminal. Ever since then, he had been obsessed with Brink's. He had followed their trucks, noted the size and times of deliveries, then robbed the safes of their customers the night of the deliveries. Only occasionally did a customer, such as the big General Electric plant, look too tough.

When Brink's moved its terminal from downtown to the North End, Tony Pino began checking out the new terminal. One night he wandered into the open garage and found the door leading to Brink's. Amazingly, there was no alarm on the door. Pino picked the lock and walked in. He opened several more doors, none with an alarm connected. For months, he crawled through the blacked-out building looking for alarms and hidden cameras. In his early prowls, fat Tony crept through the pitch-dark rooms with a paper bag over his head—a precaution against infra-red cameras. He found nothing, to his surprise, joy and disgust—disgust that any organization could be so cheap as to leave millions of dollars practically unguarded. The only alarm—a wireless type he couldn't fix—was on the vault itself.

Pino began gathering a gang to take advantage of the situation. He had been working regularly with Richardson, Geagan and Maffie. The other members of the present gang were thieves he had known, and occasionally worked with, for years. For instance, he and O'Keefe had first been arrested together when he was 7 and "Specks" was 6. Each new member of the gang was added with the consent of the others.

One member Pino had a hard time getting accepted was the man who supplied tonight's driver, Joseph Sylvester "Barney" Banfield, 40. Banfield worked for Joseph F. McGinnis, an important figure in the Boston under-world, and one whose real role in the Brink's robbery is still something of a mystery. McGinnis, 46, a big, balding bull of a man, was reputed to be a partner of Raymond Patriarca of Providence, head of New England's largest Italian crime family. McGinnis knew, and probably owned, key people in government and law enforcement. One of McGinnis's principal functions, it appears, was to grease some key palms if that became necessary. The big man was not popular with most members of the gang.

He had the reputation of being the cheapest man alive and one who would cheat his partners at every opportunity. Besides providing protection from the law, McGinnis's task in this caper would be to dispose of evidence and help get rid of the stolen money. For this, Pino moved heaven and earth to let McGinnis and Banfield each have a full share in the job. That was like giving McGinnis two shares, because he owned Banfield. Literally—he kept Barney chained in his cellar when he got drunker than Joe thought he should.

Pino admitted to one gang member that he needed McGinnis to fix a deportation case against him. The police and FBI, caught up in the myth of organized crime that required a "godfather" for every effective gang, thought McGinnis masterminded the whole operation. He didn't, but it's certain that, as O'Keefe later told writer Bob Considine, McGinnis had "almost hypnotic control" over Pino, "because Pino's life's ambition was to be another McGin-nis." Pino admitted to writer Noel Behn that at the time of the Brink's job, he was in business with McGinnis. They located "scores," then sold information about their location, and advice on how to take them, to other crooks. McGinnis always managed to stay away from the action.

Inside the Brink's terminal, in the middle of the action, the robbers took off their chauffeur caps, put on rubber masks of comic book characters Captain Marvel and Captain Marvel, Jr., then replaced the caps. The inside of the terminal was almost totally black. The men moved through the maze of rooms easily only because each of them had been in the building so often they knew it as well as their own homes. Altogether, the robbers had been in Brinks at least 74 times before this night. In most cases, Pino had acted as tour guide. Even O'Keefe, who got into the Brink's enterprise comparatively late, toured the inside of the terminal more than 30 times.

O'Keefe came to another locked door. He found the proper key by feeling the notches Pino had filed in it and opened the door. Another robber wedged the doors slightly open. The idea, Pino had explained, was to leave the doors looking closed to anyone who saw them, but still make possible a speedy exit if needed.

O'Keefe opened a third door, and the robbers moved silently outside the cage where the Brinks men were still sorting money. They moved silently because all were wearing rubbers over their shoes, as Pino had decreed. All except O'Keefe, who normally followed the fashions set by movie badmen like Richard Widmark and Humphey Bogart. O'Keefe decided to wear his new crepe soled shoes and to hell with what Tony Pino said.

The robbers, standing outside the cage, watched the Brink's people closing another business day. For a long moment, nobody said anything. Each of the four Brink's employees went on counting money until he happened to look up and see seven pistols aimed through the cage. Each seem to be paralyzed by the sight. Then one of the robbers said, "Okay, boys, put them in the air."

The Brink's men slowly raised their hands, except for one who had been kneeling near the vault and was wearing a shoulder holster. The robbers began to sweat.

"None of us were killers," Mike Geagan said later. "We planned this so nobody would get hurt—we wouldn't and neither would anyone else." Geagan had been using a gun most of his life, but, he explained, "A gun gives you power. You can use it to make people do what you tell them. But it never crossed my mind to use a gun to hurt somebody."

"Come on, come on," one of the robbers said, "Get 'em up." The kneeling man raised his hands.

The fifth Brink's man, who had stepped into another room after Costa gave his signal, reappeared. He gasped.

"That's right, this is a stickup," said one of the Captain Marvels. "Please put them in the air and do as you're told and no one will get hurt." The fifth man raised his hands.

"Get over here and open this gate," a robber demanded.

No one moved.

Jazz Maffie was getting ready to climb the grating. On one of his reconnaissance trips, he had already proved that he could get over it in seconds. Then one of the Brink's men said to the kneeling man with the shoulder holster, "Open up, Charlie. Open it up."

Charlie Grell got up and, keeping his hands away from the gun, opened the gate.

Geagan dashed in and began piling empty money baskets in front of the window so nobody outside could see what was happening. The other bandits disarmed the Brink's men while one straddled the alarm button on the floor. Gusciora herded the Brink's people to one corner, tied their hands and feet and put a strip of adhesive tape over their mouths.

Baker took a pry bar he'd been carrying and tried to open a metal box containing the General Electric payroll—reputed to be a million dollars. Other masked men were putting cash into the burlap bags they'd brought. Some even put in coins, although taking anything but paper money was a waste of time and effort. No one was watching the approaches to the money room.

A buzzer sounded. Gusciora lifted the tape from one Brink's employee's mouth.

"What does that mean?" he asked.

"It means somebody wants to get in," the man said.

O'Keefe grabbed the coat of a robber near him and motioned him to follow. They got as far as the garage but saw that the man who pushed the buzzer was a watchman of some sort and had given up trying to get in. He was strolling away and seemed quite unalarmed. They went back to the money room.

The robbers reluctantly left the steel box containing the G.E. payroll. They couldn't open it, and they couldn't carry it. The dragged their sacks of money down to the entrance where the truck would meet them and organized a human conveyer belt. Geagan opened the door a crack. It was the signal to bring up the truck.

Pino snapped open a canvas door in the side of the truck, and the robbers began hurling in money sacks. The robbers piled in after them. As Sandy Richardson, the last man to leave, got to the truck, Pino asked where the metal box was.

"We couldn't get it," Richardson said.

"What do you mean, you couldn't get it?"

"We couldn't get it. Now get out of the way and let me on."

"That box is what started it all. That box has got a million smackers in it. I been dreaming of that box for six years!"

"Let me on, for God's sake."

Pino began screaming and kicked at Richardson. Big Jazz Maffie grabbed Fat Tony from behind, clapped a hand over his mouth and lifted him, all 300 pounds of him, off the floorboards. Richardson jumped aboard and Banfield gunned the engine. Behind the truck was a car driven by Jimmy Costa and containing Faherty and Geagan, who couldn't fit in the truck after the money was loaded.

There was a lot of money to count, but most of the thieves had more important work immediately after the robbery—establishing their alibis. Jazz Maffie had been taking bets in Jimmie O'Keefe's Restaurant and told the hatcheck girl to show his wife to the table he had reserved when she came in at 7. Then he slipped out and was picked up by Pino and Banfield. Now he slipped back into the restaurant and joined his wife as if he'd been there all along. Joe O'Keefe and Gusciora began bar-hopping in their usual haunts with a couple of girl friends. Faherty was in another restaurant diligently engaged in tying one on, his usual nightly activity, after helping Jimmy Costa dispose of the costumes. And Mike Geagan was busy washing the diapers of his infant daughter.

Tony Pino called his lawyer and told him he was coming over after he stopped at his aunt's. Before he could leave, though, he got a call from Joe McGinnis, who had not taken part in the actual robbery.

"I'm talking to Lieutenant Crowley," McGinnis said, "and if you want an alibi, get your ass over to the store quick."

McGinnis was talking to James Crowley, commander of the robbery division of the Boston PD, when Pino arrived at his liquor store. Pino bought a bottle of Metaxis ("because nobody forgets a name like Metaxis") and asked McGinnis what time it was. McGinnis said 7 o'clock (it was actually 7:40). Crowley didn't have a watch, and later remembered he had been with McGinnis and Pino at 7. Pino then took the bottle to his aunt.

Banfield went to a garage owned by his employer and busied himself wiping fingerprints off the truck. Only Richardson and Baker stayed with the money at the home of Jazz Maffie's parents. By 10:30, they had counted more than a million dollars of "good" money and two and a half bags remained to be counted. "Bad" money—$1,000 bills and new bills with serial numbers in sequence—was to be destroyed, along with checks and money orders. McGinnis took the two and a half uncounted bags and later swore there was no usable currency in them.

The actual total, according to the FBI, was $1,218,211.29 in cash and $1,557,183.83 in checks and money orders. The precision is deceptive. The loot included seven "sealed packages," such as phone company receipts, which had never been counted by the owners. Nobody will ever know the exact total. It was the largest return from a robbery in U.S. history up to that time. Although no one was shot, assaulted or even touched, J. Edgar Hoover called the robbery "the crime of the century." He was not just looking at the money. The smoothness and precision of the operation aroused grudging admiration of the robbers all over the country. And admiration of crooks, grudging or not, was the bane of Hoover's existence.

McGinnis's reputation led the Boston FBI office to suspect him and

Pino, one of his few friends. That led them to keep a close watch on Pino's associates. It wasn't close enough.

Within a few days, the money had been split up and distributed in various places. Joe McGinnis held most of it. Each robber was to get $100,000, but several of them, after they picked up their shares from McGinnis, noticed that they had been shorted between $2,000 and $5,000. Then McGinnis claimed that instead of the $800,000 he had been given, he got only $400,000. With Pino's backing, he demanded money back.

O'Keefe and Gusciora missed that development. They had decided to take a trip to St. Louis, where Gusciora had relatives, leaving the bulk of their money with Maffie. The FBI knew about the trip and notified police chiefs along the way. On their way back, the two Boston thieves couldn't resist the temptation to break into a couple of places in the hick towns they were passing through. One was a sporting goods store in Pennsylvania, where they stole several guns. They drove to the next town and burglarized a clothing store. At the next stop, they were caught.

The Pennsylvanians wasted no time when they realized they had two of the suspected Brink's robbers. Gus Gusciora pleaded guilty and ended up in the Western Pennsylvania Penitentiary, where the ill treatment he received ruined his health. Joe O'Keefe pleaded not guilty and went to a county jail, for "loitering with known criminals" (Gusciora), where he sat in a nearly windowless cell with nothing to do. Following that 90 days, he got three years in the same jail for violation of the Uniform Firearms Act.

Just before the federal statute of limitations ran out, the government convened a federal grand jury, which heard 65 witnesses, including all the gang members but Faherty. Nobody said anything. Maffie and O'Keefe were sent to jail for contempt, as were O'Keefe's sister, brother and brother-in-law. All were later released, but the legal expenses bankrupted the honest members of the O'Keefe family. O'Keefe himself went back to the Pennsylvania jail for another year. The federal grand jury returned no indictments, and the federal statute of limitations ran out. The state statute had three more years to go.

When O'Keefe got out, he faced a burglary charge. Free on bond, he came back to Boston looking for his money.

Joe O'Keefe was seldom taken seriously by the bigger hoods around Boston. He was short, skinny, balding and spoke with a lisp, but he affected the mannerisms of a movie tough guy. It was easy to laugh at him.

Easy, but not wise.

Maffie was the first to find out. When O'Keefe came looking for his money, big, tough Jazz stared at Joe's .45 automatic, then broke down and cried. It was all gone, he said. O'Keefe considered killing him on the spot.

"But then I figured that if Jazz lived, he might get lucky again and eventually pay me what was coming to me. I figured, too, that through him I could present my case to the others better. I told him to stop blubbering and give me a breakdown on what he had spent on my legal fees. He made some figures on the back of an envelope and finally said that it came to about $41,000. I gave him the benefit of the doubt. It still meant that I had better than $50,000 due me."

O'Keefe went back to Pennsylvania to be tried for burglary. He was convicted, but appealed and was released on bail. He returned to Boston and began looking up gang members. He didn't get any help.

"I grabbed Jazz again and took him to McGinnis's liquor store. It was a Saturday morning. In ten or fifteen years, McGinnis had never missed being in that store on Saturday if he wasn't in the can."

He wasn't there. O'Keefe didn't know it, but McGinnis was in the can. The feds had found the still in New Hampshire where he made bootleg liquor. As they waited, Maffie told O'Keefe he was losing money from his bookie business, but O'Keefe said he could go only if he conned another member of the gang into taking his place. Maffie got on the phone and conned Baker. Finally, O'Keefe learned what happened to McGinnis and released Baker.

Next, he and a new partner, John Carlson, kidnapped Jimmy Costa. O'Keefe went to Pino and told him his brother-in-law would cost $25,000 for starters. Pino offered $2,500 as a down payment, and Costa was released.

Now it was the gang's turn. As O'Keefe was going home a few nights later, a car sped past the one he was driving and sprayed it with sub-machinegun bullets. O'Keefe was not hurt, but he went to Carlson and got another .45 automatic. O'Keefe, like most Boston crooks at the time, had a gun only when he needed it for a job. The police frequently questioned people with records, and possession of a firearm by a previously convicted felon meant a quick trip to jail.

O'Keefe called on Pino and accused him of setting up the ambush. Pino professed ignorance. Not wanting to kill his boyhood chum in cold blood, O'Keefe left.

He went to Henry Baker's vending machine company. When Baker showed up, he pulled a pistol halfway from his pocket to intimidate little Joe. Joe pulled his all the way out. Baker ran, and O'Keefe fired a couple of half-hearted shots to speed him on his way.

A week later, June 16, 1954, as he left his car, O'Keefe sensed trouble and ducked behind a car hood. A burst of machinegun fire followed. He reached over the car hood and fired back. There was nothing half-hearted in his shooting this time. The assailant backed up his car and took off without lights. Then O'Keefe noticed he had been hit in the wrist and chest. Neither wound was serious, but he went to Carlson, and his partner got him to a doctor who wouldn't talk.

From Carlson, he learned that the machinegunner was "some guy named Elmer Burke."

"He was the cold, crazy New York assassin the newspapers called Trigger," O'Keefe told Bob Considine. "We don't use names like that generally. His name was Elmer."

Burke's favorite weapon was a military M-3 submachinegun, a tinny weapon designed for mass production. The troops called it the "grease gun," because it looked like one. It fired the same .45 slugs as the classic Thompson, though, and killed just as efficiently. Burke would kill anyone for money, but he was in Boston because he was wanted in New York for killing his best friend. "He killed a number of his friends," O'Keefe said. "He was funny that way."

Nobody knew it at the time, but the gunfight between Burke and O'Keefe proved to be the turning point in the Brink's case. O'Keefe knew his former associates had not only cheated him, but planned to kill him. He began wondering what he owed them.

The police caught Burke and found his submachinegun. Possession of a machinegun could bring a life sentence in Massachusetts. Burke was "gabby," O'Keefe told Considine. The killer admitted shooting at O'Keefe. The police went after O'Keefe and arrested him for parole violation. The alleged violation dated from 1947. O'Keefe was sent to the county jail in Springfield, at the other end of Massachusetts, for security.

Shortly after that, John Carlson disappeared and is believed to have been murdered.

Then Elmer Burke made a spectacular jail break underworld sources said Anthony Pino had engineered. For almost a year, he hid out in North Carolina with an ex-con named Duke Connolly and his wife. Then one of the Connolly children was found wandering the streets of Wilmington, Delaware and the second was picked up in Baltimore. Authorities checking their home found that Duke and his wife had disappeared, and they found Elmer Burke living in their house. Burke was executed in Sing Sing January 9, 1958.

Meanwhile, Joe O'Keefe was sitting in a jail in western Massachusetts. He was broke, his relatives were destitute and his erstwhile colleagues, except for his buddy, Gusciora, were prospering. Worst of all, his former friends had tried to kill him. In a short time, the state statute of limitations would run out and they'd be safe. The U.S. statute of limitations had run out three years before, but FBI agents were still dropping in on O'Keefe to ask him about the Brink's robbery. O'Keefe faced another 20 years in prison in Pennsylvania. Burke had convinced him that he owed his partners nothing. He sent word to them that unless he received some money, he might discuss some of his memories. Instead of money, he received the news that McGinnis was going to arrange to have him committed to a mental hospital.

O'Keefe passed on some news of his own: he'd changed his mind about talking with the FBI.

On January 6, 1956, eleven days before the statute of limitations ran out, O'Keefe told two FBI special agents all he knew about the Brink's robbery. The next day, six of his colleagues were in jail. Faherty and Richardson escaped the dragnet but were captured four months later. Banfield had died of alcoholism in 1955. Gusciora was moved from Pennsylvania to Boston to stand trial, but began having dizzy spells soon after he reached his home town. On July 9, he died of a brain tumor.

The death of O'Keefe's last friend among the robbers killed any hope that he might change his mind. During the trial, he testified for 31 hours, over seven days, and the jury believed him.

At the sentencing, defense counsel Paul Smith pleaded in vain that, in spite of the publicity, the crime was simply armed robbery, and an armed robbery in which no one was hurt or even pushed. The publicity the robbers got worked to their detriment. Judge Felix Forte gave each defendant except McGinnis life for armed robbery, eight to ten years for breaking and entering, and two years for conspiracy.

He had instructed the jury that McGinnis could not be found guilty of armed robbery or breaking and entering, but only of being an accessory to those acts. So now the judge sentenced McGinnis for being an accessory to armed robbery committed by each of the others, including Banfield and Gusciora, now dead. He sentenced McGinnis to nine life terms.

In the silence that followed, the only voice heard was that of McGinnis. He turned to a court attendant and asked, "Why doesn't he give me nine more lives?"

Massachuetts released O'Keefe in 1960 and refused to extradite him to Pennsylvania.

POSTSCRIPT: "THE BRINK'S JOB"— HOLLYWOOD STYLE

About 28 years after Tony, Specks and the boys made their biggest score, a movie company came to Boston to celebrate the event. (It was the second film treatment of the robbery, the first being Universal's *Six Bridges to*

Cross.) Director William Friedkin said he was not going to be a stickler for historical detail. Before he finished shooting, though, he did learn a lot about crime that even his experience making "The French Connection" hadn't taught him.

No one could argue with his statement about historical detail. True, the company did construct 70 sets to make the Boston of 1978 look like the Boston of 1950. They even partially reconstructed sleazy old Scollay Square, demolished ten years previously. On the other hand, the movie makers eliminated four members of the gang altogether, because, as Friedkin said, eleven characters is too many.

Joe O'Keefe had been asked by some Hollywood type to sell movie rights when he was paroled in 1960, and he told the would-be producer to take a walk. Tony Pino, Jimmy Costa, Jazz Maffie and Sandy Richardson, showed less contempt for money. Maffie and Richardson also served as consultants during the filming. Consequently, O'Keefe scarcely appears in film, and the character who bears his name is completely different. O'Keefe, whose only part in World War II was a short stint in the Merchant Marine (with time off for a little thievery in London), became a shell-shocked former soldier brought into the caper for his expertise with explosives.

Friedkin's real enthusiasm was for his atmosphere scenes of North End Boston.

"Where else could you find faces like these?" asked casting director Lou DiGiamo, pointing to shots of the local people he hired as extras, as if he were showing off souvenir pictures of a visit to a New Guinea village.

The film company's pride in the atmosphere shots was so well known that shortly before shooting stopped, three armed men entered the production office, handcuffed four film editors and made off with 13 reels of atmosphere shots. They offered to return them for $600,000. The movie company refused and countered with $20,000. The robbers rejected that, so the film was shown with fewer street scenes than planned. The police suspected the robbers might include one or more of the known criminals Friedkin hired to coach his actors in the art of breaking and entering.

A year later, a certain Edward Q. Colombani, also known as Spanish Eddie, who had taught star Peter Falk how to pick locks, was arrested in New York. The charge: plotting a $2 million holdup of a Brink's car at LaGuardia Airport.

Spanish Eddie, the teacher, apparently learned something during his brief movie career.

Notes

Chapter One

The main source of information on military operations was *The Compact History of the Revolutionary War* by R. Ernest and Trevor N. Dupuy. William P. Cumming's and Hugh Rankin's *The Fate of a Nation* is a valuable source of contemporary documents, and Michael Pearson's *Those Damned Rebels* gives the view from the British side. Harold Peterson's *The Book of the Continental Soldier* and *Arms and Armor in Colonial America* provide information on military equipment on both sides.

5   "Especially delighted . . ." See Cumming and Rankin, *The Fate of a Nation*, for Gates' letter about Jane McCrea. Pages 147-8.

5   "When he took Ticonderoga . . ." Dupuy and Dupuy, *Compact History* . . ., page 198.

5   "On July 27 . . ." Cumming and Rankin, pages 147-8; Dupuy and Dupuy, page 212; Pearson, *Those Damned Rebels*, pages 245-6.

6   "Burgoyne thought . . ." Dupuy and Dupuy, pages 212-4.

7   "We shall win . . ." This frequently quoted statement may have been a patriotic invention by someone who didn't understand the situation.

7   "In a country where . . ." Every free male of military age in each colony was a member of the militia. Each colony held regular musters and had laws prescribing weapons and equipment to be kept in the militiaman's home. Until the French and Indian War, the militia did almost all of the fighting against European and Indian enemies. And even in that war, militia units played a significant, perhaps indispensable part.

7   "Many years before . . ." For the rise of William Johnson, see Eckert, Allan W., *The Conquerors*, Little, Brown and Company, Boston: 1970. For the end of the Johnson dynasty, Dupuy and Dupuy, page 206.

8   "St. Leger found his way . . ." A somewhat Holywood-ish treatment of these events in the Mohawk Valley appears in Walter Edmond's *Drums Along the Mohawk*.

8   "Guy Johnson, commanding . . ." Dupuy and Dupuy, page 208.

9   "As soon as he took command . . ." Cumming and Rankin, pages 147-8.

9   "Morgan's Riflemen . . ." Peterson, *The Book of the Continental Soldier*, pages 222-3.

9   "That was unfortunate for the British . . ." Morgan later commanded American forces at Cowpens, a tactical masterpiece that practically annihilated Banastre Tarleton's forces and eliminated that cruel young cavalry leader as a factor in the war in the South.

10   "The rifle . . ." Peterson, *Continental Soldier*, pages 38-44, also Peterson, *Arms and Armor in Colonial America*, pages 159-222, and Peterson, *Treasury of the Gun*, pages 128-45.

10   "Personal disaster . . ." Prebble, John, *Culloden*, pages 19, 63-5, 350

12   "It was a Pyrrhic victory . . ." Dupuy and Dupuy, page 350.

12   "By October 7 . . ." *Ibid.*, pages 255-6

13   " 'Don't hurt him . . .' " Pearson, page 281

Chapter Two

The most important sources for Aaron Burr's life were Milton Lomask's *Aaron Burr: The Years from Princeton to Vice President, 1756 - 1805* and *Aaron Burr: The Conspiracy and Years of Exile, 1805 - 1836*. Nathan Schachner's *Aaron Burr* also provided a good overview of Burr's life as did *Aaron Burr: Portrait of an Ambitious Man* by Herbert S. Parmet and Marie B. Hecht. James Thomas Flexner's *The Young Hamilton* provided the most information on Hamilton's early life. There is a wealth of information on the mature Hamilton, some of the best sources being Jacob Cooke's *Alexander Hamilton*, John Miller's *Alexander Hamilton and the Growth of the New Nation*, Clinton Rossiter's *Alexander Hamilton and the Constitution*, Samuel Konefsky's *John Marshall and Alexander Hamilton, Architects of the Constitution* and Richard Morris's *Witness at the Creation* and *Seven Who Shaped our Destiny*. Morris also edited *Alexander Hamilton and the Founding of the Nation*, a valuable collection of contemporary documents. The complete *Federalist Papers* may be found in Benjamin Fletcher Wright's *The Federalist by Alexander Hamilton, James Madison and John Jay*. Henry Adams' *History of the United States During the Administration of Thomas Jefferson* is the classic history of Jefferson's terms as president and puts Burr's career in perspective. Adams discovered diplomatic papers in Britain, France and Spain that indicate treasonable intentions on Burr's part. In the century since Adams did his research, however, new correspondence has been discovered, especially by Walter McCaleb, that indicate that Burr was a liar and a confidence man but no traitor. Harold Syett's and Jean Cooke's *Interview in Weehawken* contains all contemporary documents pertaining to the duel. And Merrill Lindsay's article in the November 1976 *Smithsonian* provides information on the duel that had been overlooked for more than a century and a half.

15   "Hamilton was born . . ." Flexner, pages 16-52; Cooke, pages 1-8.
16   "Aaron Burr, son . . ." Lomask, Milton, *Aaron Burr . . . 1756-1805*, pages 3-63.
16   "As Hamilton . . ." Schachner, *Aaron Burr*, pages 48-50; Lomask, *Aaron Burr, 1756-1805*, pages 50-1, says Burr falsely told the commanding officer new orders required his withdrawal.
17   "It was a frustrating . . ." Cooke, *Alexander Hamilton*, pages 48-9; Miller, *Alexander Hamilton & The Growth of the New Nation*, pages 151-83.
18   " 'The people . . .' " Cooke, page 49.
18   "Hamilton contacted . . ." Wright, *The Federalist . . .* page 7.
18   "Their [Hamilton . . .]" *Ibid.*, page 86
18   " 'The complete independence . . .' " *Ibid.*, 491
19   "He occasionally . . ." Adams, *History of . . . Thomas Jefferson*, page 132. It should be noted that Adams got the quotation from a letter by Hamilton to James A. Bayard. (See Schachner, page 195.) Hamilton, of course, is not the best character witness for Burr.
19   "He took . . ." Lomask, *Aaron Burr . . . 1756-1805*, pages 218-21; Schachner, pages 154-9.
19   "Hamilton was a master of invective . . ." Schachner, page 184.
19   " 'a man of profound . . .' " Miller, page 347.
20   " 'To be the proconsul . . .' " *Ibid.*, page 483.
21   "As he said in 1799 . . ." Miller, page 497.
21   "Hamilton went so far . . ." *Ibid.*, 498.
22   "Frustrated . . ." *Ibid.*, pages 500-1.
23   "Hamilton said . . ." Schachner, page 184.
23   "Adams recommended . . ." *Ibid.*, page 148.
24   "He wrote . . ." *Ibid.*, page 193.
24   "Hamilton took up . . ." *Ibid.*, pages 200-6; Lomask, *op. cit.*, pages 268-95.

24 "Burr had earlier written . . ." Parmet and Hecht, page 158.
25 "In the 1960s . . ." Lomask, *Aaron Burr . . . 1756-1805*, pages 287-8
25 "The Federalists caucused . . ." *Ibid.* pages 291-4.
26 " 'I beg leave . . .' " Syrett and Cooke, *Interview in Weehawken*, page 48.
26 "Hamilton sent . . ." *Ibid.*, pages 52-4.
28 "The .54 caliber . . ." Lindsay, *Trick Pistols Shed New Light on Famed Burr-Hamilton Duel* in *Smithsonian*, November 1976, pages 94-8.
28 "At least 10 days . . ." Syrett and Cooke, page 151.
28 "In a paper . . ." *Ibid.*, pages 100-2.
29 "As Pendleton . . ." *Ibid.*, pages 151-2 and Lomask, *op. cit.*, page 354.
29 "Hamilton sighted . . ." Syrett and Cooke, page 154.
29 " 'With his pistol . . .' " Lindsay, *Smithsonian*, page 96.
29 " 'Col. Burr . . .' " Syrett and Cooke, 141-2.
30 "Crowds paraded . . ." Schachner, page 255.
30 "(It must . . .)" Adams, pages 130-3
31 "On the opening day . . ." Schachner, page 261; Lomask, *op. cit.*, page 361.
31 " 'Mr. Burr . . .' " Adams, page 576; Lomask, *Aaron Burr, 1805-1836*, pages 49-50; Schachner, page 290.
32 "Walter Flavius McCaleb . . ." Lomask, *op. cit.*, page 112; Schachner, page 287.
33 "With a small fleet . . ." Lomask, *op. cit.*, page 39.
33 "To discredit Burr . . ." Schachner, pages 304-5.
33 "According to its . . ." Lomask, *op. cit.*, pages 104-5.
33 "Wikinson, who has . . ." Frantz, Joe B., *Texas: a Centennial History*, pages 36-7.
33 "As Agent 13 . . ." Lomask, *op. cit.*, page 17.
33 " 'Burr is . . .' " Lomask, *op. cit.*, page 13.
34 "Wilkinson instituted . . ." Lomask, *op. cit.*, pages 182-5; Schachner, pages 364-73.
34 "George Hay . . ." Lomask, *op. cit.*, pages 241, 247-51; Chidsey, Donald Barr, *The Great Conspiracy*, page 103.
35 "Earlier . . ." Lomask, *op. cit.*, page 245; see Jefferson, *Writings,*, pages 532-8 for his special message to Congress on the "Burr Conspiracy."
35 "But Hay . . ." Schachner, page 443.
35 "Wilkinson had given . . ." Lomask, *op. cit.*, pages 115-22 and 164-6. The style of the letter was certainly not Burr's, and no copies of any version exist in Burr's handwriting, although there are several in the handwriting of his follower, Jonathan Dayton. Wilkinson admitted in court that he had tampered with the letter. Even with changes, Marshall said it contained no evidence of treason.
35 "At the trial . . ." Schachner, page 442.
35 "There! . . ." *Ibid.*, page 511.

Chapter Three

David Nevin's *The Texans* was the major source of information on the history of Texas as a Mexican state and before. It and Walter Lord's *A Time to Stand* were major sources for the fighting at the Alamo and the campaign that followed. Both are good, but Lord's casualty figures seem more realistic, and Nevin is clearer about where the Alamo defenders were before the battle. Bowie, for instance, had established real roots in San Antonio de Béjar, his late wife's home town. Joe Frantz's *Texas: A Bicentennial History* offers a lot of human interest about the Texas revolution. Hudson Strode's *Timeless Mexico* does the same for Mexican history and Antonio López de Santa Anna. "Recuerda el Alamo!" in the October 1975 issue of *American Heritage*, was especially valuable. It was taken from *With Santa Anna in Texas: A Personal Narrative of the Revolution*, a book published late in 1836 by Jose Enrique de la Peña, a young lieutenant colonel of engineers (*Zapadores*) and gives a complete view of the battle by a Mexican participant.

36 "A Mexican staff officer . . ." Lord, *A Time to Stand*, page 102.
37 "In the fort . . ." Frantz, *Texas*, page 63.
37 "They neglected . . ." *Ibid.*, pages 34-48.
39 " 'Were I made . . .' " Nevin, *The Texans*, page 64.
39 "At one point . . ." Strode, *Timeless Mexico*, page 141.
39 "By 1828 . . ." Nevin, page 62.
39 "A Kentucky-born . . ." Nevin, page 65.
39 "Santa Anna, he told . . ." *Ibid.*, page 71.
40 "Cós' 100 Dragoons . . ." At New Orleans in 1815, the last battle of the War of 1812 (actually after the peace treaty was signed) Andrew Jackson, leading an outnumbered army with a large proportion of rifle-armed frontiersmen, destroyed a British army led by Edward Pakenham. British dead came to more than 2,000, including Pakenham; American dead totaled 13.
40 "Percussion rifles . . ." Peterson, *The Treasury of the Gun*, pages 114-22.
40 "More volunteers . . ." Lord, pages 41-61.
40 "In the roll . . ." *Ibid.*, pages 214-9.
40 "Colonel Benjamin Miliam . . ." Frantz, page 63.
40 "Sam Houston . . ." Nevin, page 51-62.
42 " 'To the People of Texas . . .' " Frantz, page 67; Nevin, page 98.
43 "He was . . ." Lord, page 115; Nevin, page 101.
44 "Lieutenant Colonel Enrique de la Peña . . ." Peña, "Recuerda el Alamo!" *American Heritage*, October 1975, page 92.
44 " 'Travis' resistance . . .' " *Ibid.*, pages 92-3.
45 " 'Our columns . . .' " *Ibid.*, page 94.
45 Page 89, "Master Sergeant Felix Nuñez . . ." Lord, pages 141-2; Nevin, page 107.
45 "Travis was seen . . ." Peña, page 95.
46 "They bayoneted Bowie . . ." Nevin, page 107.
46 " 'Some seven . . .' " Peña, page 96.
46 "His losses . . ." Nevin estimates 1,500, which is far too high. To achieve this, each Texan would have had to have killed nine or 10 Mexicans. And only about 1,800 Mexicans actually took part in the assault.
47 "Houston would have agreed . . ." Dunnigan, James F. and Nofi, Albert A., *Dirty Secrets*, page 88.
48 "Colonel John Wharton . . ." Nevin, page 140.
48 "As Houston . . ." Nevin, page 141.

Chapter Four

Wayne Gard's *The Great Buffalo Hunt* is one of the few easily available books giving much detail on the Adobe Walls fight. Stanley Vestal's *Dodge City, Queen of the Cow Towns* and Cy Martin's *The Saga of the Buffalo* each have valuable bits about the fight and, like the Gard book, give plenty of detail about buffalo hunting and the followers of that strange profession. Martin's book contains a sketch of the whole town of Adobe Walls. Dee Brown's *Bury My Heart at Wounded Knee* provides the Indian point of view. Walter Prescott Webb puts the western movement in perspective in *The Great Plains*.

Vestal raises an interesting point on page 36: "Only the simple-minded savage wondered why men would kill off native animals that took care of themselves in order to breed less hardy creatures that had to be taken care of." The answer, of course, is that the buffalo not only took care of itself, it took care of the Indian. The less hardy cattle were preferred because the Indians didn't have any.

53 "People in town . . ." Gard, *The Great Buffalo Hunt*, pages 147-9; Vestal, *Dodge City* . . ., page 66.

54 "The whole town . . ." Martin, *The Saga of the Buffalo*, page 123 has a sketch of the whole town, drawn by an observer.
54 "Buffalo hunter Josiah Wright Mooar . . ." Vestal, page 44.
54 "The Triple Alliance . . ." According to some estimates, Paraguay's pre-war population of 2,000,000 was reduced to 200,000.
55 "The movement stopped . . ." Webb, *The Great Plains*, Page 140-202.
55 "The Pioneers' secondary weapons . . ." Although usually considered an Indian weapon, the hatchet called the tomahawk was invented by Europeans primarily to trade with the Indians. Colonial militia adopted it as an alternative to the bayonet or the sword. The Indians did not consider the knife a weapon before their contact with European settlers. There was a reason they called white people "long knives."
55 "The flintlock . . ." Peterson, *The Treasury of the Gun*, pages 117-85; Vestal, pages 37-8; Martin, page 96.
56 "A buffalo hunter got . . ." Martin, page 104; Vestal, page 37; Gard, page 114.
56 "One hunter . . ." Vestal, page 42; Martin, page 102.
56 "Army officers . . ." Gard, page 94.
56 "An Indian hunting ground . . ." Vestal, page 36.
58 "Quanah Parker . . ." Brown, *Bury My Heart* . . ., page 265.
58 " 'I am a warrior . . .' " Gard, page 160
59 "The last reported magical . . ." The medicine was produced in the so-called "Simba War." It was intended to frustrate the bullets of the Congo (later Zaire) Army, particularly its white mercenaries.
59 "Sometime after midnight . . ." Vestal, pages 67-8.
60 " 'I got up . . .' " Brown, page 266.
60 "Billy Dixon later . . ." Raine and Barnes, *Cattle, Cowboys and Rangers*, pages 125-6.
61 "As the fighting continued . . ." Gard, page 172.
62 "On the third day . . ." *Ibid.*, page 178.
62 "That seemingly . . ." Monaghan, *The Book of the American West*, page 249.
62 "Before they were finished . . ." Gard, page 179.
62 "A year after the Adobe Walls fight . . ." Akehurst, *The World of Guns*, page 76.

Chapter Five

Robert Utley's *Cavalier in Buckskin* was a valuable source for both Custer's career and the battle. Mari Sandoz' *The Battle of the Little Bighorn*, based as it is on both government records and interviews with survivors and their children, is perhaps the best source for the battle itself. It flows smoothly and swiftly. Evan Connell's *Son of the Morning Star* is not as fast a read, but it's a treasure trove of Custeriana.

64 "Colonel John Gibbon . . ." Sandoz, *The Battle of the Little Bighorn*, page 16.
65 "Because Custer . . ." Utley, *Cavalier in Buckskin*, page 175-6.
67 "Custer did earn . . ." Brown, *Bury My Heart at Wounded Knee*, pages 138-9.
67 "With his wife . . ." Utley, page 115.
67 "He had, however . . ." Connell, *Son of the Morning Star*, page 33.
69 "During the Washita campaign . . ." Connell, pages 200-2.
69 "There are indications . . ." Utley, page 107-8.
69 "The more I see of him . . ." *Ibid.*, page 108.
71 "In 1866 . . ." Keith, *Sixguns*, page 16; Peterson, *The Treasury of the Gun*, pages 184-5.
73 "Actually, the Gatlings . . ." Ellis, *The Social History of the Machine Gun*, page 74; Van Doren, "Dr. Gatling and his Gun," *American Heritage*, October 1957, pages 51 and 105-7.
73 " 'They frequently . . .' " Connell, pages 257-8.

73 "three years after . . ." Ellis, pages 82-4. Also Van Doren, page 105.
74 "A witness . . ." Ellis, page 86.
74 Page 135, "That morning, Custer's Crow Scouts . . ." Sandoz, pages 50-2.
75 "The Arikara scouts . . ." Connell, pages 269-70.
76 "An Indian woman . . ." Sandoz, page 66.
77 "When the Indians thought . . ." Stands in Timber, "Last Ghastly Moments at the
    Little Bighorn," *American Heritage*, April 1966, pages 15-21, 72-3.
77 " 'We saw a good many Indians . . .' " Sandoz, Page 142; Utley, page 191.
78 "In St. Louis . . ." Connell, pages 284-5.
79 "Indians? . . ." Rosenberg, "There are No Indians Left Now but Me," *American
    Heritage*, June 1964, pages 19-23 and 106-9.

Chapter Six

The main source for this chapter is James D. Horan's *Desperate Men: Revelations from the
Sealed Pinkerton Files*. Horan's *Authentic Wild West: The Outlaws* is also valuable, as it
reproduces documents and contemporary newspaper stories. Paul Trachman's *The Gunfighters* has a good brief section on the Northfield robbery.

87 "There's a time . . ." Horan, *Desperate Men*, page 111; Trachtman, *The Gunfighters*,
    page 75.
87 "Allen started . . ." Horan, *Desperate Men*, page 110; Horan, *The Outlaws*, page 67
    (quoting Northfield newspaper account of the robbery).
88 "He passed it . . ." Trachtman, page 78.
89 "One of them yelled . . ." Horan, *The Outlaws*, page 73; Horan, *Desperate Men*, page
    115.
89 " 'Hold on . . .' " Trachtman, page 80
89 "For four days, the outlaws . . ." Posses, usually called by a county sheriff or a town
    marshal, but sometimes spontaneously formed, were the usual way of enforcing the
    law in all rural areas. This amateur law enforcement was still being practiced in the
    Great Lakes states in the 1930s.
90 " 'Do you men . . .' " Horan, *Desperate Men*, page 122.
90 "by contrast, the amateurs . . ." Bob, Emmett and Gratton Dalton, cousins of the
    Youngers, came to a similar end in 1890 at the hands of the citizens of Coffeyville,
    Kansas. The situation has been repeated time after time in states as different as
    Montana and New York. It's even more common in fiction—for example, the end of
    the Bradley gang in Stephen King's *It*.

Chapter Seven

Robert M. Utley's *Billy the Kid: A Short Violent Life* provided the basic information on the life
of the outlaw, which is in danger of being buried in legendary accretions. James D. Horan's
Authentic Wild West: The Gunfighters was also most valuable, as it reproduces letters and
other documents.

93 "Billy the Kid was born . . ." Utley, *Billy the Kid*, pages 1-16; Horan: *The Gunfighters*,
    pages 10-17.
96 "One of the nastiest . . ." For a taste of this, see Walter Noble Burns, *The Saga of Billy
    the Kid*, pages 1-54.
96 "Another version . . ." see James D. Horan's *The Authentic Wild West: The Gunfight-
    ers*, page 5.
96 "He also retaliated . . ." Utley, page 22.
97 " 'He was very handy . . .' " *Ibid.*, page 32.

97   " 'He spent all his . . ." *Ibid.*, page 32.
98   "Will Chisum . . ." *Ibid.*, page 33.
98   "The .41 Colt Thunderer . . ." Hogg and Weeks, *Pistols of the World*, pages 63-4; Keith, *Sixguns*, pages 29-31.
98   "Morton, Evans and Fred Hill . . ." Horan, pages 28-37.
100 " 'No,' Roberts said . . ." *Ibid.*, page 72.
101 "Dudley stationed . . ." Horan, pages 42-3.
102 "Billy Bonney . . ." Utley, page 97-8.
103 "One of them was . . ." Paulita always denied that she was personally involved with Billy, but their relationship was well known in Fort Sumner. One rumor falsely held that Pete Maxwell had betrayed Billy to keep him away from Paulita.
104 "Wallace wrote back . . ." Horan, page 55.
104 " 'Testify before . . .' " Utley, page 118.
104 "He wrote to Carl Schurz . . ." *Ibid.*, page 119.
105 "It's dangerous . . ." Hatcher, *Textbook of Pistols and Revolvers*, page 79.
106 " 'That's a lie . . .' " Utley, page 132.
106 "Exactly what happened . . ." It seems likely that *both* the rustlers and the posse shot Carlyle.

Chapter Eight

To Die in the West by Paula Mitchell Marks is one of the latest and probably one of the most complete books on Wyatt Earp and the O.K. Corral fight. Perhaps because the evidence she presents is so damning, Marks seems to go out of her way to show Earp in the most favorable light. Sometimes that is simply not possible.

In *Wild, Woolly & Wicked*, Harry Sinclair Drago explodes the many lies Earp told about his adventures in Kansas. It seems the "town-taming marshal" was really only a low-ranking, somewhat crooked policeman in most towns where he was charged with enforcing the law. Even in Dodge City, he never was more than an *assistant* town marshal.

As always, James D. Horan provides reproductions of documents and verbatim newspaper reports in *The Lawmen* volume of his *Authentic Wild West* series. This is especially helpful in dealing with as mendacious a character as Wyatt Earp.

110 "One report . . ." Marks, *To Die in the West*, page 102.
110 "John Mangiaracina . . ." Kansas City (Mo.) *Star*, November 17, 1950.
111 "So was Wild Bill . . ." Hickok was also a terrible liar, but that didn't become well known until long after his death.
111 "He was, as. . ." Marks, page 33.
111 "Born to a family . . ." *Ibid.*, pages 30-5.
112 "That's because . . ." Drago, *Wild, Woolly & Wicked*, pages 144-50.
112 "His name . . ." Drago, pages 207, 212.
112 "Not because . . ." Wyatt, no town-tamer, had left Wichita under a cloud.
114 "There were rumors . . ." Cunningham, *Triggernometry*, pages 414-6; Marks, pages 105-6.
115 "Ike Clanton . . ." Marks, pages 146 and 272-3; Horan, *The Lawmen*, page 223.
116 "Allie's account . . ." Marks, pages 141-2.
116 "I told them . . ." Horan (verbatim Earp testimony) page 224; Marks, page 151.
116 "He said . . ." Marks, page 151.
117 "Virgil Earp stated . . ." *Ibid.*, page 152.
117 "The Earps, as we've seen, . . ." Virgil Earp was later to claim that Frank Stillwell, murdered by his brothers, confessed just before dying that he had killed Morgan Earp.
117 "On September 9, 1881 . . ." *Ibid.*, pages 197-8.
118 "He confronted . . ." *Ibid.*, page 181.

118 "Ike was not reassured . . ." *Ibid.*, page 182.
119 "Doc Holliday walked in . . ." *Ibid.*, pages 194-7.
119 " 'Are you heeled? . . .' " *Ibid.*, pages 205-6
120 "B. H. Fallehy . . ." Horan, pages 218-9; Marks, page 211.
120 "Martha King . . ." Marks, page 220.
120 "Addie Bourland . . ." *Ibid.*, page 225.
121 "Wyatt Earp . . ." Horan, page 228.
121 "According to McGivern . . ." McGivern, *Fast and Fancy Revolver Shooting*, page 233.
123 "There is some mystery . . ." Horan, page 298, note 19.
123 "The idea that a lone man . . ." The shotgun's extreme lethality compared with that of a revolver was well known on the frontier.
124 "One of the cowboys . . ." Cunningham, page 123.
124 "According to Big Nose Kate . . ." Marks, 366-7.

Chapter Nine

Three books provided the basic information for this chapter. Altina Waller's *Feud* is the product of a trained historian who has examined court and other government records. Most of what live sources she uses are from West Virginia, where she worked when writing this account. That may be responsible for what seems to be a slight Hatfield bias. Truda Williams McCoy's *The McCoys* is the product of a highly intelligent woman—a teacher and a writer— who was not a historian. As a "real McCoy," she was able to get information over the course of years from participants—information that nobody else has been able to get. Most of the dialogue quoted here come from McCoy's book. The actual words spoken may have been slightly different, but probably not very different. McCoy is considered, by qualified people, to be a master of mountain vernacular. She, obviously, has a McCoy bias. Waller and McCoy balance each other in outlook. Virgil Carrington Jones, a popular historian, holds the middle ground with his *The Hatfields and the McCoys*.

129 "That will rouse . . ." McCoy, *The McCoys*, page 141.
131 "When the Civil War . . ." Waller, *Feud*, pages 17-33.
132 " 'We hear you've enlisted . . .' " McCoy, pages 6-11.
132 " 'You can say . . .' " Waller, page 51.
132 "The problem was land . . ." *Ibid.*, pages 38-9.
133 "Ranel McCoy lost . . ." McCoy, pages 13-9.
133 "Feeling ran high . . ." *Ibid.*, pages 20-4; Waller, page 66.
133 "Anse, the sly old devil . . ." *Ibid.*, pages 32-3; Waller, page 67.
134 "Tolbert McCoy . . ." Waller, page 71.
134 "Roseanna was afraid . . ." McCoy, pages 44-52.
134 "After a long . . ." *Ibid.*, pages 58-9.
135 "Tolbert McCoy got into . . ." *Ibid.*, pages 69-78.
135 "Sally McCoy . . ." *Ibid.*, pages 81-7.
136 "Another raid . . ." *Ibid.*, pages 113-4.
136 "One night when . . ." McCoy, pages 114-5; Waller, page 156. Waller believes it was Mary Daniels and her daughter who were whipped; McCoy says it was Mary Daniels and her mother. Since the old woman was supposedly crippled for life, it's reasonable to assume her family remembered the incident vividly. This is one instance where reliance on family tradition is more fruitful than reliance on court records. (The incident was never brought to the attention of the courts.)
137 "Wallace escaped . . ." Jones, *The Hatfields and the McCoys*, pages 70-76.
137 "In at least one instance . . ." Waller, page 165.
138 "Pikeville was strongly Unionist . . ." *Ibid.*, pages 194-5.
138 "In 1870 . . ." *Ibid.*, pages 89-90.

139   "Unknown to the posse members . . ." McCoy, pages 174-7.
139   "His message: . . ." *Ibid.*, page 188.
139   "A week later . . ." *Ibid.*, pages 188-90.
140   "One, Ellison Mounts . . ." *Ibid.*, page 148.
140   "One, Dan Cunningham . . ." *Ibid.*, page 198.

Chapter Ten

Helena Huntington Smith's *The War on Powder River* and her *American Heritage* article, "The Johnson County War" were major sources for this chapter. Paul Trachtman's *The Gunfighters* was also extremely helpful. The original newspaper articles reproduced in James Horan's *Authentic Wild West: The Outlaws* were helpful. But in that book and in his *Desperate Men*, Horan seems to rely too much on information from the Pinkerton detective agency, including such proven nonsense as the culpability of Jim Averill and the status of Nate Champion as "King of the Outlaws." Both Horan accounts, however, are superior to that of Robert Elman in *Badmen of the West*, which presents, without a grain of salt, Frank Canton's mendacious account. Even Struthers Burt, who defends the big ranchers in his immensely readable *Powder River, Let'er Buck*, ridicules (page 286) Canton's autobiography. Some surprisingly useful information was found in Stephen Bach's *Final Cut*, the story of a disasterous attempt to make a movie about the war on Powder River. Bach, at the time senior vice president of United Artists, had to research the war.

142   " 'Me and Nick . . .' " Helena Huntington Smith, "The Johnson County War," *American Heritage*, April 1961, pages 74-5.
144   "One looks like . . ." The name scratched out is said to be Frank Canton in May, *History of the American West*, page 151.
145   "The county coroner . . ." Bach, *Final Cut*, page 152.
145   "Walter, Baron . . ." *Ibid.*, page 138.
146   "Managers took . . ." Smith, 52; Raine and Barnes, *Cattle, Cowboys and Rangers*, page 232.
148   "Even those . . ." Bach, page 145.
148   "His name . . ." Trachtman, *The Gunfighters*, page 215; May, page 148.
148   "The big ranchers on Powder River . . ." Burt, *Powder River, Let'er Buck*, pages 246 and 285-6.
149   "The first targets . . ." Trachtman, page 208; Monaghan, *Book of the American West*, page 295.
149   "According to the *Cheyenne Leader* . . ." Article reproduced in Horan, *The Outlaws*, page 231.
149   "Tom Waggoner . . ." Burt pages 287-9; Trachtman, page 208; May, page 149.
149   "One of two men . . ." Burt, page 287; Monaghan, page 295; May, page 149.
150   "The Cheyenne clubmen. . ." Smith, page 53; Trachtman, page 208.
150   "Wolcott may . . ." Bach, page 152.
151   "Dr. Charles Penrose . . ." Trachtman, pages 209-10.
153   "At dawn . . ." *Ibid.*, page 214.
153   "At one point. . ." *Ibid.*, pages 219-20.
154   "At dawn on the 13th. . ." *Ibid.*, page 222.
154   "They made part . . ." *Ibid.*, page 223.
155   "Actually, it settled. . ." Smith, page 77; May, page 151.
155   "As one historian. . ." Monaghan, page 298.

Chapter Eleven

The Portland *Morning Oregonian* provided most of the information for this chapter. Tracy and his travels were the top story in virtually every issue of the *Oregonian* from June 10 through August 7, 1902. Three of James D. Horan's books were also helpful—*Desperate Men, The Authentic Wild West: The Gunfighters* and *Pictorial History of the Wild West*. Horan's principal source, particularly in *Desperate Men*, is the New York *World*. The *World's* correspondent, though, appears to be less prolific and less familiar with the territory than the *Oregonian's* team, although somewhat more imaginative. All of the dialogue in this chapter comes from the *Oregonian*, whose reporters interviewed the participants (except Tracy) soon after the conversations took place. The Oregon Historical Society in Portland and the Portland Police Department were very helpful, the latter sending material entered in the department's "mug book" the day Tracy was arrested.

Chapter Twelve

The Great Pursuit by Herbert Molloy Mason, Jr. gives a blow-by-blow description of the fighting in Columbus as well as of Pershing's pursuit of Villa. It also gives a good capsule summary of the Mexican Revolution. *Pancho Villa: Intimate Recollections by People Who Knew Him* by Jessie Peterson and Thelma Cox Knoles contains dozens of memories of the revolutionary leader by friends and enemies, American and Mexican, and covers every phase of Villa's life. Standard histories of Mexico by Alba, Kanell, Meyer and Sherman, Parkes and Strode added perspective and color.

171 Page 294, "I was awakened . . ." Peterson and Knoles, . . .*Recollections* . . ., page 205.
172 " 'Halt . . .' " Mason, *The Great Pursuit*, page 12.
173 "The machinegun . . ." Smith, *Small Arms of the World*, pages 120-1 and 292-4.
173 "After the fight . . ." Hatcher, *Hatcher's Notebook*, pages 89-91.
174 " 'By the time . . .' " Peterson and Knoles, page 206.
174 " 'I remember a couple of Customs men . . .'" John Nance Garner was Vice President of the United States in Franklin D. Roosevelt's first term.
175 " 'Mount up a troop . . .' " Mason, page 19.
175 "Altogether, almost 200 . . ." Mason, page 20: the troops passed nearly 100 bodies on the way back. Peterson and Knoles, page 208: Chadborn tells of nearly 100 Mexican bodies in Columbus being burned.
175 "General Villa . . ." Peterson and Knoles ix-x; Mason, pages 38-9; Kandell, *La Capital*, pages 427-8.
176 "Anita Brenner . . ." Mason, pages 27-8.
177 "One day . . ." Peterson and Knoles x-xii; Elman, *Badmen of the West*, page 194.
179 " 'Companeros of the plow . . .' " Monaghan, *The Book of the American West*, page 419.
180 "Villa realized . . ." Mason, pages 39-40.
181 "When Obregon arrived . . ." Strode, page 244.
181 "Villa himself . . ." Parkes, page 341.
184 "Then López . . ." Mason, page 64.
186 "One wild rumor . . ." *The New Yorker*, November 27, 1989, pages 108-20, "La Cabeza de Villa," Mark Singer.

Chapter Thirteen

This chapter is largely based on Nat Brandt's article "Sergeant York" in the August/ September 1981 issue of *American Heritage*, pages 56-64. The quotations are from a recording York made after the movie about his life was released in 1941. The incident of the die-hard German machinegunner throwing a grenade was mentioned in *Guns and the Gunfighters* by the staff of *Guns & Ammo Magazine*, page 28.

195   "York died . . ." In a way, York resembles Cincinnatus, the Roman hero who returned to the plow he had left in mid-furrow when called to war. But York, far more reluctant to leave the farm, seems to have been even happier to return to it.

Chapter Fourteen

Three books were especially helpful for this chapter: Jay Robert Nash's *Bloodletters and Badmen*; *Organized Crime in America*, edited by Gus Tyler, and *The American Way of Crime*, edited by Wayne Moquin, with Charles Van Doren. Nash, a former newsman and editor from Chicago, attempted an encyclopedic history of American crime from the earliest times. Although it's based entirely on documentary sources the accuracy of *Bloodletters* is not beyond criticism. Sometimes the documents (like *Wyatt Earp, Frontier Marshal* or the "confession" of W. D. Jones) are not reliable. On crime in an around Chicago, which Nash has been able to personally research, *Bloodletters* is a gold mine. Both the Tyler and Moquin books are collections of documents, ranging from Congressional hearings to memoirs of participants of criminal enterprises.

200   " 'The p-p-place is . . ." Nash, *Bloodletters and Badmen*, page 521.
201   " 'I'm no hood . . .' " Nash, *The Dillinger Dosier*, page 175.
202   " 'We stay with the whores . . .' " Nash, *Bloodletters*, page 129.
203   "In spite of popular belief . . ." Tyler, *Organized Crime in America*, pages 344-7 and 355-61; Moquin, *The American Way of Crime*, pages 99-106.
203   "Gaetano Mosca . . ." Tyler, page 326.
203   "The Mafia is not . . ." Tyler, page 327.
203   "Mori wrote . . ." Tyler, pages 327-8.
204   "He also loved flowers . . ." Nash, *Bloodletters*, pages 409-10. Charles MacArthur, husband of actress Helen Hayes, and Ben Hecht wrote *The Front Page*, a not-unrealistic picture of Chicago journalism in the 1920s. MacArthur and Hecht based their characters largely on fellow reporters and editors. Once, when MacArthur was playing pool with his editor, Walter Howey, O'Bannion appeared.
     "I forbid you to go with that murderous bastard," Howey told MacArthur. "Go home and get some sleep."
     "Deanie will see that I get home," MacArthur replied. "Deanie's my sandman." And he left with O'Bannion.
204   "It's worthwhile . . ." Nash, *Ibid.*, page 409.
204   "Once an automobile . . ." *Ibid.* page 411.
205   " 'Hello, boys . . .' " *Ibid.*, page 413.
205   "They let . . ." *Ibid.*, page 603.
207   "General John T. Thompson . . ." Helmer, *The Gun that Made the Twenties Roar*, pages 11-101; Ellis, *The Social History of the Machine Gun*, pages 149-55.
208   "That was the last straw . . ." Machinegun Jack McGurn is sometimes given credit for organizing the massacre. Given the importance of the operation and McGurn's some-what limited resources (mental included) that seems unlikely.
208   "He acquired . . ." Halper, *The Chicago Crime Book*, pages 55-77.

Chapter Fifteen

John Treherne's *The Strange History of Bonnie and Clyde* provided the basic information for this chapter. Treherne examined letters, interviewed family members of the bandits and interviewed the surviving law officers who tracked the "Barrow gang" down. Strangely, he is the only writer who has. In *The Dillinger Days*, for instance, John Toland credits J. J. Smith, an Oklahoma newpaperman for the information on the ambush of Bonnie and Clyde. Smith was not at the scene; his base was hundreds of miles from the ambush; and he was never as intimately concerned about the couple as Treherne's informants. Toland doesn't credit it, but a large amount of his information came, directly and indirectly, from the FBI.

The Oklahoma City Public Library was very helpful in the attempt to determine if a traffic policeman was murdered on duty in July 1933 or at any time that year. (None was.)

211 Page 358, "The sidewalks . . ." The following story is from Nash, *Bloodletters and Badmen*, page 40.
213 "Bonnie 'screamed . . .' " Treherne, page 53.
213 " 'I want you to be a man . . .' " *Ibid*., pages 54-5.
214 "Clyde deposited her . . ." *Ibid*., page 70. Fults said it was a barn; Bonnie's mother, a church, which probably seemed to her to be a more respectable place to be abandoned.
215 "Author . . ." *Ibid*., page 72.
215 " 'If Clyde . . .' " *Ibid*., page 81.
217 "Two years later . . ." *Ibid*., page 94, reproduction on page 95.
217 "He took a train . . ." *Ibid*., pages 97-8. The two mothers said Clyde drove him, but Texas police identified Bonnie and Clyde in their home state when Clyde was supposedly en route to Michigan.
217 " 'You're a little late . . .' " *Ibid*., page 104.
220 "Everybody in town . . ." *Ibid*., page 126.
221 "The version Clyde used . . ." Smith, *Small Arms of the World*, pages 638-44.
222 " 'We lived in . . .' " Treherne, page 160.
222 "During Autumn . . ." *Ibid*., page 160.
223 "At one point . . ." *Ibid*., page 178.
223 "Hamer . . ." Caro, *The Years of Lyndon Johnson: Means of Ascent*, pages 325-8.
224 "Once, as young cowboy . . ." Harrison Kinney, "Frank Hamer: Texas Ranger" *The American Gun*, Spring, 1961 pages 82-3.
224 "The FBI was later . . ." Toland, *The Dillinger Days*, pages 294-6.
225 "Ted Hinton wrote . . ." Treherne, pages 186-8
225 "The Story of Bonnie . . ." Treherne, pages 192-4. Toland confuses this with "The Story of Suicide Sal."
228 " 'I hated . . .' " Kinney, page 89.
228 "Irvin Methvin . . ." This is Ted Hinton's version of what happened. Hinton, unlike Hamer or any of the Methvins, had no axe to grind. It also seems to be the most logical, in view of the elder Methvin's abduction, his subsequent rage and sudden quiet after talking to Hamer.
228 "The FBI . . ." Toland, page 296.

Chapter Sixteen

John Toland's *The Dillinger Days* was extremely helpful. In contrast to his treatment of Bonnie Parker and Clyde Barrow, Toland researched Dillinger thoroughly. Unfortunately, the FBI was able to influence what he found by such means as its charges against Loesser and other alleged accessories to Dillinger's crimes. Nash's *Bloodletters and Badmen* provided a balance for Toland's FBI bias. Powers' *G-Men: Hoover's FBI in American Popular Culture*, a unique study of an American phenomenon, provided invaluable background. Also useful was Curt Gentry's *J. Edgar Hoover: The Man and the Secrets*. The essential book for anyone interested in Dillinger, though, is Nash's *The Dillinger Dossier*.

229 "Nervous Purvis. . ." Nash, *The Dillinger Dossier*, page 22.

230 "Purvis tried to strike . . ." From a lecture by James Metcalfe, one of the agents at the Biograph, to senior journalism students at the University of Notre Dame in the spring of 1950. Metcalfe, who wrote rhymes for the Hearst newspapers at the time, opened with his standard talk about writing, but the students, tipped off that he had been at the Biograph shooting, peppered him with questions about Dillinger. The former special agent soon relaxed and spent the next hour telling FBI war stories.

231 "Whether Nash was . . ." L.L. Edge, a Kansas City writer, says persons in a position to know (former gangsters? cops?) told him Nash tried to slip away when he saw Miller with his Thompson, but Reed shot him in the back of the head—the first shot fired in the massacre. Edge, *Run the Cat Roads*, page 4.

233 " 'Better go back . . .' " Toland, *The Dillinger Days*, page 136; Nash, *Bloodletters and Badmen*, pages 168-9.

234 " 'I think somebody's . . .' " Nash, *Bloodletters*, page 169.

234 " 'That bird sure . . .' " Toland, page 145.

235 "Tucson detective . . ." *Ibid.*, page 194.

235 "James Metcalfe . . ." Metcalfe lecture.

235 "John Toland . . ." Toland, page 209.

236 "According to J. Edgar Hoover . . ." Hoover, *Persons in Hiding*, page 82.

236 "Red Hamilton . . ." Powers, *G-Men*, page 119.

237 "Van Meter . . ." Toland, page 228-38.

238 "They said he tried . . ." *Ibid.*, pages 248-9.

239 "She may have been . . ." Nash, *The Dillinger Dossier*, pages 65-6.

239 "Hoover, trying . . ." *Ibid.*, page 30.

239 "Purvis, about 100 feet. . ." *Ibid.*, pages 38-43.

240 "Wanatka ran . . ." Toland, page 284.

240 "The Director had already . . ." Powers, page 120.

240 "Even Melvin Purvis . . ." Nash, *Dillinger*, page 58.

241 "According to Purvis . . ." Toland, pages 318-9; Nash, *Dillinger*, page 87.

242 "Hoover wanted . . ." Powers, pages 94-112.

242 "FBI folklore . . ." Sullivan, *The Bureau: My Thirty Years in Hoover's FBI*, pages 26-33. Charlie Winstead was one of the first "hired guns"—former lawmen that Hoover recruited in the 1930s to beef up his force of lawyers and accountants. Few had any college. Most, like Winstead, were southwesterners addicted to Stetsons, cowboy boots and personally owned weapons (in Winstead's case, a Smith and Wesson .357 Magnum). Most, like Winstead, ended up out of the Bureau before retirement age or in the boondocks (in Winstead's case, New Mexico, before he quite the Bureau in 1942). Gentry, pages 169-70. The "hired guns" didn't fit the image of the Bureau Hoover tried to project. If "hired guns" shot the man outside the Biograph, the Director had another reason for giving no individual credit.

242 "The FBI gave her . . ." Gentry, page 176 (the $5000) and Metcalfe, *op. cit.*, (the fur coat and good wishes)

242 "Charles C. Smith . . ." Edge, pages 215-6.

243 "They didn't understand . . ." Charles E. Petty, "The FBI Ammo Tests," *The American Rifleman*, June 1990, pages 34-7 and 83-6.

243 "After he'd gone a few miles . . ." This is Metcalfe's version of the story. Another version has Nelson turning the car over to Chase after shooting the two agents. Given Nelson's super-macho attitude, Metcalfe's version seems the more likely.

245 "According to George McKnight . . ." McKnight was a veteran reporter and the author a brand-new cub on the Kansas City *Sun Herald* in the fall of 1950.

245 "When O'Leary was released . . ." Nash, *Dillinger*, page 135.

246 "Charlie Winstead, the agent . . ." Tom McDade, one of the agents chased by Baby Face Nelson, said Winstead and Clarence Hurt, former Oklahoma City chief of

detectives and another "hired gun," told him they had shot Dillinger. Herman Hollis, killed by Baby Face Nelson, had fired and missed, they said (Gentry page 174). Winstead told William C. Sullivan (Sullivan, pages 26-33) he fired three shots after Dillinger ducked into a crouch and started to run. Three wounds on the body of the man shot at the Biograph could have been inflicted if the victim had crouched low and ducked his head. If so, the women hit in the legs could have been wounded *before* the bullets hit the street and ricocheted. The fourth bullet to hit the supposed Dillinger had been fired from the front. It entered at the clavicle area and exited at the eighth rib. The upper part of the victim's body would have had to have been nearly horizontal.

246   "According to Nash . . ." A sketch in Nash's *The Dillinger Dossier*, page 102, shows what could have been the path of the ricocheting bullets. In the sketch, the bullets strike the body at about a 45 degree angle but ricochet from the street at a very acute angle. Because of surface irregularities, the path of a ricochet is difficult to predict. Generally, though, a bullet tends to rebound from a surface at the same angle it strikes. If that happened in this case, the ricocheting bullets might have passed over the women's heads instead of striking them in the legs.

246   "She said she once ran a poolroom . . ." *Ibid.*, pages 200-1.
247   "It has been charged . . ." Powers, pages 127-33.
247   "Homer Cummings said . . ." *Ibid.*, page 121.

Chapter Seventeen

As far as the literary world goes, Dutch Schultz, the biggest individual mobster New York ever had, is practically a non-person. No books (with the exception of E. L. Doctorow's entertaining but unhistorical *Billy Bathgate*) have been written *about* him. He appears in many, many books, however, because he is the key figure in New York's Prohibition and Depression underworld. Even more than "Charley Lucky" Luciano and certainly more than Frank Costello, gangland revolved around Schultz before the Dutchman's death. Helpful in this chapter were *The Mobs and the Mafia* by Hank Messick and Burt Goldblatt; *Organized Crime in America*, edited by Gus Tyler; *The American Way of Crime*, edited by Wayne Moquin with Charles Van Doren; *The Valachi Papers*, by Peter Maas; and *The Rise and Fall of the Jewish Gangster in America* by Arthur Fried. *The New York Times* in the days following Schultz's shooting and on the release of Charlie Workman from prison was invaluable.

251   "He had a dispute . . ." Nash, *Bloodletters and Badmen*, page 337.
252   "According to J. Richard . . ." Moquin, *The American Way of Crime*, pages 155-6.
253   "As soon as Luciano . . ." Maas, *The Valachi Papers*, pages 103-4; Moquin, pages 85-93.
253   "A few months after . . ." Messick and Goldblatt, *The Mobs and the Mafia*, page 110.
254   "The credentials . . ." Maas, pages 108-14; Messick and Goldblatt, page 110.
254   " 'I started down . . .' " Moquin 157-8.
255   "Eventually, they . . ." Messick and Goldblatt, page 94.
256   " 'Madden was in . . .' " Moquin, 154-5.
257   " 'Remember that Weinberg . . .?' " Maas, 143.
258   "The other man was probably . . ." Fried, *The Jewish Gangster*, page 190-1.
258   "Nevertheless, the bartender . . ." *The New York Times*, October 24, 1935.
259   "Dr. Earl Snavely . . ." *The New York Times*, October 24, 1935.
259   "He called for a Catholic priest . . ." *New York Times*, October 25, 1935.
259   "A police stenographer . . ." E. L. Doctorow, in *Billy Bathgate*, changed Schultz's ravings so that instead of the meaningless blather of delirious man, they provided clues to where his wealth was hidden.
260   "When, in 1984 . . ." McGinnis, *Blind Faith*, pages 155-234.
260   "The letters LCN . . ." Messick and Goldblatt, pages 188-9.

Chapter Eighteen

Most of the information for this chapter came from two books, each of them essentially written by the robbers. The first was *The Men Who Robbed Brink's* by Joseph "Specks" O'Keefe, as told to Bob Considine. The second, *Big Stick-Up at Brink's!*, is the result of hundreds of hours Noel Behn spent with the remaining robbers. Not surprisingly, O'Keefe exaggerates his importance somewhat, and the other robbers make it sound as if he had little to do with the robbery and was a ridiculous figure afterwards. Actually, he scared them spitless—so much they hired an assassin to get rid of him. Looking at the case objectively, O'Keefe is the key person. If his former friends hadn't arranged for his murder, the Brink's robbery would still be one of the great unsolved cases of our time. And if Elmer Burke hadn't run away when O'Keefe returned his fire, that might still be true. Yet, in spite of this case and dozens like it since the Northfield bank robbery in 1876, experts still tell us that "amateurs" (like O'Keefe) can't cope with "professionals" (like Burke).

263 " 'like the rest of us . . .' " Considine, *The Men Who Robbed Brink's*, page 46.
265 "Pino admitted to one gang member . . ." Behn, *Big Stick-Up at Brink's*, page 228.
265 "He didn't, but . . ." Considine, page 45.
265 "They located 'scores' . . ." Behn, page 118.
266 " 'None of us were killers, . . .' " *Ibid.*, page 90.
266 " 'Come on . . .' " Behn, pages 340-2; Considine, pages 5-8.
267 " 'We couldn't get . . .' " Behn, pages 343-4.
268 "Before he could leave . . ." Considine, page 78.
268 "The actual total. . . ." Behn, page 361.
269 "Maffie was the first . . ." Considine, pages 111-2.
270 " 'But then, I figured . . .' " *Ibid.*, page 112.
270 " 'I grabbed Jazz . . .' " *Ibid.*, page 115.
270 "O'Keefe went to Pino . . ." *Ibid.*, pages 117-8.
271 " 'He was the cold, crazy . . .' " *Ibid.*, pages 127-8.
271 " 'He killed . . .' " *Ibid.*, page 132.
272 "He turned to a court . . ." *Ibid.*, page 258.
273 "On the other hand . . ." Tom Buckley, "At the Movies," *New York Times*, December 15, 1978.
273 "Joe O'Keefe had been asked . . ." Considine, page 277-8.
273 "O'Keefe, whose only . . ." Vincent Canby, Review of *The Brink's Job*, *New York Times*, December 8, 1978.
273 "Where else could . . ." Nancy Pomerene McMillan, "Brinks is Robbed Again," *New York Times*, July 2, 1978.
273 "The film company's pride . . ." *New York Times*, July 29, 1978.
273 "They offered . . ." *New York Times*, August 8, 1978.
273 "A year later . . ." *New York Times*, June 9, 1979.

Bibliography

Books

Adams, Henry, *History of the United States of America During the Administrations of Thomas Jefferson*, The Library of America, New York: 1986

Akehurst, Richard, *The World of Guns*, Hamlyn Publishing Group, Ltd., London: 1972

Alba, Victor, *The Mexicans: the Making of a Nation*, Frederick A. Praeger, Inc., New York: 1967

Alba, Victor, *The Horizon Concise History of Mexico*, American Heritage Publishing Company, New York: 1973

Ambrose, Stephen E., *Crazy Horse and Custer; The Parallel Lives of Two American Warriors*, Doubleday & Co., Inc., Garden City, New York: 1975

Auto-Ordnance Corporation, *Handbook of the Thompson Submachine Gun*, Bridgeport, Connecticut: 1940

Bach, Steven, *Final Cut: Dreams and Disaster in the Making of Heaven's Gate*, William Morrow and Company, Inc., New York:1985

Behn, Noel, *Big Stick-Up at Brink's!*, G. P. Putnam's Sons, New York: 1977

Bowers, Claude G., *Jefferson and Hamilton: The Struggle for Democracy in America*, Houghton Mifflin Company, Boston: 1925

Brown, Dee, *Bury My Heart at Wounded Knee: An Indian History of the American West*, Holt, Rinehart & Winston, New York: 1970

Brown, Dee, *The Westerners*, Holt, Rinehart and Winston, New York: 1974

Brown, Stuart Gerry, *Thomas Jefferson*, Washington Square Press, Inc., New York: 1963

Burns, Walter Noble, *The Saga of Billy the Kid*, Garden City Publishing Co., Inc., Garden City, New York: 1925

Burrows, William E., *Vigilante!* Harcourt Brace Jovanovich, New York: 1976

Burt, Struthers, *Powder River: Let'er Buck*, Farrar & Rinehart Incorporated, New York: 1938

Caro, Robert A., *The Years of Lyndon Johnson: Means of Ascent*, Alfred A. Knopf, New York: 1990

Chalfant, William Y., *Cheyennes and Horse Soldiers*, University of Oklahoma Press, Norman, OK: 1989

Chidsey, Donald Barr, *Louisiana Purchase*, Crown Publishers, Inc., New York: 1972

Chidsey, Donald Barr, *The Great Conspiracy*, Crown Publishers, Inc., New York: 1967

Coit, Margaret L., *The Life History of the United. States—1789-1829*, Time Life Books, New York: 1963

Connell, Evan S., *Son of the Morning Star; Custer and the Little Bighorn*, North Point Press, San Francisco: 1984

Considine, Bob, *The Men Who Robbed Brink's*, Random House, New York: 1961

Cook, Fred J., *Mob Inc.*, Franklin Watts, Inc., New York: 1977

Cooke, Jacob E., *Alexander Hamilton*, Charles Scribner's Sons, New York: 1982

Crawford, Mary Caroline, *Romantic Days in the Early Republic*, Little, Brown & Company, Boston: 1912

Cressey, Donald R., *Theft of the Nation: The Structure and Operations of Organized Crime in America*, Harper & Roe, Publishers, New York: 1969

Cumming, William P. and Rankin, Hugh, *The Fate of a Nation: The American Revolution Through Contemporary Eyes*, Phaidon Press, Ltd., London: 1975

Cunningham, Eugene, *Triggernometry: A Gallery of Gunfighters*, The Caxton Printers, Ltd., Caldwell, Idaho: 1989

DeVoto, Bernard, *The Year of Decision: 1846*, Little, Brown and Company, Boston: 1943

Drago, Harry Sinclair, *Wild, Woolly & Wicked*, Bramhall House, New York: 1970

Dupuy, R. Ernest and Dupuy, Trevor N., *The Compact History of the Revolutionary War*, Hawthorn Books, Inc., New York:1963

Eckert, Allan W., *The Conquerors*, Little, Brown and Company, Boston: 1970

Edge, L. L., *Run the Cat Roads: A True Story of Bank Robbers in the 30's*, Dembner Books, New York: 1981

Ellis, John, *The Social History of the Machine Gun*, Pantheon Books, New York: 1975

Elman, Robert, *Badmen of the West*, The Ridge Press, Secaucus, New Jersey: 1974

English, T. J., *The Westies*, G. P. Putnam's Sons, New York: 1990

Flexner, James Thomas, *The Young Hamilton, A Biography*, Little, Brown & Company, Boston: 1978

Frantz, Joe B., *Texas: A Bicentennial History*, W. W. Norton & Company, Inc., New York: 1976

Fried, Arthur, *The Rise and Fall of the Jewish Gangster in America*, Holt, Rinehart and Winston, New York: 1980

Gard, Wayne, *The Great Buffalo Hunt*, Alfred A. Knopf, New York: 1959

Gentry, Curt, *J. Edgar Hoover: The Man and the Secrets*, W. W. Norton & Company, New York: 1991

Guns & Ammo Magazine staff, *Guns and the Gunfighters*, Bonanza Books, New York: 1982

Hamilton, Allan McLane, *The Intimate Life of Alexander Hamilton*, Charles Scribner's Sons, New York: 1911

Hatcher, Julian S., *Hatcher's Notebook*, Telegraph Press, Harrisburg, Pennsylvania: 1966

Hatcher, Julian S., *Textbook of Pistols and Revolvers: Their Ammunition, Ballistics and Use*, Small Arms Technical Publishing Company, Plantersville, South Carolina: 1935

Helmer, W. J., *The Gun That Made the Twenties Roar*, The Gun Room Press, Highland Park, New Jersey, 1969

Hogg, Ian, *The Complete Machine-Gun: 1885 to the Present*, Exeter Books, New York: 1979

Hogg, Ian and Weeks, John, *Pistols of the World* (Revised Edition), DBI Books, Inc., Northfield, Illinois: 1982

Hoover, J. Edgar, *Persons in Hiding*, Little, Brown and Company, Boston: 1938

Horan, James D., *Desperate Men: Revelations from the Sealed Pinkerton Files*, G. P. Putnam's Sons, New York: 1949

Horan, James D., *The Authentic Wild West: The Gunfighters*, Crown Publishers, Inc., New York: 1976

Horan, James D., *The Authentic Wild West: The Outlaws*, Crown Publishers, Inc., New York: 1977

Horan, James D., *The Authentic Wild West: The Lawmen*, Crown Publishers, Inc., New York: 1980

Horan, James D. and Sann, Paul, *Pictorial History of the Wild West*, Crown Publishers, Inc., New York: 1954

Hudelston, F. J., *Gentleman Johnny Burgoyne: Misadventures of an English General in the Revolution*, The Bobs-Merrill Company, Indianapolis: 1927

Jefferson, Thomas, *Writings*, The Library of America, New York: 1984

Jones, Virgil Carrington, *The Hatfields and the McCoys*, Ballentine Books, New York: 1948

Kanell, Jonathan, *La Capital*: The Biography of Mexico City, Random House, New York: 1988

Keegan, John and Wheatcroft, Andrew, *Who's Who in Military History*, William Morrow and Company, Inc., New York: 1976

Keith, Elmer, *Sixguns*, Bonanza Books, New York: 1961

Konefsky, Samuel J., *John Marshall and Alexander Hamilton: Architects of the American Constitution*, The Macmillan Company, New York: 1964

Lodge, Henry Cabot, *Alexander Hamilton*, Houghton, Mifflin Co., Cambridge, MA: 1898

Lomask, Milton, *Aaron Burr: The Years from Princeton to Vice President, 1756-1805*, Farrar, Straus, Giroux, New York: 1979

Lomask, Milton, *Aaron Burr: The Conspiracy and Years of Exile, 1805-1836*, Farrar, Straus, Giroux, New York: 1982

Lord, Walter, *A Time to Stand: A Chronicle of the Valiant Battle at the Alamo*, Bonanza Books, New York: 1987

Lowenthal, Max, *The Federal Bureau of Investigation*, William Sloane Associates, Inc., New York: 1950

Lyon, Peter, *The Wild, Wild West*, Funk & Wagnalls, New York: 1969

Maas, Peter, *The Valachi Papers*, G. P. Putnam's Sons, New York: 1968

McDonald, Forrest, *Alexander Hamilton: A Biography*, W. W. Norton & Company, New York: 1979

McCoy, Truda Williams, *The McCoys: Their Story*, Preservation Council Press of the Preservation Council of Pike County, Inc., Pikeville, Kentucky: 1976

McGinnis, Joe, *Blind Faith*, G. P. Putnam's Son's, New York: 1989

McGivern, Ed, *Fast and Fancy Revolver Shooting*, Willcox & Follet Co., New York: 1938

Marks, Paula Mitchell, *To Die in the West*, Simon & Schuster, New York: 1989

Martin, Cy, *The Saga of the Buffalo*, Hart Publishing Company, Inc., New York: 1973

Mason, Herbert Molloy, Jr., *The Great Pursuit*, Random House, New York: 1970

May, Robin, *History of the American West*, Exeter Books, New York: 1984

Messick, Hank and Goldblatt, Burt, *The Mobs and the Mafia*, Galahad Books, New York: 1972

Meyer, Michael C. and Sherman, William L., *The Course of Mexican History*, Oxford University Press, New York:1979

Miller, John C., *Alexander Hamilton and the Growth of the New Nation*, Harper & Row, New York: 1964

Mills, James, *The Underground Empire*, Doubleday & Company, Inc., Garden City, New York: 1986

Mitchell, Lt. Col. Joseph B. and Creasy, Sir Edward, *Twenty Decisive Battles of the World*, Macmillan, New York: 1954

Monaghan, Jay (editor), *The Book of the American West*, Bonanza Books, New York: 1963

Montross, Lynn, *War Through the Ages*, Harper & Row, New York: 1960

Moquin, Wayne (ed.), *The American Way of Crime*, Praeger Publishers, New York: 1976

Morison, Samuel Eliot, *The Oxford History of the American People*, Oxford University Press, New York: 1965

Morris, Richard B., *Seven Who Shaped Our Destiny*, Harper & Row, New York: 1973

Morris, Richard B., *Witnesses at the Creation: Hamilton, Madison, Jay and the Constitution*, Holt, Rinehart and Winston, New York: 1985

Morris, Richard B. (editor), *Alexander Hamilton and the Founding of the Nation*, The Dial Press, New York: 1957

Nash, Jay Robert, *Almanac of World Crime*, Doubleday, Garden City, New York: 1981

Nash, Jay Robert, *Bloodletters and Badmen*, M. Evans and Company, Philadelphia: 1973

Nash, Jay Robert, *The Dillinger Dossier*, December Press, Highland Park, Illinois: 1983

Nevin, David, *The Texans*, Time-Life books, New York: 1975

Parkes, Henry Bamford, *A History of Mexico*, Houghton Mifflin Company, Boston: 1969

Parmet, Herbert S. and Hecht, Marie B., *Aaron Burr: Portrait of an Ambitious Man*, The Macmillan Company, New York: 1967

Pearson, Michael, *Those Damned Rebels: The American Revolution As Seen Through British Eyes*, G. P. Putnam's Sons, New York: 1972

Peterson, Harold L., *Arms and Armor in Colonial America, 1526-1783*, Bramhall House, New York:1956

Peterson, Harold L., *The Book of the Continental Soldier*, Promontory Press, Stackpole Company, Harrisburg, Pa.: 1968

Peterson, Harold L., *The Treasury of the Gun*, Ridge Press/Golden Press, New York: 1962

Peterson, Harold L., *The Remington Historical Treasury of American Guns*, Rutledge Books/Benjamin Company, New York: 1966

Peterson, Jessie and Knoles, Thelma Cox (eds.) *Pancho Villa: Intimate Recollections by People Who Knew Him*, Hastings House, New York: 1977

Pileggi, Nicholas, *Wiseguy: Life in a Mafia Family*, Simon and Schuster, New York: 1985

Powers, Richard Gid, *G-Men: Hoover's FBI in American Popular Culture*, Southern Illinois University Press, Carbondale and Edwardsville, Illinois: 1983

Pratt, Fletcher, *Battles that Changed History*, Doubleday, Garden City, New York: 1956

Prebble, John, *Culloden*, Secker & Warburg, London: 1961

Purvis, Melvin, *American Agent*, Doubleday, Duran, New York: 1936

Raine, William MacLeod and Barnes, Will C., *Cattle, Cowboys and Rangers*, Grosset & Dunlap, New York: 1930

Rosa, Joseph G., *The Gunfighter, Man or Myth?*, University of Oklahoma Press, Norman, Oklahoma: 1969

Rossiter, Clinton, *Alexander Hamilton and the Constitution*, Harcourt, Brace and World, Inc., New York: 1964

Sandoz, Mari, *The Battle of the Little Bighorn*, J. P. Lippincott Company, Philadelphia: 1966

Schachner, Nathan, *Aaron Burr, A Biography*, A. S. Barnes & Company, Inc., New York: 1961

Schachner, Nathan, *Thomas Jefferson, A Biography*, Thomas Yoseloff, New York: 1951

Smith, Helena Huntington, *The War on Powder River*, University of Nebraska Press, Lincoln, Nebraska: 1966

Smith, W. H. B., *Small Arms of the World: A Basic Manual of Military Small Arms*, Telegraph Press, Harrisburg, Pennsylvania: 1960

Stewart, Edgar I., *Custer's Luck*, University of Oklahoma Press, Norman, OK: 1955

Strode, Hudson, *Timeless Mexico*, Harcourt, Brace and Company, New York: 1944

Sullivan, William C. with Brown, Bill, *The Bureau: My Thirty Years in Hoover's FBI*, W. W. Norton & Company, New York: 1979

Syrett, Harold C. and Cooke, Jean G. (editors) *Interview in Weehawken: the Burr-Hamilton Duel As Told In the Original Documents*, Wesleyan University Press, Middletown, Conn.: 1960

Toland, John, *The Dillinger Days*, Random House, New York: 1963

Trachtman, Paul, *The Gunfighters*, Time-Life books, New York: 1974

Treherne, John, *The Strange History of Bonnie and Clyde*, Stein and Day, New York: 1984

Turner, Alford E. (ed.) *The Earps Talk*, Creative Publishing Company, College Station, Texas: 1980

Turner, Frederick Jackson, *The Frontier in American History*, Robert E. Krieger Publishing Company, New York: 1976

Tyler, Gus, *Organized Crime in America*, University of Michigan Press, Ann Arbor, Michigan: 1962

Utley Robert M., *Billy the Kid: A Short and Violent Life*, University of Nebraska Press, Lincoln, Nebraska: 1989

Utley, Robert M., *Cavalier in Buckskin; George Armstrong Custer and the Western Military Frontier*, University of Oklahoma Press, Norman, Oklahoma: 1988

Utley, Robert M. (ed.), *Life in Custer's Cavalry; Diaries and Letters of Albert and Jennie Barnitz, 1867-1868*, Yale University Press, New Haven, Connecticut: 1977

Vandenberg, Arthur Hendrick, *The Greatest American, Alexander Hamilton*, G.P. Putnam's Sons, New York: 1921

Vestal, Stanley, *Dodge City: Queen of Cowtowns*, Bantam, New York: 1952

Vestal, Stanley, *Sitting Bull: Champion of the Sioux*, Houghton Mifflin Company, Boston: 1932

Waller, Altina L., *Feud: Hatfields, McCoys and Social Change in Appalachia, 1860-1900*, The University of North Carolina Press, Chapel Hill, North Carolina: 1988

Walsh, George, Public Enemies: *The Mayor, the Mob and the Crime that Was*, W. W. Norton and Company, New York: 1980

Webb, Walter Prescott, *The Great Plains*, Ginn and Company, New York: 1931

Wills, Garry, *Explaining America: the Federalist*, Doubleday & Company, Garden City, New York: 1981

Wills, Garry, *Inventing America: Jefferson's Declaration of Independence*, Doubleday & Company, Inc., Garden City, New York: 1978

Wise, David, *The American Police State*, Random House, New York: 1976

Wise, William, *Alexander Hamilton*, G. P. Putnam's Sons, New York: 1963

Wright, Benjamin Fletcher (ed.) *The Federalist by Alexander Hamilton, James Madison and John Jay*, The Belknap Press of Harvard University Press, Cambridge, MA: 1961

Magazines

American Heritage, June 1956, *Burgoyne and America's Destiny* Reginald Hargreaves

American Heritage, August 1956, *How They Killed the Buffalo*, Wayne Gard

American Heritage, February 1957, *The Man Who Killed Custer*, Stanley Vestal

American Heritage, October 1957, *Doctor Gatling and His Gun*, Philip Van Doren Stern

American Heritage, February 1958, *Classmates Divided*, Mary Elizabeth Sergent

American Heritage, August 1960, *The Wild, Wild West*, Peter Lyon, and *Reading, Writing and History*, Peter Lyon

American Heritage, February 1961, *The Storming of the Alamo*, Charles Ramsdell

American Heritage, April 1961, *The Johnson County War*, Helena Huntington Smith

American Heritage, June 1964, *"There Are No Indians Left But Me,"* Marvin and Dorothy Rosenberg

American Heritage, April 1966, *Last Ghastly Moments at the Little Bighorn*, John Stands in Timber

American Heritage, August 1971, *Shoot Out in Burke Canyon*, Earl Clark

American Heritage, December 1974, *The Galloping Ghost*, Robert S. Gallagher

American Heritage, February 1975, *Pistols for Two . . . Coffee for One*, James R. Webb

American Heritage, August 1975, *The Fateful Encounter*, James R. Webb

American Heritage, October 1975, *Recuerda el Alamo!*, Jose Enrique de la Peña

American Heritage, April 1977, *Destruction of a Giant*, Jack Dempsey with Barbara Piatelli Dempsey

American Heritage, August/September 1981, *Sergeant York*, Nat Brandt

American Rifleman, June 1990, *The FBI Ammo Tests*, Charles E. Petty

Gun Digest, 1992, *Guns of the Philippine Wars*, William Weir

Military History, April 1985, *Santa Anna's Signal*, Kevin D. Randle

New York Times Magazine, February 18, 1968, *The Sad Ballad of the Real Bonnie and Clyde*, John Toland

Smithsonian, November 1976, *Trick Pistols Shed New Light on Famed Burr-Hamilton Duel*, Merrill Lindsay

Smithsonian, February 1991, *The Life—and Legend—of Billy the Kid*, Jake Page

Smithsonian, July 1991, *Barbed Wire, the Cutting Edge in Fencing*, H. Brooks Walker

The American Gun, Spring 1961, *Frank Hamer—Texas Ranger*, Harrison Kinney

Newspapers

Kansas City Star, November 17, 1950

New York Times, June 12, July 25, 1932; January 17, February 4, April 7, May 24-26, 1934; May 24-26, 1934; April 16 through October 31, 1935; January 18, 1950 through December 20, 1956; July 2, 1978; July 29, 1978; August 8, 1978; June 2, 1979

Oklahoma City *Daily Oklahoman* January 1 through December 31, 1933

Portland *Morning Oregonian*, June 10, 1902 through August 7, 1902

Index